Elsevier *Global Energy Policy and Economics* Series

European Energy Industry Business Strategies

Editor: Atle Midttun

Elsevier Science Internet Homepage

http://www.elsevier.nl (Europe)
http://www.elsevier.com (America)
http://www.elsevier.co.jp (Asia)

Consult the Elsevier homepage for full catalogue information on all books, journals and electronic products and services.

Elsevier Titles of Related Interest

MIDTTUN
European Electricity Systems in Transition
ISBN: 008-042994-7

WANG
China's Oil Industry and Market
ISBN: 008-043005-8

Related Journals

Free specimen copy gladly sent on request, Elsevier Science Ltd., The Boulevard, Langford Lane, Kidlington, Oxford, OX5 1GB, UK

Energy
The Electricity Journal
Energy Economics
Energy Policy
Resources and Energy Economics
Resources Policy
Utilities Policy

To Contact the Publisher

Elsevier Science welcomes enquiries concerning publishing proposals: books, journal special issues, conference proceedings, etc. All formats and media can be considered. Should you have a publishing proposal you wish to discuss, please contact, without obligation, the publisher responsible for Elsevier's energy and power publishing programme:

Lynne Clayton Honigmann
Publisher, Materials Science and Engineering
Elsevier Science Ltd
The Boulevard, Langford Lane   Phone: +44 1865 843462
Kidlington, Oxford   Fax: +44 1865 843920
OX5 IGB, UK   E.mail: l.honigmann@elsevier.co.uk

General enquiries including placing orders, should be directed to Elsevier's Regional Sales Offices - please access the Elsevier homepage for full contact details (homepage details at the top of this page).

Elsevier *Global Energy Policy and Economics* Series

European Energy Industry Business Strategies

Edited by

ATLE MIDTTUN

2001

ELSEVIER

AMSTERDAM – LONDON – NEW YORK – OXFORD – PARIS – SHANNON – TOKYO

ELSEVIER SCIENCE Ltd
The Boulevard, Langford Lane
Kidlington, Oxford OX5 1GB, UK

First edition 2001.

British Library Cataloguing in Publication Data

Midttun, Atle, 1952 –
    European Energy Industry Business Strategies. — (Elsevier
    global energy policy and economics series)
    1. Energy industries – European Union countries 2. Energy
    industries – Government policy – European Union countries
    3. Energy industries – Deregulation – European Union countries
I. Title
333.7'9'094
ISBN 0-08-043631-5

Library of Congress Cataloging in Publication Data

Midttun, Atle, 1952 –
    European Energy Industry Business Strategies / Atle Midttun.
      p. cm. – (Elservier global energy policy and economics series)
    ISBN 0-08-043631-5 (hardcover)
    1. Electric industries – Europe. 2. Electric industries – Deregulation – Europe.
    3. Deregulation – Europe. I. Title. II. Series.

HD9697.A3 E856 2001
333.793'2'094–dc21

                                        00-064681
                                            CIP

ISBN: 0 08 043631 5

Transferred to digital printing 2005
Printed and bound by Antony Rowe Ltd, Eastbourne

Contents

Preface

This book on business strategies in the energy industry is a follow up of a publication entitled *European Electricity Systems in Transition*[*]. After studying the de-regulation process at the national and European level, the next logical step was to take a closer look at the business strategies that have developed in the new liberalising markets.

Like the previous, this book is also based on national case studies, undertaken by energy specialists in each country. It is our hope that this joint effort has served to pinpoint core strategic issues facing the electricity and energy industry today. However, we have also wished to focus on some of the major challenges facing national regulators and decision-makers in the wake of strategic moves by energy industry.

We are grateful to the Norwegian Research Council for funding the Nordic studies as well as supporting the publication of this book.

* Published by Elsevier Science, 1997, ISBN 0-08-042994-7

About the Contributors

Jan Willem FABIUS graduated in 1969 from the Leiden University in the Netherlands with a Masters Degree in Law and a Bachelors Degree in Information Technology. Mr Fabius hold positions for more than 20 years as managing director of a German Gas Trading Corporation (PAM Gas GmbH, 1977-1985)) and a Dutch Utility (EDON nv, 1985-1997). From 1997 on Mr Fabius is managing partner of "European Energy Consult" in the Netherlands. European Energy Consult advises foreign companies about the Dutch energy sector. His research focuses on the emerging liberalisation of the gas and electricity market in the Netherlands and in Europe, such as strategic positioning, business development, new products and services and power trade.

Jan Terje HENRIKSEN works as research assistant at the Norwegian School of Management, BI. In addition, he is currently writing a Thesis for the completion of his MSc in Energy Management at the same institution. He has also carried out studies at the Energy and Resources Group of the University of California at Berkeley and holds a Bachelor degree in Mechanical Engineering from the Oslo College of Engineering, specialization in Offshore Engineering Design.

Jose Claudio Linhares PIRES holds a Ph-D in Economics from the IE-UFRJ (Institute of Economics of the Federal University of Rio de Janeiro) with a focus on the restructuring and regulation of energy and telecommunications industries. He is consultant of the United Nations Development Program (UNDP) in the Brazilian National Development Bank (BNDES) where he has been producing several papers about the regulation and restructuring of infrastructure sectors in Brazil. He is also the author of many articles and book chapters about these topics.

Professor Luiz Pinguelli ROSA is a Full Professor and presently the Director of the Graduate School of Engineering (COPPE), of the Federal University of Rio de Janeiro (UFRJ). He teaches and conducts researches at the Energy Planning Program in the field of energy and the environment and the efficient use of energy. He has a Ph.D. in Physics and developed studies in Physics of Nuclear Reactor, Theoretical Physics, Energy and Technology. Has more than 150 articles, book chapters and reports published in Brazilian and international publications, has oriented more than 50 thesis of students in M.Sc. and D.Sc. Is a Member of the Brazilian Society of Physics, Brazilian Society to the Progress of Science, Latin-American Society of Energetic Planning. Has been invited to participate as a conferencist by institutions as UNU, PUGWASH, OLADE, IAEA, ENEA, IFN, AFA. Has participating as representant of the Brazilian Government to the UNIDO events about IPCC.

Rolf W. KÜNNEKE is associate professor in the 'Economics of Infrastructures' program of Delft University of Technology, The Netherlands. His research interests are in the fields of the economic organization of liberalizing gas and electricity markets, network economics and industrial organization.

Atle MIDTTUN is Professor at the Norwegian School of Management and Co-director of its Centre for Energy and the Environment. He is currently a visiting professor at the University of Michigan. He holds a PhD from Uppsala University (Sweden) and a Magister Artium from the University of Oslo (Norway). His research focuses on energy and Environmental Policy issues especially their regulatory and industrial organisation aspects. He has been the editor of a number of books, including Approaches and Dilemmas of Economic Regulation (forthcoming), European Electricity Systems in Transition (published by Elsevier Science) and The Politics of Energy Forecasting. He is also the author of an extensive collection of journal articles on these topics.

Augusto Rupérez MICOLA works as researcher at the Centre for Energy and the Environment of the Norwegian School of Management. He holds a MSc in Energy Management and Economics from the Norwegian School of Management, plus a Master and a Bachelor, both in Business Administration and Economics from the Barcelona University (Spain). He has also pursued studies in Political Science and Economics at Uppsala University (Sweden).

Lionel CAURET holds a Ph-D in Economics from the CIRED (Ecole des Hautes Etudes en Sciences Sociales and CNRS), with a focus on the power systems and the demand side management. He has also been a research engineer at the Centre d'Energétique / Ecole des Mines de Paris for five years. Presently, his main activities as a project manager at

INESTENE concern the analysis of power and gas markets world-wide face to the liberalisation, the strategies of utilities and ESCOs, the modelling of load curves, the technical and economical assessment of energy saving potentials and the environmental impacts.

Joar HANDELAND is Master of Business and Administration from the Norwegian School of Management (NSM). He worked for some three years as a researcher at the Centre for Energy and Environment at NSM focussing on structural changes and strategic developments in the Nordic energy sector. He is currently working as a Strategy Consultant with Andersen Consulting in Oslo, where he works within the Energy and Finance sectors.

John JUREWITZ is Director of Regulatory Policy for the Southern California Edison Company, the local California distribution subsidiary of Edison International. Mr Jurewitz holds a Bachelors Degree in Economics from the University of San Francisco and a Masters and Doctoral Degree in Economics from the University of Wisconsin, Madison. Before joining Edison in 1978, Mr Jurewitz taught as an assistant professor of Economics at Williams College and Pomona College. Mr Jurewitz is an expert in electric utility regulation and has testified extensively on a wide variety of topics before the California Public Utilities Commission, the California Energy Commission, the California State Legislature, and the Federal Energy Regulatory Commission. He has also addressed numerous state regulatory bodies within the U.S. as well as internationally regarding electric industry restructuring. Mr Jurewitz continues to teach courses in Energy Policy, and Environmental and Natural Resource Economics at Pomona College and the Claremont Graduate University.

Terje OMLAND work as a researcher at the Centre of Energy and Environment at Norwegian School of Management. He has a Master of Business and Economics from Norwegian School of Management, with specialisation in information technology. He works now several projects related to structural changes and strategic developments in the Nordic energy sector

Steve THOMAS holds a BSc (Chemistry, Bristol) 1971. He is currently a Senior Fellow, Energy Programme, SPRU, University of Sussex. Steve Thomas works on issues of public policy related to energy. His main focus is the UK and Western Europe, but he also worked extensively on Eastern Europe and the Former Soviet Union, Brazil, Mexico and South Africa. His main current research interests include:

Liberalisation and restructuring of electricity supply industries;
Policy towards and the economic performance of nuclear power;

Liberalisation and restructuring of gas industries in Europe;
Energy transition problems in Eastern Europe and the Former Soviet
Union; and
Structure and policies of the power station equipment supply
industry.

He has published widely including books, academic journals, trade journals and articles in the popular press. He also contributes to policy debates in radio and television broadcasts.

Maarten ARENTSEN is associate professor energy and environment and vice-director of the Center for Clean Technology and Environmental Policy (CSTM) of the University of Twente (Netherlands). He is a political scientist by education and holds a PhD from the University of Twente. His research and publications focus on policy impact evaluation especially regarding energy conservation, innovation of energy supply and renewable energy.

Lutz MEZ is political scientist and holds a diploma in political science and a PhD from the Department of Social and Political Sciences, Free University of Berlin, Germany. He is co-founder and deputy director of the Environmental Policy Research Unit. In 1993/94 he was visiting professor at the Department of Environment, Technology and Social Studies, Roskilde University, Denmark. His mayor research area is environmental and energy policy with particular reference to nuclear and electricity policy.

Lutz Mez is author of numerous articles and chapters in internationally edited books. Some relevant books or editions: Umweltpolitik und Staatsversagen, Berlin: edition sigma 1997; Electricity in Eastern Europe: 10 years after the Chernobyl disaster, Berlin: Heinrich-Böll-Stiftung 1997, 2nd ed. 1998; RWE: Ein Riese mit Ausstrahlung, Cologne: Kiepenheuer & Witsch 1996; Die Energiesituation in der vormaligen DDR, Berlin: edition sigma 1991; Der Atomkonflikt, Reinbek: Rowohlt 1981; Energiediskussion in Europa, Villingen-Schwenningen: Neckar Verlag 1979ff

Prof. Mauricio Tiomno TOLMASQUIM has a Doctor of Science degree in Economics from the École des Hautes Études en Sciences Sociales, in Paris. He is, at the moment, Chair of the Energy Planning Program (PPE) of the Institute for Research and Graduate Studies (COPPE) at the Federal University of Rio de Janeiro (UFRJ). He is also President of the Brazilian Society for Energy Planning (SBPE) He has published widely including books and academic journals. He is member of the Steering Committe of the International Human Dimensions of Global

Environmental Change Programme (IHDP) and the Chairman of the Brazilian Academy of Science Committee on the Human Dimensions of Global Change. His research interests include: Electricity and Petroleum sectors reform, business strategies in competitive electricity industries, energy efficiency, energy demand and supply simulation models, the greenhouse effect and environmental economics.

Introduction

The European Union's electricity deregulation policy, which started to be implemented in February 1999, has created a basis for new strategic configuration of European energy companies. Traditional restraints on energy companies in terms of sectoral and geographical limitation and organisational form are extensively softened or have partly been taken away. In most European countries the regulatory regimes are now opening up for integration of electricity companies with oil and gas companies into broader energy companies; joint ventures between telecommunication companies and electricity companies as well as integration of electricity into broad infrastructure companies, including also water and transport. By breaking down national barriers to trade, the deregulation process also encourages European energy companies to make new engagements in markets outside their traditional supply areas, and for the most advanced liberal markets also increasingly across national boundaries.

Nevertheless, competition in the European deregulated electricity markets is very much competition under institutional diversity. Firstly, this is due to the partiality of the EU deregulation and the subsidiarity in applying this partial market opening to various national contexts. This implies that market rules and market institutions are extensively shaped to national taste. Secondly, institutional diversity can also be found at the firm level, as national and even sub-national idiosyncrasy also characterises the players in the electricity markets. The market players are companies with varying mixes of public and private ownership, with varying financial constraints, and with different combinations of political and commercial mandates.

As a consequence of the high diversity, both at the regulatory regime and firm level, the European scene is therefore one of multiplicity of strategic configuration and strategic developments. This diversity at the national regulatory and at the company level points at a co-evolution of regimes and company configuration along several different paths, which again makes the strategic context for European electricity industry complex and segmented.

The diversity of regulatory style is also matched by diversity at the structural level. The scale of European electricity industry does to a large extent reflect the scale of national markets, although modified by different traditions for national and regional organisation. Small states thereby tend to have industrial players at a scale that is highly incongruent with the industrial scale of companies in larger states. The structural asymmetry of national industrial configuration therefore implies challenges to small states in large markets where they are vulnerable to takeovers and where governments thereby lose control over traditional partners in energy policy and energy–industrial development.

In the longer run, the deregulation policy does not only pose challenges to competitively exposed companies, but also to society and regulatory authorities. At least three major challenges can be foreseen: the challenge of competition, the challenge of cross-sectoral operation and the challenge of environmental policy.

As far as competition is concerned, the increasing integration of electricity companies, following the strategic challenges of European deregulation, may in the medium and long term face the European community with problems of market concentration even at the European level. This development may then in the next round undermine the competitive pressure on the firms, which was the main factor motivating the deregulation reform. A pessimistic view is that European competition is at best a transitory phase from national monopolies on the path to European oligopolistic alliances, and with the accelerating pace of European mergers and acquisitions it will take strong anti-trust intervention from the EU authorities to counteract such a scenario.

As far as cross-sectoral operation is concerned, the deregulation and competitive exposure basically induces companies to experiment with combinations of industrial activities in order to gain competitive advantage. Indeed, as already mentioned, leading European electricity companies are now orienting themselves more broadly and redefining themselves into energy—and even 'infrastructure'—firms. However, the multi-sectoral complexity of advanced strategic business configuration challenges regulatory authorities to assess the strategic interaction effects of cross-sectoral engagements, especially as far as the pricing of natural monopoly services in grid access is concerned. Furthermore, the basic idea behind the deregulation reform is that regulation must remain 'light', as it might otherwise become a cost-burden as well as an unnecessary limitation on commercial experimentation. How well the EU and state regulatory apparatus will be able to devise advanced regulatory strategies to cope with the complexity of industrial structuration is still an open question.

The challenge of environmental policy under deregulation basically has to do with the fact that the dissimilarities of ecological vulnerability and abatement costs imply that collective strategies through unanimous multilateral agreements are hard to achieve, as the commercial interests of European nations and 'national champions' are too diverse to find a common ground. It may, in fact, be argued that with weak central governance at the relevant market level, the ability to take effective measures in environmental regulation is weakened by the liberal, deregulated regime. The fact that companies with different resource-bases—which would be highly unequally hit by common measures—compete in the same market exposes the more polluting company to very high 'green costs' and thereby easily undermines their competitiveness.

The book highlights the strategic and regulatory challenges of European deregulation in nine chapters. While the book's main focus is on the business strategies within the emerging deregulated electricity markets, regulatory implications are discussed, particularly in the final chapter.

Chapter I spells out some of the central strategic issues facing the electricity industry in its new competitive context. Classical themes such as national styles versus globalisation; scale and scope versus flexible specialisation; horizontal versus vertical integration; static versus dynamic efficiency, and business and public interest are briefly discussed, as a prelude to the following empirical investigation of actual business strategies pursued by electricity and energy industry.

The main part of the book consists of seven national case studies of business strategies. The selection of European cases ranges from the early liberalisers like the UK and the Nordic countries to France, which only very reluctantly moves towards competitive exposure of its industry. Within these two extremes, countries such as Germany, the Netherlands and Denmark take up middle positions.

Although mainly focused on European experiences, the book includes both US and Latin American/Brazilian chapters. The motivation for including these studies in a European-oriented book is twofold:

Firstly, US companies are the major foreign investors in the European electricity industry, which makes them directly relevant on the European scene. Similarly, Latin America is one of the major arenas for European electricity industry's foreign engagements. Including this market is therefore also highly relevant for understanding the strategic positioning of European electricity/energy industry.

Secondly, the two non-European cases serve to create contrasts to the European scene. Among other things, the US case illustrates a highly dynamic arena for mergers and acquisitions which is yet unparalleled in Europe except perhaps in the UK. The Brazilian/Latin American case illustrates the strategic and regulatory challenges of large-scale privatisation dominated by foreign multinationals.

A final chapter sums up the national patterns in a comparative analysis of market structures, business strategies and regulatory styles. This chapter also raises, and briefly discusses, some of the regulatory challenges that face the future governance of European energy markets.

Chapter I
Perspectives on Commercial Positioning in the Deregulated European Electricity Markets

ATLE MIDTTUN

The commercial re-positioning of the European energy industry follow-ing deregulation raises fundamental strategic issues. This chapter will elaborate on some of the underlying theoretical issues of economic or-ganisation as a prelude to the following national case studies and the final comparative analysis.

I. Globalisation/Europeanisation or National Styles: Competition under Institutional Diversity

The tension between globalisation and/or Europeanisation, on the one hand, and path dependency/national styles of industrial organisation, on the other, is fundamentally built into the European electricity market deregulation. On the one hand the deregulation project has a vision of an integrated European market with competition on equal terms for all. On the other hand, national interests have limited the competitive scope and tailored their deregulation to national taste according to the so-called subsidiarity principle.

More theoretically formulated, the so-called convergence perspective argues that, on facing a common competitive market, companies will tend to scale up and converge in function and organisational structure. Against the convergence perspective the national business systems lit-erature argues that industrial development is highly shaped by national styles and national institutions.

One of the most clearly articulated proponents of the convergence perspective is Kenichi Ohmae (1985, 1995) whose basic argument is that

1

as the 21st century progresses, industry, investment, individuals and information flow will be relatively unimpeded across national borders. In this situation, he argues, the strategies of modern, multinational companies are no longer shaped and conditioned by reasons of state, but rather, by the desire—and the need—to serve attractive markets wherever they exist and to tap attractive pools of resources wherever they sit. He claims that the capital markets in most developed countries are flush with excess cash for investment and that the investors will look for multinational companies with their competencies to play key roles in local developments, rather than support local industry. The global orientation of financial sources will, therefore, also serve to support large globally converging firms. Modern commercial dynamics, such as that which is being unleashed by the present European electricity market deregulation, pushes companies to spread across borders in a new way, tapping into global or at least European markets for technology, investment and consumers. In this context, Ohmae argues that national diversity will diminish rapidly and that the nation states no longer have a market-making role to play.

Yet another type of argument in favour of strategic convergence—the so-called institutional isomorphism argument—is put forward by the new institutionalist school in organisation theory. The basic argument here is that national differences are challenged by international learning, co-operation and/or dominance. This constitutes forces towards cross-national harmonisation of strategies and organisational models, or what Di Maggio and Powell (1991) have termed institutional isomorphism. They point out three mechanisms through which institutional isomorphic change occurs.

1. Changes towards organisational convergence may occur as mimetic processes, where changes in relevant reference nations act as a signal to own change, perhaps in response to uncertainty;
2. organisational convergence may also occur through what Di Maggio and Powell call coercive isomorphism, where the need for political legitimacy acts as a driving force for institutional isomorphism; and
3. isomorphism may be closely associated with normative pressure arising from professionalisation.

Against the globalisation and institutional isomorphism arguments a national business systems literature launches a competing perspective with a core argument that differences in major national, regional and sectoral institutions generate significant variations in how firms and markets are structured and operate. On this basis, the national styles literature argues that analytical perspectives that reduce this variation to unidimensional convergence are missing out essentials.

This general argument is developed under several labels: business systems (Whitley, 1992), social systems of production (Campbell *et al.*, 1991) and modes of capitalist organisation (Orru, 1994). The essence of this literature is again that industrial development proceeds differently in different countries, as national industrial 'milieus' draw on specific traditions and competence in their national surroundings.

Implicitly, and sometimes also explicitly, the national styles literatures draw on a broader path dependency argument that points out that industrial systems cannot develop independently of previous events (David, 1993). Local positive loops serve to propagate traditional patterns into future strategic decisions. This implies a development with several equilibrium points, where small events at one point in time may play an important role for future development by determining the course of a long-term development. The path dependency and national styles literatures thus foresee that institutional, social and organisational factors will continue to reproduce differences in strategic orientations that may reproduce themselves even under international competitive conditions.

Applied to the European electricity market deregulation, we find elements that fit both positions: the Commission's ambition to develop an internal market with pan-European competition clearly launches a programme with strong drivers towards harmonisation of markets and with strong isomorphic pressures on the competing companies.

However, two major factors serve to make competition in the European deregulated electricity markets very much of a competition under institutional diversity. Firstly, the partiality of the EU deregulation and the subsidiarity in applying this partial market opening to various national contexts implies that market rules and market institutions are extensively shaped to national taste. Secondly, national and even sub-national municipal idiosyncrasy also characterises the players in the electricity markets. The market players are companies with varying mixes of public and private ownership, with varying financial constraints, and with different combinations of political and commercial mandates.

The very cautious pace of market opening spelled out in EU's electricity directive, and the plurality of models open to national choice, indicated a soft tone vis-à-vis national vested interest. The member states were here clearly given the possibility to limit competition both in generation and supply, allowing them considerable control over the construction of new capacity and the fuel mix. The result has been a variety of regulatory trajectories and energy policies running side by side in Europe:

The Nordic deregulation took a radical, direct and structural approach with an emphasis on full-free trade competition between several decentralised actors.[1] Major parts of the Continental European development, however, seems to take a more gradual 'contestable market' path, where market deregulation rather takes the form of gradual market opening under few structural constraints. The English and Welsh reform could be characterised as somewhere in between, with radical change in ownership structure, but without sufficient market deconcentration and consumer participation to fulfil strong free-trade criteria in the first round. However, with the recent opening up of the market to small-scale consumers this has changed.

The analytical possibility-space for a European market-development may be described in terms of a two-dimensional matrix with degree of market opening to competition along the horizontal axis and the geographical expansion of the market along the vertical axis (Fig. I.1). The Continental European development can be seen to follow a path from national monopolistic planned economy (square III) towards a European

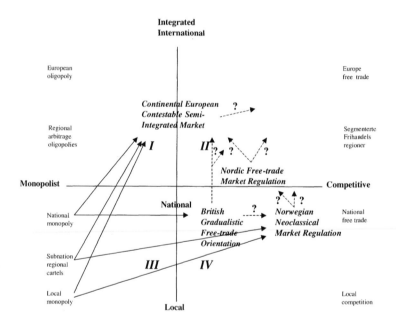

Fig. I.1. Market opening and competition.

This is a conceptual model and the rankings are highly judgmental.

---

[1] It should be noted, however, that the radical deregulation in Norway did not include the ownership of hydropower facilities. Public ownership to such resources continued to be protected by special concession laws.

semi-competitive and semi-integrated market system (between squares I and II). There is reason to expect that this peculiar mixture of competitive and restraining regulation will characterise the strategic context for years to come, even if the European liberalisation project in a longer time-perspective may provide full integration with open trade between national markets (square II). However, even in the case of extensive market opening in Europe, mergers, acquisitions and other forms of strategic integration may limit competition.

As opposed to the Continental development, where the attempt has been to deregulate and internationalise in the same movement, the British and Norwegian deregulation projects were one-country projects, where the move was along the horizontal dimension (from square III to IV) rather than along the vertical dimension. Norway then subsequently moved into a Nordic market, when Sweden and Finland, and gradually Denmark also followed it in deregulation six to nine years later.

From a globalisation and isomorphism perspective it might be argued that this development contains strong convergence elements. Firstly, convergence through internationalisation and institutional harmonisation; but secondly also convergence in regulatory style as all systems have adopted some market elements.

However, from a national styles position, it is easy to point out strong national elements, both in the institutional specification/delineation of competition and in the type of openness that is established between the national market and its environment. In addition to differences in market scope and regulatory regimes, the European scene is also characterised by extensive differences in company ownership and in competitive exposure of companies within their domestic markets.

This again obviously affects mandates, financial positions and conditions for capital accumulation. Municipalistic organisation may typically imply a local focus, where companies are oriented at serving local needs and are influenced by municipal political processes, including local needs to extract dividend to finance other non-commercial sectors. Etatist organisation exposes the company to state policies, where industrial strategy has traditionally been more developed than at the municipal level. Companies in oligopolistic or semi-oligopolistic positions do, of course, have many of the privileges of state companies, without the latter's political constraints. Companies exposed to free trade, such as smaller and medium-sized private companies in the Nordic market, are obviously pressured to develop high static efficiency and are vulnerable to takeovers.

Nevertheless, one might argue from a global convergence perspective that the commercial forces unleashed by the deregulation are sufficient to establish a dynamic of their own, leading beyond the current institutional restraints.

II. Scale, Scope and Functional Configuration of European Energy Industry

In spite of the institutional diversity and following national regulatory idiosyncrasy, deregulation of European electricity markets has created a basis for new strategic configuration, as traditional limitations on sector, geographical, organisational and economic scale and scope diminishes.

In most European countries, the regulatory regimes are now opening up for sector reconfiguration by allowing electricity companies to take new positions in other sectors or value chains. Therefore, we are seeing integration between oil and gas companies, merging into broader energy companies. We are also seeing joint ventures between telecommunication companies and electricity companies to utilise the electricity grid for transmission also of telecommunication.

By building down national barriers to trade, the deregulation process also encourages expansion of geographical scope. We therefore see European energy companies making new engagements in markets outside their traditional supply areas. Regional and municipal companies have engaged themselves in other regions and areas within their country, but also within other European countries.

Organisationally, European companies have increasingly adopted the shareholder model, although remaining dominantly publicly owned. However, some companies have also been privatised and/or sold out to foreign interests. In addition, companies have developed subsidiaries and a more complex profit-centre structure in order to manage multiple alliances and commercial engagements.

II.A. Scale and scope vs flexible specialisation

There is a large volume of literature on the challenges of industrial configuration. However, this literature includes seemingly contradictory positions, notably in the choice between scale and scope and flexible specialisation. On the one hand, the scale and scope literature argues for large size and complex engagements. On the other hand, the flexible specialisation literature recommends focus and small-scale concentration.

The advantages of scale and scope-argument goes back to classical economics (Ricardo, 1971; Smith, 1933) and includes such arguments as the indivisible input argument, the set-up-cost argument, the division of labour argument, as well as a market power argument (Koopmans, 1957).

The indivisible input argument refers to the case that some specific capital goods are indivisible in the sense that it becomes very costly or even physically impossible to scale it down to a smaller size. Under-utilisation of maximum capacity of the most efficient scale will therefore burden an economic actor with higher production costs than a competitor that is able to scale up to harvest scale advantages. The set-up cost argument implies that initial investments in organisational competencies and material structures dictate a certain volume to minimise fixed costs. This may have to do with designing organisational routines, qualifying personnel, etc. If these activities have scale advantages, there may be considerable advantages for actors capable of applying these resources to large series. The advantage of specialisation-argument, which was pointed out already by Adam Smith (1933), refers to the fact that the ability to fully develop specialised skills may dictate sufficient volume to support the necessary division of labour and the necessary critical mass to maintain an attractive context for creative professional development.

With Ricardo (1971), Smith's notion of advantages from specialisation of labour is transferred to advantages from specialisation and trade. Assuming systematic differences in productivity for a given commodity between countries, Ricardo showed how both countries might profit from trade (Ricardo, 1971). Transcending Ricardo's assumption of nationally based industry, and assuming, with modern industrial organisation, that companies may stage international operations and co-ordinate multiple resources and technologies across national boundaries, then Ricardo's classical trade theories may be transformed into arguments for multinational strategic organisation. A major criterion for scaling and scoping up, for a multinational company, may thus be to internalise Ricardian trade-advantages within the company. Similarly, the later Hecksher Ohlin theory of international trade, based on the comparative advantage of production based on abundantly available resources (1967), may also be internalised within a single multinational company, and thus made relevant in a business strategy context.

With an increasing tendency towards centralisation and oligopolisation of key sectors of the economy, there may be arguments for scaling and scoping up beyond the efficiency arguments listed above. Companies with sufficient size to take dominant market positions may profit from working the markets so as to increase their own profitability on other companies' behalf.

The classical theories of scale and scope traditionally referred to the production plant, focusing on operative efficiency at the material–technological level. With Alfred Chandler's analysis of the competitive advantage of US multinationals in the middle of the 20th century, scale and scope issues were systematically also applied at the organisational level (Chandler, 1977). Chandler saw the ability of American companies to build synergy between international market channels, as facilitated by their introduction of the multidivisional structure. Through the development of a professional middle management that linked large systems together through its 'modern' organisational models and through its more advanced organisational technology, the US companies were able to integrated large-scale transport systems and large-scale production systems with advanced multinational marketing on a hitherto unprecedented scale.

The classical and Chandlerian scale and scope position has, however, been met by a more recently developed counterposition. Sabel and Piore (1984) have, in their pathbreaking work 'The Second Industrial Divide', argued that more craftsman-like modes of production might, through their flexibility and quality, outcompete the large-scale production systems. Today's demand for highly sophisticated products built on permanent innovation, according to Sabel and Piore (1984), increasingly leads to avoidance of mass production and development of a more flexible production strategy, to reduce production costs while maintaining the flexibility necessary to thrive in economic uncertainty. This means that companies have to organise so that skills and technology can be constantly realigned in order to produce a rapidly shifting assortment of goods and services.

Sabel and Piore's (1984) argument implies that flexible specialisation is in the form of networks of technological sophistication; highly flexible manufacturing firms may in many cases meet today's demand for permanent innovation better than large-scale multinationals. The flexibility of small-scale networks makes them able to accommodate ceaseless change, rather than seek to control it. This strategy is, as Sabel and Piore state, 'based on flexible–multi-use–equipment; skilled workers; and the creation, through politics, of an industrial community that restricts the forms of competition to those favouring innovation'. Among the characteristics of flexibly specialised industries is the production of a wide range of products for highly differentiated markets and the constant adaptation of goods/services in response to changing tastes and in order to expand markets. This can be managed by developing flexible and widely applicable technologies, such as general-purpose machines rather than large, dedicated machine systems, so that product innovation is not held back by massive capital investment in rigid technologies, and workers possess the skills to produce and develop a wide range of products. The strategic imperative is a strategy that combines both differentiation and efficiency.

Future prosperity, Piore and Sabel argue, depends on the development of flexible technologies, flexible organisational practices, skilled workforces and management, and economies of scope rather than of scale. Vertical disintegration is important because Piore and Sabel envisage production through flexible specialisation as the sum of the production of many specialised firms in networks that can adapt quickly to changing market demands, rather than of a single firm as is the case in a mass production system. The spread of flexible specialisation, in other words, amounts to a revival of craft forms of

Table I.1. Porter's integrated strategy model.

	Uniqueness in the customer's eye	Low cost
The whole industry	Differentiation	Cost leadership
Only a segment of industry	Differentiation-focus	Cost leadership-focus

Source: From Porter (1980).

production that—according to Sabel and Piore—were marginalised at the first industrial divide at the turn of the 20th century.

Porter's (1980) discussion of basic competitive strategies can be seen as an attempt to build bridges between the scale and scope and flexible specialisation positions. By distinguishing between a generic cost-based strategy targeted at mass markets and a quality-based strategy targeted at more exclusive market niches (Table I.1), Porter leaves room for simultaneous coexistence between both positions.

II.B. Horizontal vs Vertical Integration

At a more specific level, business strategy must address not only the degree, but also the type of scale and scope. Vertical and horizontal integration here constitutes the two major alternatives. Vertical integration involves decisions that define the boundaries of the firm over its generic activities on the value chain from raw materials to the consumer, whereas horizontal strategy aims at identifying and exploiting interrelationships across distinct but related business units in the value chain. Given limited resources, the two strategic orientations are to some extent competing alternatives.

Seen from an existing firm in a given value chain, vertical integration may be directed forward towards the consumer side or backwards towards the supplier side, and it may cover one or several steps in the value chain. Furthermore integration may also occur in many degrees, ranging from full organisational to lighter associational forms. Hax and Majluf (1991) summarise the essential decision criteria for decisions over vertical integration under four main headings: cost reductions, defensive market power, offensive market power, and administrative and managerial advantages.

The benefits from vertical integration include providing autonomy in supply and demand that shields the firm from foreclosure and unequitable exchange relationships; protects retention of exclusive rights to the use of specialised assets; and guards against important attributes being distorted or degraded. Furthermore, vertical integration also raises entry or mobility barriers.

Vertical integration may also enhance the firm's offensive market power by increasing opportunities for entering new businesses and by providing access to new technology. In addition, vertical integration may also promote differentiation strategy by control of interface with end customers and improvements in market intelligence. Furthermore it may also facilitate a more aggressive strategy to gain market share.

As far as costs and benefits are concerned, the benefits from vertical integration include internalisation of economies of scale, lower transaction costs by integration, and better control with quality and guards against strategic behaviour from suppliers. On the other hand, vertical integration implies increased fixed costs and correspondingly greater business risk, higher capital investment requirements, and the possibility of increased overhead costs.

Up against the pros and cons of vertical integration, the firms will have to also consider possible horizontal strategies. The core issue motivating horizontal integration is the potential synergism across businesses, which could be exploited in order to add value beyond the simple sum of business contributions.

Horizontal integration is traditionally discussed under three basic headings (Porter, 1980): tangible relationships, intangible relationships and competitor interrelationships. Tangible relationships arise from opportunities to share activities founded on the actual sharing of concrete assets or managerial capabilities in one or more activities of the value chain. However, this must be weighed up against costs of co-ordination and compromise. Intangible relationships involve the transfer of management know-how among separate value chains to further competitive advantage. This involves interactions across independent strategic business units that are placed in different industries, but retain generic similarities such as same generic strategy, same type of buyers, similar configurations of the value chain and similar important value activities. However, intangible relationships are more difficult to apprehend and exploit than tangible relationships. Competitor interrelationships stem from the existence of rivals that actually or potentially compete with the firm in more than one business unit. This type of multipoint competition expands the scope for competitive analysis and leads to a focus on retaliatory action to enhance one's own competitive position.

There is obviously also a trade-off between horizontal and vertical strategy in so far as limited human and financial resources imply that a choice has to be made between competing horizontal and vertical alternatives. As pointed out by Hax and Majluf (1991) evaluation of this trade-off in principle involves the mapping of all the firm's business units, and the breadth of their engagement in the value chain, as well as the firm's horizontal engagements across business units for every stage of the value chain.

II.C. Functional configuration in European energy industry

For electricity companies, the above trade-off between scale and scope and flexible specialisation, as well as the trade-off between vertical and horizontal strategy, would in principle involve mapping their vertical engagement in the electricity value chain, from production, R&D, whole-sale, grid management and distribution to various customer segments. But it would also involve mapping parallel engagements in production, R&D wholesale, etc. in other value chains. To facilitate an empirical analysis of re-configuration in European electricity industry with respect to vertical and horizontal integration, we have constructed a scheme for multidimensional ranking. The scheme standardises the overview of strategic configuration along two dimensions: vertical and horizontal integration, and then differentiates between various multi-sector combinations: electricity, energy and miscellaneous (Fig. I.2).

Based on these typologies, the scheme allows us to differentiate between several strategic configurations:

Quadrants IV and III on the left hand side present a simple typology of horizontal and vertical integration in electricity supply and generation industry. Quadrant III-c here represents niche specialisation within a single function, such as small-scale generation, local sales companies, etc. Quadrant III-b also represents functional specialisation, but at large scale.

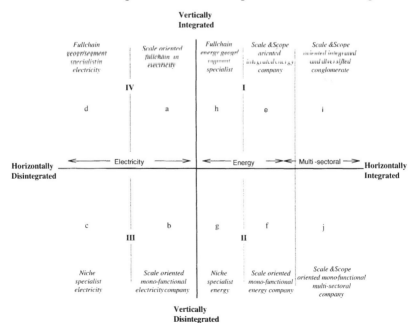

Fig. I.2. Variations of horizontal and vertical integration in value chains.

Quadrants IV-a and IV-d and both represent vertically integrated approaches within the electricity value chain. IVd represents a small-scale approach, e.g. within a restricted geographic area, whereas IV-a represents a large-scale orientation.

The right side of Fig. I.2 represents wider integration into electricity and other related sectors. Analogous to quadrants III and IV, the quadrants II and I represents various mixes of scale/specialisation with different degrees of vertical/functional integration. Quadrants I-h and I-e represent, respectively, full-chain specialist or scale- and scope-oriented integrated energy companies. Quadrants II-g and II-f represent, respectively, a niche specialist in energy or scale-oriented mono-functional energy companies.

Finally, the far right section represents further diversification beyond energy, both integrated and diversified conglomeration in 'I-i' and monofunctional multi-sector companies in 'I-j'.

Obviously ambitious scale and scope positions in this matrix must be carefully balanced against the costs. Both vertical and horizontal integration in the I-e and IV-a positions often imply flexibility losses as the flexibility to diversify is reduced and the ability to tap different distributors and suppliers is curtailed. Integration may also create higher exit barriers and larger volatility in earnings and may also create great difficulties in getting rid of obsolete processes. Furthermore, vertical integration in the I and IV positions forces the firm to maintain a balance among the various stages of the value chain, which may imply excess capacities should the firm risk unfulfilled demand simultaneously.

At administrative and managerial levels, both vertical and horizontal integration imposes administrative discipline through direct dealing with providers. It may also provide increased interchange of information with external sources. However, both vertical and horizontal integration may also involve administrative and managerial penalties as it may force the use of internal incentives as opposed to market incentives, which may be more difficult to handle than external incentives. Integration may also impose additional burdens in the organisational structure, managerial processes and systems in order to deal effectively with increased heterogeneity and complexity.

III. Static and Dynamic Efficiency, Human Resources and Organisational Form in Strategic Configuration

III.A. Static and dynamic efficiency

The challenge of deregulation, competition and strategic reconfiguration raises extensive demand on energy companies both in terms of securing cost efficiency in an increasingly competitive market economy, and in securing organisational, functional and technological innovation to be dynamically efficient in the long run. Balancing the short-run cost efficiency against the long-run dynamic innovation is extremely difficult as it implies a juxtaposition of two seemingly irreconcilable theoretical worlds.

Static efficiency is traditionally synonymous with productive efficiency and relates to the calculated ratio of what is produced with what is required to produce it. The concept of productive efficiency is rooted in the notion of the production function that the volume of output depends on the volume of inputs used in production. Under static conditions, a given volume of output can be produced with different combinations of factors. The actual combination of inputs depends on their relative prices, which determine the least-cost combination. Static efficiency thus means going as far as possible in productivity within resource and technological constraints.

As implied in the very concept, dynamic efficiency focuses on a dynamically shifting sequence of optima that result from new technological and organisational knowledge. Furthermore, under realistic cognitive assumptions these theoretical optima cannot possibly be fully defined. In spite of a more recent focus by neoclassical economics, it is the Austrian tradition that has paid most attention to dynamic growth. In this tradition the ability to further dynamic innovation and industrial restructuration is considered to be far more important for economic growth and welfare than marginalistic resource optimisation. In Schumpeter's (1943) perspective, economics should, therefore, be more concerned with disequilibrium and creative destruction than with marginalistic equilibrium analysis. With their rejection of the equilibrium concept and concentration on a dynamic process perspective, the Austrian analysis is, in essence, entirely incompatible with any static understanding of economic activity. In fact, because of the focus on innovation and limited knowledge, the concept of process, in the Austrian understanding, establishes a fundamental indetermination of economic activity that defies any concept of equilibrium and thus of optimality (Ioannides, 1992).

The radical uncertainty and the dynamic focus make the Austrian approach process oriented and concerned with innovation and learning. As dynamic innovation presents the economic actors with radical uncertainty, the Austrian tradition is therefore less willing than neoclassics to take up strong, deductively-based normative positions.

To some extent, the static vs dynamic efficiency issue has parallels to the issue of single and double loop learning in cognitive theory as applied to organisations (Argyris, 1978; Bjercke, 1998). In single loop learning—corresponding to static efficiency—the issue is one of adapting a system to an existing set of decision-rules—in the case of static efficiency, the known criteria for optimisation of the production system. In double loop learning, on the other hand, there is a feedback between the mental models, strategy, structure and decision-rules and continuous commercial experience (Fig. I.3).

From a business strategy perspective the challenge is to balance the static and dynamic perspectives against each other. Instead of simply maximising within fixed constraints, the question is how firms can gain competitive advantage from changing constraints. Instead of only deploying a fixed pool of factors of production, a more important issue is how firms and nations improve the quality of factors, raise the productivity with which they are utilised and create new ones. Nevertheless, static efficiency must simultaneously be maintained in order to secure a sufficient cash flow to support the company's dynamic strategy. With an analogy to the learning model, the company must simultaneously maintain single loop static and double loop dynamic efficiency strategies.

III.B. Strategy and human resources

The issue of balancing off static and dynamic efficiency also has implications for the management of competency within the firm. Although the traditional view sees labour as merely an input factor in the production function (Mansfield, 1977), the current literature points out that the ability to develop human resources and maintain competencies at a high level can be a unique source of sustained competitive advantage. This is especially true when its components have high internal and external fit (Baird and Meshoulam, 1968; Lengnick-Hall and Lengrick-Hall, 1988).

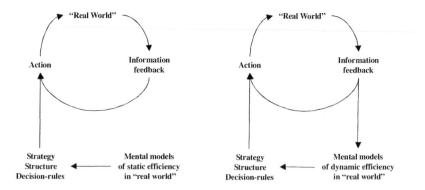

Fig. I.3. Single and double loop learning applied to efficiency.

Source: Bjercke (1998) and Argyris and Schön (1978).

Human resources may then become a strategic lever that can have economically significant effects on a firm's results. This literature therefore shifts the focus from labour as a production and cost factor towards human resources as a central factor in value creation.

Unlike capital investments, economic scale, or patents, a properly developed human resources (HR) system is an 'invisible asset' (Itami, 1987), which creates value when it is so embedded in the operational systems of an organisation that it enhances the firm's capabilities. This interpretation is also consistent with the emphasis on 'core competencies' developed by Prahalad and Hamel (1990), who argued that conventional measures of economic rents such as the difference between the market and book value of assets (i.e. Tobin's q) reflect 'core competence–people-embodied skills' (Hamel and Prahalad, 1994).

A major point to be aware of is that much of the human resource management literature refers to a specific systemic coupling between personal competencies and the firm. Firm-specific human assets refer to special skills, knowledge, or personal relationships that are only applicable in a given firm. These socially complex resources are hard to replicate because they are embedded in complex social systems (Lippman and Rumelt, 1982; Barney, 1991). This has to do with the complexity of many social and cognitive processes involved (Coff, 1997).

Choice of a human-resource- or labour-cost-based focus may also have implications for strategic organisation. This is in part Stabell and Fjelstad's (1995) point of departure in their critique of Porter's value chain model and their argument for a supplementary alternative 'value shop' model that, they claim, is better suited to high quality professional services utilised to serve a customer or client problem.

While the value chain is designed to produce a standard product in large numbers, the value shop schedules activities and applies resources in a fashion that is dimensioned and appropriate to the needs of the problem. The value shop describes organisations where resources and activities are assembled to solve a customer or client problem. The classical value shop is the professional service, such as in medicine, law and engineering. The primary activities of the value shop are, therefore, also often couched in terms and sequenced in a form that is unique to each speciality and profession.

The human resource and labour logic and their respectively linked value shop and value chain configurations may be considered both as complementary and competing perspectives. In the first respect they may be seen as a strategic repertoire that serves to meet the needs of different functions in a commercial process. The relative weight of these perspectives may also vary across sectors or industry. Given the interplay between both standardised functions and more dynamically evolving competence-demanding activities, energy industry, like many other sectors may display an overall value-creating configuration that is a combination of different generic configurations. Parts of the activities can be organised as chains with a focus on labour as a cost-factor, and parts as shops with a human competency focus. As Stabell and Fjelstad (1995) argue, overlapping and multiple value configurations open the potential for important synergies.

III.C. Organisational form

The management of complex dynamic efficiency and advanced human resources, in the form of complex multifunctional configuration with several value-logics within the firm, raises extensive challenges to strategic organisation. Generally speaking, three ideal types of organisation are profiled in the literature of economic organisation: hierarchy, markets and networks. As discussed by Powell (1981), these three modes of organisation have different properties in terms of their normative basis, means of communication, flexibility, methods of conflict resolution, amount of commitment among the parties and tone or climate.

Market-based organisation provides flexibility and efficiency through competition, etc. Hierarchic-based organisation provides stability and coherence through the systematic combination of goal-setting and authoritative instruction-rights. Network-based organisation provides semi-flexibility through coalitions and relational means. However, the three types my also be combined so as to give the electricity company a greater repertoire of control and flexibility in its strategic operation.

Combining these three mechanisms provides a functional matrix of organisational solutions that allows for a tighter fit between strategic ambitions and the operational organisation to fulfil them. Combinations may be reached by choosing intermediary forms such as co-ordinated free market, liberalised co-ordination, co-ordinated hierarchy, etc. (Arentsen and Künneke, 1996). However, combinations may also be made by positing one form within another, such as market-driven profit-centres within a hierarchic corporation, or positing hierarchic command-structures along one dimension within a network structure along other dimensions.

The possibility for energy companies to orchestrate strategic integration through an extended organisational matrix may allow better tradeoffs between costs and benefits of various strategic designs. Instead of treating integration and flexible decentralisation as exclusive alternatives, the question is one of relating functions vertically or horizontally to almost a continuum of organisational forms, ranging from tightly integrated hierarchy to uncoordinated markets (Stinchcombe, 1984).

With a broad menu of organisational forms available, energy companies may position themselves so as to better overcome the aforementioned dilemmas of strategic choice. By loosening the couplings between units into a network, rather than hierarchic form, they may to some extent succeed in maintaining some of the vertical and horizontal integration implied in the scale and scope position. The looseness of the couplings allows them, at the same time, to gain advantages from flexible specialisation through looser, network-based coupling of the units.

Similarly, flexible organisation may allow the company to handle its wider stakeholder relations while at the same time serving its stockholdership. Although the stakeholdership may be maintained through relatively loose semi-network ties to societal interests, the core production system may be more tightly integrated through stronger hierarchic organisation.

The interplay between tight hierarchical and loose network-based coupling may also give the company scope for handling the partly contradictory challenges of static and dynamic efficiency. The latter function may typically rely on fairly loosely controlled activities, with freedom to experiment within given economic constraints. Successful innovations may then be incorporated into the tighter integrated core business.

Transaction-cost theory, which argues for complementariy dependence on transaction characteristics such as the specificity of the engagement between the transacting parties and the frequency of transaction (Williamson, 1975) provides one of the central guidelines to optimise on organisational form. However, organisation theory, such as Scott (1981) and Mintzberg (1989), supplements the extremely rationalistic Williamsonian position with a range of 'softer' motivational elements that have also proven to be critical factors in organisational development.

IV. Business and Public Interest

The historic public service orientation of much of the European energy industry implies that this sector traditionally carries a stronger commitment to public welfare than is customary in most other sectors of the economy. This public commitment is partly carried on into the new deregulated market context through special regulatory regimes and other arrangements to govern the local, regional and national grid management and system operation. These functions are traditionally defined natural monopolies, and hence cannot be exposed to 'normal' competition.

At the same time, however, the market-oriented deregulation implies that the electricity industry is now being exposed to general competition. There is, thus, a tension between commercial and public service-orientation running right through the industry. This tension between public interest and business interest is partly solved by a new division of labour between the firm and the regulatory authorities. However, regulatory intervention is in many cases clearly imperfect, and public interest must, therefore, continue to rely extensively on self-regulatory restraint by the companies and ad hoc intervention by the regulatory apparatus.

IV.A. Stockholdership vs stakeholdership

As far as the self-regulatory restraint by the companies is concerned, the business strategy literature recurs back on the issue of stakeholdership, as opposed to the traditional stockholder-perspective of the firm. While the traditional classical/neoclassical model of the firm sees it primarily as responsible for maximising the value of its shareholders' investment, a wider stakeholder perspective recognises that the modern corporation has a responsibility to serve the interests of multiple stakeholders. These include its stockholders, but also its employees, communities, customers, suppliers, and the broader society in which it is located.

The stockholder-model has its roots in two central pillars of classical and later neoclassical theory: individualistic, hedonistic actor assumptions; and structural assumptions that select self-interested behaviour (Smith, 1933; Ricardo, 1971). The structural assumption of market competition, which also characterises both classical and neo-classical economics, introduces a context of 'Darwinian' functional selection of the fittest. In line with this, a fundamental premise behind deregulation is that selective mechanisms, built into competition rules, will force firms, even if they should not be hedonistically motivated, to act as profit-maximising agents in order to survive in a competitive world.

Later development of the theory of the firm to encompass large-scale managerial organisation (Williamson, 1979; Coase, 1988; Chandler, 1992) and non-managerial ownership (Jensen and Meckling, 1976) maintained the hedonistic profit-seeking point of departure of the classical literature. In this literature the orientation of the firm as a whole now, emerges as a consequence of strategic interaction within the firm, which is again decomposed into an arena for maximising individuals.

Against the hedonistic, utility-oriented stockholder perspective stands the stakeholder orientation. For more than a decade—since Freeman (1984) published his landmark book *Strategic Management: A Stakeholder Approach*—the stakeholder approach to understanding the firm in its environment has been a powerful heuristic device. This device has broadened management's vision of its roles and responsibilities beyond the profit-maximisation function to include interests and claims of non-stockholding groups. The basic notion is that corporations have an obligation to constituent groups in society other than stockholders and beyond that prescribed by law or union contract (Jones, 1980).

There has, however, been extensive discussion over how wide the stakeholder-set should be defined. Freeman's now-classic definition, 'A stakeholder in an organisation is any group or individual who can affect or is affected by the achievement of the organisation's objectives' is among the broadest. In contrast, Clarkson (1995) offers one of the narrower definitions of stakeholders as voluntary or involuntary risk-bearers. Scholars who have attempted to narrow the definition of stakeholder have emphasised the claim's legitimacy based upon contract, exchange, legal title, legal right, moral right, at-risk status or moral interest in the harms and benefits generated by the company actions.

Among the more thoughtful and comprehensive discussions of the stakeholder concept is that offered by Mitchell *et al.* (1997). Departing from Cyert and March's (1963) notion of organisations as coalitions of individuals and organised 'sub coalitions', Mitchell *et al*, (1997) develop the concept of stakeholder salience reflecting the power, legitimacy and urgency various stakeholders have with respect to influencing the firm's decisions. Mitchell *et al.*'s proposition is that stakeholders' salience may be defined in relation to their possession of three critical attributes: power, legitimacy and urgency. They predict that the salience of a particular stakeholder to the firm's management is low if only one attribute is present, moderate if two attributes are present and high if all three attributes are present.

IV.B. Infrastructure and commodification

In spite of its departure from the crude profit maximising idea, also the stakeholder-model relies fundamentally on motivation through competitive exposure. Without competition, the firm is hardly endogenously motivated to serve its environment except for political or normative pressure through public ownership or regulatory bodies. In other words, competition remains the final driver that motivates the stakeholder-oriented firm to take broader societal interests into consideration.

Given the natural monopoly characteristic of large parts of the electricity industry, the competitive exposure necessary to provoke a strong stakeholder-orientation is missing. However, even traditional natural monopoly segments of the electricity industry are becoming more and more competitively exposed, as technological and institutional innovation allows further commodification of traditional infrastructure industry.

One major premise for today's de-coupling of grid service and trade is clearly information technology, which allows systematic computation of transactions between dispersed suppliers and customers. This technological development obviously allows a commodification of infrastructure in so far as it allows free contracting and hence competition. Although certain elements of the traditional infrastructure remain hard to commodify directly, indirect competition between alternative networks, as markets develop and between sectors, opens up the market for substitute competition. Gas and electricity markets are, for instance, becoming more and more integrated and in some cases appear as close substitutes. In this way, the commercial dynamics and customer- orientation may come to characterise sectors in spite of the character of their infrastructure. In this sense it may be argued that the natural monopoly characteristics of a sector is a positional concept. Although central positions with connections to several networks may approach commodification and the following exposure to commercial dynamics, natural monopoly applies primarily to mono-functional periphery positions.

With the exposure to more market-like commercial dynamics, as well as to more competitively-oriented regulatory design, we are likely to see further commodification of infrastructure. It follows that we will then also increase our reliance on commercial dynamics as a guarantor of public/ customer interest. With multifunctional utilities with multiple use of grid systems, traditional mono-sectoral natural monopoly regulation will become increasingly difficult to maintain.

The increasing complexity of commercial dynamics in the European energy markets is thus creating extensive challenges both to energy companies and to energy regulators. By investigating strategic adaptation of the energy industry in ten countries we seek to shed light on major patterns of strategic behaviour and on some of the strategic dilemmas that face both the energy industry and governments that regulate the energy markets.

Literature

Agyris, C. and Schön, D. (1978) *Organizational Learning*. Oxford, Blackwell Publishers.

Arentsen, M.J. and Künneke, R.W. (1996) Economic organisation and liberalization of the electricity sector: in search of conceptualization. *Energy Policy* 24(6): 541–52.

Baird, L. and Meshoulam, I. (1968) Managing two fits of strategic human resource management. *Academy of Management Review* 13: 116–28.

Barney, J. (1991) Firm resources and sustained competitive advantage. *Journal of Management* 17: 99–120.

Bjercke, G. (1998) Learning processes in international joint ventures. PhD Dissertation. The Norwegian School of Management, Sandvika.

Campbell, J.L., Hollingsworth, R. and Lindberg, L.N. (1991) *Governance of the American Economy*. New York, Cambridge University Press.

Chandler, A.D. (1977) The visible hand: the managerial revolution in American business. Cambridge, MA, Belknap Press.

Chandler, A.D. (1992) Managerial enterprise and competitive capabilities. *Business History* 34(1): 11–41.

Clarkson, M.B.E (1995) A stakeholder framework for analyzing and evaluating corporate social performance. *Academy of Management Review* 20: 92–117.

Coase, R. (1988) The nature of the firm: Influence. *Journal of Law, Economics and Organization* 4: 33–47.

Coff, R.W. (1997) Human assets and management dilemmas: coping with hazards on the road to resource-based theory. *Academy of Management Review Mississippi State,* April 1997.

Cyert, R.M. and March, J.G. (1963) *The Behavioural Theory of the Firm.* Englewood Cliffs, NJ, Prentice Hall.

David, P.A. (1993) Path dependence and predictability in dynamic systems with local network externalities: a paradigm for historical economics. In: Foray, D., Freeman, C. (eds) *Technology and the Wealth of Nations.* London, Pinter Publishers.

Di Maggio, P. and Powell, W.W. (1991) The iron cage revisited: institutional isomorphism and collective rationality in organizational fields. In: Di Maggio, P., Powell, W.W. (eds) *The New Institutionalism in Organizational Analysis.* Chicago, University of Chicago Press.

Freeman, R.E. (1984) *Strategic Management: A Stakeholder Approach.* Boston, Pitman Publishers.

Hammel, G. and Prahalad, C.K. (1994) *Competing for the Future.* Boston, MA, Harvard Business School Press.

Hax, A.C. and Majluf, N.S. (1991) *The Strategy Concept and Process.* New Jersey, Prentice Hall.

Ioannides, S. (1992) *The Market, Competition and Democracy.* Aldershot, Hants, Edward Elgar.

Itami, H. (1987) *Mobilizing Invisible Assets.* Boston, Harvard University Press.

Jensen, M.C. and Meckling, W.H. (1976) Theory of the firm: managerial behavior, agency costs, and ownership structure. *Journal of Financial Economics* 3(4): 305–60.

Jones, T.M. (1980) Corporate social responsibility revisited, redefined. *California Management Review* 22(2): 59–67.

Koopmans, T.C. (1957) *Three Essays on the State of Economic Science.* New York, McGraw Hill.

Lengenick-Hall, C.A. and Lengenick-Hall, M.L. (1988) Strategic human resource management: a review of the literature and a proposed typology. *Academy of Management Review* 13: 454–70.

Lippman, S.A. and Rumelt, R.P. (1982) Uncertain imitability: an analysis of interfirm differences in efficiency under competition. *Bell Journal of Economics* 13: 418–38.

Mansfield, E. (1977) *Principles of Microeconomics.* New York, W.W. Norton & Company.

Mintzberg, H. (1989) *Mintzber on Management.* New York, The Free Press, Macmillan.

Mitchell, R.K., Agle, B.R. and Wood, D.J. (1997) Toward a theory of stakeholder identification and salience: defining the principle of who and what really counts. *Academy of Management Review* 22(4): 853–86.

Ohlin, B. (1967) *Interregional and International Trade,* rev. edn. Cambridge, MA, Harvard University Press.

Ohmae, K. (1985) *Triad Power.* New York, The Free Press/Macmillan.

Ohmae, K. (1995) *The End of the Naton State: the Rise of Regional Economies.* London, Harper Collins Publishers.

Orru, M. (1994) The faces of capitalism. Paper presented at the Sixth Annual International Conference on Socio-Economics. HEC, Paris.

Piore, M.S.and Sabel, C.F. (1984): The Second Industrial Divide.

Porter, M. (1980) *Competitive Strategy.* London, The Free Press, Macmillan.

Powell, W.W. (1981) Neither market nor hierarchy: network form of organization. *Research in Organizational Behaviour* 12: 295–336.

Pralahad, C.G. and Hammel, G. (1990) The core competence of the corporation. *Harvard Business Review* 63(3): 79–89.

Ricardo, D. (1971) *On the Principles of Political Economy, and Taxation* (edited with an introduction by Hartwell, R.M.). Harmondsworth, Penguin Books.

Schumpeter, J. (1943) *Capitalism, Socialism and Democracy*. London, George Allen & Unwin Ltd.

Scott, R. (1981) Organizationa: rational, natural and open systems. Englewood Cliffs, New Jersey, Prentice Hall.

Smith, A. (1933 (1776)) *An Inquiry into the Nature and Causes of the Wealth of Nations*. London, J.M. Dent & Sons.

Stabell, C. and Fjelstad, Ø. (1995) On Value Chains and Other Value Configurations. *Working Paper 1995/20 The Norwegian School of Management*. Norway, Sandvika.

Stinchcombe, A.L. (1984) Contracts as hierarchical documents. Work Report No. 65, Bergen, Institute of Industrial Economics.

Whitley, R. (1992) *European Business Systems: Firms and Markets in their National Contexts*. London, Sage.

Williamson, O. (1975) *Markets and Hierarchies: Analysis and Antitrust Implications*. New York, Free Press.

Williamson, O.E. (1979) Transaction cost economics: the governance of contractual relations. *Journal of Law and Economics* 22: 233–261.

Chapter II
Nordic Business Strategies

ATLE MIDTTUN, JOAR HANDELAND, JAN TERJE HENRIKSEN,
AUGUSTO R. MICOLA and TERJE OMLAND

I. The Nordic Model and its Structural Preconditions

The Nordic countries have been pioneers in the market exposure of the electricity sector, together with England and Wales. Yet, as opposed to England, they have not privatised the electricity industry, but maintained it under dominant public ownership. The Nordic electricity market therefore displays business strategies forged under the Nordic pragmatic public ownership under 'advanced' commercial conditions.

The Nordic countries have dominant public ownership models with considerable variation. The Norwegian electricity industry represents the most 'pure' application of the public sector model. Sweden and Finland come closer to a mixed economy model, with a larger share of private ownership. The Danish electricity industry represents a special variant of the Nordic model, characterised by a large share of consumer ownership.

The decentralised municipal ownership served to make the Nordic public ownership model well suited to free trade. In this respect, the Norwegian reform, the Nordic forerunner, clearly could build on almost ideal–typical structural conditions. With more than 94 generators and 205 suppliers[1] (ENFO, 1999) it barely moderately concentrate electricity generation and was a completely open market for supply (Fig. II.1). The Swedish model is far more centralised, with Vattenfall alone controlling 50% of electricity generation (Fig. II.2).

The sequencing of the Nordic electricity market reforms is, therefore, important. Although the Norwegian reform was confined to the country's

---

[1] Vertically-integrated companies are included in these numbers.

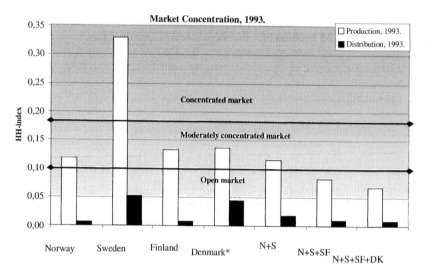

Fig. II.1. Concentration in the Nordic electricity markets 1998.
Source: Annual reports from the 20 biggest companies in each country, 1998.
Note: All data on Denmark in this table dates from 1995.

national boundaries, the Swedish reform opened up directly for a joint Norwegian–Swedish market. It thereby evaded the structural problem of the oversized Vattenfall, as the joint Norwegian–Swedish market barely figured as moderately concentrated for electricity generation. When Finland integrated into this market in 1998, both generation and supply in the new joint Nord Pool market area could be classified as open. The inclusion of Denmark in 1999 strengthened this openness even further (Fig. II.1).

In this chapter we shall present basic features of the structural transformation of the Nordic electricity industry, including ownership patterns.

A second section discusses Nordic models of strategic configuration. This section pinpoints typical patterns of scaling up for competitive advantage, linking up in flexible networks for innovation and the use of complementary resources, etc.

A third and final section draws some preliminary comparative observations on Nordic electricity industry strategies.

II. Structural Transformation of the Nordic Electricity Industry

Although the Nordic electricity markets share several structural characteristics and are gradually being exposed to similar market conditions, they have responded rather differently to the commercial challenges of deregulation. A combination of industrial traditions and ownership patterns are brought in to explain the Nordic variety.

II.A. Electricity Industry transformation in Sweden

In spite of the new competitive pressures since the 1990s, the public ownership model still remains dominant in Sweden. However, there has been a strong increase in foreign ownership and, partially as a consequence, a further consolidation and development of electricity industry clusters has taken place. The largest Swedish companies have played a major role in the transformation process, integrating smaller companies into their organisations. Medium-sized companies have been less active.

II.A.a. Ownership development

Institutional[2] and industrial ownership in the Swedish electricity industry have declined in generation and supply by 11% and 13%, respectively (Table II.1). This is due to ownership changes in the major companies Sydkraft, Gullspång and Graninge, which were previously dominated by industrial and institutional owners. However, the two paper and pulp companies Stora and MoDo have kept their institutional ownership shares constant, which currently constitute more than 50% in each of them.

Table II.1. Ownership structure in Sweden, 1994 and 1997.

	State (%)	Municipal (%)	Industry (%)	Institutional (%)	Foreign (%)	Other (%)
Production 1994	54.8	17.3	5.0	12.0	6.82	4
Production 1997	54.7	16.5	0.2	5.8	19.75	3
Change	−0.1	−0.7	−4.9	−6.2	12.9	−1.0
Votes 1997	54.7	19.2	0.6	4.5	19.3	2.0
Distribution 1994	30.9	44.6	6.2	9.3	5.75	3
Distribution 1997	36.9	35.7	0.0	2.6	22.55	2
Change	6.0	−8.8	−6.2	−6.7	16.8	−1.0
Votes 1997	36.1	39.5	0.0	1.3	21.8	1.3

Source: Annual reports from the 20 biggest companies in Sweden, 1994 and 1997. The table is based on market shares of the 20 largest generators and 20 largest suppliers. All data on ownership is, where possible, as a rule traced back to first-order ownership outside the electricity industry. This implies that an electricity company's share in another electricity company is not counted as cross-ownership within the sector, but is decomposed into the various ownership categories behind the owner company. Exceptions to this rule are explicitly noted in the text.
By supply we mean supply of electricity to end consumers. Wholesale of electricity to other suppliers or to very large industrial clients is thus not included.

---

[2] By institutional, we mean financial investments such as banks, pension funds, etc.

State ownership in Vattenfall, with its vast generation resources in hydro and nuclear power, remains strong and shows no change in the period. Following Vattenfall's growth in supply by 9,591 GWh, mainly through acquisitions, the Swedish state strengthened its position.

Municipal ownership has shown a downward trend throughout the period, both for generation and particularly for supply. This is because of the disinvestment of municipal shareholdings in the two large companies: Gullspång and Sydkraft. Overall, however, the increase in state ownership more or less balances out the decline in municipal ownership. Public ownership thereby retains its dominant position in Sweden, with a generation share decline of only 2% and no change in supply.

Following rapid acquisitions by IVO, EdF, PreussenElektra, Statkraft and HEW in major Swedish companies such as Gullspång, Sydkraft and Graninge, there has been a significant change in foreign ownership, which is now a major factor in the Swedish electricity industry. The aggregated data shows that, for the 20 largest suppliers and generators, however, the voting rights of foreign companies exceed 20% both in supply and generation (Table II.1). Sweden thereby takes the lead among the Nordic countries as an arena for foreign investment in the electricity industry.

II.A.b. Clustering in the Swedish electricity industry

Throughout the 1990s we have seen the consolidation of three major groups in the Swedish electricity industry, with ties to new foreign part owners (Fig. II.2). The two groups with major foreign owners are Birka Energi and what can be called the Sydkraft sphere. The last major group is Vattenfall, which alone is as big as the other two combined.

The Sydkraft group controls a generation capacity of more than 27 TWh and supply of more than 14 TWh, and is now increasingly foreign owned. The growth of foreign control in Sydkraft has come after the reduction in institutional municipal and industrial ownership.

The German company PreussenElektra entered as a Sydkraft owner in 1991 with 10%, and at present owns 17.6% of the shares and 27.3% of the votes. The Norwegian Statkraft bought Sydkraft shares in 1996 as the French company EdF sold out, as did the German company Hamburgische Elektrisitetswerke (HEW).

EdF fought with PreussenElektra for control over Sydkraft in the mid-1990s, with the acquisition of 7% of the shares in 1994. However, the French state company sold out during 1996 and instead entered the medium-sized Swedish company Graninge, buying the shares of the industrial investor Skanska (29.2%).

Sydkraft has acquired supply outlets in southern Sweden such as

Malmø Energi, Ørebro Energi and Båkab. Through Sydkraft's 19.9% ownership of the medium-sized Swedish company Graninge, with a 2.5 TWh generation and supply, and through PreussenElektra's ownership in both Sydkraft and Graninge (13.3%), Graninge has a tie to the Sydkraft sphere, although of a rather loose character.

However, a direct ownership share of 29.9% in Graninge by EdF and an agreement with another big owner, the Versteegh family (19%), most likely points at a rather independent strategy for Graninge, under the leadership of the French state company. Still, PreussenElektra's and Sydkraft's holdings in Graninge may limit EdF's ability to pursue independent strategies.

The second large Swedish group, Birka Energi AB, with a generation of more than 21 TWh and a supply of more than 24 TWh, was formed through the merger of Gullspång and Stockholm Energi, and came into effect on 1st January 1999. Its large Finnish owner IVO/Fortum has heavily influenced Gullspång, which has grown considerably over the last five years through the acquisitions of Uddeholm Kraft from the Swedish gas-supplier AGA and Skandinaviska Elverker from the Incentive Group. Stockholm Energi has, during the last two years, made connections to this group through the jointly-owned trading company Birka Kraft, before it chose to merge with Gullspång into Birka Energi. IVO/Fortum of Finland and the Municipality of Stockholm now own the cluster on a 50/50 basis.

The third Swedish strategic centre is the formidable Nordic giant Vattenfall, with more than 70 TWh of generation and 30 TWh of supply. Vattenfall has continued its strategy of balancing vertically by buying up suppliers throughout the 1990s. This includes companies such as Flens Energi, and Nacka Energi Marknads AB. Since 1995 Vattenfall has also been active acquiring Finnish suppliers, thereby increasing its vertical balance (supply/generation) and gaining a foothold in the Finnish market. The two main companies in Vattenfall's Finnish portfolio are Lapuan Sähkö and Hämeen Sähkö, the former being Finland's number five supplier.

Vattenfall's acquisition of 49% of Oslo Energi supply adds to the company's present engagement in the Norwegian market and affirms its broad presence in all Nordic markets.

II.A.c. Structural transformation of Swedish companies: a summary

As indicated in Fig. II.3, the Swedish transformation has primarily affected the larger companies: Sydkraft, Gullspång Stockholm and to some extent Vattenfall as well as some smaller suppliers that have been acquired.

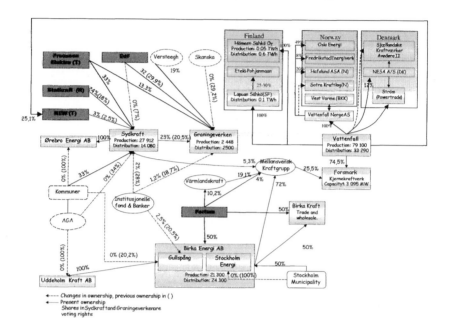

Fig. II.2. Ownership clusters in the Swedish electricity industry, 1990–1998.
Source: Annual reports from Swedish electricity companies, 1997–1999 and press
briefings (TDN Power and Reuter Business Briefing, 1998–2000).

Medium-sized companies have, relatively speaking, been more stable.
These companies, such as Skellefteå Kraft, Tekniska Verken i Linköping,
Göteborg Energi and Telge Energi, have traditionally had strong municipal owners that considered reliable electricity supply a municipal duty.
Throughout the 1990s these companies were very reluctant to expand
through mergers and acquisitions. However, this could be about to
change because at least one of the companies, Göteborg Energi, has stated
its willingness to reach the critical size necessary in a competitive market. One of the discussed solutions is a merger with Vattenfall's activities in the region.

The restructuring of the Swedish electricity industry in the 1990s was
largely based on acquisitions of privately-owned companies such as
Båkab, Uddeholm and Skandinaviska Elverker (SEV), and on acquisition
of small supply companies with grids bordering on larger companies.
Further large-scale restructuring and transformation of the Swedish electricity industry will probably depend on the readiness of Swedish municipalities, who own virtually all of the remaining medium-sized
companies, to sell out or merge.

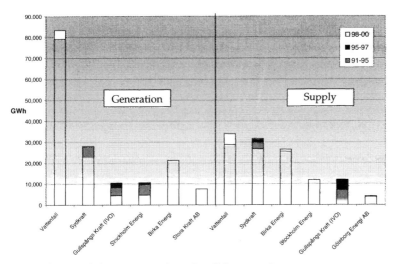

Fig. II.3. Structural change among large Swedish companies.
Source: Annual reports from Swedish Electricity companies, 1991–1999 and press briefings (TDN Power and Reuter Business Briefing, 1991–2000).

II.B. Transformation in the Finnish electricity industry

The response of the Finnish electricity industry to the competitive challenge of deregulation has included consolidation and regrouping of clusters, as well as foreign takeovers.

The pattern of consolidation of traditional clusters refers to the Finnish forestry industry's integrated operation of its electricity generation. The forestry industry is thereby able to secure long-term electricity supply at a self-cost basis.

New clustering has occurred among Finnish suppliers in order to face the market power of the generator side. However, generators have challenged the supplier clustering in the form of both alternative clustering and takeovers.

II.B.a. Ownership development

The ownership development in the Finnish electricity industry in the 1990s is characterised by a sharp decline in municipal ownership of supply companies, increased state ownership in supply and increased foreign ownership in both supply and generation (Table II.2).

The drastic decline in municipal ownership of supply companies is matched by a parallel expansion of the State power company IVO/ Fortum into supply. Starting with hardly any supply in the early 1990s, IVO has responded to the market reform by acquiring large suppliers

Table II.2. Ownership structure in Finland.

	State (%)	Municipal (%)	Industry (%)	Institutional (%)	Foreign (%)	Other (%)	PVO (%)
Production 1994	36.6	15.2	27.0	5.7	0.4	5.7	10.2
Production 1997	35.9	17.0	19.1	6.1	8.1	4.7	9.1
Change	−0.8	1.8	−8.9	0.4	7.8	−1.0	−1.1
Supply 1994	0.0	91.2	1.4	1.2	0.0	6.2	0.0
Supply 1997	17.6	67.3	3.1	2.4	7.8	1.8	0.0
Change	17.8	−23.9	1.7	1.2	7.8	−4.3	0.0

Based on market shares of the 20 largest generators and 20 largest suppliers. All data on ownership are, where possible, as a rule traced back to first-order ownership outside the electricity industry. This implies that an electricity company's ownership of shares in an other electricity company is not counted as cross-ownership within the sector, but is decomposed into the various ownership categories behind the owner company. Exceptions to this rule are explicitly noted in the text.
Finland represents one of the exceptions to the rule of first-order ownership. In the table, this is shown as PVO-ownership and represents Pohjolan Voima Oy's (PVO) ownership in nuclear power generator Teollisuuden Voima Oy (TVO).
Source: Annual reports from Finnish electricity companies, 1994 and 1997.

such as Länsivoima Oy, Uudenmaan Energia and Tuusulanjärven Sähkö. By far the most important of these has been the gradual acquisition of 65% of Länsivoima, which has made the company an IVO subsidiary. At the end of 1997, IVO had acquired 4,600 GWh of supply, thereby significantly increasing its supply capacity from a mere 400 GWh in 1994.

Besides the expansion of Finnish State ownership in supply through IVO, increase in foreign ownership is the second factor behind decline in municipal supply ownership in Finland. The total foreign owned supply in Finland in 1997 was 2,305 GWh or approximately 8% of the supply of the 20 largest companies among the 20 biggest suppliers. This is due to the acquisitions in Hämeen Sähkö and Kainuun Säkhö by the Swedish companies Vattenfall and Graninge, respectively.

In response to the Nordic market reforms, foreign ownership in Finnish electricity companies also increased on the generation side. This can be attributed to the forestry companies UPM-Kymmene Oy and Enso Group Oy (now merged with Swedish Stora) and the energy company Neste Oy. All three are major Finnish producers, in addition to being leading actors of their respective industries at the European level. Total public ownership in generation (state and municipal) has been relatively stable in generation (52–53%) but has declined in supply (91–85%). This 6% decline in publicly owned supply is largely explained by the increased foreign shareholdings in the period. The decline in public shareholdings in generation during this period is attributed to increased capacity by private companies, particularly the forestry industry.

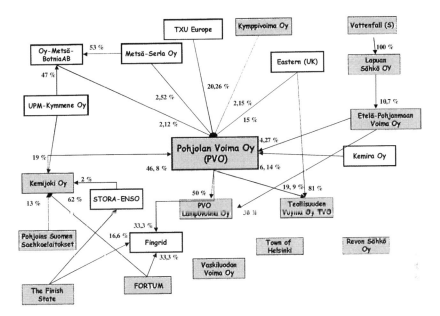

Fig. II.4. Strategic clusters in Finnish electricity generation.
Source: Annual reports from Finnish electricity companies, 1998 and press briefings
(TDN Power and Reuter Business Briefing, 1999).

II.B.b. *The industrial ownership cluster*

In response to the emerging Nordic electricity market reforms, there has
been a further consolidation of co-ordinated industrial power generation.
In this system, a number of industrial firms have transferred their electricity generation to centrally organised power companies in return for ownership shares and specific rights to draw on resources at special prices. The
three companies, Teollisuuden Voima Oy (TVO, Industrial Power),
Pohjolan Voima Oy (PVO, Northern Power) and Teollisuuden Voimansiirto
Oy (TVS, the Industrial Power Transmission and Purchasing Company),
were instrumental in this co-ordination. Combined with an extensive generation capacity of individual firms, the co-ordinated industrial generation
system has developed an internal merit order system and strengthened its
relative independence of the external market. Fig. II.4 gives an overview
of the industrial cluster and other major Finnish generators.

The market reform in Finland has led not only to consolidation of traditional practices, but also to major changes. One of the major organisational consequences of the Finnish market reform has been the merger
of the public and industrial high-tension grids. Suomen Sähköverkko, or
Fingrid, is the result of a pooling of the two Finnish central grids into a
larger national company. The grids were merged in 1997 and Finnish

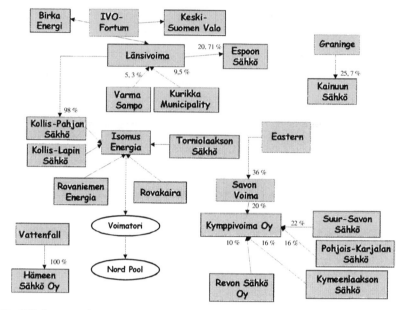

Fig. II.5. Strategic clusters in Finnish electricity supply.
Source: Annual reports from Finnish electricity companies, 1998 and press briefings
(TDN Power and Reuter Business Briefing, 1999).

industry is now a part-owner of Fingrid of one-third through PVO. In
addition, the Finnish state owns one-sixth, insurance companies own one-
sixth and IVO/Fortum owns one-third. Thus, directly and through IVO's
share, the Finnish state controls 50% of Fingrid, while the rest is controlled by industry and institutional companies.

II.B.c. Ownership clustering among public suppliers

Apart from the consolidation of the industrial cluster, there has also been
extensive grouping among public companies, in both supply and generation. Anticipating the Finnish reform, ten suppliers created a common
purchasing company, Kymppivoima Oy (Tiokraft), where they collabo-
rated to negotiate better prices with generators (Fig. II.4). Kymppivoima
represented about one-third of total supply (10 TWh) and covered one-
quarter of the national customer base (Midttun 1997).

During 1995, Vattenfall, Graninge and IVO started acquisitions of
some of the member companies in Kymppivoima, reducing the owners
of Kymppivoima to only five. These and the municipalities behind them
have made an attempt to consolidate the local ownership in
Kymppivoima, founding Itä-Suomen Energia (East-Finnish Energy).

Kymppivoima has also sought to strengthen its position by buying into

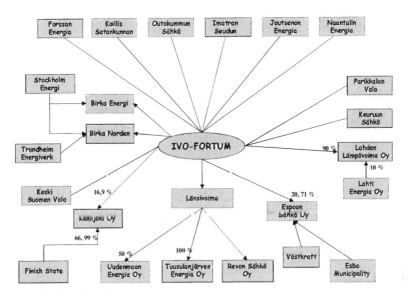

Fig. II.6. IVO and associate companies.
Source: Annual reports from Finnish electricity companies, 1998 and press briefings
(TDN Power and Reuter Business Briefing, 1999).

PVO, the core of the industrial cluster, as a way of securing a steady supply of electricity for its owners.

A strategic cluster of growing importance and interest is Isommus-Energia Oy, which originated as a procurement company, like Kymppivoima, for five regional suppliers in the north provinces of Oulu and Lapland. This company has since May 1998, also taken over the handling of the owners' electricity sales to end customers. However, the ongoing consolidation of the Finnish electricity industry has also had its consequences for Isommus-Energia. In December 1998, IVO acquired one of the Isommus-Energia partners Kollis-Pohjalan Sähkö Oy, an acquisition that could result in a similar development for Isommus to that of Kymppivoima. Isommus is again a member of Voimatori Oy, which handles all trading on the spot market on its behalf. Nine regional procurement companies and 25 local electricity companies are members of Voimatori. All of these but one are municipally owned.

II.B.d. The IVO-Partner alliance

The collaboration between suppliers has been met by clustering on the generation side. IVO made an attempt to forge closer connections with local suppliers through the IVO-Partners chain (Fig. II.5). We may, therefore, speak of an IVO cluster, which consists both of suppliers acquired through takeovers and of looser partnerships, the so-called IVO Partners.

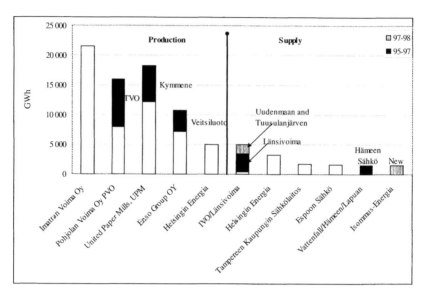

Fig. II.7. Structural change of large Finnish companies.
Source: Annual reports from Finnish electricity companies, 1995–1997 and press briefings (TDN Power and Reuter Business Briefing, 1995–1998).

This constitutes a countermove to the Kymppivoima strategy and has in fact several former Kymppivoima participants as members. The IVO Partners alliance is a concept where the member co-operates in marketing. Moreover, there is an opening for further development of common operations and services. So far 11 companies have chosen to join the partnership, four of which are controlled by IVO.

II.B.e. Transformations in the Finnish case

To sum up, Figure II.6 shows that the consolidation on both the generation and supply sides indicate that the market reform had led to considerable structural changes.

The massive impact of the mergers in the forestry industry is striking. UPM and Enso have added 50% to their generation capacity as a result of them. It is, however, as previously mentioned, not entirely correct to show PVO and TVO in just one column. For instance, PVO only controls 56.8% of the output; the rest belongs to other owners.

Fig. II.6 also highlights the growth of IVO/Fortum in supply. After the acquisitions of Länsivoima, Uudenmaan and Tsuulansjärven, IVO is by far the biggest Finnish supplier. Vattenfall and Isommus-Energia are interesting newcomers as both have further growth potential. If the sales operations of Isommus-Energia are successful, more municipal participants are expected in the company. Further success for Vattenfall in its takeover strategy might also soon place it more prominently in the Finnish electricity industry.

The considerable size differences between generators and suppliers produce clear scale advantages for the former in their rivalry for power.

II.C. Industrial transformation in Norway

Considering Norway's early deregulation in 1991, the restructuring of supply and generation came remarkably late. An early organisational move was, however, taken by generators who formed export cartels to face trading with monopolised continental markets.

More recently, and in parallel with Swedish and Finnish industrial restructuring, Norwegian suppliers started integrating into regional clusters, all over the country. These groups have various degrees of integration and mixes of political and commercial interest. On the other hand, all of them clearly represent attempts of scaling up to meet larger commercial pressures.

Given the 'soft' and flexible mode of integration, regional clustering has not implied dramatic ownership transfers. The Norwegian commercial restructuring has, until recently, been characterised by a negotiated approach with extensive political overtones.

II.C.a. Ownership development

Ownership patterns in Norway from 1990–97 showed a remarkable steadiness. Generation and supply were characterised by only minor adjustments (Table II.3). However, in late 1997 and in 1998 the pattern changed and we can observe more active restructuring.

The most prominent ownership change recently has been Statkraft's 20% acquisition of the municipal company Oslo Energi Produksjon. In spite of the decline for strategic reasons of the amount of electricity generated by the state, Table II.3 registers a stable share for state ownership.

The change in foreign ownership in the Norwegian electricity industry mostly refers to changes in the ownership of the two companies listed on the Stock Exchange, Hafslund and Norsk Hydro. A mere registration of ownership changes, however, tends to underscore structural developments without ownership change.

II.C.b. Clustering in the Norwegian electricity supply industry

Following increased pressure of the liberalised market, clustering of municipal suppliers increased, in many cases leading to consolidation of large regional groups in the Norwegian electricity industry. So far, the

Table II.3. Ownership structure in Norway.

	State (%)	Municipal (%)	Industry (%)	Institutional (%)	Foreign (%)	Other (%)
Production 1994	41.1	48.9	2.2	0.0	4.63	3
Production 1997	41.0	48.5	0.6	2.9	3.86	3
Change	0	−0.4	−1.5	2.9	−0.8	−0.2
Votes 1997	39.7	50.0	2.9	0.5	4.1	0.9
Distribution 1994	0	100.0	0	0	0	0
Distribution 1997	0.1	99.2	0.1	0.2	0.13	0
Change	0.1	−0.8	0.1	0.2	0.1	0

Based on market shares of the 20 largest generators and 20 largest suppliers. All data on ownership is, where possible, as a rule traced back to first-order ownership outside the electricity industry. This implies that an electricity company's ownership of shares in another electricity company is not counted as cross-ownership within the sector, but is decomposed into the various ownership categories behind the owner company. Exceptions to this rule are explicitly noted in the text.
Source: Annual reports from Norwegian electricity companies, 1994–1997.

clusters have mainly involved sales operations and marketing, but we may expect further integration into common companies.

One of the major reasons for the 'soft' regional Norwegian clustering strategy is probably that it is hard to transfer ownership on a large scale in Norway for both legal and political reasons. Structural transformation in the Norwegian case has therefore largely been a clustering process based on both commercial and political 'logic'.

In western Norway, Bergenshalvøens Kommunale Kraftselskap (BKK) was merged with Bergen Lysverker in 1996 into one of the biggest verti-cally-integrated companies in Norway (Fig. II.8). So far, the company has expanded to the north through acquisitions in exchange for shares in BKK. In the south, BKK has bought 22% of the local vertically-integrated company Sunnhordland Kraftlag, but has had no luck in acquiring fur-ther shares. More recently, in the autumn of 1998, BKK bought two ad-jacent suppliers, Osterøy Energi and Sotra Energi, in the latter case challenging Swedish Vattenfall, and 49% of the local supplier Hurum Kraft, which operates in the greater Oslo area.

Apart from the electricity business, BKK also owns assets in the natural gas (Naturgass Vest), heat (BKK Varme) and telecom (El-Tele Vest) indus-tries. To support its growth strategy and acquire capital, BKK has allowed Statkraft to buy into its sales and generation/grid subsidiaries (Fig. II.8).

Further north in the western county of Møre og Romsdal, a smaller regional consolidation has taken place as small, supply-based companies with limited generation resources have merged. It is expected that the electricity industry in most of this county will be merged into one or two regional companies.

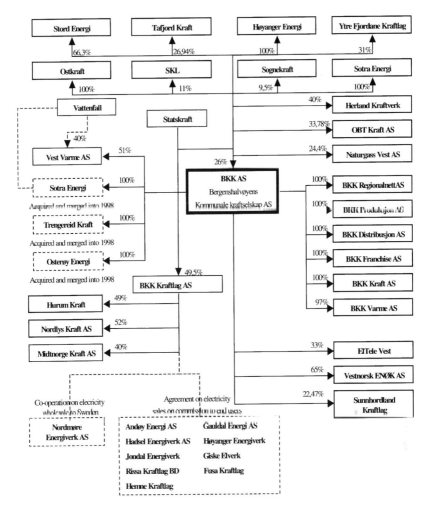

Fig. II.8. The strategic configuration of BKK AS.
Source: Annual reports from Norwegian electricity companies, 1998 and press briefings
(TDN Power and Reuter Business Briefing, 1999).

In the south-west, Lyse Energi has been formed in a merger of five
local companies and their commonly-owned generator. The new firm will
be a regional giant and a possible national actor with a generation of 5
TWh and a supply of more than 3 TWh to 117,000 customers.

In the south, five owners have formed the regional group Interkraft,
formerly Sørkraft. They are vertically-integrated municipal companies.
Interkraft has so far concentrated its activities in trading and selling electricity outside its owners' concession area. Inside, the owners have so far

purchased electricity on their own behalf and sold electricity to customers under their own name.

In northern Norway, five local and regional companies have pooled resources on product development, marketing and logistics into a new company: Elinor. The members of Elinor have approximately 5700 GWh of supply and hold a significant electricity generation capacity. It is expected that the present co-operation is only a step towards full integration.

A second large cluster in eastern Norway, DIN Energi AS, was founded by a merger of the sales units of Asker og Bærum Energiverk, Drammen Kraft Omsetning Kongsberg Energi and Buskerud Energi AS. This new company will have a customer basis of 110,000, supply 3600 GWh of electricity per year and operate in the western suburbs and adjacent areas of Oslo. Part owner of DIN Energi, through a 47% share is Hafslund ASA, which in turn is controlled by Oslo Energi Holding (31.52%), Vattenfall (11.83%), Statoil (11.58%) and Østfold Kraft AS (4.44%) all potential competitors.

This cluster also has strong ties with a parallel generation-oriented cluster. In 1996 Statkraft bought 20% of Oslo Energi Produksjon and, in 1997, the latter bought 30% of Drammen Kraft Produksjon (now merged with Buskerud Kraft Produksjon AS). A cluster has formed as Oslo Energi also has a share of 31.52% in Hafslund, which owns 47% of DIN Energi, the result of a merger of former Drammen Kraft Omsetning and Asker og Bærum Omsetning. DIN Energi has three other owners, including Energiselskapet Buskerud AS, which holds 51% (Fig. II.9).

In eastern Norway, the vertically-integrated county company Akershus Energi bought several local supply companies and controls

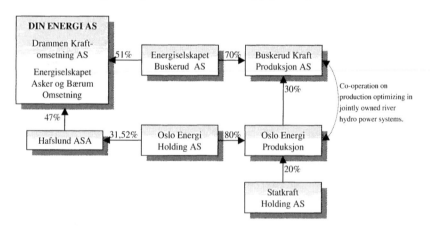

Fig. II.9. Ownership clusters in Norwegian el-generation.
Source: Annual reports from Norwegian electricity companies, 1998 and press briefings (TDN Power and Reuter Business Briefing, 1999).

most of the supply to Akershus County, east of Oslo. In addition, Akershus Energi is forming a cluster with suppliers in adjacent areas. So far, the company controls 2,500 GWh of retail supplies.

Oslo Energi has been engaged in the formation of a trade and sales company in eastern Norway. This is to be formed in joint ownership with Østfold Energi and Akershus Energi, which is controlled by Østkraft. Supplies to end-customers have apparently been the first target and the three together supplied 11,800 GWh in 1998. The cluster links to the DIN Energi cluster through the co-operation and possible merger with Hafslund grids and Østfold's regional and supply grids, respectively. A second link is Oslo Energi Holding's 31.52% ownership of Hafslund. That way, the whole Oslo area could be consolidated on the supply side in a single company/cluster. Fig. II.10 is an overview of the biggest recent clusters in eastern Norway.

In 1999, the Swedish state company Vattenfall bought 49% of Oslo Energi and thereby acquired a strong foothold in the Norwegian supply market. Vattenfall will include its almost 40,000 Norwegian customers in Oslo Energi. This may enhance Oslo Energi's role in the regional context.

Like Sweden, Norway enjoys, to some extent, large rivers where several generators operate joint power plants or have generation capacity that

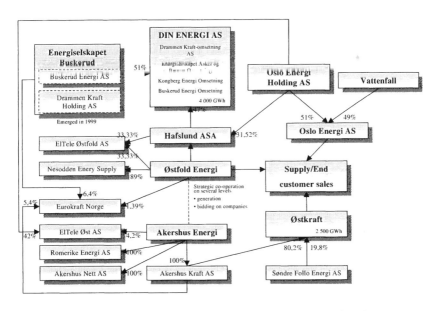

Fig. II.10. Ownership clustering in the east Norwegian electricity supply industry.
Source: Annual reports from Norwegian electricity companies, 1998 and press briefings (TDN Power and Reuter Business Briefing, 1999).

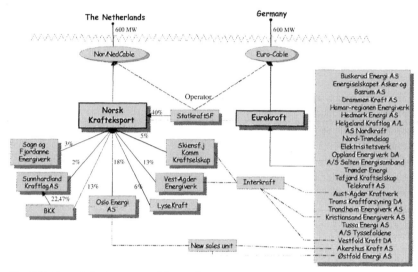

Fig. II.11. Export clusters among Norwegian generators.
Source: Annual reports from Norwegian electricity companies, 1997 and press briefings
(TDN Power and Reuter Business Briefing, 1998).

need co-ordination to ensure maximum output. However, the largest resources in the Norwegian system lie in the huge mountain reservoirs, many
of which could be operated independently. Although some of the major
dams were established as joint ventures between Statkraft and the regional
generator, clusters of joint owners in common river systems play a smaller
role than in Sweden.

II.C.c. Clustering in the Norwegian generation and export industry

The targeting of export markets is characterised by co-ordinated strategies in clusters. Two groups were formed in connection with two cable
projects from Norway to the European continent: Norsk Krafteksport and
Eurokraft. These groups gather companies across other clusters and are
intended to export electricity (Fig. II.11).

The rationale behind this clustering has partly been the provision of
access for many companies to a limited set of export licences. In addition, they also serve to co-ordinate Norwegian interests against Continental monopolists. Statkraft will soon operate a third cable connection.

II.C.d. Transformation in the Norwegian case

In conclusion, a compilation of the biggest Norwegian generators and
suppliers in graphs (Fig. II.12) indicates extensive restructuring of the

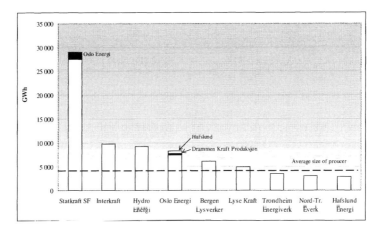

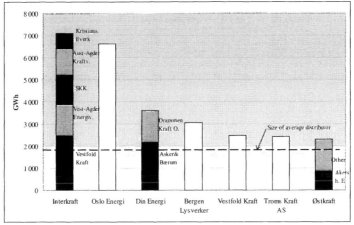

Fig. II.12. Structural change in large Norwegian electricity industry companies.
Source: Annual reports from Norwegian electricity companies, 1991–1997 and press briefings (TDN Power and Reuter Business Briefing, 1991–1998).

supply industry in a 'soft' form. However, none of the supply clusters includes transfer of the grids' ownership.

All three supply clusters make a heavy impact (Fig. II.12). Interkraft has the potential to be the larger supplier, but is weakened by internal conflict: DIN Energi is currently the real number two, after Oslo Energi. Østkraft, with 2.300 GWh of supply, is currently the sixth largest. Since the plans for co-operation between Oslo Energi, Østfold Energiverk and Østkraft are not yet known, and may be offset by Vattenfall's acquisition, they cannot be included in the figure.

II.D. Industrial transformation in Denmark

In the Nordic context, Denmark has been a latecomer in the deregulation of electricity markets. However, extensive strategic reorganisation has taken place during the late 1990s in anticipation of future competitive exposure. On the one hand, suppliers have been integrating, particularly in the Jutland area, in order to gain scale and bargaining power. On the other hand, some generators have prepared export strategies in the opening European market.

Danish generators have a double motivation for taking an active part in Nordic and continental trade. With its dominant thermal system, Denmark represents a complementary position to the large Nordic hydro-systems and may gain from further exploitation of it. Given its location at the German border, it represents a gateway for trade from the Nordic system to central Europe, and Danish generators may find themselves in a position to reap gains from bridging the two systems.

II.D.a. Ownership development

The Danish system stands out as special in the Nordic context. It is characterised by the total absence of state ownership. The majority of Danish electricity suppliers are municipally-owned (48.6%) or consumer-owned (46.4%) (Table II.4). The exception is the Zealand company NESA, listed on the Copenhagen Stock Exchange and controlled by municipal, foreign and institutional owners. The foreign ownership consists of Swedish Vattenfall's 10.5% share in the company.

Among the ten large centralised generators, which account for more than 80% of the total, 48% are owned by consumers through supply companies and 48.9% are owned directly by municipal owners. As with suppliers, minor shares belong to foreign and institutional owners through NESA.

II.D.b. Clustering in the Danish electricity supply industry

In spite of Denmark's late deregulation, the Jutland and Fyn area have been exposed to a major restructuring of the supply and generation in-

Table II.4. Ownership structure in Denmark.

	State (%)	Municipal (%)	Industry (%)	Institutional (%)	Foreign (%)	Consumer (%)
Production 1997	0	48.9	0	1.2	1.52	48
Supply 1997	0	48.7	0	2.2	2.79	46.4

Source: Annual reports from Danish electricity companies, 1997.

dustries in anticipation of the liberalisation of the Danish and European markets.

The mergers in the Danish electricity supply industry have proceeded swiftly and without much debate. This is in contrast to Norway and Finland, where municipal owners are very reluctant to give up control over the local electricity companies. The Danes seem to have become aware that they have to join forces to survive in a backdrop of increasing competition and market liberalisation of retail supplies. The scaling-up has been almost exclusively located in the Jutland and Fyn area, mostly because Zealand has traditionally been more concentrated.

The mergers in Jutland (Fig. II.13) are limited to the north and southeast. In north Jutland, the merger of ENV (Elforsyningen Nordvendsyssel) and HEF (Himmerlands Elforsyning) in a new company, Nordjynsk Energi, has formed the biggest supplier in the region with an annual supply of 1,351 GWh. In south Jutland and Fyn, four mergers of approximately the same size and two smaller ones have been accomplished. First, Vest Energi, is the result of the merger between SAEF and Esbjerg's Municipal Supply Company, and supplies 1,250 GWh annually. Second, ESS, the merger of Elforsyningen Sønderjylland Syd and Haderslev og Omegn Elselskap, supplies 1,083 GWh annually. Third, Energi Fyn, the merger of Effla and Vestfyn Elforyning, supplies 1,018 GWh annually. Fourth, TreFor, the merger of three municipal electricity supply companies in Fyn, supplies 1,005 GWh annually. The last two mergers are EnCon and Sydvest Energi, both supplying about 800 GWh annually. The latter is a merger of Energiselskapet EASV and Midtsønderjyllands Energiforsyning, whereas the former is a merger of five smaller local suppliers.

In addition to the above mergers, suppliers have grouped into purchasing organisations in Jutland/Fyn. This grouping covers virtually the whole region. Unlike in Norway and Finland, these organisations are not based on geographical vicinity or adjoining grids but gather companies scattered throughout the area.

The organisation of supply in such co-operations seems motivated by cost and learning advantages. Most members are not large enough to support their own market management units or attract competition among generators. In March 1999, there were four purchasing organisations: DanEl, DISAM, Elisa and Scan Energi. The two largest, DanEl and DISAM, purchase about 4.5 TWh annually and co-operated with Nordic partners to acquire market management skills. Only eight of 71 supply companies in Jutland/Fyn have agreed to participate in purchasing organisations. These are, however, very small; combined, they account for 0.5 TWh of supplies.

As shown in Fig. II.13, both mergers and grouping of purchasing

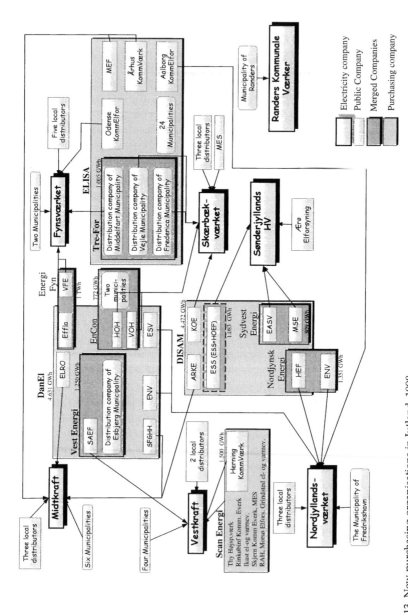

Fig. II.13. New purchasing organisations in Jutland, 1998.
Source: Annual reports from Danish electricity companies, 1997 and press briefings (TDN Power and Reuter Business Briefing, 1998).

organisations present cross-ownership ties with generators. For instance, Dan El's members are linked to five different generators: Midtkraft, Nordjyllandsværket, Skærbækværket, Fynsværket and Vestkraft. The suppliers are now free to purchase electricity from any generator. Such organisation would have been difficult to achieve prior to the abolition of the suppliers' purchase obligation, but this made suppliers more independent and resulted in increased competition.

Four big companies (NESA, SEAS, NVE, Nordvestsjællands Energiværk and København Belysningsvæsen) dominate Zealand. Of these, NESA has been the most dynamic in adapting to the liberalisation process, notably by entering a partnership with Vattenfall to exchange electricity and build power plants in joint venture with Sjællandske Kraftværker (SK). This latter is, in turn, 52% owned by NESA. For example, the Avedøre II coal-fired CHP plant currently under construction is jointly owned by Vattenfall and SK. In return, Sjællandske Kraftværker is given rights to hydro-power generation in Sweden. Another example is what seems like a countermove to NESA's alliance with Vattenfall.

København Belysningsvæsen, NVE and SEAS have formed a new electricity sales company with Swedish Sydkraft. Each owner holds 25% of the shares in the new company, Elektra Energihandel A/S, which will primarily concentrate on big customers in the Danish electricity market.

II.D.c. Strategic adaptation in Danish electricity generation

New relationships between supply and generation have emerged with the reorganisation of the Danish electricity companies and the emerging Danish market reform. Traditionally, suppliers have received the bulk of their electricity from centralised generators where they are major owners. With market liberalisation, suppliers are gaining the right to buy power wherever they want. Already the five liberalised big consumers have made huge savings on their electricity bill by freely choosing the cheapest supplier, and it is expected that this will apply to forthcoming liberalised consumers as well.

Nevertheless, suppliers own Denmark's 10 large central generators, or 77% of the market. These ties make for some ambiguity as to the commercial positioning between generators and suppliers. In addition, there are 32 decentralised power plants owned by the centralised companies and 458 decentralised CHPs owned mostly by supply companies or directly by industrial companies (Dansk Elforsyning, 1998).

As with supply case, companies in the Jutland and Fyn areas have been the most active in adapting to the market that is reforming the generation business. The large Jutland generation and system-operation company Elsam pursues a foreign-trade-oriented strategy, much like some

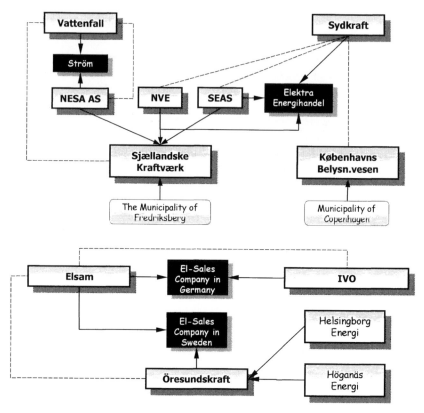

Fig. II.14. Danish sales co-operations with foreign participants, February 1999.
Source: Annual reports from Danish electricity companies, 1997 and press briefings
(TDN Power and Reuter Business Briefing, 1998).

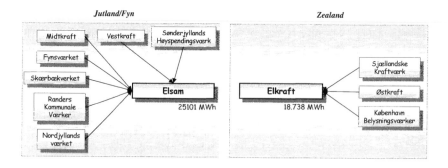

Fig. II.15. Organising of the electricity generation in Denmark.
Source: Annual reports from Danish electricity companies, 1997 and press briefings
(TDN Power and Reuter Business Briefing, 1998).

Norwegian generators, and has established wholesale operations with Öresundskraft in Sweden and IVO in the German market. The company has also set up a separate office in the city of Ratingen to carefully monitor the development of the German electricity liberalisation process. Elsam, with an annual generation of 20 TWh, recently stated that their new target market area is Scandinavia, Germany and the Netherlands (TDN Power 1999). The company's trade strategy has been developed in collaboration with the supply companies. As suppliers group into purchasing companies and merge to increase buying power, generators appear to be seeking new markets for electricity in order to strengthen bargaining power at home. The commercialisation of the Danish generation-coordination companies is facilitated by division of their grid ownership and systems operation functions into separate companies.

The large generator and system-operator Elkraft, operating in the Isle of Zealand, remains more locked into a self-supply strategy, where every generator carries enough installed effect to cover peak load within its area and where the suppliers are loyal to their traditional generator within predefined boundaries. The exception to that is NESA, which has taken steps towards co-operation with new entrants. NESA has entered into a sales co-operation with Swedish Vattenfall to form the joint company Ström. This firm intends to offer tailor-made energy supplies to Danish industry, public entities and individual customers. This has not been well received by the other electricity companies on Zealand, and other electricity companies in the Elkraft area have stated that the initiative jeopardises the whole Elkraft co-operation (TDN Power 1999). In Jutland/Fyn, both are generators through Elsam, and all suppliers are prepared to compete freely for big customers. In contrast, the attitude in Zealand is that the segment belongs to Elkraft and that breaking this tradition would endanger the foundation of the traditional electricity supply there.

Nevertheless, as a counter-move to the NESA–Vattenfall grouping, the other three suppliers on Zealand have entered a deal with Sydkraft, the second largest Swedish generator, to form a joint trading firm in which each will own 25% (Fig. II.14). The company is supposed to operate in Denmark and energy trading will be the core business area. Anticipated competitive pressure is obviously driving even the Zealand companies to transcend old policy traditions (Fig. II.15).

II.D.d. Transformations in the Danish case
The deregulation of the Danish electricity industry has lagged behind other Nordic countries. Furthermore, Danish energy policy has traditionally been strongly environmentally focused and continues to be so under the new market reform. According to the White Papers Energi 2000

(1990) and Energi 21 (1996), energy from renewable sources shall cover 12–14% of Danish energy consumption by 2005, and Energi 21 projects this number to rise to 30% by 2030. Special measures are, therefore, being worked out to sustain environmental policies under the new market conditions, hereunder to specifically support wind power (Meyer, 1999).

Nevertheless, the anticipated reform had already led to structural changes in the industry, even before being decided. In the Jutland and Fyn regions the members of the purchasing organisations, DanEl, Disam, Elisa and Scan Energi, accounted for 98.41% of all electricity sold in 1998. The major mergers involved 38.23% in the same regions and increased in 1999 as new companies joined in. The scope of structural changes in the Zealand region cannot match those in the Jutland/Fyn regions. So far, no mergers have occurred, and only co-operation in sales concentrates on the big customers. The Elektra (Nordvestsjællands Energiforsyning, SEAS and København Belysningsvæsen) organisation will, if it handles all customers, account for 42.9% of the supplies in Zealand, while NESA alone supplies 40.7%.

On the generation side, well-developed plans and alliances prepare Danish companies for advanced trading in the Nordic energy market, and between this market and the partially opened continental markets. The geographical location of Denmark, between the Nordic and continental markets puts Danish industry in a position to harvest arbitrage between them.

III. Strategic Configurations

The structural transformation of the Nordic electricity industry discussed in the previous section can be interpreted in the light of several strategic motivations. In this section we shall relate more systematically the Nordic patterns of industrial organisation to a business-strategy perspective.

The discussion particularly focuses on how companies with apparently similar resources and preconditions can motivate different patterns of industrial configuration. More specifically, we shall analyse how large companies, supposedly with sufficient scale to internalise resources for advanced commercial activity, take very different positions on how to balance internal hierarchic and external market governance.

We shall also discuss various forms of scaling up of small-company clusters and the motivation of this variety. They differ with respect to both how and in which functions they achieve integration. One of the interesting features of Nordic strategic configuration is the interface between the many small companies and the advanced market areas, which are both hallmarks of Nordic reforms. We shall here particularly focus on how the emergence of new market-management expertise has made it possible to combine small-scale and local customer interface with scale-based advanced market-management of power purchasing and risk management.

To a varying extent and in different forms, the Nordic electricity market also provides examples of new sectorial integration. We shall briefly discuss how Nordic electricity firms are actively integrating into gas and petroleum corporations and vice versa. Similarly, we shall discuss new strategic engagement by electricity companies in the telecommunications industry, often based on utilisation of the electricity grid for multiple purposes.

III.A. Strategic configuration in large companies

Large companies employ both fission strategies, where generation and supply are de-coupled into separate business units, and integration (fusion) strategies, with a focus on channelling transactions within the company. In between we find semi-integration.

III.A.a. The fission model

In the fission model, a company splits its various functions into strategic business units, with external trading relations between them. This implies, for example, that the generation and supply units of the same company are allowed to trade freely on the open market, without any preference for internal trade. Fission thus implies internalising external marketplaces (symbolised by the market cross and exemplified by Nord Pool and the arenas for more specific market products, OTC) into the company, and reduces the management of the parent company primarily to financial matters (Fig. II.16).

Fission necessitates building full-scale trading competencies, with market trading management units, in both supply and generation units, so that they can undertake separate and perhaps conflicting transactions. However, these units may draw on a common market analysis, undertaken by a separate analysis unit serving both trading units.

Among the larger Nordic electricity companies, Oslo Energi—a vertically-integrated electricity company including all traditional parts of the electricity value chain—comes closest to this ideal type. During a major reorganisation of Oslo Energi in 1996, the grid was separated and turned into an independent company, owned directly by the city of Oslo. The remainder of Oslo Energi has been turned into a holding company, Oslo Energi Holding—of which the city of Oslo is also the sole owner—and into two companies where generation and supply are placed, and in which the holding company owns the majority of the shares. There is no

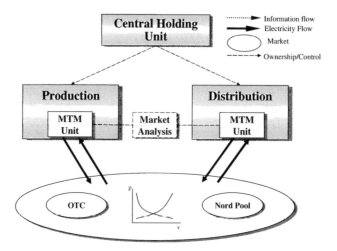

Fig. II.16.The fission model.

co-operation between the units in terms of preferential trading. Oslo Energi Produksjon (the generation unit) trades with whoever offers the best price for its electricity, whether the buyer is internal, in Nord Pool, or in the bilateral market. The same applies for the supply unit, which gives no preference to Oslo Energi's generation unit.

Independent management of the strategic business units has allowed Oslo Energi to pursue different strategies for its generation and supply units. The generation unit has sought to integrate itself into a wider generator group. On the one hand, it has acquired 33% of the generation company Drammen Kraft Produksjon. On the other hand, Oslo Energi has allowed Statkraft to acquire 25% of Oslo Energi Produksjon, even though Oslo Energi's supply unit faces Drammen Kraft as one of its major competitors in the end-user market.

III.A.b. The integrated (fusion) model
At the other end of the continuum, the integrated (fusion) model implies that business units maximise internal transactions and minimise external trade. Contracts in external markets are only resorted to when there is excess capacity or demand. The ideal case is thus for a company to have an internal balance between generation and supply, so that most transactions can be internalised (see Fig. II.17). In this case, trading competencies can be accumulated in a single unit that serves the whole company and balances its portfolio on behalf of both the supply and the generation side.

Vattenfall's current trading practices have many of the characteristics

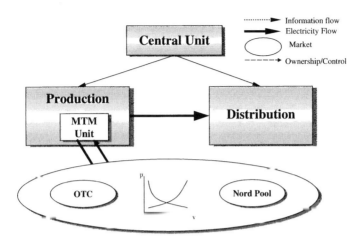

Fig. II.17. The integrated (fusion) model.

of the fully integrated model. Although the company has a strong imbalance between its generation capacity and supply needs, it is oriented towards internalising flows between generation and supply. For a long time, Vattenfall has actively sought supply outlets to balance its huge generation surplus, either by acquisition or through development of partnerships and long-term contracts. Seen from the point of view of contractual supply partners, the ties to generation create long-term price stability and give access to the supplementary services that a large generator can provide.

Instead of using the Nord Pool market price as a reference point for optimising generation and supply portfolios, Vattenfall, therefore, bases its trading decisions on the joint effects on its mix of generation facilities and supply obligations. Vattenfall's main interplay with Nord Pool and the bilateral/trilateral markets is, therefore, linked to selling excess capacity or demand for hedging purposes. So far, Vattenfall's trade activities have been mostly restricted to physical trade, with little engagement in financial trading. But as increasing end-user competition in Sweden has led to an overall increase in the need for financial hedging in many markets, so also Vattenfall has started to prepare for more complex trading strategies.

III.A.c. The semi-integrated model

The semi-integrated model (see Fig. II.18) is a hybrid of fission and fusion, where the company has an organised internal market for preferential internal trading, in which all units of the vertically-integrated company can ask for a price. The internal market unit will provide external

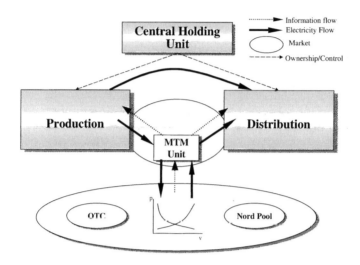

Fig. II.18. The semi-integrated model.

references for internal transactions between the supply and generation units, which means that the internal pricing is at least as good as the external market price. The internal market unit will also facilitate supplementary trade between the company and external markets, but internal trade will be favoured, in which the internal units incur no extra transaction costs.

Birka Energi, formerly Stockholm Energi AB (SEAB), is an example of the semi-integrated strategy. Only one part of the company deals with external markets, thereby reducing transaction costs and allowing for an internal concentration of trading competence. The internal trading unit does not set prices for heat generation, as there is no external market for this product.

Like Vattenfall, SEAB has followed a strategy of balancing supply and generation with an implicit orientation towards internal trade. The company therefore bought hydropower capacity throughout the 1990s, in order to meet future supply needs at stable prices. However, the market still has a significant place in SEAB, as generation does not fully match supply, and active involvement in external markets is therefore necessary. In addition, and unlike Vattenfall, external trade is always an alternative for the units. The semi-integrated approach therefore implies that external prices are used as benchmarking and exit options for internal trade, mediated through specialised market competence within the company.

III.A.d. Strategic motivation

The three strategies, integrated (fusion), semi-integrated, and fission, obviously strike different balances between scale/scope and flexible specialisation. Fission allows greater specialisation within the firm, and achieves this by looser market-based coupling between the units. Integration, on the other hand, seeks synergies through internalisation of complementary market positions.

The advantage of fission lies in the observability of single-unit performance and, thus, in the incentive for optimisation at the unit level. Static partial efficiency is therefore improved. Furthermore, there may be advantages in strategic independence, in leaving each unit to pursue its aims and alliances independently of other units. Fission thereby invites separate dynamic strategic developments, and thus may be more geared to adapting flexibly to market possibilities. This strategic independence also allows each unit to undertake its specific balancing of stockholder versus stakeholder interests. Nevertheless, the reason for maintaining some company integration may be that it can thereby mobilise financial strength to support all the individual units. However, fission might be a first step towards selling off parts of a company that are not locked in by concession laws.

The advantages of integration lie in its ability to create synergy between units and in the avoidance of external transaction costs. Integration provides incentives for optimisation of total company resources through a more united pursuit of a common strategy, as opposed to the partial-efficiency focus of fission. By its concerted orientation, integration provides a basis for coherent branding strategies, as well as more unitary and hence more forceful stakeholder profiling. Successful branding may attract not only customers, but also competent labour, and may thus enhance the firm's management of human resources. Integration can thus mobilise more forcefully towards a common dynamic target, but may fail to focus and differentiate. Furthermore, integration may be motivated by the ability to mobilise market power.

Semi-integration seeks to maximise the advantages of both integration and fission at the same time. If successful, it may gain synergies of co-ordination along with local efficiency and flexibility.

III.B. Building scale and competence by new market management

The Nordic electricity market reforms have introduced power markets and power trade as a core part of the electricity system. With the resulting demand for specialised competence in risk management and financial instruments, the trading activity has emerged as a major new business area both within larger energy companies and outside their boundaries, in new companies, with a focused specialisation on this segment of the value chain.

The new market companies have developed several profiles. While some have taken active trading positions, others have limited themselves to brokerage or to portfolio management on behalf of specific customer groups. In some cases we have also seen long-term buffering strategies to level out electricity price fluctuations, taken by the new market managers on behalf of their customers.

Unlike the traditional companies in which the physical values of the grid and generation capacities are the most valuable assets, the strategic core of the new market companies is knowledge of marketplace functioning and how to handle it. As specialised units focus on market management, these new companies can aggregate scale and scope in this function, at a level that can only be matched by the biggest Nordic companies.

As already mentioned, there are several sub-functions of market management (see Fig. II.19). The brokerage and market arena function creates a meetingplace for sellers and buyers where they may find counterparts in the electricity trade. The brokerage services are often supplemented by some degree of counselling with a basis in market analysis, which may be considered a separate function in itself. Brokers may inform their clients about market development, and even offer systematic forecasting and risk-simulating services, or the counselling unit may itself directly supply customers with market analyses. More operative engagement by the new market actor in managing the client's market strategies will amount to direct portfolio management, which may be considered another major sub-function. Finally, direct trading by the market management company on its own behalf may be seen as another distinct function, where the company uses its analytical and transaction competencies to speculate on its own behalf.

As indicated in Fig. II.19, the new market managers trade with each other and against the Nord Pool markets, as is also often the case with their clients.

Although there are obvious synergies between these sub-functions, there are also role conflicts between several of them. For example, being a trader on your own behalf at the same time as offering brokerage obviously leads to questions of neutrality in the brokerage function. Portfolio management may create similar interest conflicts, in that the market manager may be suspected of favouring his portfolio clients while executing his brokerage function. To counteract these interest conflicts, the new market managers have either abstained from certain functions, or have created internal divisions with independent mandates. The driving forces for integration in spite of role conflicts are scale and scope advantages. Underlying the brokerage, counselling, portfolio management and trading functions is a common market analysis, which would be costly to replicate. There are also obvious information advantages from integrating the full range of market management functions within one organisation.

III.B.a. Brokers

The brokers have offered services on both physical and financial contracts in what is referred to as the OTC market. For the OTC market to work, the broker needs a vast network of clients to be able to effectively match two parties. The brokers have therefore actively sought customers to add to their new market arenas, partly in direct competition with Nord Pool.

The advantage for the market actors of using a broker is that the broker, rather than acting directly on the marketplace, may acquire know-how of their specific supply situation and can couple matching companies effectively. Other advantages are that when big volumes are involved, the trading may be handled more discretely and the volume does not drive the Nord Pool spot market price, which is a reference price for all electricity trading. Brokers may also be better able to handle specialised requests and contracts.

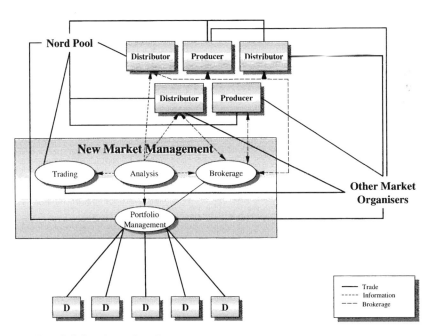

Fig. II.19. Sub-functions of market management.

In the Nordic energy market there are several big brokers, almost all with a Norwegian background, although they may have international owners. This includes companies such as Skandinavisk Kraftmegling, Markedskraft, TFS, Spectron and CBF.

III.B.b. Traders

The trader takes a position in the financial market on their own account and thus this holds a market risk of its own. This market risk stems from speculations on price movements, typically in futures and other term markets. As the market matures, trading margins decrease due to information technology and increasing professionalism among the actors, and only the best traders will survive and make money.

The new entrants in trading are often companies with experience from other financial or energy markets, which are able to make a profit on better risk management and margin handling than other actors. In addition to the pure speculative trading by specialised traders, both the suppliers and the generators in the Nordic electricity market have taken trader positions to hedge against physical supply obligations and future generation.

III.B.c. Portfolio managers

Brokers and traders have, as already mentioned, sought to expand the scale and scope of their businesses through portfolio management on behalf of supply companies and energy customers. Portfolio management is a service typically used by small supply companies and industrial companies with limited resources. Such companies cannot afford to have a separate analysis unit and without this unit the risk increases when trading on the pool or in the bilateral market. The use of portfolio managers varies with the market development. The Swedish market has so far only seen real competition in the industrial segment, and a portfolio management service has therefore been most common for these clients. In the Norwegian market there has been full competition for both industrial and household customers and both industrial companies and supply companies have used portfolio managers.

Brokers who already have an established analysis unit can move into portfolio management by offering the small suppliers management of their portfolio of supply obligations. They will typically involve the supplier in determining an explicit risk profile. The portfolio risk will then be monitored in continuous contact between the portfolio manager and the supplier. Portfolio management allows the analysis function as well as the operative trading to be 'outsourced' to a specialist, while the client remains in charge of the basic trading strategy. However, the relative influence between the client and the portfolio manager varies from strict contracts in which the manager is given no freedom, to agreements where the portfolio manager is free to handle the portfolio as he sees best.

Even though several types of actors can possibly act as a portfolio manager, this function requires appropriate neutrality from other competing activities. This may, in some cases, imply a full division of the firm. Typical portfolio managers are brokers, but traders also fill such functions.

III.B.d. Multi-market traders, advanced financial actors and new market arenas

Electricity market liberalisation has attracted actors from other traditional free markets such as the currency exchange market and the stock market. These actors draw on financial instruments and financial analytical traditions and experience in other highly competitive markets.

S E Banken (Sweden) and Morgan Stanley (UK) are so far the only banks involved in power trading directly on the Nord Pool. The banks bring with them several assets in electricity trading. They are traditionally good at trading on margins and also, in combining various markets for hedging and arbitrage. In addition, the banks bring with them a portfolio of customers who need to hedge their electricity demand or diversify hedges in various markets.

Given the fact that Norway liberalised the electricity market five years ahead of Sweden, it might seem odd that Swedish banks are ahead of the Norwegian banks in entering into electricity trade. Differences in the traditional linkages between the banking sector and the industry may provide a more plausible explanation. Sweden has always had a strong banking system with tight links to the industry without supported industry with capital, whereas the banks and private capital in Norway have been weaker.

III.C. Linking external market management with local supply networks: a new combination of scale and flexibility

Small suppliers do not have the financial strength to carry the cost of an analysis unit of their own, and thus could easily lose out in competition with larger suppliers, unless they have trading assistance. As trading becomes more and more specialised, many small suppliers therefore have found outsourcing of the trading function to the new market-managers to be an attractive option. The development of specialised market-managers has thus allowed a complementary, small-scale flexible supplier

strategy to emerge. Small local supply companies indirectly achieve economies of scale, while at the same time maintaining their anchoring with
their local customers, and their synergy with the local supply/supply
network.[3]

Suppliers can choose various degrees and forms of outsourcing (see
Fig. II.20). As a minimum outsourcing strategy, they can buy risk-analy-
sis services and then act independently based on this information. The
most elaborate form of outsourcing involves not only portfolio management, but also marketing and invoicing, which may involve a network
of partner companies. The only part of the electricity value chain left
to a local supplier is then the service function, which requires a local
presence.

The gains from outsourcing are several. First, local presence is maintained while synergies with other functions can still be exploited. Second, outsourcing allows local ownership to be preserved, which is also
an important element in the very traditional Norwegian electricity supply industry. Third, small suppliers can thus utilise scale and scope advantages, and earn a return on capital for their owners. The alternative
to outsourcing would be a merger or takeover, or development of
tighter ties to a bigger company, for instance through a commission
agreement.

One example of a Norwegian company offering outsourcing services
is Norsk Markedskraft. Originally a broker, portfolio manager and service provider for Nordic suppliers, Markedskraft now also handles risk
and portfolio management and, through a subsidiary, invoicing services.
Markedskraft draws on its broad skills in risk and portfolio management
to achieve scale and scope advantages by having many local companies
as customers, then pooling these into a single invoicing system.

III.C.a. The growth of regional semi-integrated groups

The Nordic electricity supply industry is decentralised, so there are many
small and medium-sized companies. While the largest Nordic companies
may have sufficient scale internally, these small and medium-sized companies are also finding it attractive to grow through regional semi-integration. Regional groups may also be seen, however, as defensive
responses to takeover strategies of bigger Nordic generators.

The local and regional public ownership of small and medium-sized
companies means that commercial motives for integration are often

---

[3] Although customers in Norway have a wide variety of suppliers—as customers in Sweden
and Finland will soon—customer loyalty to the traditional supplier is expected to remain
strong.

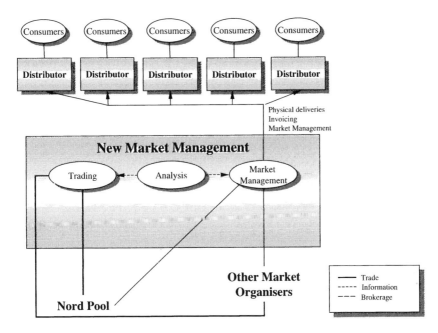

Fig. II.20. Outsourcing market management.

strongly blended with politics. As already mentioned, regional integration has been 'soft' in most cases: politically negotiated, with extensive use of flexible organisational means such as partnerships and network-based co-operation, gradually moving into stronger organisational forms.

The regional groups have so far mostly focused on supply activities, but have taken several organisational forms, including joint-purchase organisations, co-operation in end-user sales, commission sales and mergers.

III.C.b. Joint-purchasing organisations

Joint-purchasing organisations allow the participants better contracts because their combined market power makes for more attractive deals. Some of these organisations have their own analysis department, but most purchase these services, or attract a partner company with the existing skills.

In Denmark there are two such purchasing organisations, Disam and DanEl. Disam was founded in 1993 as a supply (not purchasing) co-operative with the aim of exercising activities that would enhance the electricity companies' opportunities to live up to future standards. However, so far, most of Disam's activities have been directed towards projects in less-developed countries, in co-operation with Danida and the

World Bank, focused on power-plant efficiency and on the establishment of electricity supply systems. With the first steps towards the freeing of the Danish electricity market in 1998, Disam took on responsibility for the electricity purchases of its members, thereby becoming the biggest electricity consumer/purchaser in Denmark, with 4.6 TWh or 13% of the total market, and 350,000 customers. After further market liberalisation in 1999, Disam became a portfolio manager on behalf of the six participating companies.

III.C.c. Co-operation in end-user supply
A further step in integration is to include not only purchasing but also co-operative supply. The co-operative organisation can then take care of all aspects of acquiring and selling electricity, including risk management, invoicing, and marketing, although this does not necessarily preclude electricity supply under the individual company names. But most of the supply activities in which there are economies of scale and scope are shared.

Typically, several small local or regional suppliers, such as Oslo Energi, form joint co-operatives or joint ventures. No assets necessarily change hands in these regional groups, and they are, therefore, more easily acceptable to local political owners.

Interkraft, consisting of five regional electricity companies in southern Norway, was one of the first formed for end-user sales. So far, Interkraft has functioned as a co-ordinating organisation, in which common products and marketing strategies are developed. The members in their own supply areas, under their own names, handle electricity supply. In addition, Interkraft has sold electricity to end-users outside of the members' areas. Closer co-operation, or a horizontal merger of the member companies, would create a Norwegian giant with 275,000 customers and an annual supply of 6–7 TWh. Interkraft Trading, in which the Finnish company Espoon Sähkö and the Dutch company Tradeon are also owners, is a separate trading unit outside the regular Interkraft co-operation. However, Interkraft has been very troubled by internal conflicts.

A similar development has occurred with the Finnish Isommus Energia, established originally as the joint-purchasing company for six electricity suppliers in Finnish Lapland. 25 supply companies, including Isommus and Kymppivoima, in turn own Voimatori, a co-operative organisation for spot and financial trading. The six members, under their own names, supplied the power delivered by Isommus to end-users. However, in 1998, Isommus became the sales company responsible for all aspects of electricity supply, for all its members.

Collaboration in end-user sales, as well as in wholesale trading, probably serves to facilitate more professional risk management and balancing of ingoing and outgoing commitments. Many of the smaller firms in the Isommus group were probably too small to trade actively on their own and without the alliance would therefore, have remained tied into long-term bilateral contracts with generators.

However, with the horizontal reconfiguration currently occurring in Finnish electricity supply, Isommus has experienced difficulties in standing alone against the big generators like IVO and Vattenfall. Like Kymppivoima, which has lost half of its ten members to either IVO, Vattenfall, or Graninge, Isommus has been attacked by IVO, and one of its members has been bought. In October 1998, IVO acquired, from the municipal owners, all shares in Koillis-Pohjan Sähkö, formerly Isommus' biggest participant, with 26,500 customers.

III.C.d. Commission sales

Another form of regional 'growth' to exploit economies of scale and scope is electricity sales on commission, useful when a takeover or merger is not possible or otherwise not suitable. The seller gets paid for each kWh of electricity sold for the supplier, which handles all market and risk-exposed transactions, including invoicing. In this way, suppliers can better exploit their market management capabilities and boost their market power. If the supplier is a generator with excess capacity, commission sales have the effect of building up a supplementary supply channel.

The regionally integrated company BKK (Bergenshalvøens Kommunale Kraftselskap) in western Norway has used sale on commission. BKK has agreements with eleven local small suppliers, which sell electricity on commission for BKK. This arrangement may preserve the local presence in the end-user interface, while yet allowing advantages of scale and scope to be exploited. Most of BKK's commission-sales agreements were signed in 1998, but already in that year BKK sold 3.6 TWh through its commissioners. (In 1997, BKK alone had 6.1 TWh of generation and 3 TWh of supply.)

III.C.e. Mergers

Merger is the strongest form of integration. A merger of several local electricity companies can be the result of an earlier co-operation process, and it may involve both horizontal and vertical elements. Scale and scope effects are both usually driving forces.

Lyse Energi is the most recent example of a regional merger of electricity companies, both vertically and horizontally. The companies now included in Lyse Energi were all local suppliers in the south-west of

Norway, each with shares in the regional generator Lyse Kraft. In the merger, the suppliers merged all their supply activities with Lyse Kraft to form Lyse Energi, a vertically-integrated regional electricity company. Lyse Energi has on average 5,500 GWh of generation annually and 5,000 GWh of supply, in Norway, thus being among the five biggest in both categories.

III.C.f. Strategic motivation

The emergence of new trading possibilities with new market managers is one of the clearest results of Nordic deregulation in the electricity market. Functions that previously were of negligible importance have now become focal points in industrial organisation, with flexible specialisation in new competency a core asset. As an alternative to the traditional industrial arena, the trading function increasingly provides scope for a whole range of new strategies, involving not only trading, but also brokerage and analysis.

The emergence of market specialists allows smaller companies to buy trading services from external suppliers. Market management as an outsourced specialised function is in many ways complementary to the small-scale supply that characterises the Norwegian market. It allows smaller local suppliers to maintain their independence without severe trading handicaps. If they manage to maintain local-customer loyalty on the downstream side, the outsourcing of trading functions may thus provide them with a sustainable niche in the commercial market.

III.D. Multi-energy combinations: working on the economics of scope, arbitrage, and customer integration

The deregulation of the electricity industry has lead to a search for synergies and business opportunities outside of the traditional sector boundaries. Danish, Finnish and Swedish electricity industry has traditionally had strong ties to district heating in combined heat and power systems and has, thereby, had a broader base for multi-sectorial expansion. This combination has emerged naturally out of the efficiency increases from 'double' use of thermal generation systems. In Norway, where the electricity system is dominated by hydropower, the industrial base is considerably narrower.

However, reforms in the Nordic electricity and the emerging European gas markets have triggered new developments towards integrated energy systems at several points of the value chain, including Norwegian companies. At the generation level, we are seeing plans for multi-fuel strategies that allow companies flexible energy input. At the wholesale level, we are observing development of alternative transport facilities through electricity and gas grids, and arbitrage between gas and electricity markets. At the end-user level, we are seeing multi-fuel marketing strategies and billing systems.

One of the consequences of this integration of the value chains is that the oil companies are moving into the electricity market, partly in competition with, but also in alliance with, traditional electricity companies. Such alliances also supply electricity companies with the opportunity to move into closer contact with parts of the petroleum sector. We are also seeing mergers that integrate petroleum and electricity in a common organisation.

III.D.a. Fortum

The most dramatic move towards an integrated petroleum–electricity strategy is the Finnish fusion of two state companies, the electricity company IVO and the petroleum company Neste, into a new energy company. Fortum, as of 17th June 1998. This was owned ≈75% by the Finnish state. Geographically Fortum's core market areas are the Nordic countries, the Baltic countries, Poland and Germany.

The new company controls Finland's largest electricity generation capacity, and has acquired extensive supply outlets both domestically and abroad. In addition, it has strong positions in the oil and gas value chain.

Combining the three energy chains (oil, gas and electricity) within the previous companies Neste and IVO into one horizontally- and vertically-integrated company gives Fortum new possibilities. It makes Fortum a total energy supplier, where customers in both the wholesale and retail markets can be offered a mix of energy sources that suits their needs. By combining the customer bases of Neste and IVO, Fortum increases its interface with its targeted markets. Its vertical and horizontal integration within the three energy chains also gives it an opportunity to engage broadly in trading across all energy commodity markets.

Through active participation in gas research and planning for gas interconnections, the company is positioning itself as a major catalyst for energy transit between eastern and northern Europe.

III.D.b. Statoil's electricity/oil customer profiling

Although more richly embedded with both petroleum resources and electricity generation capacity, the Norwegian state has showed far less initiative than the Finnish state in orchestrating multi-fuel integration. Thus, so far, the two Norwegian state-owned companies, Statkraft and Statoil, have remained separate.

Nevertheless, Statoil has taken steps on its own to engage in electricity retail sales by exploiting synergies from its petroleum sales activities. In May 1998, Statoil started marketing and selling electricity to their residential heat customers, to Premium Club Cardholders and Domino Card cash customers. Premium Club is Statoil's bonus card system for private customers purchasing gas from Statoil's gas stations, while the Domino Card is a nationwide bonus-card alliance of retailers of different products. In total this involves a base of 800,000–900,000 potential customers in Norway and 3 million in the Nordic countries. By the end of 1998, Statoil had acquired 40,000 household customers and some industrial customers, which places the company among the 15 biggest electricity suppliers in Norway. Statoil is also learning the electricity retail business through its 50% ownership in Melhus Energi Omsetning, a small electricity sales company.

The processing of new customers is divided among the Gas Business Development (GBD) department and the Retail Marketing unit. The GBD department is responsible for wholesale trading and handling of all aspects of contact with the local grid operator, such as reporting the customer's change of supplier and metering of consumption. The Retail Marketing unit handles all direct contact with the customer, such as billing, marketing and service functions. For both the trading and marketing functions, Statoil could rely on strong existing competencies.

Statoil has built up its own trading unit for electricity purchases and wholesale trading, in addition to expanding their household marketing department. The electricity trading unit, which is organised under the Gas Business Development department, buys market analysis from external companies since the electricity sales are so far not big enough to support this activity.

At the generation level, the most prominent of Statoil's plans are the initiatives for gas-fired power plants in Norway through the companies Naturkraft and Industrikraft. The former is a joint venture with Statkraft SF and Norsk Hydro, each participant holding 33% of the shares, and there are plans to build two power plants of 600 MW. Industrikraft is a joint venture with metals generator Elkem (40%) and forestry company Norske Skog (40%), where there are plans to build a CHP plant in conjunction with Norske Skog's factory in Skogn (mid-Norway). The Industrikraft power plant will imply closer links between electricity generation and energy consumers, while Naturkraft is a pure electricity generator that will sell its power on the open market.

III.D.c. Hydro's multi-fuel strategies

Norsk Hydro is the Nordic company that, by its traditional structure, is perhaps best positioned for a broad multi-fuel engagement in the energy field. Norsk Hydro ASA has traditionally been involved in the oil, gas and electricity value chains. In addition to its energy generation, Norsk Hydro is engaged in agriculture, aluminium, magnesium and petrochemicals. Its own electricity generation is used as input in an energy-intensive product range. Some of the crude products from the oil and gas activities are used as feedstock in agriculture and petrochemical generation. The generation of fertiliser in particular requires a rather high consumption of natural gas.

Norsk Hydro's vertical integration varies between the different chains. Their main focus in electricity has historically been to generate electricity to cover their own needs. The situation is still much the same today, but there has been a gradual move towards more electricity trade. However, as experience in trading has increased, it is becoming an independent business segment as well as a support function.

Hydro has for several years tried to connect the gas and electricity value chains, by producing gas-based electricity. This includes participation in the previously mentioned Naturkraft consortium with Statkraft and Statoil, as well as on their own plans to establish gas-fired power plants in Norway.

Facing strong domestic obstacles to its fuel integration strategies at home, Norsk Hydro has focused on fuel integration abroad. The company has plans for installing a 490 MW gas-fired power plant in the Netherlands. It will be integrated with the steam system in a fertiliser plant owned by Norsk Hydro's agriculture division. Some of the generated electricity will be used in the plant and surplus electricity will be sold on the market.

Like Statoil, Hydro is also engaging in downstream inter-fuel integration, but its move here is in an earlier phase and less forceful. The Hydro Texaco chain in Norway constitutes Norsk Hydro's involvement in the Norwegian retail market in the oil chain, and this is also the vehicle for electricity sales to the Norwegian household market.

Norsk Hydro also sells electricity to the retail market in Sweden through the subsidiaries Norsk Hydro Kraft AB, which covers the wholesale market and industrial customers in the retail market, and Hydro Energi Syd (previously Blekinge Energi), which covers small scale end-users in Sweden.

III.D.d. Electricity–gas integration in Sweden

In Sweden, several of the electricity companies have integrated horizontally into natural gas supply. However, with Swedish national priorities set on increasing bio-fuel generation, natural gas utilisation has been politically unwanted and thus no big-scale gas-fired power plants or gas grids have so far been set up. The most prominent of the gas supply ventures have been undertaken by Vattenfall and Sydkraft. Vattenfall, through its majority ownership of Vattenfall Naturgas AB, controls the only gas grid for import from Denmark, and sells gas wholesale to local and regional suppliers. So far this is Vattenfall's only engagement in the petroleum value chain. However, following the restructuring of Vattenfall Naturgas in 1997, when Ruhrgas (D), Statoil (N), DONG (DK) and Neste (SF) became shareholders, further integration can be expected, as the objective of the acquisitions is to develop the natural gas market in Sweden (Vattenfall, 1997).

III.D.e. Danish electricity–gas integration

There are no integrated energy companies in Denmark, either horizontally or vertically. This could however, soon change following industry restructuring and state initiatives in both sectors. Dansk Undergrunds Consortium (DUC) is in charge of oil and gas recovery from all fields on the Danish continental shelf with Mærsk Olie and Gas AS as the field operators. All gas generated on the shelf is sold to Dansk Naturgas A/S, a subsidiary of state company DONG (Dansk Olie og Naturgas A/S), and thus the only wholesaler of gas in Denmark. In addition there are five regional gas supply companies supplying gas to end-users. Attempts to consolidate the gas industry have been made and the Danish state has offered to buy all five regional suppliers, but to date (1999) only one, Naturgas Syd, has accepted.

According to press briefings (TDN Kraft 18.11.1998) plans exist to merge the electricity generator and the gas supplier on the island of Fyn (Fynsværket and Naturgas Fyn). This possible merger could trigger wider national mergers if it is successful, especially considering the close ties between gas and electricity, because many electricity generators use gas as fuel, and more are expecting to convert. In addition to the state's consolidation attempt in gas supply, the electricity generation's co-ordinating organisations, Elsam and Elkraft, are attempting to merge generation and wholesale operation in their respective areas. These two mergers could also expand to a wider energy consolidation process.

III.D.f. Strategic background and implications

Synergies and scale are obviously driving forces behind the multi-fuel development. Trading units and market analysis may be utilised for multiple purposes, and there are branding and service advantages in creating a customer interface with broader multi-fuel applications.

However, multi-fuel strategies, at least at a mass level, are broad and demanding and imply mobilising competencies and positioning across traditional domains. Building up multi-fuel engagements may therefore involve considerable capital investments. One way to limit the transition costs may be to proceed by horizontal strategies in specific functions such as Statoil's retailing venture.

Besides the scale and synergy issue, multi-fuel strategies may be motivated by facilitating positioning across energy markets with different degrees of openness. Barriers on trade in one fuel may be overcome by routing through another so as to serve the company's total positioning.

III.E. New electricity–telecom interfaces: synergies and competing networks

With the deregulation of both the telecommunication and electricity industries there has also been a move towards utilising the electricity grid as an alternative grid for telecommunication. The core motivation for integration of the electricity and telecommunication value chains, from the telecommunication side, has been to secure alternative telecommunication transmission channels to circumvent the grids controlled by the old telecommunication monopolists. Even though third party access is generally given through the old telecommunication grids, disagreeable prices and strategic positioning makes it attractive for newcomers to seek alternative channels.

From the electricity industry, the major motivation has been to capitalise on synergies through utilising the electricity grid as a multi-system carrier linked to other grids. Such synergies could build on a tradition of internal communication within the electricity industry to secure the operation of electricity plants. This practice could now be widened to encompass general communication, utilised by new entrants in the telecom markets without grids of their own.

III.E.a. Overview of major Nordic electricity–telecom initiatives

Electricity–telecom initiatives in the Nordic countries vary both according to geographical scope and functional engagements. Initiatives for electricity–telecom integration have been taken in all Nordic countries as illustrated by the following examples:

- *EniTel*, owned by Statnett SF (33.12%), Skiensfjordens Kommunale Kraftselskap AS (8.04%), Troms Kraftforsyning DA (6.70%) and 45 regional electricity companies (EniTel, 1999), is one of the major Nordic groups. EniTel has a basis in the national electricity-grid, but with gradual regional integration and with sub-sea–international cabling engagements with the Swedish company Telia. The EniTel group has primary orientation towards infrastructure provision. Customers are telecommunication operators and communication intensive firms (EniTel and Orkla Finans, 1998).

- The *ElTele* group consists of six operative regional units, which are owned by electricity companies in their respective regions (ElTele AS, 1998). Some of the major owners are: Alta Kraftlag (100% of ElTele Nord), Oslo Energi Holding and France Telecom (49.15% and 33.99% of ElTele Øst, respectively), Fredrikstad Energiverk, Hafslund and Østfold Energi (each 33% of ElTele Østfold), Lyse Energi (85% of ElTele Rogaland) and BKK, Haugaland Kraft and Sunnhordaland Kraftlag (each 33% of ElTele Vest) (ElTele Øst, 1999). Additionally, it has established two regional subsidiaries in the ElTele Group, ElTele Vesstfold and ElTele Midt-Norge, subsidiaries of ElTele Østfold and ElTele Øst, respectively. The ElTele group has a basis in the regional grid and an alliance with the Norwegian National Rail Administration for access to the central railroad grid. The ElTele group has a broader functional orientation than EniTel, which includes infrastructure operation and to some extent telecommunication operation. This is made possible through partnership with France Telecom. The services of the ElTele group is offered to a narrow customer base, consisting of communication-intensive firms.

- *Sydkraft Telecom,* a subsidiary of Sydkraft, has a broad functional engagement within its regional area towards its targeted customers: energy companies in the Malmö region. Their nets are regional and local. The local nets function as access nets for monitoring and controlling energy use. Sydkraft Telecom has functions within infrastructure provision and infrastructure operation and, to some extent, within telecommunication operational services. They have operational services to end-users as part of energy monitoring and control. Sydkraft Telecom does not function as a telecommunication operator as such.

- *Powercom,* a joint venture by Eltra and Nesa, has a national and international extension in Denmark with a primary orientation towards infrastructure provision at the central level (Powercom, 1999) Their objective is to sell transmission capacity to telecommunication service companies, based on surplus capacity on their power transmission lines.

III.E.b. Strategic comments and comparative remarks

A common feature for all companies discussed above is their focus on targeted customers. Faced with the complexity of full telecommunication, all companies are aiming at entry into this new business segment by targeting a niche customer segment. EniTel has their focus on telecommunication operators and communication-intensive companies. ElTele has a focus of telecommunication-intensive corporations. Sydkraft Telecom's targeted customers are energy companies within their region, and Powercom aims for customers that request a national grid.

In addition, the companies have sought expansion into telecommunication by routing connections over grids within their exclusive control. The electricity sector's move into telecommunication, when oriented to more than infrastructure provision, has been through partnerships with telecommunication companies. This has allowed grid access to a complementary knowledge base and human capital in a highly knowledge-intensive field.

The move into telecommunication represents a move into a highly sophisticated technological area, where technical breakthroughs may fundamentally change commercial opportunities. Research into signal technology that may eventually allow the electricity grid to be directly used as a telecommunication grid may suddenly revolutionise communication routing in favour of the electricity industry. However, competing air communications may win through and make the electricity grid a far less attractive vehicle.

IV. Concluding reflections on Nordic business strategies

IV.A. Diversity or globalisation

Comparing Nordic strategic organisation we can observe considerable variety in economic organisation. Reflecting on the classical discussion of national styles versus globalisation one may ask to what extent these strategies are sustainable as strategic equilibrium and to what extent they are transitory positions towards a common optimal mode of organisation.

Oslo Energi's reintegration into different configurations with Statkraft in generation and with Vattenfall in supply seems to indicate that the fission strategy, in the longer run, is a transitory strategy towards partition and re-integration in other models. However, other specific patterns, such as the Finnish electricity–industry complex, or the Norwegian small-scale end-user interface, coupled with a new segment of market specialists, may under certain conditions represent more durable organisational patterns.

One way to bridge the national styles versus globalisation positions may be to interpret them at two levels: functional and institutional. Given the decentralised character of the Nordic, and particularly Norwegian, electricity industry, it should come as no surprise that the commercial exposure in deregulated electricity markets has implied considerable scaling up as a general functional orientation. However, the scaling up has been conducted by very different institutional means. Notably, the Danish and Norwegian scaling up have taken much 'softer and collaborative' forms than the Swedish and Finnish.

At least in the short run, we therefore observe national institutional forms supporting the national style argument, but at the same time a general concentration process supporting the common optimal organisation model.

IV.B. Organisational models

Given the need to differentiate according to both functional needs and national styles of strategic configuration, it comes as no surprise that we can observe network, market and hierarchic organisation in the transformation of the Nordic electricity industry. One may observe organisational developments towards market organisation, as in the Oslo Energi fission model; towards hierarchic integration, as in the vertical integration strategies of the big Swedish companies; and towards various network solutions, as in the Norwegian and Finnish supplier integration.

The political lock-in to local public ownership, which is particularly prominent in the Norwegian case, has created a need for network organisation in order to scale up functions where volume and competency demands larger system integration. As previously noted, this has implied a functional combination of small-scale suppliers with large-scale market managers into a peculiar mix of small- and large-scale organisations, based on functional specialisation within the value chain. Norwegian companies, such as Skandinavisk Kraftmegling, Markedskraft and others, have specialised in trading as the complexity of this function and the emergence of new market arenas has demanded new specialised competencies. While this solution may solve immediate co-ordination and scaling needs, the question is how it will function in dynamic competition with challenges from more hierarchically consolidated companies.

IV.C. Competency challenges

In terms of competencies, the Nordic market development has understandably created a great need for extensive trading. The emergence of new market managers can in this perspective be viewed as representing centralisation, which is necessary not only for scale reasons, but also for rationing on scarcity of competency.

Given the early Norwegian market reform and the advanced organisation of the Nordic market, Norwegian actors had an early start in developing trade competencies. This competency was also developed in specialised trading outside of the traditional electricity industry. Some of these traders/brokers and portfolio managers are now playing prominent roles in larger Nordic and north European markets. However, whereas Nordic companies in this way have developed advanced electricity trading competencies, it remains to be seen how this may be exploited in further market positioning. On the one hand, Swedish banks are entering the market with a wider trading expertise, while the integration of electricity trading into broader banking has been fairly limited in Norway. On the other hand, large European companies may buy into the Norwegian competency by acquiring new trading skills through takeovers, as the acquisition of 51% of Skandinavisk Kraftmegling by a German company, EnBW Gesellschaft für Stromhandel GmbH, illustrates. The large financial resources of, e.g. of large German utilities, open up for this. These options illustrate how the competence-economy raises challenges not only to development, but also to further maintenance and integration of expert knowledge.

IV.D. Multi-energy and multi-industrial engagements

The Nordic electricity industry also illustrates the challenges of inter-fuel and inter-sectorial integration once public sector demarcations are abandoned. There are, as already noted, examples of energy and industrial diversification in several directions. We have seen forceful broad energy-strategy moves by Finnish Fortum to integrate the electricity and petroleumvalue chains into a broader energy strategy. More modest engagements by Norwegian petroleum companies into electricity trading are in striking contrast to this, as the Norwegian resource-potential for inter-fuel strategies is extremely good and far better than the Finnish.

The Finnish paper and pulp industry is also unique in its systematic engagement in electricity generation, through an organised internal electricity pool. Other Nordic companies like Hydro have more individual strategies, but not on a similar scale.

Moves by various electricity company consortia into telecommunication based on synergies from multiple use of grids is another example of cross-sectorial integration. This development may be observed in all Nordic countries, and often includes partnerships with telecommunication companies that wish to penetrate the semi-liberalised telecommunication markets through alternative grids. Given the complexity of telecom markets and telecom technology, the electricity industry here faces an extensive challenge, and will probably for the foreseeable future need extensive support form telecommunication partners, at least for strategies that involve advanced configurations.

IV.E. Stakeholdership and dynamic configuration

The strategic organisation of the Nordic electricity industry also poses some difficult challenges in redefining stakeholdership under dynamic configuration. Stakeholdership in the Nordic context has traditionally been handled through a dominant public ownership of the electricity industry. However, with the challenges from a broader European competition, the Nordic decentralised public sector model is confronted with an increasing need for structural transformation.

Confronted with competition on a larger European scene, the Nordic decentralised public ownership model, which has traditionally carried the stakeholdership in this sector, seems to be running into serious contradictions. The more that public-owned Nordic companies engage outside of their polity, the less is the rationale for their public ownership. The more the companies activate themselves beyond their home-base, the more are the interests of its political owners transformed into ordinary stockholder interests. To the extent that Nordic public companies fully involve in European competition, the decentralised public ownership mode loses much of its meaning. Public ownership tends to lose its distinctive character once the field of operation transcends the owner's polity-domain.

In other words, the development from static to dynamic efficiency, where companies position themselves outside their national boundaries, tends to undermine the basic motivation for public ownership, and certainly the motivation for decentralised public ownership irrespective of the public company's ability to achieve static efficiency.

While the Nordic electricity industry, with its large hydropower resources and efficiently run nuclear stations, may survive economically under almost any conditions, it is highly questionable whether it is able to reap the full welfare effects of the new market regime with the present ownership and organisational structure.

Generally speaking, the extensive public ownership seems to have made for less structural change by mergers and acquisitions than one would expect in a highly capital-intensive industry such as the electricity industry under private ownership. It thereby continues to support a fairly decentralised Norwegian, Finnish and Danish electricity industry, whereas concentration in Sweden seems to have gone further. It seems likely, however, that as the European market emerges, Nordic companies will have to integrate wider across national boundaries. In the process they may have to diminish the role of public ownership and develop new forms of stakeholdership to accommodate their new commercial positions.

Literature

On-line databases and news services

Reuters Business Briefing, News releases 01.01.1993–28.02.1999.
TDN Kraft, Online News Service, News releases 01.01.1993–28.02.1999, http://kraft.tdn.no

Annual reports

Electricity

Annual reports for the 20 largest suppliers and 20 largest producers in each of the Nordic countries (Norway, Sweden, Finland and Denmark), 1994–1999. For a complete list of companies see Appendix A.
Annual reports from larger European electricity and energy companies:
PreussenElektra (G), VEBA (G), RWE (G), Hamburgische Electricitätswerke (G),VEAG (G) Electricité de France (F), National Power (UK), SEP (NL), UCPTE, CENTREL and Statoil (N).

Telecommunications

AB Stelacon (1998) *Marknaden för telekommunikation i Sverige*, Bromma, Sweden, Bild 20, p. 52.
ElTele AS (1998) *http://www.eltele.no*, January 1999.
Eltele Øst (1999) List of ownership shares of the ElTele group, January.
EniTel and Orkla Finans (1998) *Prospectus EniTel asa*, Oslo, pp. 9–10.
EniTel (1999) *Aksjonærer og eierandeler etter kapitalutvidelse; Oversikt tildelinger*, List of ownership shares of EniTel prior to the second phase of share issuing to financial institutions at the end of 1998, January.
Powercom (1999) *http://www.powercom.dk*, January.
Powercom (1999b) Translated from Powercom's internet page *http://www.powercom.dk/ powkunder.htm*

Statistical sources

Danish Association of Electricity Companies (1996–1998) *El & Energi*.
Danish Association of Electricity Companies (1998) *Statistik, Dansk Elforsyning 1997*.
Kraft Journalen AS (1995–1999) *Kraft Journalen*.
Ministry of Industry and Energy in Finland (1990–1999) *Energy Review*.
Nordel (1985–1997) *Annual reports*.
Norwegian Association of Electricity Companies (1995–1999) *Energi*.
Norwegian Association of Electricity Companies (1999) *Internet Resource*, http://www.enfo.no.
Official Statistics of Norway (1997) *Electricity Statistics 1995*.

Publications

Danish Energy Agency, Ministry of Environment and Energy (1998) *Energistatistik 1997*.
Meyer, Niels I (2000) "Green certificates markets in Europe with focus on the Danish situation" *Paper presented at the Salzburg Conference* Salzburg.
Midttun, Atle (1997): European Electricity Systems in Transition Oxford: Elsevier
Swedish Association of Electricity Companies (1995–1999) *ERA, elektricitetens rationella användning*.
Swedish Association of Electricity Companies (1997) *Statistik 1995*.

Chapter III
Corporate Strategies in the British Electricity Supply Industry

STEVE THOMAS

I. Introduction

In 1990, the British electricity supply industry was re-structured, privatised and competition was introduced.[1] The companies that were to operate in the system were either new, or their activities so completely different to those they carried out under the old regime that they must be regarded as essentially new. In this chapter, the policies that these companies have followed since 1990 are examined, and the motives and strategies of the companies that have entered the British electricity market since then are analysed.

At the time the industry was privatised, there was an expectation in the minds of most people that, after a period of adjustment, a stable new structure would soon emerge. This has proved not to be the case and, ten years after the reforms took place, there is no sign that the flow of unexpected developments is slowing down. This has made planning in the sector difficult and few companies have been able to pursue consistent long-term strategies. The threat of takeover, and pressure from shareholders, especially institutional investors, to increase profits has forced the companies to respond to short-term pressures, often disrupting strategies. Regulatory action to reduce the market power of the larger companies has also eroded their core business and in most cases, corporate attention has had to focus on protecting existing markets rather than building new ones.

---

[1] For an account of the privatisation of the British industry and of its subsequent development, see Surrey (1996).

I.A. The policy background

In order to understand the policies followed by the companies involved in the electricity sector, it is important to sketch the political background that has applied to the sector. Margaret Thatcher, first elected as Prime Minister of the UK in 1979, was the main driving force behind a privatisation programme that saw many of the publicly owned assets transferred from national ownership to private shareholders. Thatcher continued in power until 1992, when she was succeeded by John Major, from the same party (Conservatives). The policies followed by Major's governments, at least in this sector, continued largely unchanged. The privatisation programme proceeded, and the somewhat *laissez faire* attitude to markets prevailed.

After it had privatised the electricity industry, the Conservative government generally maintained a non-interventionist stance in the industry. As a result, gas was allowed to enter the generation market at a very rapid rate. This had a very damaging effect on the market for British coal. Transitional protection for the coal industry was provided via coal contracts between the nationalised British coal company and the two large generation companies, which largely maintained the volume of purchases but at significantly lower prices. The political furore that resulted when these contracts came up for review and the much lower volumes of coal that would be required became apparent did force the government to act to force the extension of the contracts for a further five years at much lower tonnage. However, it was clear even then that this additional transitional support was not likely to prevent the demise of the British coal industry; it merely postponed it.

On the question of structure, the government was less passive, especially on the question of vertical integration, that is, separation of the electricity industry into the four component sectors: generation, transmission, distribution and supply. De-integration appears to have been one of its key principles in determining the post-privatisation structure of the industry. In 1996, it prevented attempts by the two large generation companies to takeover the regional electricity companies (RECs) (in the new structure these were responsible for both distribution and supply). It also required the RECs to sell the National Grid Company, which they were given joint ownership of after privatisation. However, on ownership, the Conservative government adopted a non-interventionist stance. It took no steps to try to retain the ownership of RECs in British hands after the Golden Shares in them had expired (described below) in 1995. In 1996, however, it did prevent the takeover of the largest electricity generation company, National Power, by an American company using the rights that its Golden Share gave it.

In the May 1997 general election, the Labour Party, led by Tony Blair, was elected with a very large majority. Its manifesto gave no hint that there would be dramatic changes to the electricity sector and, unlike earlier Labour administrations, there was no commitment to nationalisation, indeed the Labour party to some extent embraced privatisation and a market economy.

Since the election, the Labour government has set in motion reviews that cover almost every aspect of the electricity system, including a review of regulation, power station fuel policy and the Power Pool. The review of the Power Pool was inevitable whichever party was in power because of the apparent reliability problems with the Pool, especially the computer software and the detailed design. However, the proposed reforms are far more fundamental than would have been needed simply to resolve the existing practical problems. The real impact of the other reviews is more difficult to gauge. This is partly because of doubts about the strength of the political will to intervene in this sector if there is not an obvious problem to solve. Nevertheless, the indications are that, in some respects, the Labour government is prepared to take a more interventionist stance. For example, it has placed restrictions on consents for new power stations burning gas and has examined in depth methods of retaining a British coal-mining sector.

However, on the issues of ownership and structure, it has, if anything, been more liberal than Major's governments were. For example, it has allowed the takeover of established supply businesses by the two large fossil fuel generation companies. How far these apparent differences represent genuinely different philosophies about the sector and how far they represent pragmatic reactions to new challenges is not clear.

II. The New Structure and its Operation

Before examining the policies of the companies, it is necessary briefly to explain the new structure and how it works. On 1st April 1990, the electricity supply industry for England and Wales was fundamentally reformed. Prior to then, a nationally owned company, the Central Electricity Generating Board (CEGB), which had a virtual monopoly of generation and owned and operated the national high-voltage transmission system, had dominated the industry. Twelve regionally based companies, also owned by central government and then known as Area Boards, operated the local low-voltage distribution system and supplied electricity to final consumers, reading meters and sending out bills. The much smaller electricity supply industries covering Scotland and Northern Ireland were also privatised at about the same time, but with a very different structure. This account concentrates on the system of England and Wales.[2]

While the reforms that took place are generally referred to in Britain as privatisation, they actually comprised a number of distinct and separate changes. The basic philosophy was to separate, or de-integrate the industry into four main component parts, generation, supply, transmission and distribution. The activities of generation and high-voltage transmission are easily understood, but the idea that distribution and supply could be separate activities is less familiar. Distribution covers the operation of the low-voltage distribution system while supply is the commercial activity of purchasing power and selling it to consumers. It was believed that generation and supply could be made competitive, while transmission and distribution were natural monopolies. In the new structure, competitive procedures were introduced for generation and supply and the barriers to entry for new companies minimised. For transmission and distribution, a new system of regulation was introduced, designed to provide strong incentives for the companies operating the monopolies to improve their efficiency, passing on many of the benefits to consumers.

In detail therefore, the reforms comprised four main elements: privatisation; restructuring and de-integration; the introduction of competition in generation and supply; and the creation of a new body for economic regulation.

II.A. Privatisation

Privatisation of the electricity supply industry was part of a much larger programme of selling publicly owned assets to private shareholders that

---

[2] In Scotland, the two regional, fully integrated companies, the South of Scotland Electricity Board (SSEB) and the North of Scotland Hydro-Electric Board (NSHEB) were previously nationally owned. They were privatised largely intact (also in 1990) as Scottish Power and Scottish Hydro-Electric, respectively. The operating nuclear plants, both of which are of the more modern of the two British designs used, were transferred to Scottish Nuclear, which was privatised in 1996, along with Nuclear Electric, as the Scottish Nuclear division of British Energy. Reflecting the integrated nature of the companies, there is still limited scope for competition in the Scottish system.

The system in Northern Ireland, which was privatised in 1992, is different again. The pre-existing, fully integrated company, Northern Ireland Electric (NIE), was also previously nationally owned and was privatised as a transmission, distribution and supply company (NIE). Its four major power stations were split between three companies. The largest plant was sold to a subsidiary of British Gas, two other plants were sold to a consortium of Tractebel (Belgium) and AES (USA) called Nigen, and the other plant was sold to its employees and management. While the structure is potentially more competitive than that created in Scotland, the generation companies were given long-term, non-competitive contracts of up to 29 years and there is therefore little competition yet.

the Conservative government, under Margaret Thatcher, followed from 1979 onwards. As with nearly all the privatisations, the new companies were floated on the London Stock Exchange through public share offers rather than being sold by auction to existing companies (trade sales). The financial scale of the companies was such that the share sales had to be phased to prevent any distortion to the rest of the stock market that might have been caused by such a large flow of capital into these new companies. The majority of the shares were sold in the first year after 1st April 1990, although 40% of the shares of the two fossil fuel generation companies were retained for a further five years. For different reasons, discussed later, the nuclear sector was not privatised until 1996 and the National Grid Company (NGC) was not quoted separately on the stock exchange until 1995.

II.B. Restructuring and De-integration

The 12 Area Boards were privatised intact and became known as Regional Electricity Companies (RECs). There was an accounting separation of the two parts of the companies, the monopoly distribution business and the potentially competitive supply business. This was intended to minimise any distortion to competition that might occur if cross-subsidies from the monopoly business to the competitive business were possible.

The CEGB was split into three generation companies and one transmission company. The generation companies were National Power and PowerGen, which took over the fossil fuel power plants, and Nuclear Electric, which took over the nuclear power plants. It had been planned that the nuclear power plants would be privatised as part of National Power, but only months before the new system was due to go into operation, the investment community made it clear that this was not acceptable. The nuclear power plants had to remain in public ownership in a new company, Nuclear Electric, until 1996 when all except the oldest units were privatised as British Energy.[3] The National Grid Company (NGC) was jointly owned until 1995 by the 12 RECs. They were then required to sell their shares on to the stock market. NGC's pumped storage generation business was also sold off in December 1995 to a US utility, Mission Energy.

---

[3] In July 1996, much of the nuclear capacity, including all the newer plants, representing about 70% of the capacity, was privatised as the Nuclear Electric division of a new company, British Energy. The older plants were transferred to a state-owned company, Magnox Electric. This has been being integrated into the state-owned fuel cycle company, British Nuclear Fuels Limited (BNFL).

II.C. Competition in generation

Competition in generation was introduced by minimising barriers to entry for new generation facilities and by requiring all large power sources (each turbine generator at each station as well as interconnecting lines from foreign systems) to trade their output through a half-hourly spot market, the Power Pool. New generation facilities were required to obtain a generation licence and to become members of the Pool. However, there were no national planning procedures aimed at matching supply and demand with which they had to comply and, essentially, any company wishing to build a new power plant had to do no more than satisfy the planning laws that would apply to any industrial facility.

This arrangement implies intense competition in generation with the owner of each plant having to place a bid for every half-hour of the day to determine whether the plant would run. In practice, competition has not been so intense because of the structure of the market and because hedging contracts or contracts for differences (CfDs),[4] which effectively bypass the Pool, are allowed. Until 1998, a significant but declining proportion of the generation market was covered by power generated by National Power and PowerGen using coal from British mines and sold to the RECs at prices which were not in any way related to the Pool price. Also, until 1996, the RECs were required to purchase all the power that could be generated at the nuclear power stations. These arrangements and other contractual obligations have meant that, until at least 1998, 90% or more of wholesale purchases of electricity were made at prices that were in no way related to the Pool price.

A review of the Pool arrangements was started in 1997. The Pool is to be abandoned in favour of more complex and flexible trading arrangements. However, until these have been implemented, it is not possible to gauge the impact of these changes.[5] It was planned that the new trading arrangements would be introduced in April 2000, but by the autumn of 2000, this target had slipped to the spring of 2001.[6] As with other major changes since privatisation, the construction of the required computer systems may cause serious practical and cost problems.

---

[4] Under a contract for difference, a generator must place a successful bid into the Pool for the plant to be dispatched and the purchaser and generator must buy and sell power through the Pool at Pool prices. However, the difference between the Pool and the CfD price is settled bilaterally between the buyer and seller, so the price at which power is bought and sold is not related at all to the Pool price.

[5] OFFER (1998a).

[6] OFGEM (1998a).

II.D. Competition in supply

The RECs were granted a single licence, the Public Electricity Supply (PES) licence, which covered both distribution and supply. New entrants to the electricity supply market are able to obtain a licence that covers just supply. In order to spread the workload associated with privatisation and to give some stability to the newly privatised companies, it was planned that competition in supply would be phased in over eight years. From 1st April 1990, consumers with a maximum demand of more than 1 MW were allowed to choose their supplier of electricity. In practice, at this time, this meant they could choose to be supplied by any of the 12 RECs, either of the two large privatised generation companies or by either of the two integrated Scottish companies, both of which could export power to England. The REC in whose territory the consumer is situated is required to allow any supplier to use their system at standard, non-discriminatory charges. Only 5,000 consumers used enough electricity to fall into this category but this represented about 30% by volume of the electricity market. In 1994, the limit was reduced to 100 kW allowing in a further 50,000 consumers and representing a further 20% of the market.

It was planned that on 1st April 1998, the limit would be removed and all consumers would be allowed to choose their supplier. It has not been possible to meet this timetable and the phasing in of competition did not begin until September 1998, a process that was completed in May 1999.[7]

II.E. The regulation system

The sector-specific regulatory system adopted for electricity followed similar principles to those that guided the systems devised for the telecoms and gas industries when they were privatised in 1984 and 1986, respectively. This system appears to place decision-making largely in the hands of a single person, a Director General of Electricity Supplies (DGES), but with the assistance of a support staff, the Office of Electricity Regulation (OFFER). In 1999, the gas (OFGAS) and electricity (OFFER) regulatory bodies were merged to form the Office of Gas and Electricity Markets (OFGEM). The Regulator is usually characterised as independent. However, he or she is appointed by the relevant government minister, with whom he or she shares most of the statutory duties, and it is hard to see how a Regulator could continue in office if he or she was not following policies that were acceptable to the government.

---

[7] OFFER (1998b).

It was intended that the competitive parts of the industry would not require special regulation while the monopoly parts of the industry would be regulated using a formula that limited the income of a monopoly service provider to a specified level. This was portrayed as a major break with the more well-established method, rate-of-return regulation under which the level of profit a company can make from a monopoly activity is prescribed, being calculated from the value of the assets employed. The regulator sets the prices for monopoly activities using a formula, commonly expressed as $RPI - X$, where RPI or retail price index is a measure of inflation and 'X' is an incentive term. In principle, under this formula, the overall income of the companies from carrying out a monopoly service is capped in real terms at the same level as the previous year minus an incentive term, 'X'. This means that if a company is to maintain its level of profits, it must increase its efficiency by 'X' per cent each year. The companies have some discretion about how they allocate their costs between consumers within this overall cap on income and some classes of consumer may benefit more from price reductions than others.

'X' is set typically to apply for four or five years forward. This period was meant to be long enough to give the regulated companies a predictable business environment in which they could plan long-term investments, but not so long that major discrepancies between actual and expected profits could arise unchecked. Although the value of 'X' is generally expected to require real prices to go down, in some circumstances, such as a perceived need for exceptional additional investments, the 'X' factor could allow price rises above the rate of inflation. This has generally been the case with the water industry since privatisation, and for some of the RECs in the first years after privatisation.

In addition to the sector-specific regulation, there are also a number of regulatory bodies that can exert some control over the industry. Her Majesty's Inspectorate of Pollution (HMIP) regulates the environmental performance of the industry (including nuclear safety). The Director General of Fair Trading (DGFT) with his or her staff, the Office of Fair Trading (OFT), is the regulatory body that oversees the operation of competitive consumer markets in general. It has played an important role in the privatised gas industry and does have powers to intervene in the electricity industry, but so far it has not been a major influence on policy.

The Competition Commission, which up until April 1999 had been known as the Monopolies and Mergers Commission (MMC) is a long established body appointed to carry out investigations into markets and into proposed takeovers, where there is concern that these might operate against the public interest. Unlike the sector-specific regulator, the Competition Commission has always operated on a 'panel' basis with a number of commissioners coming to a decision on each investigation. It has no powers to initiate investigations, but operates under instruction from a government minister and now from the sector-specific regulator. It has a number of roles in the electricity industry. It has examined proposed takeovers of the British electricity companies, and if the DGES and the regulated companies cannot agree on the regulatory pricing formula, the Competition Commission undertakes an investigation. Within the Competition Commission, there is now a utility panel that deals specifically with utilities. The government minister (at present, the Trade and Industry minister) makes the final decision on any Competition Commission recommendations on the basis of its report although he or she is not obliged to follow its recommendations.

III. Factors Conditioning the Corporate Policies Followed

A number of factors have conditioned or restricted the policies that the privatised electricity companies have followed.

III.A. The Golden Share

One of the features of the overall privatisation programme of the Conservative governments from 1979 onwards was the use of a device known as a Golden Share.[8] This was designed to give the government some control over privatised companies that operated in sectors it believed to be of strategic importance to the British economy. A Golden Share was meant to address the fear that key national resources would fall into foreign hands and their reliability compromised. For the electricity supply industry, NGC, National Power and PowerGen have open-ended Golden Share protection. The government took a Golden Share with a term of ten years for British Energy, expiring on 30 September 2006, and the RECs were given five-year Golden Share protection, expiring in April 1995.

The terms of Golden Shares are specific to each company but, typically, they require that no company be allowed to own more than 15% of the stock without government approval. This gives the government power to veto takeover bids for privatised companies. In some cases, where the company's activities are of strategic national importance or where it is not clear when (or if) the markets in which they will operate will become fully competitive, the duration of the Golden Share is open-ended. In others, for example, where the markets in which the companies will operate are still immature but there is a good prospect they can be made competitive within a given timescale, the Golden Share has a fixed

---

[8] The Golden Share cannot be traded and has no monetary value. For a more detailed examination of the Golden Share, see McHarg (1998).

duration. After this period has expired there are no special restrictions on the ownership of the companies.

These distinctions are, however, not always precise or immutable, and the rationale behind the application of the Golden Share is not clear. The RECs were given Golden Share protection only until 1995, three years before the last major step in introducing competition in the supply market was expected to be completed. In July 1997, the Labour government relinquished its Golden Share in the privatised telecoms company, BT, a company that at the time of privatisation was seen as a long-term strategic national asset, but which now, because of technical progress, is seen to operate in a competitive market.

The Golden Share does not offer absolute protection, because the government is not obliged to use its power to veto takeovers. For example, the Conservative government relinquished the Golden Share in a privatised oil company, Britoil, to allow it to be taken over by British Petroleum. It also allowed the Jaguar car company to be taken over by the Ford Motor Company, and VSEL (a shipbuilding and engineering company) to be taken over by GEC. When the government does decide not to block a takeover, it might try to impose conditions on the new owner of the company. However, this is not always successful and, for example, when BP was allowed to take over Britoil, undertakings from BP that there would be no job losses were not enforced. Because of the rather arbitrary way in which the Golden Share has been applied and the mixed success its use has had, doubts have been arisen in recent years about the usefulness of Golden Shares. This is reflected in the apparent anomaly that, in 1990, National Power and PowerGen were given open-ended protection, while in 1996, British Energy was only given Golden Share protection for a limited duration. Nuclear power stations would seem, on the face of it, to be of more strategic importance than fossil fuel power plants.

III.B. A new corporate culture and rapidly developing market conditions

It is not possible to argue that by 1990, the old system had failed, prices were reasonable, the nationalised companies made large profits and the reliability of the system was very good. However, there was a common perception that the nationalised industry philosophy was out-dated and inefficient. The procedures and philosophy of the old companies were therefore often despised in the new companies, which were keen to present themselves as dynamic, market-led companies. The previous priority of long-term planning, aimed at ensuring the public interest was protected, was abandoned in favour of short-term commercial success.

While the companies spent sizeable sums of money on public relations aimed at maintaining their image as responsible, ethical companies, no-one should have been in doubt that they were now profit-led businesses in which the interests of directors and shareholders came first. This was well illustrated by the massive pay increases and bonuses the directors of the companies took, often increasing their pay by up to ten times the equivalent position in the nationalised companies. In spite of the fact that this was one of the least significant factors in final electricity prices, directors' ('fat cats') pay has been by far the main issue of public debate since privatisation. Directors have shown no sign of responding to public revulsion at the scale of pay increases.

The companies have also been under intense scrutiny from financial institutions and business analysts particularly in the early years after privatisation. Through their ability to influence share price, these institutions had the financial power to force changes to companies if they did not like the way they were being run. They were looking for strong evidence that the privatised companies were responding positively to their new role and had shed their nationalised industry practices in favour of tough, profit-centred policies. There were thus strong pressures to reduce staffing levels and cut out those expenditures that did not have immediate pay-offs. As a result, in the ten years since privatisation, employment in the electricity supply industry has halved, and most of the large Research and Development laboratories and research programmes that the CEGB maintained or sponsored have been shut down (see Tables III.1 and III.2).

The UK was the first developed country to attempt to reform its electricity supply industry on strongly competitive grounds and there was therefore no precedent from which the companies could learn. Conditions have developed rapidly and generally not predictably. This has meant that the British companies have had to devote their management time to responding to these changes in conditions in order to protect their home base. This has often left little senior management time to devote to diversification into other sectors or other countries.

III.C. High technical competence but limited commercial expertise

The CEGB and the Area Boards developed a strong reputation for reliable technical operation of the system, but their commercial credentials were limited. The CEGB's record in managing construction sites and contractors was poor, with new power stations almost invariably coming online late and over-budget. They also had little experience in purchasing equipment and fuel on the world market because of a long tradition of buying only from British sources, to conform to (unwritten) government policy. Almost all coal purchases (which then accounted for more than 75% of British

Table III.1. Employment in the British electricity supply industry.

	88/89	89/90	90/91	91/92	92/93	93/94	94/95	95/96	96/97	97/98	98/99
The CEGB and its successors											
CEGB	47631										
National Power		16977	15713	13277	9934	6955	5447	4848	4474	4348	4445
PowerGen		9430	8840	7771	5715	4782	4171	4148	3367	3456	6216
Nuclear Electric		14415	13924	13300	12283	10728	9426				
British Energy								6572	6366	5724	5389
National Grid		6442	6550	6217	5666	5127	4871	4565	4414	4218	3628
Total	47631	47264	45027	40565	33598	27592	23915				
The RECs											
East Midlands	7478	7478	7382	8243	8684	7914	6458	5099			
Eastern	9843	9970	10001	9877	8415	7003	6403	6113			
London	7060	6920	6691	6581	6258	5532	4908	4404			
MANWEB	5423	5551	5483	4623	4533	4604	4582	3245	2975		
Midlands	7702	7738	7729	7643	7370	6207	5815	5114	4864		
Northern	5313	5439	5528	5364	4826	4714	4456	3882	3601		
NORWEB	8243	8249	8203	7917	7977	8255	8247	8195			
SEEBOARD	6450	6343	6340	6257	6039	5339	4680	4278	4146		
SWALEC	3803	3770	3767	3632	3166	3350	3218	2979			
SWEB	5653	5641	5676	5553	5569	5400	5005	3254			
Southern	8154	8233	8362	8340	7642	7391	7091	6728	6661		
Yorkshire	7169	7153	7126	7105	6850	5764	4924	4294			
Total	82291	82485	82288	81135	77329	71473	65787	57585			

Source: Company Annual Reports.

Figures quoted represent the average number employed during the financial year.

In 1995/1996, the assets of Nuclear Electric and Scottish Nuclear were redivided with the newer plants going to British Energy (privatised in 1996) and the older plants going to Magnox Electric (absorbed into BNFL in 1998). Employment figures for Magnox Electric are not available. The figures for British Energy are therefore not directly comparable with Nuclear Electric and the total figure cannot be calculated accurately.

Some staff from National Power and PowerGen have been transferred to Eastern Electricity as a result of 6000 MW of plant disposals as required by the regulator.

From 1996/1997 onwards, figures are not available for the RECs that are no longer independent companies.

In 1998, PowerGen changed its reporting period from April–March to calendar years. The figures shown under 1998/99 refer to the nine months from March 1998 to the end of December 1998. The figures for this year include former employees of East Midlands.

electricity generation) were from the nationalised British coal company, the National Coal Board (subsequently renamed *British Coal*). All major equipment purchases were made from British-based companies, such as GEC and NEI Parsons. One of the most powerful criticisms made by those that advocated privatisation was that, because the CEGB

Table III.2. Research and development in the British electricity supply industry.

	88/89	89/90	90/91	91/92	92/93	93/94	94/95	95/96	96/97	97/98	98/99
CEGB	201										
National Power		22	26	17	20	26	26	57	31	39	49
PowerGen		5.1	14.2	12	10	9	8	7	6	6	5
Nuclear Electric		116	95	71	64	51	48				
British Energy									20	22	21
National Grid Co.		7	7.4	7.7	7.9	8	8.3	8.4	7.9	7.8	8.4
Total	201	150	143	108	102	94	90				

Source: Company Annual Reports.
Some R&D is carried out by RECs, but it is often not costed in the annual reports. The total of identified R&D is less than £10 m.
In 1995/1996, the assets of Nuclear Electric and Scottish Nuclear were redivided with the newer plants going to British Energy (privatised in 1996) and the older plants going to Magnox Electric (absorbed into BNFL in 1998). No R&D figure for British Energy was reported for 1995/1996 and no R&D figures for Magnox Electric are available.
The figure of £7 million for the NGC in 1989/1990 is imputed—no actual figure was reported.
In 1998, PowerGen changed its reporting period from April–March to calendar years. The figures shown under 1998/1999 cover only the nine months from March 1998 to the end of December 1998.

effectively had no choice over its suppliers, these deals meant that fuel and equipment were purchased more expensively than they could have been, at the expense of the electricity consumer.

The Area Boards purchased almost all their power needs from the CEGB on terms over which they had little say. They also had the monopoly right to supply all consumers within their territory, so they had no scope to develop commercial expertise in two of the main areas of their business in the new system. On purchases of equipment, they were under similar constraints to buy from British suppliers as the CEGB. The one area in which they had some commercial expertise was in retailing consumer electrical goods (white goods). All the Area Boards operated chains of retail stores for these products, which also served as centres where electricity bills could be paid and advice given. However, these shops were not noted for their creativity and innovation in retailing and were often criticised by other retailers on the grounds that they were cross-subsidised by the main distribution and supply businesses. Nearly all the RECs have closed or sold off these chains, because they are not regarded as core businesses and are probably too small to compete effectively against the main retail outlets for these products. This business is therefore not considered further in this paper.

IV. The Development of the Industry since 1990

IV.A. Regulation in practice

The main statutory duties of the regulator have been to promote competition in the industry wherever possible, and to set prices for the monopoly services. The duty to promote competition has meant that the DGES has monitored closely the operation of the generation market, including the Power Pool. He has required the dominant generators to sell off some of their plant to reduce their market shares, and has placed limitations on their bidding strategies when he felt their dominant position was allowing them to abuse their market power. He has overseen the progressive introduction of competition in the supply market.

When OFFER was set up in 1989, there were conflicting pressures on the regulatory bodies created to oversee the privatised utility industries, particularly on the extent of the powers and resources available to them. On the one hand, the general public probably did not believe that a lightweight regulatory body would have the capability to devise formulae that would prevent excessive profits being made. There was also scepticism about the likelihood of competition emerging without strong regulatory prompting. In order for it to be effective, OFGAS, the regulatory body for gas, had found it necessary to grow from only a handful of staff when it was created in 1986 to about a 100 by 1990.

On the other hand, the government was strongly averse to setting up large, unwieldy regulatory bodies comparable to the US state utility commissions. Stephen Littlechild, who was the DGES from 1989–99, had been heavily involved in the design of the privatisation programme and is widely credited with inventing the regulatory formula. He was seen as a significant influence on Conservative government thinking. His instincts were that government intervention was generally counterproductive and there was a suggestion that competition would be so effective that the need for special regulatory arrangements for the electricity sector would soon wither away. This claim did not seem realistic and OFFER started out with over 250 staff, a level that it has maintained since.[9]

The Conservative government set the initial regulatory formulae in 1990 that determined the prices for the three monopoly activities, transmission (for three years), supply to franchise consumers (for four years) and distribution (for five years). These allowed the companies to raise their prices in line with inflation and, for distribution, to increase

---

[9] Unlike OFGAS, OFFER is responsible for dealing with individual consumers' complaints and about half of its staff is involved in this activity, so at the time of its creation, its staffing levels were comparable with those of OFGAS.

them in real terms. The government also set the terms of the three-year contracts from British Coal to the large generation companies (British-mined coal then made up the bulk of generation) and from the generation companies to the retail suppliers. In the event, these initial regulatory formulae and transitional contracts proved very generous to the electricity companies, who were able to make large profits during the period they applied. They also gave a strong signal to potential investors in the British electricity system that the British regulatory system was weak.

As the initial regulatory formulae expired, the DGES took over the job of setting the pricing formulae and began to increase the cost pressures on the companies. The first review, published in 1992 to apply from 1993, saw the 'X' factor for NGC increased from 0 to 3,[10] while under the second, in 1994, to cover supply to franchise consumers, the 'X' factor increase from 0 to 2.[11] However, it was the distribution review in 1995 that marked a real turning point. The 1990 formulae varied from REC to REC, with all RECs allowed to at least maintain their charges in real terms. Some were allowed to increase them by up to 2.5% per year. The process of negotiating the 1995 review was a complex one described later. The result was that the distribution formula for the RECs from 1995–2000 required one-off real price cuts of 11–17% in 1995/96 and 10–13% in 1996/97, followed by cuts of 3% per year for the following years.[12] The 1997 transmission review seemed even tougher requiring an initial price cut of 20% followed by annual reductions of 4%.[13]

The DGES has also, probably against his instincts, intervened in the apparently competitive generation market, because he believed it was not operating competitively. In 1994, he became so dissatisfied that he capped the Pool price from 1994–96[14] and forced the two large fossil fuel generators to sell a significant quantity (6 GW) of old coal-fired plant to increase competition in the Pool, an undertaking that was only finally fulfilled in 1996.[15] While the DGES has no formal powers to enforce a price cap or force plant sales, he was able to use the threat of a referral to the MMC to achieve his aim. He could have requested an MMC investigation into whether the electricity market operated in 'the public interest'. Such an investigation would have been lengthy and would have taken up a large amount of management time of the generation

---

[10] OFFER (1992).
[11] OFFER (1993).
[12] OFFER (1995a).
[13] OFFER (1997).
[14] OFFER (1995b).
[15] OFFER (1995c).

companies. The uncertainty about the outcome would mean that it would be difficult for the companies to make major strategic decisions while the investigation was underway. The DGES was therefore able to persuade the two large companies to sell the plant to increase competition in generation and comply with a Pool price cap as a way for them to avoid an MMC investigation.

Littlechild was appointed for a five year term from 1989 and had his contract renewed for a similar period in 1994, but he left his post almost a year early. This was in part to allow the amalgamation of regulation in gas and electricity that the Labour government had proposed. In addition, while he has had no public disagreements with the Labour government, he is not likely to be as in tune with its policies as he was with those of the previous administration. The new Director General of both Electricity Supply and Gas, Callum McCarthy, took on his joint role from 1st January 1999. It is not yet clear how his policies will differ from those of his predecessor.

A review of regulation was instigated in 1997 and a consultation document produced in March 1998.[16] The responses were reviewed by government and broadly confirmed in a further paper published in July 1998.[17] There have been a number of changes to regulation, such as the merger of the gas and electricity regulatory bodies and the appointment of advisers to the DGES to limit his apparent personal power. In 2001, the single person regulator for gas and electricity will be replaced by a panel of four, to be known as the Energy Markets Authority. His prime duty has also changed from the promotion of competition to the protection of consumers. Littlechild consistently argued that the best way to protect the interests of consumers was to promote competition, so this apparently significant change may not in practice have much impact. However, there will not be any change to the basic principles of regulation, with '*RPI − X*' continuing to be the method of setting prices for monopoly activities.

IV.B. The distribution and supply sectors

When the Area Boards, which became the Regional Electricity Companies (RECs) in 1990, were created in 1947, they were meant to be reasonably similar in size, as measured by power sales. However, there are inevitable differences arising from the characteristics of the terrain and customer base in which they operate. It is therefore useful to examine their core businesses, distribution and supply, to assess their starting base.

---

[16] DTI (1998a).
[17] DTI (1998b).

Table III.3. The RECs' territories—distribution network in 1995/96.

REC	No. customers (000s)				Customer density	Distribution network			Metres / customer
	Area	Dom	Other	Total		U'ground	O'head	Total	
Eastern Group	20.3	2800	400	3200	158	52.5	35.5	88.0	27
East Midlands	16.0	2083	186	2269	142	42.4	25.4	67.8	30
London	0.7	1721	241	1962	2950	29.8	0.1	29.9	15
MANWEB	12.2	1252	112	1364	112	23.4	21.4	44.8	33
Midlands	13.3	2032	175	2217	166	37.5	27.3	64.8	29
Northern	14.4	1342	113	1455	97	24.2	17.2	41.3	28
NORWEB	12.5	1976	206	2182	175	44.7	14.6	59.3	27
SEEBOARD	8.2	1814	184	1998	244	32.2	12.7	44.9	22
Southern	16.9	2369	233	2602	154	42.7	28.9	71.6	27
SWALEC	11.8	874	90	964	82	13.4	18.6	32.0	33
SWEB	14.4	1172	132	1304	91	18.4	29.1	47.6	37
Yorkshire	10.7	1903	148	2051	192	38.2	15.9	54.2	26
Total	151.4	21338	2220			399.4	246.7	646.1	

Source: Doyle and MacLaine (1996).

IV.B.a. The distribution businesses

Table III.3 shows that London is clearly a very different territory to the other RECs, with a small area, a high proportion of its cable underground, and a customer density more than ten times that of the next most concentrated REC. Of the other RECs, Eastern stands out as the largest in terms of area, number of consumers and length of circuit, while SWALEC and SWEB are more sparsely populated than the other RECs. The climate in England and Wales is not extreme, but the low customer density in the SWEB region and relatively mountainous regions in the two Welsh regions (MANWEB and SWALEC) means that maintaining the distribution network in these regions is relatively expensive.

This factor seems to have been reflected in the regulatory pricing formula for distribution that the UK government imposed to run from 1990 to 1995. This allowed SWALEC and MANWEB to significantly increase their prices each year by 2.5% more than the rate of inflation, while SWEB was allowed 2.25%. By comparison, the other RECs were allowed to increase their prices upto 1.5% per year. Subsequently, it became clear that this special treatment was not required and the 1995 review of distribution pricing largely reclaimed the extra revenue SWALEC, SWEB and MANWEB were allowed.

IV.B.b. The supply businesses

The supply business of Eastern stands out amongst the RECs because of its residential market. It is much larger than those of other RECs, representing 20% of demand in England and Wales. The residential market dominates Eastern's sales, representing 60% of its sales compared with 38% for England and Wales as a whole (see Table III.4). Its sales per residential consumer are high, largely because of the relative affluence of consumers in the area. However, its sales to other consumers are low per consumer, reflecting the limited industrialisation in the region. SWEB, SEEBOARD, and Southern also have above average sales per residential consumer, although in the case of SWEB, this reflects the limited extent of the gas network in the region, which means that a significant number of houses are heated using reduced price off-peak electricity. Since this is sold at about one-third of the normal tariff rate, this high consumption may not be a very profitable business.

The MANWEB region stands out because of the high proportion of sales going to non-residential customers and because of the high consumption per non-residential customer. Yorkshire, Midlands, East Midlands, SWALEC and Northern also sell a high proportion of their output to relatively electric-intensive industry.

IV.C. Generation

The CEGB's fossil fuel power stations were split very carefully between National Power and PowerGen taking account of fuel used, age of plant, technology and location so that the cost bases of the two companies matched as far as possible. PowerGen got off to a faster start in 1990 than

Table III.4. The RECs' territories—customer base in 1995/96.

REC	Maximum demand (GW)	Units distributed (TWh)			Consumption per customer (MWh)		
		Resid	(%)	Other	(%)	Resid	Other
Eastern Group	6.4	18.6	(19)	12.4	(8)	6.7	31.1
East Midlands	4.7	8.7	(9)	16.4	(11)	4.2	88.4
London	4.2	6.5	(7)	14.2	(9)	3.8	59.0
MANWEB	3.1	4.9	(5)	13.6	(9)	3.9	121.6
Midlands	4.9	8.8	(9)	16.3	(11)	4.3	93.3
Northern	2.7	4.8	(5)	10.5	(7)	3.6	93.0
NORWEB	4.3	8.0	(8)	14.9	(10)	4.1	72.1
SEEBOARD	3.9	8.4	(9)	7.6	(5)	4.6	41.2
Southern	5.0	10.9	(11)	16.9	(11)	4.6	72.4
SWALEC	2.0	3.2	(3)	8.3	(5)	3.6	91.7
SWEB	2.7	5.8	(6)	7.7	(5)	5.0	58.4
Yorkshire	4.3	7.1	(7)	16.1	(10)	3.7	108.9
Total	48.8	95.7	(100)	154.9	(100)	4.5	69.8

Source: Doyle and MacLaine (1996).

National Power and since then has often been the more innovative. For example, PowerGen was first, in 1990, to order a CCGT plant, and it placed a bid for a REC ahead of National Power in 1995. It has also advertised extensively in order to increase public awareness of the brand name, presumably mainly in preparation for its entry into the retail electricity market for households. In part, the early lead by PowerGen was because National Power was knocked out of its stride by the re-organisation within the company necessitated by the last minute withdrawal from privatisation of the nuclear plants, which were to have been owned by National Power. This meant the company had to find a new chairman to replace the expected candidate, Lord Marshall (whose main expertise lay in nuclear power), leaving them somewhat lacking in direction for a key period in 1989/90. It may also have been that National Power was expected to inherit the CEGB mantle as the solid base for the British industry while PowerGen, being the smaller company, had to 'try harder'.

The nuclear power plants in Britain were owned, from 1990–1996 by two nationally owned companies, Nuclear Electric for England and Wales and Scottish Nuclear for Scotland. These companies were remarkably successful in operating the existing plants more efficiently than the CEGB. By 1996, it was possible to privatise the newer nuclear power plants from England, Wales and Scotland in a new company, British Energy. After a difficult period during privatisation, British Energy became a highly successful company. The older nuclear plants still could not be sold and remained in public ownership in Magnox Electric. In 1998, this company was absorbed into the nationally-owned fuel cycle company British Nuclear Fuels Limited (BNFL), which, by 1999, was also a candidate for privatisation.

Since 1990, a large number of companies have entered the generation business in England and Wales. Some have built large power plants that are dispatched through the Pool (generally plants that can supply more than 100 MW to the public supply system must be centrally dispatched). Others have built much smaller plants such as combined heat and power (CHP) and renewables, which are 'embedded' in the local distribution system. However, at the beginning of 1999, the daughter companies of the CEGB, that is, National Power, PowerGen, British Energy and Magnox Electric, still retained about two-thirds of the generation market.

IV.D. Transmission

Britain was one of the first countries to build a comprehensive, national high-voltage grid and much of today's grid was in place by 1960. With limited demand growth over the past 30 years, the main task for the operator of the grid continues to be one of maintenance and improving

Table III.5. The National Grid system.

	400kV	275kV	132kV	Total
Overhead lines				
Route th km	5180	1579	198	6958
Circuit th km	9526	3610	378	13518
Underground cables				
Route th km	232	279	86	630
Circuit th km	295	429	114	876

Source: National Grid Co (1990) Annual Report, NGC, London.
Total includes a small amount of circuit operating at 66 kV or less.

efficiency with existing assets rather than extending the system to new consumers or new power sources (see Table III.5). It jointly owns the interconnectors to France (1988 MW DC) and to the AC link to Scotland. At the time of privatisation, the Scottish link had a peak capacity of 750 MW and this has been increased progressively to 1200 MW and in 2000 to 2200 MW.

V. The Nature of the Electricity Industry

In order to understand the policies adopted by the companies, it is useful to examine the characteristics of the businesses that make up the electricity supply industry. One of the most striking factors to emerge since 1990 has been the way in which the four component parts of the industry have been revealed as very different in nature in terms of the skills required, the risks involved and the determinants of success. Indeed, as experience accumulates, the industry may break up into even smaller parts. For example, metering may become an entirely separate business, as is already the case in the gas industry.

Generally, corporate diversification strategies now look to identify a core business and, from this, move into other businesses that will yield synergies. These might be technical synergies, that is, businesses where existing technical skills can be applied, or commercial synergies, that is, businesses that mutually reinforce each other's market position. Core competencies are also identified and, where skills are required that are not within the group's core competencies, these activities are often subcontracted out. For example, an electricity supply company might choose to subcontract its IT requirements to a specialist company.

V.A. Generation

In character, the generation business has most in common with high-technology continuous processes, such as metals manufacture or chemicals production. The generation business was always seen as the heart of the electricity supply industry. This was because of the technologically sophisticated nature of the equipment, the high capital cost of plant, the large amount of cost-reducing technology change that has occurred during the history of the electricity supply industry and the major role generation cost plays in setting the price of electricity. Typically generation represents about 60–70% of the final cost to consumers of electricity.

Large-scale generation in a competitive market has been revealed by privatisation to be one of the riskiest of industrial activities, having the potential for high losses as well as high profits. There is ample evidence in recent years of how errors in technology selection, poor site management, poor plant operation and maintenance, and changes in fuel prices can all render an expensive power plant, perhaps costing billions of pounds, uneconomic or 'stranded'. In a monopoly non-competitive system, any costs resulting from a stranded investment would be passed on to final consumers, but in a competitive market, they should fall on shareholders.

The fact that electricity cannot effectively be stored means that there is a high priority on plant reliability—output that cannot be produced because a plant has broken down can never be recovered. However, the strategic responsibilities are less on companies operating in competitive markets than monopoly generators. In a monopoly generation system, the owner of the power plants will be held responsible if the system fails because there is insufficient generating capacity and its commercial position and reputation will be seriously damaged. In a competitive market, no single company can have the market power to ensure supply security, and system failures cannot generally be blamed on individual companies.

These severe risks mean that power plant construction projects in a competitive market are likely to be charged a high interest rate on the capital, and be depreciated over a short period of time. Typically, a monopoly publicly-owned utility would have been required to make a real rate of return on capital of less than 10% and perhaps as low as 5%, as was the case with the CEGB, and depreciate the plant over 30–40 years. Now, a competitive generation project might be charged a real rate of return of 15% and the plant depreciated over only ten years. This severely restricts technology choice, making it unlikely that capital-intensive projects, such as nuclear power plants, large-scale hydroelectric plants and clean-coal technologies, would be chosen. In practice, gas-fired power plants using combined cycle gas turbine (CCGT) technology seem to have overwhelming advantages over other large-scale options.

There has been little sign that generation companies will use their technical capabilities to diversify into industrial activities outside the electricity industry. Commercial synergies for generators may exist in two directions, integrating horizontally into power station fuel supply and vertically into electricity supply to final consumers. Integrating a gas supply and electricity generation business may provide a hedge against volatile fuel prices, both for gas producers and electricity generators. For example, in the UK, a company with its own supply of gas can choose to sell the gas directly, export the gas to mainland Europe, or use it to generate electricity, depending on which will offer the highest profits. So, a rise in gas price may make electricity generation from gas uneconomic, but may make the supply of gas to final consumers more profitable. Integration into coal supply is less attractive for electricity generators because of the lack of alternative markets for coal other than electricity generation.

Vertically integrating into electricity supply to final consumers may reduce the risk of investment in generation because of customer inertia. Electricity is a standard product and this factor largely precludes any market protection through product differentiation (so-called 'green' electricity may be an exception). Selling power into a spot market or on short-term contracts is highly risky and if, for example, fuel prices move against a generator, it will be forced to sell at a loss, or not generate at all. Large final consumers are very price-sensitive, typically contracting for power on an annual basis, selecting each year the cheapest supplier. Smaller consumers are less price-sensitive and may carry on buying power for several years at prices above the lowest available.

The companies most likely to enter the generation market may be fuel suppliers and manufacturing companies with significant power and perhaps process steam or hot water requirements that can be met by a small- to medium-scale power plant. Fuel suppliers will be able to ensure a market for their product, and perhaps add value to it. In a competitive generation market, industrial electricity generators may be able to supply themselves with power at more predictable and lower prices than the market, either selling surplus power to the grid at a profit or purchasing any additional power needs from the market.

V.B. Transmission

Charges for use of the transmission network (in Britain, this covers lines operating at 275 kV and above) comprise less than 5% of a typical electricity bill. In a country such as Britain, with a complete grid, where all consumers are already served and where demand is growing slowly, the investment required in new transmission lines is very limited and the transmission business is one primarily requiring maintenance, repair and some replacement of a capital stock. It uses complex technologies and requires sophisticated skills to co-ordinate the activities of a large number of consumers and producers. However, technological change is limited and the skills are well established.

Transmission is currently a natural monopoly and, unless regulation is weak, in commercial terms should be a low risk, low return business. The only way in which the business can grow significantly is through takeover of other transmission systems. There is some risk that the business could decline if decentralised energy options, which do not use the transmission network, continue to increase in significance. These options include renewables, combined heat and power and, for the future, fuel cells.

In technological terms, the reliability of an electricity supply system is crucially dependent on the high-voltage network and any failure due to lack of investment or poor maintenance will cause severe consequences with repercussions on the national economy and welfare. This was clearly illustrated in New Zealand in 1998, when failures in the national transmission system led to large-scale electricity disconnections in Auckland lasting for a period of nearly three weeks.[18] It is likely that the commercial reputation of the company involved will suffer severe long-term damage as a result of this.

There do not appear to be any businesses that provide obvious commercial synergies with transmission. Liberalisation of electricity supply systems almost invariably requires that ownership of the grid be separated from the potentially competitive parts of the system, generation and supply, for which ownership of the grid could be used to (unfair) advantage. The clearest technical synergies are with low voltage electricity distribution and telecoms. There is a significant overlap with electricity distribution in terms of the skills and equipment required, while the commercial characteristics of being a regulated business are also similar. In the UK, now that the RECs have been required to make a more strict division between their distribution and supply businesses, it is possible that NGC would want to purchase monopoly distribution businesses.

A number of transmission companies have used their infrastructure as a way of developing a telecoms business, by adding optical fibre cables to the existing pylons. However, the commercial characteristics of telecoms are very different to electricity transmission. In a liberalised market, supplying telecoms services is a high-risk business where customers are very cost-sensitive and where losses are likely to be made while the business is being developed. The most appropriate strategy for a transmission company may be to do as NGC in Britain did, to develop its telecoms business through a subsidiary company and, when the

---

[18] FTE (1998b)

business is well established, separate off the business. There has been some speculation that NGC would seek to capitalise on its co-ordination skills to takeover air traffic control in Britain, if this is privatised.

V.C. Distribution

The distribution business (the low-voltage network, in Britain covering lines operating at 132 kV and below) is a much larger business (comprising 15–25% of a typical final bill, smaller consumers paying a higher proportion) than transmission. The purchase by National Power in 1998 of the supply business of Midlands Electricity made that company the first example of a company that operates an electricity distribution network as a stand-alone business. Distribution had always previously been carried out by a company that had the responsibility to supply electricity to final consumers. As noted above, there is a strong overlap in terms of skills and technology between electricity distribution and transmission. The distribution network in Britain is well established and mature, with little need for extension. It should be a low risk, low return business with little growth potential other than by takeover, but with high penalties if the system fails. This was illustrated in Brazil, in 1998, when a series of system failures in the Rio de Janeiro area was blamed on the local distribution network. The reputations of the members of the international consortium, that had recently taken over the company, including Electricité de France, AES and Houston Industries, were damaged.[19]

There is a strong technical synergy with other industries that require network delivery, usually underground, of utility products to final consumers, such as gas, water, telecoms and other cable services. However, as with transmission, unless regulation is lax enough to allow a monopoly business to cross-subsidise a competitive business (generation or supply), it is difficult to see businesses with commercial synergies. In Britain, there was some concern that there was not sufficient corporate separation between supply and distribution, both carried out by the RECs, leading to a risk of unfair cross-subsidies, and in 2000, the RECs, license was split into two separate parts. This allowed more effective separation of the businesses and by autumn 2000, four of the RECs had sold their supply businesses.

V.D. Supply

Supply was the least recognisably separable element of the electricity supply industry prior to privatisation in Britain. This was because the

---

[19] FTE (1998a).

companies involved, the Area Boards, had no control over the main elements of the business, purchasing electricity in bulk and marketing to final consumers. The CEGB dictated the wholesale tariff, while final consumers had no choice over their supplier of electricity. The Area Boards simply passed on their costs to the consumers.

It has since become clear that electricity supply is a very different business to any of the other three elements in the electricity supply chain. It is a high turnover, but low capital and low margin business, and, as the supply market is opened to competition, it becomes an increasingly high risk business. In principle, an electricity supplier needs little more than a telephone and a computer to operate a supply business. It need own no network facilities or power plants, and meter reading and billing can be subcontracted to specialist companies.

Supply, including metering and billing, is the smallest element of electricity bills ranging from about 1% for the largest consumers to about 7% for small consumers.[20] However, the supply company represents the main interface of the industry with the final consumer and, in some respects, negotiates on behalf of consumers with the generation sector. A competitive supply sector was therefore seen as an essential element if the British electricity privatisation was to be judged a success.

VI. Policies in the Electricity Supply Industry

In order to examine the strategies of the electricity industry companies since 1990, it is useful to divide the period into three sections. From 1990 1995, the income and profits of the companies were largely determined by the contracts and regulatory formulae set by the government in 1990. There was a semblance of competition through the Pool and through competition to supply large consumers, but this was highly restricted and could have only a minimal effect on the profitability of the industry. The companies were protected from takeover by Golden Shares and were able to begin to experiment with business development and diversification strategies.

From 1995–1998, the transitional measures were beginning to unwind and the force of competition was being felt. Regulatory pressures on monopoly businesses became very much more intense, and scrutiny from investors, keen to maintain 'shareholder value' became more intrusive. As a result, the companies had to become more cautious in their business strategies, often restricting themselves to core businesses. Government

---

[20] In 2000, when a stricter separation of distribution and supply was imposed, some costs previously allocated to distribution were transferred to supply and for a residential consumer, the supply component of the bill increased to about 15 per cent.

protection of companies by Golden Shares began to be relaxed and many of the companies were taken over.

From 1998 onwards, competitive forces were much less restricted and regulatory pressures on monopoly businesses continued to increase. A major restructuring of the industry began to take place. The RECs were no longer independent and generally had limited control over their destinies. The generation companies and the NGC began to focus on the USA as an area in which to grow, with a series of attempts to take over or merge with US electric utilities.

VI.A. Policies from 1990–1995

VI.A.a. The RECs

In retrospect, and by comparison with what has followed, the period from 1990–1995 saw relatively few significant changes to the RECs' businesses. Golden Shares protected the companies from takeover, and the generous distribution and supply price formulae together with their ownership of NGC allowed them to increase their profitability by 50% (see Table III.6). While this was achieved in part by a 20% reduction in employment, the job losses were far less severe than those in the generation companies, which more than halved their manpower (see Table III.1).

Distribution remained at the heart of the RECs' businesses and, while privatisation did allow some fresh thinking on how the business should operate, it remained largely unchanged in character. From 1990–1995, the companies were able to make comfortable profits without having to institute ambitious cost-saving programmes. Indeed, if costs had been cut dramatically, profits would have been embarrassingly high. This would have invited a very tough regulatory formula from 1995 to claw back the cost savings for consumers, given the earlier public outcry against excessive profits. From a corporate point of view, the prudent strategy appeared to be to postpone cost-saving measures until they were required to meet more stringent regulatory targets.

While liberalisation did not enforce a corporate split between supply and distribution, it did require an accounting split between the activities and competition in supply was partially introduced. Under the terms of their licences, a REC is required to sell distribution services to any licensed supplier of electricity supplying to an eligible consumer within that REC's territory, at standard and non-discriminatory rates. From 1st April 1990, eligible consumers were those with a maximum demand of more than 1 MW (covering about 5,000 consumers or 30% by volume of the market). These could choose to purchase their power from any licensed supplier, rather than from their local REC. On 1st April 1994, the limit was reduced to 100 kW (bringing in a further 45,000 consumers or 20% by volume) and, in 1990, it was planned that, in 1998, all classes of consumer (the remaining 22 million consumers) would be given choice.

The impact of the RECs' exposure to this competitive market was limited, because the supply business made up only about 10% of their operation and only 30% was initially open to competition, rising to 50% in 1994. At least until 1993, all the potential suppliers were buying from National Power and PowerGen on essentially the same terms, that is, the ones imposed by government in 1990. There was therefore little scope for one supplier to undercut another by much. The sector of the market that was open was nevertheless strongly competed over, with National Power and PowerGen moving in powerfully. However, the RECs that lost market share lost very little in terms of profits (see Table III.7).

These first two stages in this opening of the market had a clear economic logic and meant that half of Britain's electricity demand was supplied in a competitive market. Such consumers are large enough to be able to accurately access competing bids, and their bills are large enough (at least £35,000 per year) to pay for the transaction costs of competition. These include a meter that transmits consumption data on a half hourly basis (about £200 per year to supply the meter and process the data produced), marketing costs and the cost of the discount necessary to persuade a customer to switch suppliers. There were major practical difficulties after the 1994 opening, particularly in the computer systems necessary to allocate costs for use of system and, as a result, billing in the first year of the opening of the 100 kW market was chaotic.[21] Nevertheless, it is clear that most consumers took advantage of the possibility of investigating changing supplier, with more than half the eligible consumers switching from their host REC.

The competitive market for large users of electricity (100 kW consumers) was driven primarily by price considerations and it is one in which customers have little loyalty to their supplier. Perhaps, as a result, the major competitors have all been the incumbent companies, the RECs and the large generators. Following the 1990 opening, the large generators were restricted to taking no more than a 15% in the share of the market in any one REC's area. This condition was relaxed in 1990 and again in 1992, and finally removed altogether. The RECs have had the advantage of ownership of the infrastructure and knowledge of the consumers, while the generators have been able to use their ownership of generation plant to give them a comparative advantage. So far, commodities trading houses operating through futures and options, and buying on the spot market have not entered the market to any great extent, perhaps

---

[21] For a brief review of some of the problems encountered, see Doyle and MacLaine (1996).

Table III.6. Profits of the British electricity companies since 1990—the CEGB daughter companies.

Financial Year	85/86	86/87	87/88	88/89	89/90	90/91	91/92	92/93	93/94	94/95	95/96	96/97	97/98	98/99
1. Annual turnover														
CEGB	8015	8156	8325	8935										
National Power					3998	4378	4701	4348	3641	3953	3948	3535	3354	3009
PowerGen					2608	2651	3009	3188	2932	2885	2933	2898	2932	2344
Nuclear Electric					2058	2202	2432	2706	2962	2889				
British Energy											1654	1896	1954	2067
National Grid					1071	1144	1320	1392	1425	1428	1487	1457	1625	1568
Total	8015	8156	8325	8935	9735	9180	10197	10354	9730	9904				
2. Pre tax profits (£m) historical cost accounting (HCA)														
CEGB	783	675	457	-3026										
National Power					178	479	514	580	677	705	806	718	731	571
PowerGen					234	272	359	425	476	545	687	577	211	-245
Nuclear Electric					-928	-14	62	109	392	1068				
British Energy											-155	61	191	298
National Grid					429	386	498	533	580	611	616	591	573	1285
Total	783	675	457	-3026	-88	1123	1433	1647	2125	2929				
3. Profitability expressed as HCA pre-tax profit divided by turnover														
CEGB	0.098	0.083	0.055	-0.339										
National Power					0.045	0.109	0.109	0.133	0.186	0.178	0.204	0.203	0.249	0.190
PowerGen					0.090	0.103	0.119	0.133	0.162	0.189	0.234	0.199	0.072	-0.104
Nuclear Electric					-0.450	-0.006	0.025	0.040	0.132	0.370				
British Energy											-0.094	0.032	0.098	0.144
National Grid					0.400	0.337	0.377	0.383	0.407	0.427	0.414	0.406	0.354	0.820
Total	0.098	0.083	0.055	-0.339	-0.009	0.122	0.140	0.159	0.218	0.296				

Table III.6. Profits of the British electricity companies since 1990—the RECS *continued*

1. Annual Turnover

Financial Year	85/86	86/87	87/88	88/89	89/90	90/91	91/92	92/93	93/94	94/95	95/96	96/97
NORWEB	985.9	1023.7	1053.3	1129	1232.1	1240.3	1318	1413.5	1470.6	1510		
E Midlands Elec	987.3	1041.1	1083.1	1165	1263.1	1326.7	1543.8	1570	1444.5	1370	1194.5	755.1
MANWEB	706.1	719.8	741.3	803.2	887.1	829.3	834.6	919.9	920	877.6	—	
Yorkshire Elec	994.8	1019.1	1044.6	1159.5	1258.1	1242.5	1342.6	1325	1307.9	1459	1332.3	
Southern Elec	1124.7	1176.9	1202.6	1334.3	1456.8	1546	1750.6	1796.5	1780.2	1680	1597.6	1767.1
SWALEC	493	500.3	501.6	549.7	604	567.2	590.2	585	605	641.9		
SEEBOARD	803.3	831.2	838.8	907.9	982.1	1047.5	1157	1220	1218.1	1195.6	—	1182
London Electricity	926.9	961.8	968.1	1045.5	1147.7	1224	1347.1	1370	1308.4	1209.4	1187.7	
Eastern Electricity	1271	1330.1	1363.1	1494.1	1616.3	1720.1	1878.1	1920	1846.3	2061	2118.8	
Northern Electric	659.6	664.2	679.5	735.4	819.7	774	813.7	882.7	1030.5	1081	902.2	954.1
SWEB	600.6	618.1	616	686.3	747.9	779.4	847.1	892	899.6	874.9	704.1	
Midlands Elec	1041.2	1061.4	1079.1	1181.1	1295.2	1329.1	1454.1	1540	1415.5	1456.9	1335.8	1347.3
Total	10594	10948	11171	12176	13310	13626	14877	15436	15247	15417	10373	6005

2. Pre tax profits (£m) historical cost accounting (HCA)

Financial Year	85/86	86/87	87/88	88/89	89/90	90/91	91/92	92/93	93/94	94/95	95/96	96/97
NORWEB	53.9	59.5	53.3	65.8	75.8	70.3	137.9	157.1	178.3	205.4		
E Midlands Elec	48.2	70.8	81.8	87	90.9	106.5	150.1	155.1	51.2	214	287.5	
MANWEB	26.3	32.4	27.4	39.5	37.7	58.9	94.7	111.2	126.3	85.8		
Yorkshire Elec	55.3	64.5	71.8	90.2	109.5	134.6	141.9	156	149	217	219.3	255.5
Southern Elec	69.3	92.4	80.8	113.8	128.2	139.6	116.3	187	222	202.1	625.1	
SWALEC	26.1	32.5	22.3	30.8	26.2	58.1	72.5	87	104	122.6		
SEEBOARD	49.5	57.9	43.5	57.9	57.6	81.4	98.4	112.7	131.7	142	—	182.8
London Electricity	85.1	95.5	89.3	112.7	126.2	141.8	142.5	145.5	186.5	172.4	276.1	
Eastern Electricity	88.5	100.5	99.9	119	120	98.9	143.1	193.4	176.8	203.3	257.9	
Northern Electric	46.8	47.7	45	58.1	66.1	64.7	98.2	111.4	128	140.7	150.8	103
SWEB	47.2	44.4	32.3	55.8	66.1	66.2	83	101.1	116.8	111.5	253.4	
Midlands Elec	65.6	68.9	63.1	76.6	85.4	103.1	142.1	167.1	195	178	266.6	184.1
Total	661.8	767	710.5	907.2	989.7	1124	1421	1685	1766	1995	2337	725.4

Table III.6. Profits of the British electricity companies since 1990—the RECS *continued*

Financial Year	85/86	86/87	87/88	88/89	89/90	90/91	91/92	92/93	93/94	94/95	95/96	96/97
3. Profitability expressed as HCA pre-tax profit divided by turnover												
NORWEB	0.0547	0.0581	0.0506	0.0583	0.0615	0.0567	0.1046	0.1111	0.1212	0.136		
E Midlands Elec	0.0488	0.068	0.0755	0.0747	0.072	0.0803	0.0972	0.0988	0.0354	0.1562	0.2407	
MANWEB	0.0372	0.045	0.037	0.0492	0.0425	0.071	0.1135	0.1209	0.1373	0.0978		
Yorkshire Elec	0.0556	0.0633	0.0687	0.0792	0.087	0.1083	0.1057	0.1177	0.1139	0.1487	0.1646	
Southern Elec	0.0616	0.0785	0.0672	0.0853	0.088	0.0903	0.0664	0.1041	0.1247	0.1203	0.3913	0.1446
SWALEC	0.0529	0.065	0.0445	0.056	0.0434	0.1024	0.1228	0.1485	0.1719	0.191		
SEEBOARD	0.0616	0.0697	0.0519	0.0638	0.0586	0.0777	0.085	0.0924	0.1081	0.1188	0.1547	
London Electricity	0.0918	0.0993	0.0922	0.1078	0.11	0.1158	0.1058	0.1062	0.1425	0.1426	0.2325	
Eastern Electricity	0.0696	0.0756	0.0733	0.0796	0.0742	0.0575	0.0762	0.1007	0.0958	0.0986	0.1217	
Northern Electric	0.071	0.0718	0.0662	0.0786	0.0806	0.0836	0.1207	0.1262	0.1242	0.1302	0.1671	
SWEB	0.0786	0.0718	0.0524	0.0812	0.0884	0.0849	0.098	0.1133	0.1298	0.1274	0.3599	0.108
Midlands Elec	0.063	0.0649	0.0585	0.0649	0.0659	0.0776	0.0977	0.1085	0.1378	0.1222	0.1996	0.1366
All RECs	0.062	0.07	0.064	0.075	0.074	0.082	0.095	0.109	0.116	0.129	0.225	0.121

Source: Company Annual Reports.

Figures for Nuclear Electric include income from a consumer subsidy, the fossil fuel levy, which was in force from 1990/91 to 1995/96 providing income of about £1 bn per year. In 1995/96, British Energy was paid a consumer subsidy, the nuclear premium, of £899 m and in 1996/97, the nuclear premium was only payable for Scotland and was £26 m.

In 1995/96, the assets of Nuclear Electric and Scottish Nuclear were re-divided with the newer plants going to British Energy (privatised in 1996) and the older plants going to Magnox Electric (absorbed into BNFL in 1998). Separate turnover and profit figures for Magnox Electric are not available. The figures for British Energy are therefore not directly comparable with Nuclear Electric and the total figure cannot be calculated accurately.

PowerGen's profits for 1997/98 were severely reduced by a write-down of asset values of £339 m. PowerGen paid £101 m windfall tax in 1997/98. A second equal sum was paid in December 1998.

National Power paid a windfall tax of £133 m in December 1997 and a second instalment of £133 m in December 1998.

National Grid made exceptional profits of £107 m and £892 m in 1997/98 and 1998/99 from the sale of some shares in its telecoms subsidiary, Energis.

The high profitability of the RECs in 1995/96 was due to the de-merger of NGC.

In 1998, PowerGen changed its reporting period from April–March to calendar years. The figures shown under 1998/99 refer to the nine months from March 1998 to the end of December 1998. The figures for this year include East Midlands Electricity.

Table III.7. Market shares of the supply market.

REC	Market shares (% of supply)					
	1 MW			100 kW		
	1995/96	1996/97	1997/98	1995/96	1996/97	1997/98
Nat Power	18	17	13	6	—	—
PowerGen	23	23	19	—	—	—
Nuclear Electric	—	—	6	—	—	—
Eastern	8	8	14	13	15	12
East Midlands	—	—	—	7	6	6
London	—	—	—	9	12	9
MANWEB	—	—	—	—	—	—
Midlands	6	—	—	8	—	—
Northern	—	—	—	7	9	10
NORWEB	6	5	5	6	—	5
SEEBOARD		—	—	7	6	6
Southern	6	5	7	8	9	12
SWALEC	—	—	—	—	—	—
SWEB	—	—	—	—	—	—
Yorkshire	7	9	8	12	12	7
Others	11	14	28	7	13	22

Source: Office of Electricity Regulation, Annual Report and Accounts (annual).

because of the fear that the potential duopoly power of National Power and PowerGen over Pool prices would leave them vulnerable to predatory action.

The main diversification strategy followed by RECs in 1990–1995 was the move into generation. In the first two years after privatisation, about 5 GW of power plants were ordered by new entrants to the generation market (see Table III.8) in the so-called Dash for Gas. However, these new companies were generally closely linked, by ownership or by contract, for the power output, to the RECs. The RECs were originally able to have a significant ownership stake in generating plant sufficient to supply up to about 15% of their power needs. The motives for the RECs in entering these agreements were relatively clear and simple. They saw ownership of these plants as a way of expanding their business and reducing their dependence on the two large generators: National Power and PowerGen.

The price of power from these new plants was not always immediately competitive with the Pool price. However, there was a strong expectation, based on preliminary quotes from National Power and PowerGen, for power contracts to run from 1993, that the wholesale price of power would rise and their plant would become economic. This expectation was not fulfilled. The RECs were confident that, even if additional costs were incurred, these could be passed on to consumers,

Table III.8. Large British independent power projects—new capacity.

Plant	Size	Order	On-line	Initial owners (% owned)	Power contracts	Power purchasers (%)
Roosecote	229	1989	1991	ABB (80), NORWEB (20)	CfD	NORWEB (100)
Teesside	1875	6/91	1993	ENRON (50), Midland (19), Northern (15), SWALEC (12)	CfD	Midland (29), Northern (23),
Brigg	272		1994	SWALEC (8), SWEB (8)	CfD	SWEB (11), ICI/ENRON (25)
Corby	406	11/90	1994	Yorkshire (75), IVO (25)	CfD	Yorkshire (100)
Peterborough	405	12/90	1994	E Midlands (40), Hawker Siddeley (40), ESB (20)	CfD	E Midlands (100)
Fellside	168	7/91	1994	Eastern (50), Hawker Siddeley (50)	CfD	Eastern (100)
Barking	1000	3/92	1995	BNFL; BICC (25.5), CU Power (25.5), Southern (22), Eastern (13.5), London (13.5)	CfD	Southern (45), Eastern (27.5), London (27.5)
Medway	675	4/92	1995	SEEBOARD (37.5), Southern (37.5), AES (25)	CfD	SEEBOARD (50), Southern, Southern
Spondon	236	4/92	1995	Courtaulds, Southern, Mission		
Keadby	710	4/92	1995	Scottish Hydro (50), NORWEB (50)		
Humber 1	793	10/94	1997	IVO (30), Midlands (25), Tomen (25), ABB (20)	CfD	Midlands, IVO, Tomen
Kings Lynn A	415	10/94	1997	Eastern (100)	CfD	Eastern (100)
Seabank	812	1/96	1998	British Gas (50), Scottish Hydro (50)	Tolling	Scottish Hydro (100)
Rocksavage	760	7/96	1998	InterGen, ICI		ICI (43), Pool
AES Barry	240		1998	AES	Merchant	
Humber 2	527	12/96	1999	IVO (30), Midlands (25), Tomen (25), ABB (20)	Tolling	
Salt End	1200	97	2000	Entergy		
Brimsdown	350	97	2000	Indeck Energy, NRG Energy		

Table III.8. Large British independent power projects—new capacity *continued*

Plant	Size	Order	On-line	Initial owners (% owned)	Power contracts	Power purchasers (%)
Sutton Bridge	772	1/97	1999	ENRON		
South Denes	410	98	2000	Amoco		
Brighton	500	98	2000	Scottish Power, SEEBOARD		
Damhead Creek	775	3/99	2000	Entergy		
Coryton	720	98	2000	Intergen		
Shotton	240	99	2001	Eastern		
Baglan Bay	500	4/99		BP Chemicals		

Source: Compiled by author.

Includes plants with output greater than 150 MW that were either in service or under construction on 1st January 1999.

The order date is the date of financial closure (if available) when the main contracts were signed.

Roosecote feeds directly into the NORWEB 132-kV system. ABB sold its 80% stake to Mission Energy in 1991.

Teesside is a CHP station at which 340 MW plus steam is delivered to the nearby ICI works.

Spondon is a CHP station supplying steam to Courtaulds.

Fellside supplies steam and power to the Sellafield site. It was originally wholly owned by BNFL, but in 1993, Scottish Hydro took a 50% stake in it. About 100 MW of power is available for Scottish Hydro's customers in England and Wales.

Eastern purchased Hawker Siddeley's share in Peterborough in September 1994.

IVO purchased Yorkshire Electric's share of Brigg in 1998.

The Rocksavage plant will supply about 400 MW to ICI's Runcorn chlorine works with the balance going to the Grid.

Gas prices for supplies to the Seabank and Humber 1 plant are indexed to the electricity Pool price.

Scottish Hydro purchased NORWEB's stake in the Keadby plant in March 1997.

In April 1997, British Energy and Elf took up 12.5% each of the equity in the Humber projects. This left the remaining 75% distributed between IVO (22.5%), Midlands (18.75%), Tomen (18.75%) and ABB (15%).

In September 1999, ENRON put the Sutton Bridge plant up for sale on its completion.

especially residential consumers who were required to purchase power from their local REC, at least until 1998. While in strict economic terms, it is clear that many of the plants now make a loss, if they are seen as an insurance policy against dominance by the two large generators it can be argued they were worthwhile investments.

The output of the plant was fully contracted for usually 15 years forward, at prices unrelated to the Pool price under contracts for differences. This contractual cover meant that these plants were not expected to set the Pool price and therefore have contributed little to competition so far. Ownership of this plant also extended the range of their business from the relatively stagnant British distribution and supply sectors into an area in which income was not controlled by the regulator. Of the 12 RECs, only MANWEB did not acquire a stake in a CCGT. Subsequently, when these investments turned out to be less profitable than was expected, a number of plants have been sold on at a loss. For example, NORWEB sold its only share in a CCGT to Scottish Hydro, and Yorkshire also sold its share in a CCGT to the Finnish company, IVO.

However, despite the restrictions on the full force of competition, the increased risk in the generation sector and the need to raise project finance was reflected in the generating technology chosen and the comprehensive contractual cover which seemed to minimise any risk. All large plants ordered since 1990 have been of the combined cycle gas turbine (CCGT) variety. CCGTs are smaller scale (typically unit size is in the range 300 to 750 MW), have shorter lead-times (typically two years) and lower capital costs (less than half the price of conventional coal plant) than other options.

The Dash for Gas, which started in 1990, came to an end in the spring of 1992, as quickly as it started, for a number of reasons. Some of the RECs were approaching the 15% limit on own generation. A political controversy was emerging over the closure of coalmines that the existing orders had contributed to (see below). Placing further orders for gas-fired plant, which would have exacerbated the mines problem, would have been politically insensitive and invited further scrutiny of the economics of the existing plants. Some of the RECs may also have looked forward to the opening of the supply market and seen long-term contracts for power with plant owned by them as too risky.

Most RECs also used their gas purchases for their new power stations as a basis to move into gas supply to large consumers, a market that was open from 1992 onwards. Many of the companies bought stakes in other companies, often in unrelated sectors, but these moves were almost uniformly unsuccessful and these acquisitions have now been sold.

VI.A.b. National Grid Company

For NGC, the period 1990–1995 was one of adjustment, but with little commercial pressure and little need to make strategic moves to defend the core business or diversify. The initial regulatory formula determining its income was generous: NGC was allowed to increase its prices in line with inflation for 1990–1993. By the standards of subsequent settlements, the 1993 regulatory settlement for the four years to 1997 was also generous, an 'X' factor of 3. However, as NGC was not then separately quoted on the stock exchange, there was no share price to act as a barometer to judge whether the efficiency targets were too lax. Nevertheless, NGC did reduce its manpower by a somewhat greater percentage than the RECs (see Table III.1) and it improved its profitability from the already high level of 1990 (see Table III.6).

Its scope to diversify was limited. Ownership by the RECs restricted its independence. In addition, its core skills were restricted to operation of an electricity transmission network and it is not likely to be allowed in Britain to integrate into the competitive parts of the electricity business. Indeed, it is not allowed to trade in electricity and it was required to sell its small generation business in 1995. Its core skill, operation of a transmission network, is still regarded in many countries as a national strategic asset which should not fall into foreign hands, and so the scope for foreign takeovers has so far been limited. Nevertheless, NGC was able to launch a telecoms subsidiary, Energis, in 1993, adding optical fibre cables to the transmission system. It made substantial losses in its first few years but this was to be expected for a company trying to build up a business from scratch that had to make substantial up-front investments. A limited amount of overseas transmission work was undertaken and discussions on new interconnectors to Ireland and Norway took place, but the restrictions against it trading in electricity mean that it is more difficult to finance such links because it cannot contract for use of the cable. By 1995, NGC was feeling increasingly restricted as a result of its ownership by the RECs and was hoping to be floated on the stock exchange as an independent company.

IV.A.c. The fossil fuel generators

National Power and PowerGen had somewhat more scope for manoeuvre in this period. They were given indefinite Golden Share protection and, in this period, there were few that would have expected a takeover of them to be allowed. Their core business, generation in Britain, was guaranteed to be profitable by the generous contracts for purchase of coal between them and British Coal, matched to contracts for sale of power between them and the RECs. Nevertheless, they did have important issues to deal with, in particular, managing the inevitable reduction in generation market share they were bound to suffer, and meeting the substantial investment requirement needed to comply with acid gas emissions targets.

For the two large generators, there has always been an ambiguity in government as to whether they should be allowed to remain large companies or be slimmed down. Some ministers were more concerned about the performance of British companies in world markets and allowing National Power and PowerGen to retain a strong position in the British market was expected to give these companies a solid base from which to compete overseas. Others were more concerned about competitiveness of the British electricity system and they saw the power of these two companies as a barrier to competition. One of the main justifications for the highly concentrated generation market structure that was created was that new entrants would rapidly come in to dilute the market.

At the time of privatisation, there was scepticism that new entrants would risk competing against the might of National Power and PowerGen, which had been given a stock of reasonably modern, reliable coal-fired plants. The companies were privatised for a fraction of the accounting value of their power plants, so essentially it appeared that competitors would have build and pay for new plant to compete against largely amortised plant. However, two unexpected factors, the availability of the CCGT and gas as a power station fuel, and the unwillingness of the RECs to tolerate such a concentrated market, were significant. These meant that the rate of entry of new generating companies probably far exceeded the expectations of even the most committed advocates of the government's plans.

In the first three years after privatisation, it was expected that National Power and PowerGen would retain their market shares, simply because it would take at least that long to build new capacity. However, the unanticipated extra output that Nuclear Electric began to squeeze out of its nuclear plants had to be bought by the RECs at the expense of the market shares of National Power and PowerGen. Imports from France were categorised by government as having been generated from nuclear power plants and, by European Community law, had to receive the same level of subsidy as British nuclear power. There were, therefore, strong incentives for the French generating company, Electricité de France (EDF), to maximise the flow of power from France to England, again at the expense of the two large generators. The integrated Scottish electricity companies had excess capacity, and exports were also deemed not to have been generated from fossil fuels. Their home markets were not at risk, so they too had an incentive to maximise exports.

Table III.9. Market shares of the generation market (%).

	1989/90	1990/91	1992/93	1994/95	1995/96	1996/97	1997/98
National Power	48	45	41	34	31	24	21
PowerGen	30	28	27	26	23	21	20
Nuclear Electric	16	17	21	22	22	17	17
Magnox Electric	—	—	—	—	—	7	7
First Hydro/NGC	*	1	1	1	1	1	1
Eastern	—	—	—	—	1	7	10
Entrants (CCGT)	—	—	—	—	10	12	14
Entrants (Other)	—	—	—	—	1	1	1
Others	1	1	1	9	—	—	—
France	—	—	—	—	6	6	6
Scotland	—	—	—	—	4	3	3
Interconnectors	5	8	8	9	—	—	—

Source: OFFER, various.

The RECs claim that a strong factor behind their ordering of CCGTs was the high prices being quoted by National Power and PowerGen for contracts for power to follow on from the 1990–1993 contracts. It is not clear whether, if lower prices had been quoted, the RECs would have not invested so much and National Power and PowerGen would have retained a higher market share (see Table III.9). Another factor behind the fall in market share of the two large fossil fuel generators was the sale of old coal-fired plant that the DGES required. While this did not occur until 1996, the main factor behind it was the DGES's perceptions of the behaviour of National Power and PowerGen bidding into the Power Pool in years after privatisation. The DGES was concerned specifically about the bidding behaviour of National Power and PowerGen from April 1993 onwards. At that time, plant owned by these companies set the Pool price for the vast majority of half-hourly periods and there was a fear that the two companies could, as a result, manipulate the Pool price.

The DGES threatened a referral of the overall generation market to the MMC. Such an investigation would have been lengthy and disruptive, and the results could have been catastrophic to National Power and PowerGen, for example, a recommendation to break up the two companies into much smaller units. Under this threat, the generators agreed to sell a large amount of existing coal-fired plants, which at that time were generally the Pool price setters. They also agreed to bid their plant such that the annual average Pool price fell at or below a specified level (2.4 p/kWh), somewhat below the prevailing Pool prices.[22] There can be debate about how effective the Pool price cap was. The generators

---

[22] OFFER (1994a).

could still, at least in theory, achieve very high Pool prices at peak demand times, thereby increasing their profits, while still complying with the price cap by bidding low at times of low demand. The highly volatile Pool price that emerged probably served to deter purchasers of power from buying directly from the Pool and potential generators from planning plant on the basis of income from the Pool. However, the sale of plant, which they managed to put off until 1996, did ultimately cause them to lose additional market share and gave market power to a new entrant (Eastern).

It was expected in 1990 that National Power and PowerGen would be required to fit flue gas desulphurisation (FGD) equipment to 12 GW of their coal plant if the acid gas emissions targets were to be met. In the event, they were able to meet this target by fitting FGD to about 6 GW of plant and ordering about 6 GW of CCGTs in the period 1990–1994 (see Table III.10).

Every megawatt of base-load gas-fired capacity they built was a megawatt of old coal-fired capacity that did not need to be retrofitted with FGD equipment, at nearly the same capital cost. It also reduced their dependence on British coal. This was a fuel source they regarded with suspicion because of the likelihood, amply demonstrated since, that their capacity to burn coal would be used by government to force them to buy British coal in order to keep a British coal-mining industry going. Building new plant also gave them a more modern image than operating a fleet of worthy, but old-fashioned coal-fired plant would have done.

Table III.10. National Power and PowerGen power projects.

Plant	Size	Order	On-line
National Power			
Killingholme A	650	1990	1993
Deeside	500	1991	1995
Little Barford	684	1992	1996
Didcot B	1360	1994	1997
Staythorpe C	1500	1997	2003
PowerGen			
Killingholme B	900	1990	1993
Rye House	740	1991	1993
Connah's Quay	1442	1992	1997
Cottam	500	1997	1999
Killingholme C	700		2003

Source: Compiled by author.
In November 1999, National Power announced that it was proposing to sell its Killingholme A plant to NRG Energy (USA).

By the time negotiations started on the renewal of the contracts between the fossil-fuel generators and British Coal (these came to an end in April 1993), much of coal's potential market had been pre-empted. This was by the gas-fired plant ordered by the RECs and the two large fossil-fuel generators, and by the extra output from the nuclear plant. This was a major political issue at the time, as the reduction in the volumes of coal required would inevitably lead to a large number of pit closures and loss of mining jobs. The coal industry still exerted a powerful emotional pull over much of the British population. Ultimately, the government did as much as it was probably then able, which was to broker further five year contracts between British Coal and the generators, but for only about two-thirds of the volume previously taken and at prices that fell by about 15% in real terms. Again these contracts were matched by contracts between the generators and the RECs for sale of power.

While the Conservative government had no interest in preserving the British coal industry, it did have an objective of privatising the coal industry, which this deal allowed it to achieve while also largely defusing a difficult political debate. For the generators, the deal was a very good one. The contracts with the RECs protected them from competition by new generators for their duration and, if their profits are a good indicator, the terms of the contracts were highly advantageous to them. How far this good outcome can be credited to the commercial skill of National Power and PowerGen and how far it was just a 'lucky break' is hard to determine. Unlike the RECs, the two large generators were quick to institute dramatic cuts in jobs and over the period 1990–1995, the companies reduced their manpower by over 60% during a period when their market share fell by about a quarter (see Table III.1). No rigorous analysis of how this reduction in jobs was achieved exists, but a number of contributory factors are clear. Both companies closed down their major R&D facilities (see Table III.2) and a significant number of small, old fossil fuel power stations that were highly labour-intensive were closed. This undoubtedly contributed to the increase in profitability of 70%, which, in turn, allowed the job losses to be managed smoothly (see Table III.6). Redundancies were all voluntary and pay-offs were generous.

VI.A.d. Nuclear Electric

Nuclear Electric faced a different but perhaps no less intense set of pressures in that period. It was guaranteed to be able to sell all the output it could produce and much of its income was guaranteed by a consumer subsidy that the government set in 1990 for the period until 1998. This initially comprised about half of its income. However, the future of much of its capacity was in doubt. Of its nuclear power plants, 3000 MW were

Table III.11. Takeover and merger bids for British RECs.

REC	Bid Date	Bidder	Bidder's business	Privati-sation Price	Take-over Price
SWEB	7/95	Southern Co	US electric utility	0.29	1.1
MANWEB	7/95	Scottish Power	UK electric utility	0.41	1.8
Eastern	7/95	Hanson Trust	Multinational	0.65	2.5
NORWEB	9/95	North West Water	UK water company	0.41	1.8
Midlands	9/95	PowerGen	UK generator	0.50	1.95
Southern	10/95	National Power	UK generator	0.65	2.8
SWALEC	12/95	Welsh Water	UK water company	0.24	0.9
SEEBOARD	11/95	Central & SW Corp	US electric utility	0.31	1.6
Midlands	5/96	Avon Energy	US utility consortium	0.50	1.7
East Midlands	11/96	Dominion Resources	US electric utility	0.52	1.3
London	12/96	Entergy	US electric utility	0.52	1.3
Northern	12/96	CalEnergy	US IPP company	0.29	0.8
Yorkshire	2/97	Yorkshire Holdings	US utility consortium	0.50	1.5
Energy Group	2/98	Texas Utilities	US electric utility		4.4
East Midlands	6/98	PowerGen	UK generator		1.9
Southern	9/98	Scottish Hydro-Electric	UK electric utility		2.5
Midlands Supply	11/98	National Power	UK generator		0.18
London	12/98	EDF	French utility		1.9
SWEB Supply	6/99	EDF	French utility		0.16
SWALEC S'ply	6/99	British Energy	UK generator		0.10
SWALEC Supply	8/00	Scottish Hydro-electric	UK electric utility		0.25
Norweb Supply	8/00	Texas Utilities	US electric utility		0.31
Swalec Distribution	9/00	Southern Co	US electric utility		0.56

Source: Press reports.

The British government blocked the bids by National Power for Southern and PowerGen for East Midlands.

The Hanson Trust demerged Eastern and Peabody Coal into The Energy Group in January 1997.

The bid for The Energy Group includes Peabody Coal and Citizens Energy, which have to be sold to meet US regulatory requirements. These companies were valued at about £1.4 bn.

Yorkshire Holdings comprises American Electric Power and Public Service of Colorado.

Avon Energy comprises General Public Utilities and Cinergy.

National Power purchased only the supply business of Midlands Electric, the distribution business is still owned by Avon Energy.

CalEnergy was taken over by MidAmerican Energy Holdings Company in December 1998. This company announced an agreed takeover bid by a group of investor companies led by Berkshire Hathaway (78%) in October 1999.

old plants of the Magnox design, all of which were beyond their design life. Whilst these plants were reasonably reliable, their operating costs were so high that income from sales of electricity did not cover them. In 1990, it was expected that most, if not all of this capacity would be retired by the year 2000. The rest of its capacity, the 6000 MW of advanced gas-cooled reactors (AGRs), was then hopelessly unreliable with an availability of about 40%. This made the plants unprofitable to run, and closure of one or more of the stations was expected. The one plant, under construction, the Sizewell B pressurised water reactor (PWR), was ordered in 1987. Nobody expected it ever to make an adequate return on the investment, and, as late as 1992, there was still a strong argument that it would be cheaper not to complete, even after five years of construction work.

Many of Nuclear Electric's employees were deeply committed to nuclear power, while others were just keen to preserve the company. This contributed to the success, on all fronts, of Nuclear Electric. It convinced the safety regulator that the Magnoxes could remain in service and it was able to maintain reliability at the stations, despite their age. Only one of the seven Magnox stations it was operating in 1990 had to be retired. The reliability of the AGRs was dramatically improved to about 75% with a corresponding improvement in economic performance. Sizewell B was completed reasonably close to the costs and schedule the company set itself in 1990. Ironically, some of the consumer subsidy, which ministers often portrayed as being earmarked for dealing with nuclear waste and decommissioning costs, was used to build the Sizewell reactor. Somewhat bizarrely, this meant that a company that was basically insolvent was able to make a major investment without any need for borrowing. From a position in 1990 when the company made a small loss, by 1995, albeit with a consumer subsidy of about £1 bn, the company made a profit of about £1 bn. As a result, it was pressing to be privatised and to be allowed to build more nuclear capacity.

VII. Policies from 1995–1998

VII.A. Ownership changes amongst the RECs—1995–1998

A key feature of the period from 1995–1998 was the rapid change in ownership in the electricity sector that followed the expiry of the Golden Share in the RECs in 1995. Despite this, the basic structure of the industry remained unchanged.

Ownership of the National Grid Company (NGC) was placed jointly with the 12 RECs in 1990. At that time, it was given a nominal value of only £800m. Partly to give NGC more commercial freedom and partly to avoid any suspicion that the RECs would use their ownership of the grid to unfairly advantage other parts of their business, the DGES later obliged them to sell most of their shares in NGC. They were required to sell them, retaining no more than 1%, during the year from December 1995, by which time the share value of the company was about £4.4 bn.

The sale price amply compensated them for the lost profits they received from NGC—at that time NGC made annual profits of about £600 m on a turnover of only £1.1 bn (see Table III.6). However, it was seen as a windfall gain to the RECs resulting from an under-valuation of the NGC by the government. The RECs could hardly argue that the increase in value was a result of changes and improvements to the NGC. The RECs were therefore required to pay back about £1 bn to final consumers from the windfall gain that the flotation of NGC represented to them in the form of a £50 rebate to each consumer on their bills. The sale of NGC has had little strategic significance for the RECs because the terms of their ownership of NGC did not allow them to influence NGC policy to any extent.

The Golden Shares applying to the 12 RECs were time-limited, expiring in April 1995. However, even before they expired, there was widespread speculation about likely takeovers. It was the publication of the proposed distribution price formula, to apply from April 1995, and the imminent expiry of the Golden Shares that began to cause those inside and outside the RECs to examine much more closely the strategic options that ownership of a REC offered. The DGES's initial distribution price review proposal[23] was published for consultation in August 1994 and, compared with the previous formula, appeared very tough. Whereas previously, RECs could raise their prices in real terms by up to 2.5% a year, the new formula required them to reduce their prices. A one-off cut in April 1995 by 11–17% was prescribed, with cuts (the 'X' factor) in the following four years of 2%.

The RECs made ritual objections that the targets were too harsh but accepted the new formulae. Far from perturbing financial analysts, this caused them to mark up the value of the RECs' shares in the belief that the targets would be easy to meet. There was an expectation that takeover bids would follow. A diversified, mainly British-based company, Trafalgar House, placed the first bid in November 1994, for Northern Electric. The imminence of the expiry of the Golden Share meant that although the government did state that it would not allow the merger before the expiry of its Golden Share, this did not deter Trafalgar House because it would have been difficult to complete the merger before then. Northern chose to try to fight off the bid partly because they believed it to be too low, but perhaps also because their executives did not want to lose their newly acquired status. Northern felt able to promise existing shareholders a large package of benefits out of the high profits it expected to make under the new pricing formula. Ultimately, the bid was withdrawn, but it represented a strong signal that the British RECs would be seen as attractive targets, especially with the distribution price formula proposed.

---

[23] OFFER (1994b).

This clear recognition within the industry that the new formulae would allow the RECs big profits forced the DGES to find a pretext to re-open the review in March 1995. In July 1995, he imposed a much tougher settlement, leaving the one-off cut in place, adding a second of 11–13% in April 1996 and increasing the '*X*' factor to 3.[24] The REC hit hardest was, not surprisingly, Northern, and it had to reduce the real price of its distribution services by 35% over five years. Even the RECs that came off lightest (Southern and Eastern) had to reduce prices by 27%. These much tougher targets were still not seen as too onerous. The fact that the income for the RECs' distribution business (90% of RECs' profits) was assured for the next five years under this formula meant that the overall income stream for the RECs was very predictable and acquiring a REC seemed to represent a low risk.

Within a day of the announcement of the revised formulae, the first bid for a REC had come in (the Southern Company of USA for SWEB) to be quickly followed by Scottish Power's bid for MANWEB and Hanson's bid for Eastern. Within six months, half the RECs had been subject to takeover bids, including the contentious bids by National Power and PowerGen in September 1995 for Southern and Midland, respectively (see Table III.11). The prospect of a generation company taking over a REC appeared to contradict the basic philosophy of privatisation, which seemed to be to create an industry without vertical integration. In fact, the position on vertical integration was always ambiguous. In the new structure, there was no attempt in 1990 to separate distribution and supply by splitting the RECs into two separate companies. In addition, the RECs were given ownership of the grid company, the RECs were allowed to move into generation to a limited extent and the generators had been allowed to compete to supply large consumers.

The Minister accepted the advice of both the DGES and the Director General of Fair Trading (DGFT) and referred both generator bids to the MMC.[25] The MMC ruled that, subject to compliance with some conditions, the mergers could be allowed. However, the Minister sided with the DGES and the DGFT, who were not convinced by the MMC's reasoning and rejected the MMC's advice and, in April 1996, refused to allow the takeovers. However, the ruling was equivocal and did not proscribe this sort of vertical integration in principle, merely saying that the time was wrong. It was argued that competition for all final consumers still had to be implemented and National Power and PowerGen still dominated the generation market.[26] The clear implication was that, once

---

[24] OFFER (1995a).
[25] Monopolies and Mergers Commission (1996a and 1996b).
[26] DTI (1996)

the generation and supply markets had developed further, integration would be allowed, and PowerGen made no secret of its continued desire to take over a REC.

Of the changes in corporate ownership of the RECs that followed the initial takeovers, the most complex have occurred at Eastern Electric. The Hanson Trust, a diversified multinational company, took this over in an agreed bid in August 1995. The Hanson Trust had long had an interest in acquiring some part of the British electricity supply industry and, before privatisation, it had tried to negotiate with the government to buy PowerGen directly rather than allow it to be sold by public flotation. Eastern purchased 4000 MW of coal-fired plant from National Power and 2000 MW of coal-fired plant from PowerGen in July 1996. This sale was via competitive tender and was required by the DGES, who was attempting to reduce the market power of the two large generation companies.[27] In February 1996, and as part of a restructuring of the whole Hanson Group, it was announced that Eastern would be floated off with a US coal subsidiary of Hanson, Peabody Coal, to form The Energy Group (TEG), a move completed in January 1997. However, only six months later, an agreed takeover of TEG by Pacificorp, an Oregon based US utility was announced.

The new Labour government, keen to show it was less passive to issues of corporate ownership than the previous government, referred this bid to the MMC in August 1997 and received a report in November of that year which broadly approved the takeover.[28] However, British procedures require that a bidder that has successfully overcome an MMC inquiry must resubmit its bid. This gives the opportunity for new bidders to enter. Texas Utilities (TXU) placed a higher bid than that of Pacificorp and, after a number of successively higher bids from the two parties, as well as expressions of interest from a number of other potential bidders, TXU took over the company in May 1998. It paid £4.45 bn for the company, compared with Pacificorp's original bid of £3.65 bn.

VII.B. The RECs

By early 1995, the RECs were under intense pressure. The DGES's initial settlement for the regulatory formula for the distribution sector was the toughest so far, but did not even recover the ground lost through overgenerous income caps in the previous five years. Even the revised settlement meant that over the ten-year period following privatisation, the

---

[27] In fact, the plant was transferred on a complicated leasing arrangement aimed at reducing Eastern's tax bill. The deal for National Power involves a much larger annual fixed payment than that involving PowerGen.

[28] Monopolies and Mergers Commission (1997).

RECs had to do little more than achieve the same rate of efficiency improvement as the despised nationalised industries were able to do in the 1980s. Nevertheless, the adjustments had to be rapid to compensate for the loss of about 25% of their distribution income in only two years. The Golden Share expired in April 1995, making them potential takeover targets for the long queue of companies looking to enter the British electricity industry. As a result, as described above, the RECs were all subject to takeover bids within two years of the expiry of the Golden Share.

In the period 1995–1998, the RECs had much less scope to adopt independent corporate strategies. Most were by then under new owners who looked at their business with different eyes. The new owners would decide corporate policies, and, particularly where the RECs were taken over by US utilities, overseas investment was more likely to be carried out under the banner of the US parent company.

Nevertheless, opportunities for diversification were arising. The residential gas market was opening up, somewhat ahead of electricity, and this represented a market RECs could easily and cheaply enter using their existing gas businesses and contacts with final consumers. Technical change, including the growth of the cellphone market, the possibility of using electricity cables as a way of delivering telecoms services and the growth of the Internet gave RECs the opportunity to develop IT-based subsidiaries. The idea of multi-utility businesses began to emerge, including services such as gas, electricity, telecoms, Internet, water and cable television.

VII.B.a. The distribution business

Inevitably, the character of the main business of the RECs, the monopoly distribution business, remained largely unchanged. From 1995 onwards, the pricing formulae for the distribution business were much tougher, and this was reflected in an acceleration in job losses (see Table III.1). For the future, the precedent set by the 1995 review means that there will be an expectation that continuing cost savings will be possible. However, the price reductions imposed in 1995 may have been achieved by a combination of one-off opportunities and taking up the backlog of cost saving opportunities that did not need to be taken up from 1990–1995.

VIII.B.b. The supply business

The prospect of the completion of the opening of the supply market to competition began to expose more clearly how poorly a supply business fits, in business terms, with a distribution business. Regulation should mean that any cross-subsidisation is not possible and the supply business, with its high risks and need for trading and marketing skills, is very different to the low-risk, engineering-based distribution business. The residential supply business is very different in character to the supply markets that have been opened so far.

For a new entrant, electricity supply to residential consumers makes no sense as a stand-alone business. The supply element of a typical household bill is about £30 per year, the other elements are either standard charges (transmission and distribution) or purchases from a competitive market (generation) in which it would be difficult for one supplier to gain any advantage over another. By comparison, the costs of competing for a new customer are high. Advertising might cost about £50 per consumer won and the discounts to undercut the existing supplier might cost a similar sum.

If costs were to be allocated accurately, it would be desirable for consumer consumption data to be metered at the same interval, 30 minutes, as wholesale prices of electricity are set. However, the meters capable of doing this, similar to those which have been used for large consumers, together with the associated computer systems, cost approximately £200 per year. This represents a substantial reduction on the cost at time of privatisation. There does not seem sufficient scope for further price reductions for this type of meter to be economically feasible for households, unless it is part of a package of electronic communications that includes other meters and network connections.

The DGES, a strong advocate of metering as a way of allocating costs appropriately, reluctantly came to the conclusion in 1995 that 'smart' meters were not viable and that 'profiling', at that time being introduced in Norway, was the only viable solution. Under profiling, consumption will continue to be metered at the same interval as now, every three months. Standard consumption patterns (so-called 'profiles') will be assumed and these will be used to allocate consumption over that period to each half-hour segment in it.[29]

In principle, the decision to open the market in 1998 had been known since 1990. However, a combination of pre-occupation in the RECs sorting out the problems that arose from the 1994 opening and waiting for the decision on profiling meant that it was not until 1996 that preparations could begin. The main element was the IT systems needed to allow consumers to switch.

Almost from the start, there was little confidence that the process could be completed on time and to cost and these fears proved well founded. A number of factors are said to have contributed. The industry places some of the blame on the regulator for the late start and for lack of leadership.

---

[29] OFFER (1995d).

The regulator, keen to avoid a public relations disaster that would have occurred if the problems of 1994 had recurred, imposed very rigorous testing on the new systems. There were problems arising because each REC had to develop its own software, but it must be able to interface with the other companies' systems. Agreeing common standards proved difficult with RECs tending to argue for the standards that complied most closely with their own existing standards. The costs may also have escalated as RECs used the opportunity to update old systems. By 1998, the DGES finally had to admit that the original timetable could not be met. The cost that would be passed on to consumers of building and operating the new systems over a five-year period had increased to £726 m, a doubling of the cost estimated by the DGES only a year previously.[30]

On the other side of the supply business, purchasing electricity in bulk, the RECs had much less scope for independent activity. As noted previously, in 1993, the government brokered five-year contracts between the RECs and National Power and PowerGen, which ensured a market share for British Coal of about 40%. By then, nuclear output was up to about 25% of the market and the RECs' own power plants, supplying about 10% of their needs, were also coming on stream. So until 1998, there was still little need for the RECs to go out into the marketplace to buy bulk electricity.

VII.B.c. Generation
After the end of the 'Dash for Gas', only Eastern continued to expand its generation activities, partly by further plant orders but mainly through its acquisition of 6000 MW of old coal-fired plant from National Power and PowerGen in 1996. The restriction that RECs could only own plant up to 15% of their needs was relaxed to allow Eastern to purchase this plant (see Table III.12). RECs were allowed to contract for only about 15% of the power needs of their franchise customers with their own plants but were able to own more capacity. The market power of National Power and PowerGen was much reduced and the RECs could no longer risk contracting for power purchases many years forward because they no longer had a captive customer base. So further orders for power plants were not attractive.

VII.B.d. Diversification into gas supply
The industrial gas market was progressively opened from 1988 onwards, initially only with very large consumers (25,000 therms per year) and then, from August 1992, medium consumers (2,500 therms per year). A

---

[30] House of Commons (1998).

Table III.12. British independent power projects—acquired capacity.

Plant	Size	Year sold	Type	Former owners	New owners
Dinorwig	1740	1995	Pumped Store	NGC	Mission Energy
Ffestiniog	360	1995	Pumped Store	NGC	Mission Energy
Drakelow C	976	1996	Coal	PowerGen	Eastern
High Marnham	945	1996	Coal	PowerGen	Eastern
Ironbridge	970	1996	Coal	National Power	Eastern
Rugeley	1026	1996	Coal	National Power	Eastern
West Burton	1966	1996	Coal	National Power	Eastern
Uskmouth	342	1999	Coal	National Power	AES
Drax	3960	1999	Coal	National Power	AES
Ferrybridge	2000	1999	Coal	PowerGen	Mission Energy
Fiddler's Ferry	2000	1999	Coal	PowerGen	Mission Energy
Killingholme A	650	1999	Gas	National Power	NRG Energy
Eggborough	2005	1999	Coal	National Power	British Energy

Source: Compiled by author.

number of RECs, including Midlands (the first), East Midlands, SWEB and Eastern (ENG) took the opportunity to enter the market (see Table III.13). However, only Eastern made much of an impact and by February 1998 it was the only REC, with 12% of the market, in the top ten industrial gas suppliers—these accounted for more than 90% of the market. The first trials to allow residential consumers to choose their gas supplier took place in the south west of England, in SWEB territory, starting in April 1996. These trials were extended and, by May 1998, all residential gas consumers in Britain were able to choose their gas supplier.

This was a highly attractive market for the RECs to enter for a number of reasons. New entrants had a substantial advantage over the incumbent supplier, British Gas Trading (BGT). This company had inherited a large number of take-or-pay gas contracts, signed from the mid-1970s onwards when its nationalised predecessor was the monopoly gas supplier. These contracts were set at prices well above the current market price. New entrants could purchase gas up to 50% cheaper than BGT's average costs (a weighted average based on the spread of its contract prices) and therefore easily offer discounts of 15–25%. However, this 'windfall' cost advantage is now diminishing as BGT renegotiates its gas supply contracts.

The RECs were reasonably well known and apparently reliable companies and consumers would have relatively few qualms about trusting such a company to supply such an essential purchase as pipeline gas. The home REC would have a particular advantage because it could target its marketing through routine contacts at low cost, and the characteristics

Table III.13. RECs' gas businesses.

REC	Gas partner	Brand name	Gas supply business
NORWEB		Energi	Launched Feb 98
Northern	CE Gas	Own brand	CE Gas (previously Sovereign) a subsidiary. Dual fuel offer. Took over Atlantic Gas N Sea gas assets.
MANWEB		MANWEB	Integrated with parent, Scottish Power's business.
Southern Electric		Own brand	
SEEBOARD	Amoco	Beacon	Beacon launched Aug 96. SEEBOARD bought out Amoco in July 1999.
SWEB		SWEBGAS	Sold residential gas business outside area to Amerada Hess, Sep 97. Business gas supplier since 93.
London Electric		Own brand	Earlier link up with Total dropped Feb 98 and business won outside London sold to Northern.
Yorkshire			Residential business launched Sep 97. N Sea equity stake. Gas purchase deal with Conoco effective Oct 98.
Eastern	In house	Own brand	Residential business launched Apr 96. N Sea equity stake
SWALEC		Own brand	Residential business launched Feb 97. Business customers supplied since 92.
Midlands	Amerada Hess	Own brand	Business customers supplied since 91 (first electricity company in market). Domestic consumer business effectively sold to Amerada Hess June 98. Commercial and industrial business sold to Agas November 98.
East Midlands		Sterling Gas	Sterling Gas launched Sep 97. Business customers supplied since 92.

Source: Compiled by author

of the consumers were well known, so it could target profitable customers. Most of the RECs competed in the first trials, keen to get experience and to establish the business early on. Even RECs which had no wish to become a long-term gas supplier had an incentive to enter the market, in the knowledge they could build a business cheaply and then probably sell it on at a profit. Entering the gas market was also a way of defending the RECs' electricity markets since some gas suppliers, especially

BGT, might move into electricity once that market was open, offering a package including gas and electricity. In many respects, gas supply was a market that the RECs could not afford not to contest and, in the end all the RECs took out gas supply licences.

Despite the large discounts on offer, the rate of switching away from BGT has been surprisingly slow and in the first year of trials in the south-west, only 20% of consumers switched despite the large discounts on offer. There has also been bad publicity because of dubious marketing tactics, especially doorstep sales, adopted by some of the new entrants, including SWEB and Northern, and surveys have shown that consumers have difficulty in knowing which is really the cheapest gas on offer.

As might be expected with a new market and with such disappointing rates of switching, there has been a considerable shakeout in the early contestants. SWEB, one of the most aggressive entrants in the early trials, and London Electric have now abandoned attempts to win customers outside their region, selling what customers they have won on to other suppliers, and are merely continuing to supply their existing gas consumers in their own territory.

It is still too early to judge which of the companies have been successful, but out of about 19 million residential consumers in Britain, by May 1998, about 1.7 million had switched away from BGT. However, there have been a significant number of consumers, about 130,000 by May 1998, who had switched away from BGT but quickly moved back. In the first three areas to open up for competition, the main new entrant by some distance is ENG, with about 6% of the market. Of the other REC based companies, Scottish Power (3%), Northern (2.5%) and Beacon (2%), are doing best.

Another gas business some RECs have entered is providing gas network connections to new customers. As most existing households are already supplied with gas, this is mainly for new housing developments and is generally in conjunction with supplying an electricity connection. The joint electricity and gas connection markets are estimated to be worth about £2 bn per year and six companies have emerged to challenge the network operator, Transco. Of these, three are based in British RECs, Eastern Pipelines, Southern Electric Pipelines and Scottish Power Gas, the parent company of which owns MANWEB.

VII.B.e. Water

Three RECs became integrated with water companies. SWALEC was taken over by Welsh Water to form a multi-utility company, Hyder, and North West Water took over NORWEB, also to form a multi-utility company, now known as United Utilities. In 1995, MANWEB was taken over

Table III.14. RECs' IT businesses.

REC	IT business
London	Tie up on mobile phones with ACC Telecom and Cellnet.
NORWEB	NORWEB Communications launched Mar 98 promoting Nor.web PowerLine technology.
Eastern Group	Promoting its own version of NORWEB's PowerLine technology. Business sold to NTL in Dec 98.

Source: Compiled by author.

by Scottish Power, the larger of the two privatised integrated Scottish electric utilities and Scottish Power subsequently bought Southern Water, effectively to form a multi-utility. However, unlike Hyder and United Utilities, there is no overlap in the geographical coverage of the three companies.

VII.B.f. IT-related businesses

The IT-related market is much more diverse and the reasons for RECs to enter the business are less compelling than for gas, although the electricity distribution network does offer opportunities to incorporate a telecoms network (see Table III.14). United Utilities was the most aggressive entrant, bundling energy and telecoms services into a single consumer package. It tried to develop its own technology, Nor.web PowerLine, in collaboration with Nortel, a Canadian-based telecoms company. This would have utilised the existing network to carry data communications, including Internet traffic and low-grade voice telecoms. However, in September 1999, it abandoned this technology as uneconomic. Eastern, through its telecoms subsidiary, was also promoting its own version of this technology, but it too abandoned it in December 1998. Nevertheless, NORWEB's telecoms subsidiary has promise. Like NGC, United Utilities will probably choose to float the company off once it is developed.

VII.B.g. Meter reading

There are now clear signs that the meter reading function, for all utilities including gas and water as well as electricity, will become more separated from the rest of the electricity supply industry. For large consumers (the 100 kW market) meter operation (installing and maintaining meters) and data collection (reading meters) has been open to competition since 1994. Although competition for small consumers will be phased in from autumn 1998, meter operation and data collection will remain a monopoly in the short term to minimise avoid the risk that problems in opening up this market would affect the process of introducing supply competition to small consumers. For large consumers, some RECs are developing competitive businesses and others are sub-contracting the function. At present, most RECs are still retaining the option to develop this business, although East Midlands and the two multi-utility companies Hyder and United Utilities seem most committed at this stage. Eastern announced in October 1999 its intention to sell off its metering business.

VII.B.h. Other UK non-utility diversification
After the first wave of largely unsuccessful diversifications, the RECs have been wary about diversifying away from their core strengths. However, United Utilities, which incorporates NORWEB, has launched a facilities' management company, Vertex, which has won contracts, for example, to operate call centres (facilities to deal with customer telephone calls).

VII.B.i. Overseas expansion
Until 1997, Midlands was the only REC to have invested significantly overseas, acquiring stakes in power plants and power companies in Portugal (1993), Spain (1995), Pakistan (1995), and Turkey (1996). These investments are estimated to be worth more than £100 m, the main part of which involves Pakistan and Turkey, but it is not possible from the accounts to establish how profitable they have been. It is perhaps significant that this overseas investment seems to have dried up after Midlands' takeover by a US utility. Eastern moved aggressively into the international arena in 1997 and is the only REC to make a concerted attempt to become a significant energy company in Europe, especially the liberalised Nordic market.

VII.C. National Grid Company
NGC was floated as an independent company in December 1995,[31] at about the same time as the company sold its pumped storage stations to Mission Energy (see Table III.12). These two events revealed the extent to which NGC was undervalued in 1990. The pumped storage stations were sold for £650 m, not far short of the total valuation placed on NGC in 1990. On the first day of trading, NGC shares were changing hands for about £2, making the overall value of the company about £4.4 bn. The review of charges for transmission services resulted in an income

---

[31] The factors behind the flotation of NGC are discussed in McHarg (1998).

cut for the transmission business of 20% for 1997/98 followed by 4% reductions in each of the following years. This was the toughest regulatory settlement so far, and, while it was unwelcome, it was not unexpected. Profits were affected proportionately but still remained healthy.

International activities (mainly in Pakistan and Argentina) were still a small proportion of turnover. Energis was still making a loss (£34 m on a turnover of £168 m), but in December 1997, NGC floated Energis as a separate company selling about 25% of the shares at about £2.90 per share. Within months, the market value of the company had risen from about £850 m at time of flotation to over £2.5 bn.

VII.D. The fossil fuel generators

The period from 1995–1998 must have been a frustrating one for National Power and PowerGen, particularly for their British operations. The companies were prevented from fulfilling a key objective of taking over a REC and thereby integrating into electricity supply, while their combined generation market share fell by a third due to factors over which they then had no control (see Table III.9). National Power managed to maintain its increase in profitability, while PowerGen's profitability was less impressive, with much of 1997/98's profits wiped out by a write-down in asset values of some of its British power plants. In 1998, PowerGen's profits were severely reduced by the renegotiation of its gas contract portfolio. This was necessary because of the steep fall in gas price since the contract for supply to Connah's Quay was negotiated and cost the company £535 m. In November 1999, National Power also announced provisions for losses on its gas contracts of £759 m.[32]

At that time, by far the most attractive form of diversification for the generators was to integrate vertically by buying a REC. The main benefit of this would be to reduce risk in their generation business because, instead of selling their output into volatile and highly price-sensitive spot markets or to supply companies, they could sell direct to final consumers. Smaller consumers in particular are much less price sensitive and show some degree of loyalty, making the market share of the generators more stable and giving a more secure base for investment in new generating capacity. The extra business would compensate for the turnover lost as their generating market share contracted. It would also give them skills in distribution and electricity retailing, which would allow them to compete to buy integrated foreign electric utilities. The key business for the generators to obtain would be the RECs' supply businesses. The RECs' distribution businesses, while being much larger and, so far, highly

---

[32] National Power (1999).

profitable, would give them little if any advantage in the generation and supply markets. However, when the option to take over RECs became available in 1995 with the expiry of the RECs' Golden Shares, the government decision blocked National Power's and PowerGen's takeover bids for RECs.

In the generation business, the RECs' CCGTs, ordered in the 'Dash for Gas', began to go on line and nuclear output continued to rise. In 1996/97, 6000 MW of old coal-fired plant was transferred from the two large generators to Eastern, further accelerating their market decline.[33] Both companies had further sites earmarked to expand gas-fired generation, but only two were proceeded with, the National Power Staythorpe site, which will not be completed until 2003, and the PowerGen Cottam site, which will be a test-bed for Siemens gas turbine technology.

In 1996, a potential bid to take over National Power by the Southern Company (USA) was blocked by the British government using the Golden Share, on the grounds that the markets were not yet fully developed. This left the door open to future bids and Golden Share protection is clearly not something National Power and PowerGen can rely on.

VII.D.a. Diversification in the UK

As long as vertical integration was proscribed, the main opportunity to diversify in the UK for the large generators was horizontally into gas. Their emerging position as large gas purchasers gave them scope to use their purchases as a basis to develop a gas business. PowerGen launched a joint venture in 1992 with Conoco and Kinetica, to transport and sell gas, at first to its own power plants, but also to final gas consumers. This business encountered some difficulties in the mid 1990s because of the collapse of the North Sea gas price and in 1997, PowerGen bought out

---

[33] Despite their market share nearly halving, there is still concern about the market power of the two large generators and proposals to force them to sell more plant. The basis for this concern is their power over Pool price setting and in 1997/98, National Power and PowerGen set the Pool price about 70% of the time, the remainder being split between Eastern and First Hydro.

The issue is not clear cut however, as the Pool price has little relevance to the price of electricity—most electricity purchases are still covered by Contracts for Differences which are in no way linked to the Pool price. For the future, it now seems likely that the compulsory Pool will be abandoned in favour of more flexible arrangements, which allow trading outside the Pool and which may not give essentially the same price to all bidders. However, if the generation market is to be truly competitive, the proportion of electricity sales that are made at prices related to some sort of electricity spot market must increase and if National Power and PowerGen continue to control the price-setting plant, this will be an unhealthy market.

Conoco and Kinetica was integrated into the PowerGen business, by which time it had a 10% market share of gas sales. National Power has not developed a significant gas trading business.

Both companies have developed cogeneration businesses and renewable power businesses. In 1998, National Power owned cogeneration plant with an electrical capacity of 487 MW and PowerGen had 178 MW. The renewables businesses took advantage of the consumer subsidy originally intended for nuclear power but broadened to include any non-fossil fuel source. In 1998, PowerGen had 90 MW of capacity in service, while National Power has 132 MW.

VII.D.b. Diversification overseas

Restrictions on their ability to vertically integrate in the UK have meant that the major opportunity for National Power and PowerGen to diversify was overseas. However, even here, their lack of experience in transmission and distribution meant that it was difficult for them to take over integrated electricity companies and their main scope was to compete for independent power projects (IPPs).

Winning contests to build IPPs is a fiercely competitive although potentially highly profitable business, often in markets such as the Indian sub-continent, where the commercial risks are high. By 1998, PowerGen had 7800 MW of capacity either in service or under construction outside Britain and had an objective of owning as much capacity overseas in 2005 as it does in Britain. The extent to which the company believes this will be achieved by expansion overseas as against contraction in Britain is not clear. The main areas for investment have been Australia, India, Indonesia, Thailand and Kazakhstan. In Europe, PowerGen has stakes in plants in Portugal and Germany (in the former German Democratic Republic).

National Power has also been active in this area, and in 1998, had 10,000 MW of capacity overseas. It owns plants in Turkey, Australia, China, Indonesia, Portugal, Pakistan and the USA and in 1998, it planned to double its annual rate of international investment to around £600 m.

VII.E. The nuclear generators

In July 1996, British Energy was floated on the London Stock Exchange. Its most urgent priority has been to reduce its dependence on British nuclear power plants. While the performance of its advanced gas-cooled reactors (AGRs) has improved remarkably since 1990, there is probably little scope for much more improvement. The British AGRs are unique, the only AGRs in the world are those owned by British Energy and there were severe difficulties in constructing the plants, in one case taking more than 20 years from start of construction to commercial operation. These factors mean that there is still a significant risk that major problems will emerge, seriously affecting the income of the company. British Energy moved rapidly to take a 12.5% stake in the Humber gas-fired CCGT under construction. It also formed a joint venture with the REC, Southern Electric, to build a number of small open-cycle gas turbine plants to provide peak power.

Overseas, its main move was to form an alliance with a US utility, PECO of Philadelphia to takeover or win contracts to operate existing nuclear power plants in North America. This venture got off to a slow start, but as liberalisation of the electricity industry proceeded in the USA, it was hoped the opportunities would increase as utilities decided not to retain a nuclear capability.

The creation of Magnox Electric was only a transitional arrangement with the company expected to be quickly absorbed into British Nuclear Fuels Limited (BNFL), the nationally owned company that provides fuel cycle and waste disposal services. The company therefore had little scope to develop distinctive business plans.

VII.F. New entrants to the generation market

Since privatisation, a large number of companies have entered the generation business in England and Wales. Some have built large power plants that are dispatched through the Pool (generally plants that can supply more than 100 MW to the public supply system), while others have built much smaller plants such as combined heat and power (CHP) and renewables that are 'embedded' in the local distribution system. While the latter development is of some interest, the analysis here will concentrate on the companies building or acquiring large plants. About 10 GW of new plants have been built, or are under construction, by companies other than the successors to the CEGB. The new plants have all been of the CCGT type, which, as argued earlier, has formidable advantages, other than the relatively low projected cost of generation, in the current market. As discussed earlier, much of this is owned or controlled by RECs and was ordered in the period 1990–1992—the 'Dash for Gas' period.

Three companies acquired capacity from the CEGB successor companies. Mission Energy (a US IPP company) purchased 2.1 GW of pumped storage capacity from NGC in 1995 and 4 GW of coal-fired plant from PowerGen in 1999. The Eastern Group (a REC) bought 6 GW of coal-fired plant, 4 GW from National Power and 2 GW from PowerGen in 1996. In both these cases, the sale of capacity was instigated by the DGES, not the companies selling the plant. Celtic Energy, the company that took over British Coal's open-cast coal mines in South Wales, tried to purchase a coal-fired plant, Uskmouth, comprising three 114 MW units. The station had been retired several years earlier and was expected to be sold for £100 m by National Power in 1997. A considerable amount of refurbishment was thought to be necessary and it was originally hoped that the plant would re-enter service in 1998. The negotiations fell through because the UK Environment Agency insisted on FGD equipment being fitted. The project was taken over by the US utility AES, renamed Fifoot's Point, and serious work, including the fitting of FGD, began in March 1999 when it was expected the plant would return to service in 2000. In August 1999, AES also bought the 4000 MW Drax station from National Power.

In November 1999, National Power announced it was selling a further 3.3 GW of its plant, subject to negotiation and regulatory approval. British Energy was to buy the 2000 MW Eggborough coal-fired power plant, while NRG Energy (the parent company of a Minnesota-based utility, Northern States Power) was to buy the 650 MW Killingholme A CCGT and the 626 MW Blyth coal-fired station. (The Blyth sale was subsequently abandoned.)

After the abrupt end to the 'Dash for Gas', there were few orders for gas-fired plant for the next three or four years. By 1995, the picture facing the new entrants was very different. On the market side, Pool prices had fallen rather than risen, competition in the supply market had been extended to smaller consumers and there was political momentum behind the extension of competition to all consumers. On the technology side, the capital costs of CCGTs were falling (about 30% real from 1990–1997) and their thermal efficiency was increasing (from under 50% to 58% in the same period). The price of gas had fallen by about 30% in real terms. The 'Dash for Gas' plants began to look uneconomic both compared to new plants that could be built and to existing coal-fired plants (the price of coal had continued to fall steeply).

However, this salutary experience did not stop further investments, although this time, a different set of players was involved. The price of gas was low because of a glut of gas from the North Sea, produced on an expectation of an even higher demand for gas than had materialised. The price of electricity had not fallen as much as the price of gas, so gas companies saw the opportunity to increase the effective price they received for their gas by converting it to electricity in new, state-of-the-art CCGTs. Two new terms entered the vocabulary of competitive generation, 'tolling' plants and 'merchant' plants.

Tolling plants, such as Seabank and Humber, convert gas to electricity for a fixed fee, with the price paid for the gas linked to the wholesale (Pool) price of electricity. They may be covered by CfDs so the plant owner is not exposed to major risk because the utilisation of the plant and the price paid for its utilisation are pre-determined. However, while the gas supplier is guaranteed a volume, the price is not pre-determined so the gas supplier is at much greater risk than previously.

Merchant plants are much more risky for the plant owner. They are not covered by CfDs and therefore the utilisation of the plant and the price paid for the electricity is dependent on the Pool price. No plants planned as merchant plants have yet been built.

The Rocksavage plant represents a different response to risk. The output of this plant is mainly supplied to an industrial consumer, ICI, which takes the risk. Rocksavage was built partly because of the dissatisfaction of ICI with the functioning of the Pool.

VIII. Policies from 1998 onwards

The first eight years after privatisation of the electricity supply industry had seen far less stability than expected. Ownership of the RECs had changed hands rapidly, the Pool had not proved a good market for power sales, and regulation had become highly controversial. By 1998, far from stabilising, the situation was, if anything, becoming less stable with, for the first time, a major restructuring of the industry beginning. A number of factors lay behind this.

- The ending of the transitional measures imposed by the government, including the coal contracts and the monopoly for supply to small consumers. At least in theory, this should have made generation and supply fully competitive markets.
- Continuing evidence, especially the NGC settlement of 1997, that regulatory pressures on monopoly services would increase. The distribution settlement negotiated by the regulator in the autumn of 1999 turned out to be severe, and profit levels for distribution are likely to fall to those appropriate for a low risk industry.
- Likely increased government pressure on the industry, as illustrated by the Windfall Tax and the moratorium on new gas power plant orders discussed below.
- A changing government perspective on industry structure, under which vertical integration of generation and supply is acceptable but vertical integration of supply and distribution is not.
- Increased opportunities to invest in electricity industries in developed countries, especially the USA.

- Evidence that the large European utilities, especially those in Germany and France, were beginning to look to invest in acquiring companies outside their own territories.

VIII.A. The RECs

VIII.A.a. Takeovers and mergers

The takeover of Eastern by Texas Utilities was not completed until May 1998, but the special nature of Eastern, as a major generator and supplier of gas, means it is necessary to consider Eastern separately from the other RECs.

By the autumn of 1998, a new round of changes of corporate ownership of the RECs was beginning (see Table III.11). This was inspired by a number of factors. In its manifesto for the 1997 general election, the Labour Party signalled its intention to levy a 'Windfall Tax' on privatised companies in all sectors. This was to reflect the fact that the companies had been sold too cheaply and had been allowed, by over-generous pricing formulae, to make excessive profits. However, the owners of the RECs were not at that time unduly perturbed. It was not clear whether the Labour Party would be elected and the utilities were confident that they could either fight off the tax or that they could significantly reduce the amount they had to pay. This proved to be a miscalculation and the Windfall Tax was levied at a much higher rate than the utilities had expected to have to pay. The level of the tax was announced in July 1997 and was payable in two instalments, December 1997 and December 1998. The electricity supply industry paid £2.3 bn, of which £1.4 bn came from RECs (see Table III.15).

Another factor was the tightening of the regulatory regime. The first wave of takeovers was prompted to some extent by the perception that the distribution review of 1995 would allow large profits for the five years it applied. Since then, the efficiency targets have got much tighter, for example, a one-off price reduction of 20% was imposed on NGC in October 1996 to apply from 1997 with 4% annual cuts in the subsequent three years.[34] Where the priority for the new owners was mainly to take the short-term profits, the new owners may have decided that the new regulatory regime has become too tough for a high level of profits to be possible and the value of the RECs will fall. As a result, some may have been looking to sell the companies ahead of the publication of the distribution price review in the summer of 1999.

---

[34] OFFER (1997).

Table III.15. The Windfall Tax.

RECs Company	Estimated tax (£m)	Generators Company	Estimated tax (£m)	Others Company	Estimated tax (£m)
Eastern	112	National Power	261	NGC	—
East Midlands	96	PowerGen	203	Scottish Power	408
London	140	British Energy	—	Scottish Hydro	17
MANWEB	97			Northern Ireland	12
Midlands	134				
Northern	118				
NORWEB	155				
SEEBOARD	110				
SWALEC	90				
SWEB	97				
Southern	165				
Yorkshire	134				

Source: K. Moore (1997) Any chance of a challenge. *Utility Week*, Reed Business Publishing, 11 July.

A third factor was the possibility that a corporate separation of distribution and supply would be enforced, coupled with the completion of the introduction of competition in supply for all final consumers. Prompted by the DGES, the government signalled in its 1998 review of regulation that it wanted to increase the separation between the supply and distribution businesses.[35] The RECs were not required make a full corporate separation between distribution and supply but the 'Chinese walls' required were strict enough that there will be little scope for synergies or cost savings from operation of the two businesses. Once competition in supply was complete, the supply business would be a relatively small but highly risky business which would only be attractive to companies operating related businesses, such as electricity generation (vertical integration) or supply of other network delivered services (a multi-utility).

By the summer of 1998, vertical re-integration was again on the agenda. PowerGen had made no secret of the fact that it retained the objective of taking over one or more RECs. In June 1998, PowerGen placed an agreed bid to buy a REC, East Midland, from its US owners. After at first denying that it was seeking to buy a REC, National Power negotiated the purchase of Midlands Electric's supply business, also from US owners. This time, the government did not block the takeovers. However, part of the deal negotiated was that the two large generators would both sell 4000 MW of coal-fired plant to further reduce their market power in generation.

---

[35] DTI (1998b).

These ownership changes were followed up by a number of further changes that had the effect of increasing vertical integration. The one remaining independent REC, Southern Electric, merged with one of the integrated, privatised Scottish utilities, Scottish Hydro-Electric in September 1998 to form Scottish & Southern Energy (SSE) plc. The French company, EDF, outbid British Energy to buy London Electric in December 1998. It followed this up by purchasing the supply business of SWEB in June 1999. British Energy finally succeeded in integrating into supply with the purchase of SWALEC's supply business from Hyder in June 1999, but it re-sold this to SSE in August 2000.

The multi-utilities were not faring well and a merger between National Power and United Utilities, the owner of NORWEB, in February 1999 only failed at the last minute. Hyder, the owner of SWALEC, formally put its electricity supply business up for sale in May 1999 selling the business to British Energy. There were also indications that the whole of Yorkshire Electric was for sale and that the supply business of SEEBOARD was on offer. It is probably no coincidence that most of the companies up for sale were reported to have done badly in the annual round of negotiations with customers in the 100 kW+ market.[36] The potential buyers were companies such as British Energy, EDF, National Power, PowerGen and Centrica (formerly the gas supply division of British Gas). The two large German electric utilities, RWE and PreussenElektra, were also reported to be interested in acquiring British electricity companies.

VIII.A.b. Supply

The final opening of the supply market, planned for April 1998, was delayed by problems in completing the computer systems necessary to allow customers to switch suppliers. In January 1998, after successive RECs had admitted they would not be able to meet the deadline, the DGES finally had to concede that no companies would be ready on the original target date.[37] Competition for small consumers began to be phased in on 1st September 1998 and was completed in May 1999.[38]

---

[36] Moore (1998).

[37] OFFER (1998c).

[38] When the announcement of a delay was made, it was expected that four RECs, Eastern, MANWEB, Yorkshire and SEEBOARD would be ready to begin to open their markets on 1st September 1998, but SEEBOARD required a delay of a further month. Two further RECs, Midland and Northern were expected to begin to open their markets in October, with the remaining six to follow in December. The process of opening each area would be carried out in three phases over a period of six months, so that all consumers would have choice by June 1999.

As a result of the non-viability of supply as a stand-alone business, it was far from clear how new entrants could easily compete with the host REC. In general, the competitors would only be able to justify entering the market if there were major synergies with other products. There was therefore considerable speculation as to whether companies such as supermarkets or gasoline companies would enter the market and use it as a means of buying loyalty to their main products. However, in the nine months after the market began to open, few of the RECs seemed to have been competing hard outside their own territories. The only new entrants that appear to be spending much money trying to gain market share were:

- British Gas Trading (formerly part of British Gas) in association with the supermarket company Sainsbury's;
- ENRON (an American energy trading company), and;
- Independent Energy (a small new company that built its business in industrial CHP plant).[39]

Given the lack of incentives for new entrants to come into electricity supply, there would appear to be two possible ways (not mutually exclusive) in which the promise to introduce competition for all consumers could be fulfilled. One is vertical integration of generation and supply, while the other would be to allow consolidation of the RECs' supply businesses into far fewer, but more powerful groups.

When the market opened, a number of the RECs did begin to develop distinctive strategies (see Table III.16). Eastern, in particular, launched a range of options to appeal to various interest groups. In some cases these were 'affinity' deals, for example with the Youth Hostel Association and charities, which will give preferential terms to members or give a donation to the charity. In others, customers will pay premium prices to support a particular energy option, for example Eastern's Lionheart brand to support British coal (later abandoned) and SWEB's Green Electron brand to support renewable energy sources. However, the public seemed indifferent to the possibility of changing supplier and showed few signs of seeking out cheaper suppliers.

The capabilities of the RECs in the other side of the supply business, bulk power purchasing, still remained largely untested. From 1990–1998, 80% or more of RECs' power needs were supplied from sources that required little or no negotiation on their part. These included government-brokered contracts with National Power and PowerGen, nuclear

---

[39] Independant Energy went bankrupt in September 2000 and was taken over by National Power.

Table III.16. Marketing electricity to small consumers.

REC supply business	Opening date		Affinity partner	Electricity
Eastern	Sep 98	Barclaycard	National offer launched December 1997 Lionheart brand to support British coal industry 'Ecopower' tariff to support 'green' technologies	
Yorkshire	Sep 98	Tandy	Indicated wish to merge supply business with other companies	
Scottish Power	Sep 98			
MANWEB	Sep 98		Green tariff to be launched jointly with its owner, Scottish Power	
Seeboard	Oct 98			
Midlands	Oct 98	Boots		
Northern	Nov 98	Daily Telegraph Granada Newcastle BS Saga		
Hydro-Electric	Nov 98		Air Miles offered	
NORWEB	Nov 98	Tesco		
SWEB	Nov 98		'Green Electron' tariff to support 'green technologies'	
London	Dec 98	Alliance&Leicester		
East Midlands	Dec 98			
Southern	Jan 99	Argos Just 1		
SWALEC	Jan 99		Indicated wish to merge supply business with other companies	
PowerGen	Sept 99	Age Concern	Special dual fuel deal for older, 'fuel poor' consumers	

Source: Compiled by author.

electricity and the output of plants in which they had an ownership share. When the National Power and PowerGen contracts expired, a number of factors made a significant long-term commitment to new power purchasing agreements risky.

- The end of the coal contracts meant that the remainder of the British coal industry was under threat again as it became clear that a renewed surge of CCGT orders would take away most of the rest of the coal market. There was speculation that gas would, by 2005, take about 80% of the British electricity market. The new Labour government moved in and imposed a moratorium on new orders for gas-fired plants and announced a review of power station fuels, largely to determine whether there was a case, on strategic grounds, to restrict further gas use. This moratorium was finally withdrawn in November 2000.

- The enforced sale of power plant totalling 8 GW by National Power and PowerGen and of a further 3.3 GW of National Power also gave scope for new entrants to come into the generation market making generation more competitive.
- The outcome of the final opening of the supply market for small consumers would show how mobile the residential electricity market would be and would determine how far ahead contracting was feasible.
- The new electricity trading arrangements to replace the Pool might change the relative attractiveness of purchasing power long-term under contract versus short-term from the market.[40]

As a result, few of the RECs appeared to be making significant commitments to purchase electricity more than a few months ahead.

A consultation document was published[41] that identified ways in which government could restrict further gas use, including use of existing legislation to deny generators permission to use further gas in power plants. It was also widely reported that an understanding had been reached under which National Power and PowerGen would buy more British coal and would sell more of their old coal-fired plant and in return, they would be allowed to take over RECs.

VIII.A.c. Distribution

It was not clear whether the REC owners are selling just the supply business as a long-term investment or whether they are merely waiting for the distribution review to make a decision whether to sell. The two parts of the consortium that took over Midlands Avon Energy, clearly did not agree on the direction they should take. GPU decided to concentrate on infrastructure while Cinergy was more interested in energy trading. As a result, Cinergy sold its share of the Midland distribution business to GPU and there was even speculation it would buy a REC supply business.

The regulator's initial proposals for price controls on the distribution sector were very tough.[42] They required initial one-off revenue reductions (P0) of more than 20%, and for some RECs, more than 35%. This was to

---

[40] OFFER (1998d).
[41] DTI (1998c).
[42] OFGEM (1999b).

be followed by annual cuts (*X* factor) of 3% in real terms for the next four years. The final proposals published in December 1999 were somewhat less severe with the Po reduced by 1 to 4% point, but the *X* factor was maintained.[43] This provoked a predictable response from utilities that the targets were too tough and would result in heavy job losses. Whether the distribution sector can absorb this revenue reduction and continue to meet '*X*' factors of 3 or more without compromise to service standards remains to be seen. The DGES must strike a fine balance in setting the income caps allowing companies sufficient income to maintain standards whilst still applying strong downward pressure on prices.

The October 1999 revisions to the distribution price review also contained more concrete proposals on the separation of the distribution and supply businesses.[44] Again, these represented a relaxation over earlier proposals. They still seem to imply separate premises, staff and management, although there is some provision for shared services. It remains to be seen whether owners of the RECs will continue to see an advantage in retaining ownership of distribution and supply in a single company. If a split between the RECs does occur, there may be a consolidation in both the distribution and supply sectors. From a regulatory point of view, there is no need to have as many as 12 businesses to allow reasonable 'yardstick' regulation of distribution. Companies with core skills in operating networks, such as the water companies, or even NGC, may choose to expand their businesses in this direction. There may also be scope to expand into Scotland. Logically, the process of de-integration, particularly of monopoly activities, which has continued in England and Wales, must be applied to Scotland if full competition is to emerge, provided the new Scottish Parliament agrees. If the two integrated companies choose to concentrate on the competitive businesses, generation and supply, the distribution businesses may come on the market.[45]

In 2000, there were signs that there would be a consolidation of the distribution sector. The owners of the adjoining London and Eastern distribution systems, EDF and TXU respectively, agreed to manage the two systems jointly. In addition, the US owners of the SWEB distribution system (Southern Co) took over the adjacent SWALEC distribution system.

---

[43] Office of Gas and Electricity Markets (1999) 'Reviews of Public Electricity Suppliers 1998 to 2000. Final Proposals' London, Office of Gas and Electricity Markets.
[44] OFGEM (1999c).
[45] The DGES suggested that the transmission businesses of the two Scottish companies be placed into separate ownership. See OFFER (1998e) and OFGEM (1999d).

VIII.B. Eastern Group

Despite changing owners three times since 1995, and enduring almost a year of uncertainty while the most recent take-over process was completed, Eastern has maintained a highly distinctive and aggressive business strategy that deserves separate attention. Table III.17 shows that, despite the uncertainty over its ownership for the first half of 1998, it has moved consistently and powerfully to take stakes throughout Europe in gas and electricity trading. Now that it is part of Texas Utilities, it is more difficult to judge the success of these ventures, but it now has a strong position in electricity supply, gas supply and electricity generation in Britain. It is now also almost invariably a prominent bidder when electricity businesses are put up for sale. TXU seems content to allow Eastern to pursue a cross-European strategy although it would not be surprising if the business was to change hands again.

VIII.C. National Grid Company

By 1997/98, NGC's business was still dominated by UK transmission activities (see Table 18). NGC's main strategic move in 1998/99 was the acquisition of two power companies in New England. In December 1998, it took over New England Electricity System for £2.5 bn followed in January 1999 by the takeover of Eastern Utilities Association for £610 m. These two primarily network companies have contiguous systems and NGC plans to merge the companies.

The share price of NGC's Energis offshoot continued to grow spectacularly and in January 1999, NGC sold a further 25% of the shares raising £1.1 bn. By May 1999, despite the fact Energis was still making small losses, the share price had risen to about £17, six times the price only 18 months earlier when NGC first sold shares, making the stock market value of Energis comparable to that of the whole of NGC. Whether these somewhat speculative share prices can be maintained or even grow further, remains to be seen.

As with the distribution sector, the possible restructuring of the Scottish market may lead to opportunities to expand there. If the two integrated companies are required or choose to concentrate on the competitive businesses, generation and supply, the transmission businesses may come on the market.

VIII.D. The fossil fuel generators

The main strategic move made by National Power and PowerGen has been the vertical integration into electricity supply described above. PowerGen

Table III.17. Significant events for Eastern group: January 1998–October 1999.

Month	Event
1998	
Feb	'Lionheart' electricity brand launched to support British coal industry
	Pacificorp renews bid for Eastern after MMC clearance and Texas Utilities launches rival bid
	Plans announced to open Eastern offices in Spain, Poland, Belgium and Germany
Mar	Agreement announced with Dutch energy distributor, Energie Noord West, to develop Dutch markets
May	Texas Utilities takes over Eastern
	Lease purchased on output of power from Norwegian plants to assist trading in the Nordic market
	Link-up announced with Barclaycard to market electricity to small consumers
	Link with Esprit Telecom announced to lease a cross-channel telecom link
	Eastern sacks 9 out of 13 of its doorstep gas sales agencies after criticism from OFGAS
June	Affinity deal signed with Youth Hostel Association to market electricity
	Reports of Texas Utilities' bid for supply business of London Electric
July	Withdraws its 30% stake (£80 m) from consortium to build coal plant in Taiwan
	Telecoms division announces development of own technology to transfer data down power lines
August	Negotiations (successfully completed May 1999) to buy stake in Finnish distributor, SVO (£40 m)
Sept	John Devaney resigns as Chairman of Eastern
	Fitting of FGD at 2000 MW coal-fired plant announced
Oct	Telecoms division expands network by 550 km (£30 m)
Nov	Purchases upstream North Sea gas interests from BHP Petroleum (£100 m)
	Reports of interest in purchasing 2000 MW of capacity from ENEL (Italy)
Dec	Government approval given for Shotton 215 MW CHP plant
	Purchases 30% of KPCL (India) power company
	Purchases 5% of Spanish utility Hidrocantabrico (£54 m)
1999	
Jan	Telecoms business sold to NTL
	Increases stake in North Sea gas field (£20 m)
	Purchases all BG's CHP capacity (53 MW) for £16 m
March	Fails in bid to buy Dutch generator (UNA)
	Acquires licence to trade electricity in Poland
April	Renewable projects in Western Scottish islands announced (£10 m)
June	500 jobs to be lost mainly from sales force
July	Eastern rumoured to be bidding for Dutch generation company, EZH
Sept	Eastern became the first British company to be a member of the Amsterdam Power Exchange
Sept	Eastern receives permission to trade in the Spanish electricity market
October	Eastern announces it will sell its metering business

Source: Utility Week, various.

Table III.18. Financial structure of National Grid—turnover (£m).

	1997/98	1998/99
Transmission		
Price controlled (RPI-X)	857	837
Post-1990 connections (ROR)	73	75
Transmission services	280	265
Other	15	18
Interconnectors	76	76
Ancillary services	119	117
Other	154	162
Energis	103	–
Total	1676	1549

Source: Annual Report and Accounts.
Income from post-1990 connections is regulated using rate-of-return (ROR) methods.

chose to buy the whole of a REC, while National Power chose to buy only the supply business. How far this was a conscious choice, as was claimed by National Power, and how far it was simply a matter of buying what was available, is not clear. However, at the time, National Power consistently denied any interest in owning a distribution business. The advantage of PowerGen's strategy was that it gives them a capability in operating a distribution system, a skill that might be valuable for diversification overseas. It also replaces some of the turnover lost in the contraction of generation market share that it experienced in Britain. An advantage of National Power's strategy was that it involved a much lower purchase price. It also meant that they did not have to manage a business, distribution, which had little or no connection with their core skills and which they might have to sell on if a split in the RECs is enforced.

The two companies do not report their activities on the same basis, with PowerGen not distinguishing international from UK activities in its turnover. It also does not report operating profit according to activity (see Tables III.19 and III.20). However, its profits from international activities were only about a third of those of National Power and the business is probably correspondingly smaller.

In the UK, National Power has a smaller share of its output being sold direct to final consumers, even before PowerGen's acquisition of East Midlands began to inflate the retail sales figures. PowerGen's gas business is much larger than National Power's. Both companies were prepared to sell a large proportion of their generating capacity, which they are not immediately replacing with new gas-fired plant, in order to integrate vertically. This suggests that the companies see any future expansion in Britain as largely coming from further purchases of REC businesses rather than rebuilding generation market share.

Table III.19. Financial structure of PowerGen—turnover (£m).

	1997/98	April–Dec 1998
Sales through the Pool	1897	1132
Retail electricity sales	622	886
Gas trading and retail	257	193
Other energy sales	156	133

Source: Annual Report and Accounts.
In 1998, PowerGen changed its reporting year from April–April to calendar years.

Table III.20. Financial structure of National Power—turnover/operating profit (£m).

	1997/98	1998/99
By class of business		
Wholesale elec sales	2291/681	2110/593
Retail elec sales	448/–7	425/12
Cogen and renewables	72/14	87/18
Eastern lease	436/215	224/209
Other 91/37	136/35	
Corporate & development	16/–157	27/–206
By geographical region		
UK operations	3136/868	2733/792
UK corp & development	16/–157	27/–206
Europe (ex UK)	1/1	59/13
Australia	130/45	119/42
USA 26/11	24/7	
Rest of world	45/15	47/13
Total 3354/783	3009/661	

Source: Annual Report and Accounts.
Income under Eastern lease is the income derived from the arrangements under which 4000 MW of coal plant was transferred to Eastern in 1996.

The 12-month period from mid-1998 onwards was one of intense activity in international markets as the two companies tried to replace the business lost in the British generation market overseas (see Table III.21). By May 1999, things were not going smoothly for either company with sharply reduced profits at PowerGen and some internal disarray at National Power culminating in the removal of the Chief Executive. There were suggestions that National Power would have to split into a company covering UK operations and a separate company for overseas investments. National Power, in particular, was beginning to look vulnerable to takeover as a result of a loss of confidence following heavy losses on investments in power plants in Pakistan.

Table III.21. Significant events for National Power and PowerGen: May 1998–November 1999.

Month	Event
1998	
May	Press reports of merger talks between PG and Houston Industries
	NP announces investment of US$125 m in Malaysian power company, Malakoff
	PG reports small increase in profits, and NP reports small decrease
	NP announces US$250 m investment in Chinese coal-fired power plants
	NP starts construction of 1500 MW CCGT at Staythorpe
	35 NP employees held captive at NP's Hub River plant in Pakistan following allegations of bribery
June	Reports that government likely to require PG to fit FGD to an old large coal-fired station
	PG places successful bid (£1.9 bn) to buy East Midlands from Dominion Resources
July	NP buys share in Kazakhstan distribution company for US$20 m
August	PG merger talks with Houston abandoned
	Reports of possible takeover bid for NP
Sept	NP announces construction of 58 MW CHP plant
	PG agrees to put 4000 MW of old coal-fired plant up for sale
Oct	NP announces construction of $350 m CCGT in Texas
	Pakistani fraud squad raids Hubco (NP owns 26%)
	NP takes 20% (ca £100 m) stake in Polish generator
	PG sells all upstream gas interests to Centrica and renegotiates gas contracts from those fields
	NP Purchases 25% (£380 m) of large Spanish utility, Union Fenosa
Nov	NP purchases Midlands' supply business (£180 m) and puts Drax (4000 MW with FGD) up for sale
	PG renegotiates contracts for gas supply to Connah's Quay
1999	
Jan	PG buys Yorkshire electric's CHP plant (120 MW in operation, 112 MW planned) for £95 m
	Reports of talks between NP and United Utilities to purchase NORWEB
Feb	PG begins restructuring of East Midlands, expected to result in 20% job losses
	PG purchases 49.9% stake in new CCGT in South Korea (£91 m)
	NP announce plans to build 500 MW CCGT in Australia (£170 m)
	Merger talks between NP and United Utilities collapse
March	NP buys Calortex gas supply company (£30 m)
April	NP signs deal to buy British coal for 5 years, mostly to be burnt in Drax
	Mission Energy buys 4000 MW of plant from PG for £1.3 bn
May	NP Chief executive resigns because of lack of confidence in NP business strategy
	Speculation about possible takeover of NP
	NP to shed up to 300 jobs
June	Regulator orders inquiry into closure of three NP power stations
	Speculation about PG bid for United Utilities
July	NP announces construction of 1650 MW of plant in USA (£1.25 bn)
August	NP announces sale of Drax plant to AES
October	NP announces new brand name, Npower, to cover all its gas and electricity supply operations
Nov	NP announces that the company will split into a UK company and an international company

Source: Utility Week, various.

Finally, in November 1999, National Power announced the expected split into a UK company and a separate international company, but, more unexpectedly, it announced further plant sales, amounting to 3.3 GW.[46] In October 2000, National Power was split into a UK-based company to be known as Innogy and an international company, the International Power Group.

VIII.E. The nuclear generators

British Energy's and Magnox Electric's activities in the UK market have been severely restricted by the government moratorium on new gas-fired power plants. Both companies have expressed a strong wish to diversify into gas-fired power plants to reduce their dependence on nuclear power (see Table III.22). British Energy has been linked with all the RECs that have come up for sale in 1998 and 1999, especially London Electric where it was a strong bidder. By May 1999, it appeared to have given up the pursuit and was buying back £400 m of shares, effectively returning the money it had earmarked for purchasing a REC to shareholders. However, in June it succeeded in purchasing the supply business of SWALEC only to re-sell it in August 2000. In November 1999, it announced the acquisition of the 2000 MW Eggborough coal-fired power station. This represented a major step towards diversifying away from nuclear power and strengthened its position in negotiating power sales contracts. British Energy was more successful in making acquisitions in the US market through its joint venture with PECO, AmerGen. By September 1999, it had agreed to buy five old US nuclear power plants, four of which each of which cost in the order £10 m, while the fifth, for a larger, newer station cost $103 m.

It is not clear what the corporate priorities of BNFL will be when it has fully absorbed Westinghouse and Magnox Electric and therefore whether Magnox Electric will become a more or less significant player in the electricity market. In 1999, the government proposed selling 49%

Table III.22. Financial structure of British Energy—turnover (£m).

	1997/98	1998/99
Electricity generation	1752	1839
Direct supply sales	188	219
Miscellaneous	14	9
Total	1954	2067

Source: Annual Report and Accounts.

[46] National Power (1999).

of its shares in BNFL and this complicates still further the picture for the Magnox stations.

IX. Conclusions

Privatisation led to a very sharp change in the corporate culture of the British electricity supply industry, away from a public service ethic to a profit-led ethic. This is well illustrated by changes in pay levels. Prior to privatisation, many in the industry regarded their job as a public service and, particularly for senior executives, while the jobs could certainly not be described as poorly paid, salaries were well below private sector levels. The heavy loss of jobs in the industry has been accomplished with no significant union opposition. In part, this is because the industry's high profits have allowed handsome pay-offs to those leaving the industry and have meant that all redundancy programmes so far have been on a voluntary basis.

In retrospect, it is remarkable how little comment the shedding of national responsibilities that went with this public service role has excited. The British deep-mining coal industry is probably past the point of no return and the prospects for further orders for nuclear power plant seem remote. Gas consumption from British fields to power stations has been allowed to increase unchecked, at least until 1998. The power station equipment companies have either gone out of business or are now part of international or foreign groups. Long-term R&D into new generation technologies, funded by the electricity supply industry, has effectively come to an end. In short, all the traditional components of a traditional energy policy have been abandoned.

These changes were unsurprising as long as government was opposed to market intervention. More surprising was the apparent indifference of government to takeover of the RECs by foreign companies and the lack of any positive steps to create companies that would be 'national champions' in overseas electricity markets. Their limited Golden Share cover suggests that government did not view the RECs as strategically important. The government did use its Golden Share to prevent the takeover of National Power in 1996, but was happy to see the UK business of National Power (and PowerGen) effectively cut in half. This is in contrast to a number of other European countries which have begun to introduce liberalisation but have been unwilling to allow the commercial position of the largest company to be damaged, for example, the Verbund in Austria, EDP in Portugal, ENEL in Italy and Endesa in Spain.

From the point of view of shareholders, the policies of the privatised electricity companies have been highly successful, at least up to 1998/99. All companies have turned in dramatically increased profits, leading to large increases in share prices. How far these increases in profits can be credited to the companies and how far they are the result of highly advantageous transitional conditions being set by the government is hard to determine. However, judged against broader criteria, such as expanding their business and preserving their independence, their performance is much less impressive. Compared with their European peers, they were perhaps hampered by not having a solid base in which losses could be underwritten, from which to speculate into new businesses. They were also under intense scrutiny from the representatives of shareholders, especially the big fund managers. It is perhaps no coincidence that, arguably the two most successful companies, Nuclear Electric and NGC, were insulated somewhat from this latter pressure at least until 1996, through public ownership in the case of Nuclear Electric and through joint REC ownership in the case of NGC.

None of the RECs was able to build a strong enough business to survive as an independent company and most are now little more than commercial properties that are being bought and sold according to market conditions. The partial exception to this may be Eastern, which, although taken over twice, has maintained a distinctive, reasonably consistent and apparently successful corporate policy.

National Power and PowerGen were assisted by the government Golden Share which protected them from takeover, but hampered by government policy which only recently allowed them to diversify into distribution and supply in Britain. This largely restricted their overseas investments to stakes in IPP, a notoriously risky and hard-fought sector. For the future, they may still prosper if they can build oligopolistic positions as integrated electricity businesses in England and Wales.

One of the striking features of the diversification policies of European electricity utilities is how little they have involved moving into other countries in Europe. Amongst the British-based companies, only Eastern in the past year has shown any serious intent to operate at a Europe-wide level. Equally, mainland European utilities only began to show interest in British companies from 1998 onwards. It may be that this is a result of a perception in Europe that Britain will remain an electricity island leading nowhere in business terms with an unpredictable and potentially regulatory regime.

In terms of the policies followed, integrating electricity generation and supply to final consumers seems to be highly favoured because of the extent to which integrating the businesses mutually reduces commercial risk. The large generators are increasingly also looking to joint promotion of CHP schemes with industrial customers as a way of increasing customer loyalty.

A presence in gas also appears important for an electricity company, although the evidence here is more equivocal. All the RECs attempted to build a gas supply presence, but a number have now sold the businesses on. It is not clear whether this was a result of losses being made, or simply that the companies did not regard them as core competencies. PowerGen and Eastern have built strong gas supply companies, but while Eastern is now strengthening its upstream position producing gas in the North Sea, PowerGen has sold its interests.

The multi-utilities have not been successful. Given the regulatory climate in Britain, which is suspicious of the same company operating a monopoly network as operates a competitive supply business, it is hard to see much future for companies supplying a wide range of final consumer services that are delivered by network. The mixture of a low-risk, low-return business such as distribution, with a high-risk business such as supply does not seem to work well even if regulation permits it. Even NGC, with its spectacularly successful Energis telecoms company, has chosen not to retain ownership of Energis because of the contrast between the low-risk grid business and the high-risk telecoms business.

Perhaps the most surprising thing about the British electricity industry since privatisation is the lack of stability, even a decade after the sector was reformed. Many people probably expected that the reforms would be followed by a short period of adjustment before a new stable structure emerged. In fact, the reforms may turn out to follow three phases. In the first, the new corporate structure becomes established, and the competition and regulation mechanisms settle down. In the second, there is a further corporate restructuring based on integration of the competitive elements of the business and full separation of the monopoly elements. A third phase may see the electricity industry further split and integrated into general industrial activity, rather than remaining a separate activity carried out only by single mission electricity companies. In Britain, the end of the first phase may be in sight and the second phase is under way, but the third phase has still to begin.

Literature

Doyle, G. and MacLaine, D. (1996) *Power as a commodity: the future of the UK electricity supply industry*, Financial Times Energy Publishing, London (pp. 164–8).

DTI (1996) *Ian Lang blocks electricity mergers* (press release P/96/313, 24 April 1996), Department of Trade and Industry, London.

DTI (1998a) *A fair deal for consumers: Modernising the framework for utility regulation*, Department of Trade and Industry, London.

DTI (1998b) *A fair deal for consumers: Modernising the framework for utility regulation – The response to consultation*, Department of Trade and Industry, London.

DTI (1998c) *Review of energy sources for power generation*, Department of Trade and Industry, London.

FTE (1998a) "Aneel bites back", *Power in Latin America*, February 1998: 15–16.

FTE (1998b) "Power crisis launched", *Power in Asia* 23 March 1998, FT Energy: 26.

House of Commons Trade and Industry Select Committee (1998) *Developments in the liberalisation of the documestic electricity market*, 10th report, HC 871, 29 July 1998.

McHarg, A. (1998) "Government intervention in privatised industries: the potential and limitations of the Golden Share", *Utilities Law Review* 9(4): 198–201.

Monopolies and Mergers Commission (1996a) *National Power plc and Southern Electric plc: A report on the proposed merger*, Cm 3230, The Stationery Office, London.

Monopolies and Mergers Commission (1996b) *PowerGen plc and Midlands Electric plc: A report on the proposed merger*, Cm 3231, The Stationery Office, London.

Monopolies and Mergers Commission (1997) *Pacificorp and The Energy Group: A report on the proposed acquisition*, The Stationery Office, London.

Moore, K. (1998) "100kW market proves too tough for some", *Utility Week*, 13 March 1998.

National Power (1999) *Strategy review and interim results 1999* National Power, London.

NGC (1990) *Annual Report*, National Grid Company, London.

OFFER (1992) *NGC transmission: use of system charges*, Office of Electricity Regulation, Birmingham.

OFFER (1993) *The supply price control: Proposals*, Office of Electricity Regulation, Birmingham.

OFFER (1994a) *Decision on a monopolies and mergers commission reference*, Office of Electricity Regulation, Birmingham.

OFFER (1994b) *The distribution price control: Proposals*, Office of Electricity Regulation, Birmingham.

OFFER (1995a) *The distribution price control: Revised proposals*, Office of Electricity Regulation, Birmingham.

OFFER (1995b) *Pool prices and the undertakings on pricing given by National Power and PowerGen*, Office of Electricity Regulation, Birmingham.

OFFER (1995c) *Text of letter from DGES to National Power and PowerGen concerning the undertakings on sale or disposal of plant*, Office of Electricity Regulation, Birmingham.

OFFER (1995d) *The competitive market from 1998: the next steps*, Office of Electricity Regulation, Birmingham.

OFFER (1997) *The transmission price control review of the National Grid: Proposals*, Office of Electricity Regulation, Birmingham.

OFFER (1998a) *Review of electricity trading arrangements: Framework document*, Office of Electricity Regulation, Birmingham.

OFFER (1998b) *Opening the electricity market in 1998* (press release), Office of Electricity Regulation, Birmingham.

OFFER (1998c) *On track for market opening* (press release, 27 April 1998), Office of Electricity Regulation, Birmingham.

OFFER (1998d) *Review of electricity trading arrangements: Interim conclusions*, Office of Electricity Regulation, Birmingham.

OFFER (1998e) *Public electricity suppliers: separation of businesses* (press release, 13 May 1998), Office of Electricity Regulation, Birmingham.

OFGEM (1999a) *The new electricity trading arrangements: OFGEM/DTI Conclusions document, October 1999*, Office of Gas and Electricity Markets, London.

OFGEM (1999b) *Reviews of public electricity suppliers 1998 to 2000: Distribution price control review: Draft proposals, August 1999*, Office of Gas and Electricity Markets, London.

OFGEM (1999c) *Reviews of public electricity suppliers 1998 to 2000: Distribution price control review: Update, October 1999*, Office of Gas and Electricity Markets, London.

OFGEM (1999d) *Review of Scottish trading arrangements, a consultation document, October 1999*, Office of Gas and Electricity Markets, London.

Surrey, J. (ed) (1996) *The British Electricity Experiment – Privatisation: the record, the issues, the lessons*, Earthscan, London.

Chapter IV
Dutch Business Strategies Under Regime Transition

MAARTEN J. ARENTSEN, JAN WILLEM FABIUS and
ROLF W. KÜNNEKE

I. Introduction

The new Dutch electricity law, passed in Parliament in August 1998, marks a milestone in the national debate on the reform of the electricity industry. Tracing the beginning of this debate is rather difficult, because the Dutch actually never stopped debating the reform issue since the establishment of the electricity industry at the beginning of the 20th century. Yet, the EU-directive on the liberalisation of the European electricity market reinforced the need for restructuring, since it was obliged to diminish national monopoly positions, to introduce market competition and to open up national borders. Although the directive holds degrees of freedom, the new Dutch electricity law reflects a rather liberal interpretation of requirements in the directive. Under the new law, restrictions on generation have been abolished; access to the grid is open for all on the base of a system of regulated access (regulated TPA); energy companies are obliged to unbundle financially and administratively transmission and transport on the one side and trade, retail and supply on the other; and all consumers are free to choose their own supplier in 2007.[1]

After the competitive market had been established on paper, the next job was to bring competition into force. Actors debated the new competitive rules of the game, the establishment of new institutions like the regulator and the Amsterdam Power Exchange, and the historical burden of stranded investments. At the company level, activities concentrated on efficiency improvement, business strategies, developing commercial orientations and skills, market position analysis, strategic alliances,

---

[1] In 1999 this schedule was adjusted to 2004 (Energy Report, 1999).

mergers and takeovers. Shareholders were in a resigned position, because privatisation was not really on the agenda in 1998. In 1999 however, privatisation was already on top of the agenda and three of the four power producers were sold to foreign companies. Liberalisation accelerated privatisation, bringing new dynamics to the Dutch electricity market. The actual structure, functioning and performance of the new market has not yet consolidated. In short, in 1999 the Dutch electricity industry was still in transition.

This chapter describes and analyses the major developments in Dutch business strategies between 1989 and mid 1999.[2] The next section starts with a brief retrospective of the background of the Dutch transitions and sketches the major features of the new, liberalised legal structure of the Dutch electricity market. Then the chapter continues with the analysis of the major developments in business strategies in generation. Generation and distribution have been vertically disintegrated since 1989, but the rather typical Dutch structure of ownership continued. Dutch generation companies are owned by distribution companies and this ownership structure is one of the causes of the debate on market power between generators and distributors. Section IV of this chapter analyses the major trends in business strategies of distribution companies. Distributors were driven by the race for market power, a race that was played in three mutual games: the game for scale, the game for scope and the game on costs. Section V describes the major trends in public service obligations that companies were and still are facing. Here it turns out that the old stakeholder-driven system has been changed to a regulatory-driven system. Section VI analyses some recent market developments, such as the establishment of the Amsterdam Power Exchange (APX) and new entrants on the Dutch market. Section VII draws some lines on the prospects of the Dutch electricity industry and Section VIII summarises and discusses the main findings.

II. Overture: Regulatory Reform and System Upheaval

The Dutch electricity system, still predominantly publicly owned, developed out of small-scale municipal electricity companies, established in the first decades of the 20th century. Technology improvements guided the electrification of the country, headed by SEP,[3] the grid coordinator since 1949. Between 1950 and 1989, electricity generation and distribution was well organised in small-scale monopolies, with clearly defined

---

[2] This chapter covers market developments until December 1999.
[3] SEP stands for *Samenwerkende ElektriciteitsProducenten* (Association of electricity generators).

positions and legally authorised tasks reflecting the public utility character of electricity supply and the company's public service obligations. Until 1989, the system was publicly owned and public service oriented in operation and performance.

In 1985, the then Dutch government started debating scale and scope of the national electricity system, to improve its economic performance (efficiency) but not releasing its overall public service orientation on security and reliability of supply and low tariffs. Before 1985 generation, transport and distribution was integrated with 14 larger generation/distribution companies in leading market positions. Ten of them had provincial ownership structures and were regionally based, and four had municipal ownership structure, operating in the urban areas in the western part of the country. The 1985 debate reinforced the need to concentrate. Distribution and generation disintegrated and mergers reduced the number of generation companies to four.[4] SEP reinforced its leading and managing position in generation, and headed the technical and economic dispatch of the power plants owned by the four generation companies. SEP also headed the high-voltage transport and import and export of electricity and the forecast of electricity demand and supply, legally obliged to do so by the Electricity Act of 1989. Distribution companies continued merging, hoping for efficiency improvements by increasing the scale of business. The mergers swallowed relatively small-scale municipally-owned distribution companies and were taken over by the provincial owned larger companies. The Electricity Act 1989 reflected and authorized this newly established structure in the electricity system as it developed between 1985 and 1989.

The Electricity Act 1989 authorised the new electricity landscape as it was redesigned by industry itself. From 1989 on, division of generation and distribution was legally obliged,[5] but the newly established legal order incorporated two rather significant tensions. Firstly, the Electricity Act 1989 separated generation and distribution, but did not change the ownership structure, leaving distribution companies in an ambiguous position as shareholder and customer of generators. Secondly, the Act opened up ways for distribution companies to produce electricity outside the central generation capacity co-ordinated by SEP. And, indeed, happened as expected: distribution companies started generating electricity, in fact rather strategically. They invested in CHP technology, in many cases in joint venture with private industry, putting pressure on the centrally coordinated electricity generation. At the time

---

[4] The initiative to disintegrate generation and distribution was actually taken by the Dutch government of that time. For a more detailed description of the debate see, Arentsen *et al.*, 1997.
[5] One of the major reasons for this structure was to improve the conditions for the development of CHP and sustainable electricity.

distributors started their investments, CHP technology became strongly supported by government for environmental reasons and, with the help and support of private industry, distributors eroded the monopolistic price setting of the generation companies by creating overcapacity in the system. SEP and the generators were forced to negotiate an agreement with distributors to manage surplus capacities. In this way distributors managed to reshuffle positions *vis à vis* generation companies favourable to their own position, but, paradoxically, the distribution companies, successfully competing generation as customers, at the same time competed themselves as shareholders.

The complex ownership–customer relationship and clearly different interest positions of generation and distribution could only be released by restructuring the national electricity market again rather shortly after the 1989 revision. Yet the ongoing European debate on liberalisation mitigated the institutional tensions in the Dutch electricity system for a couple of years. In between, Dutch public authorities took advanced positions in the European debate on liberalisation, guided by a change in the domestic political climate. The social liberal coalition took over power in 1994, replacing the conservative coalition, in power for two decades and dominated by Christian democrats. The new coalition, strongly advocating liberalisation and deregulation, launched a White Paper on energy, designing new orders for the national energy system on electricity and gas by the end of 1995.[6] In fact, the White Paper reflected liberalisation proposals developed and discussed by the European Union to harmonise the internal electricity and gas market. The Dutch Parliament accepted and approved the liberalisation ideas proposed by the social liberal coalition, marking the point of no return that accelerated the process of restructuring the national electricity supply industry. At the same time the EU accepted the final draft of the EU liberalisation directive and the Dutch government took the next step in designing the new structure for the national electricity market that finally resulted in a proposal of a new electricity law by the end of 1997, and the inauguration of this law in 1998.

As stated in the introduction, the new electricity act-proposal reflects a rather liberal interpretation of the EU directive 96/92/EG. Table IV.1 illustrates the main changes in the value chain of electricity as proposed by the new electricity act.

The act obliges an administrative and financial unbundling of generation, trade and supply on the one hand and transmission and distribution on the other. Access to the grid is arranged as regulated TPA and the market will be liberalised in step, beginning in 1999 (650 giant

---

[6] *Derde Energienota*, Dutch Parliament 1995–1996, 24 525, nrs. 1–2.

Table IV.1. The old and new electricity regime in the Netherlands.

Value chain	Before 1998	After 1998
Generation	• Long-term strategic and operational planning • Central economic and technical dispatch	• Free and unconditional except standard legal obligations
Transport/Services	• *De facto* SEP monopoly • Technical dispatch by SEP, from 1989 on also economic dispatch • Internal rules electricity industry	• Monopoly of the grid company • Free access based on a system of regulated TPA • Independent system operator
Distribution	• Geographic monopoly distribution company	• System of licenses to supply captive customers • Tariff regulation and efficiency measures
Wholesale	• *De facto* SEP monopoly on import and export[7]	• No restriction, but imports on the base of reciprocity
Retailing	• Not operational, integrated with distribution	• Free with the exception of grid companies • Stepwise free choice electricity supplier
Products and services	• No (commercial) services in combination with electricity supply allowed	• No restrictions on products and services

consumers > 2 MW, representing 34% of the market), next in 2002 (some 56,000 small industrial consumers up to 3*80 Amp, representing 27% of the market) and finally in 2007 (some 6.7 million households, representing 39% of the market). The act also launched the regulator for market control and tariffs and introduced privatisation as a theme, but did not really open the discussion yet.[8] The political debate in Parliament was rather restricted, but full of ideological rhetoric. The political opposition (Christian democrats and left wing parties) objected to the act

---

[7] The Electricity Act 1989 did allow for direct import of electricity by giant consumers, but the tariff structure on transport made the imports de facto inefficient, leaving SEP in a de facto monopoly position.
[8] The new Electricity Act maximizes privatisation to one-third of the shares of distribution companies and to half of the shares of generation companies.

on ideological grounds, but didn't succeed in rejecting *liberalisation*. Parliament only changed the tariff structure for captives, making efficiency improvement accessible before they actually enter the liberalised electricity market in 2007. In 1999 the act became operative and from that time on competition was launched in the Dutch electricity market. In November 1999, the minister for Economic Affairs published an Energy Report in which the acceleration of the eligibility of customers was announced. Contrary to the original ideas, the Energy Report suggested the eligibility of the middle group of smaller industrial consumers before 2002 and eligibility of all Dutch consumers not in 2007 but in 2004 at the latest.[9]

The structural changes in the Dutch electricity system during the last fifteen years basically reflected the need to improve efficiencies. Dutch prices were among the lowest in Europe in the early nineties, but still too high, as was proven by the distributors with their CHP-investments. They offered electricity two cents under SEP tariffs and, in no time, they managed to conquer a market share of some 22%. Liberalisation didn't change the transition process that started after 1985, but reinforced the need to improve efficiencies. As a result, Dutch distributors persisted in the merger process and the four remaining Dutch producers, were challenged by the 'efficiency regime' of SEP, forcing them to generate as efficiently as possible. At the operational level, generation and distribution continued to co-operate as in the old days, but at the strategic level, they stipulated market power in the debate to merge the four generation companies as one giant national generator. The debate on the establishment of one giant Dutch producer is one of the two manifestations of the power game that has been played by the Dutch energy companies over the last fifteen years. The second manifestation is the increase in business scale and scope of distribution companies. From 1989, on generators and distributors disputed power dominance in the Dutch market, a dispute that was finally resolved by the failure of the merger of the four generation companies into one giant national producer in early 1998. The generators were defeated, but Dutch distributors still had to settle their mutual dispute on control of the Dutch market. The next two sections of this chapter analyse both parts of the power game in more detail, starting with the structural changes in generation.

III. Structural Changes in Generation

The potential of Dutch generators to enter the European market was one of the major concerns in the liberalisation debate in the Netherlands.

---

[9] *Energy Report*, 1999, p. 26.

None of the four generation companies was expected to develop independently as an European player and, as Fig. IV.1 illustrates, even as one company (GPB), Dutch electricity generators still rank among the group of smaller generators in Europe.

The Dutch electricity market was assumed to be easily accessible and Dutch generators an easy and relatively cheap target for foreign investors. Table IV.2[10] lists some production data of each of the four Dutch generation companies.

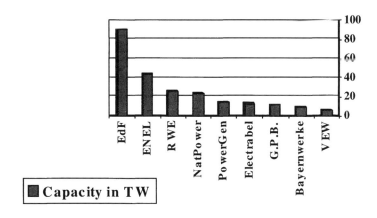

Fig. IV.1. Power producers in Europe.

Only one Dutch giant generation company was assumed to have some European potential, and for that reason generators were impelled to concentrate and to merge into one company. The Dutch government started debating the merger of the four generation companies and facilitated its establishment by prospecting financial support and tax releases if the merger succeeded. This financial support was severely needed, because of the rather restricted solvency position of Dutch generators (see Table IV.3). The strong regulatory protection Dutch generators enjoyed in the past released the need of solid equity positions and, consequently, urged the need for additional support to facilitate the transition towards liberal market conditions.

In addition to the argument to build a strong Dutch generator as an European player, financial arguments, especially the stranded investments, pushed Dutch generators to merge. From 1989 on, SEP had taken a leading and central position in generation. Both at the operational and

---

[10] Unless otherwise indicated, all data listed in this chapter are taken from the 1996 and 1997 annual reports of the generation and distribution companies.

Table IV.2. Generation capacity in MW and electricity production in GWh 1994 and 1997 in the Netherlands.

Company	Generation capacity in MW		Production in GWh	
	1994	1997	1994	1997
EPON	4284	4978	16.200	19.400
UNA	3527	3472	12.100	12.200
EZH	2532	2282	12.400	11.600
EPZ	4567	3858	16.900	14.800
IPP's	3935[1]	5220	19.621[1]	22.638
GKN[2]	56	0,0	300	0.0

[1] 1995 figures.
[2] GKN is the nuclear plant in Dodenwaard, no longer operative (since 1997).

Table IV.3. Dutch Power Producers 1997.

in ƒ min	EZH	EPZ	EPON	UNA	Total	SEP
Net turnover	1.536	2.346	1.818	1.555	7.255	370
Depreciation	282	244	318	337	1.181	172
Personnel	145	187	105	107	544	36
Other costs	418	1.099	282	344	2.143	95
Financial expense	−28	−107	−140	−105	−380	−99
Net profit	132	97	73	109	411	−85
Total assets	2.324	2.914	3.146	3.067	11.451	2.312
Capital and reserves	917	698	581	732	2.928	243
Personnel	1.015	1.526	1.041	970	4.552	279
Capacity MW	2.281	3.855	4.978	3.472	14.586	253
Net generation TWh	11,2	14,6	19,3	12,3	57,4	

at the strategic level, SEP dominated decision making. SEP also dominated the import and export contracts and was decisive in strategic planning of demand and supply of electricity. SEP dominated the four generation companies in other fields as well. SEP was the actual operator of the high-voltage grid and contracted for gas imports from Norway and the Nordic cable operators to import Norwegian hydropower. SEP also initiated the erection of a large coal gassification plant in the Southern part of the country, which had a highly experimental generation capacity and was not expected to be competitive in a liberal electricity market. The cost of these investments were shared by the generation companies, which they reflected in the tariffs. If the four generators didn't merge, the SEP contracts, responsibilities and investments had to be settled another way, but alternatives were scarce. So both the survival of an independent national generation capacity in the European market and the stranded investments were strong arguments to push the merger in generation.

In April 1998, after eighteen months of negotiation, the merger terminated. The debate foundered on two themes: supply contracts after 2001 until 2008 and the so-called gassification contracts. The distribution companies, participating as shareholders in the merger debate, insisted on clear tariffs after 2001. Present supply contracts of generators ended in 2002 and the distributors insisted on a price agreement for the new contracts after 2001. The generators refused, arguing that prices after 2001 had to reflect the market conditions at that time, which, of course, were hard to forecast in 1998. With the gassification contracts, distributors attempted to increase their power over generation in the liberal market, by contemplating the giant generator as their own generation capacity by supplying fuels (gas) to be converted to electricity by the generator and to be traded and sold by the distribution companies. In this way distributors could both control the market power of the generator, in between earning money by fuel supply and electricity trade, and at the same time still keep all their options open to develop independent company strategies for generation and trade. This distributor's rather typical and specific interpretation of an open and competitive market was too obvious to succeed and one of the main reasons for the failure of the merger.

The generation companies were left in a rather awkward position, because they had to develop a new business orientation and they had to settle the stranded investments. The problem of stranded investments was solved in collaboration with the Dutch government. By the end of 1998 the Dutch government signed an agreement with the generators on the stranded investments. To reimburse the stranded investments, the generators were allowed to charge for the transmission of electricity and in return the Dutch government took a share of 50% plus one share in the national grid company (Tennett) that was established at about the same time. Furthermore, the agreement allowed the four generation companies to agree mutually upon the share each generation company had to take in the stranded investments. However, the companies couldn't agree upon this issue themselves, and therefore the Dutch government forced each generation company, by law, to take its share in the financial burden. The EU did not approve this settlement of stranded investments and therefore other options were considered. In November 1999 an advisory board, commissioned by the Minister for Economic Affairs and headed by Herkströter, recommended the separation of the stranded investments into three different parts. It was recommended that the Dutch state should pay for district heating and the experimental coal gassification plant, the running import contracts should be sold by auction and the power producers each take a share in the final part of the stranded investments.

In regard to business orientation, the Dutch generators continued to improve their efficiency and their poor financial position. The next graphs list some figures on 1996 and 1997. Until mid 1999 the companies concentrated on slimming the organisation, basically by early retirement (see Fig. IV.2), and on improving the financial performance.

However, the basic problem Dutch generators are facing is to increase their financial performance, to be able to respond to the over-capacity in the Dutch market in the short term. Companies have to find ways to reduce the costs of production and at the same time to increase their profit position. The cost of a Dutch centrally generated kWh is still too high to be competitive in a liberal market. Companies are forced to develop more offensive innovation strategies, but they severely lack equity capital (see Fig. IV.3 and IV.4).

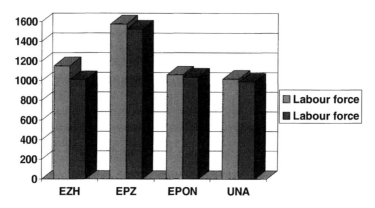

Fig. IV.2. Labour force statistics for four generators.

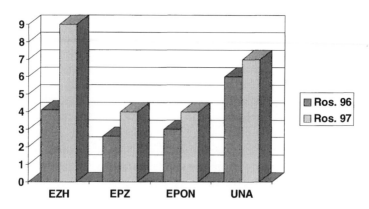

Fig. IV.3. Return on sales 1996 and 1997 for four generation companies (rounded figures).

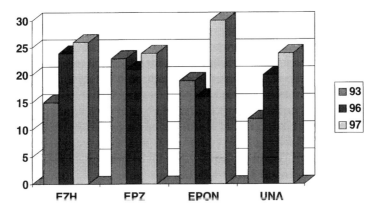

Fig. IV.4. Solvency of four generation companies (rounded figures).

Lack of capital may force companies to extend the life cycle of all production plants, including the outdated and most polluting plants. Some of these plants have been closed to respond the 1990 acidification agreement with the Dutch government, but some are still in operation.

In regard to the future, the continuation of four independent Dutch generation companies is highly unlikely, partly because of their rather complex ownership structure. As Table IV.4 reveals, two generators are owned by combinations of municipalities and provinces and two are owned by distribution companies. Early in 1999 it became clear that EPZ would be vertically integrated with PNEM/MEGA and the three other generators were offered for sale. UNA was taken over by an American company, Reliant, who paid about US$2 billion for the company. EZH was the second company taken over, by the German company PreussenElektra in 1999. In November 1999 EPON, the third generation company, was taken over by the Belgian company Electrabel.

Table IV.4. Shareholders of generation companies 1997.

Company	1997
EPON	NUON 50%,
	EDON 50%
UNA	Province Noord Holland
	Municipality of Amsterdam
	Municipality of Utrecht
	Province of Utrecht
EZH	Province Zuid Holland 15%
	Municipalities 85%
EPZ	PNEM/MEGA 67%
	Delta 33%

The once dominant SEP has been dismantled, and the transport and system operation activities have continued under a new name, Tennett. This organisation is the new national grid operator and the new owner of the high-voltage grid. The Dutch state takes a share of 50% plus one in Tennett and the new company is in charge of the technical dispatch at the highest voltage level and for transport on the 380 kV and 220 kV-grid. The short-term challenge of this newly established company is to handle the increasing number of electricity suppliers and the diversifying fossil and renewable-based generation technologies that will be connected to the grid, and at the same time to maintain and to ascertain the reliability of electricity supply as in the old pre-liberal era.

IV. Structural Changes in Dutch Distribution

Dutch distributors won the game of market dominance they started in 1989, but they still had to play their mutual game of market power. This power play among distributors was basically played in three games: the game of business scale, the game of business scope and the game of costs. This section tells this part of the power game in the Dutch market.

IV.A. The game of scale: Merger mania in distribution

Between 1985 and 1999, distributors continued enlarging the scale of business.[11] These mergers started to respond to the 1985 efficiency push of the Dutch government. As a result, the number of Dutch distribution companies drastically decreased from 1985 on, as is illustrated in Table IV.5.

The efficiency push launched by the Dutch government in the 1985–1989 period motivated several locally operating and municipal owned companies in the rural eastern half of the country to accept a takeover offer of the bigger, provincial owned distribution companies. In this way,

Table IV.5. Concentration and horizontal integration in distribution.

	Electricity/gas	Mono-gas	Total
1950	225	118	343
1985	82	76	158
1994	29	12	41
1995	28	11	39
1996	23	11	34
1997	20	11	31
1998	16	10	26

[11] The logic of this process has been elaborated upon by Arentsen *et al.*, 1997.

NUON, EDON, PNEM and MEGA took over a lot of small-scale distribution companies to enlarge their company scale and to improve efficiencies in work processes. At the same time, the generation activities of these larger distributors were disposed of and continued as independent generator (see above), allowing the distributor to concentrate on distribution and to develop new strategies into other fields of business (see below). As a result, the larger distribution companies dominated the rural areas of the country in the beginning of the 1990s. These companies primarily distributed electricity, but also had substantial activities in gas distribution. The distribution companies in the western urban part of the country responded to these developments with the establishment of two large companies, ENECO and ENW, uniting several smaller, locally operating distribution companies under a new name. Table IV.6 lists the background of the larger distributors.

Table IV.6. Background of the five largest distribution companies.

Merger of:	Resulted in:
EGD (Groningen, Drenthe) and Ijsselmij (Overijssel, Drenthe)	EDON
PGEM (Gelderland and Flevoland) and PEB (Friesland)	NUON
PEN (Noord Holland) GEB Amsterdam, GEB Haarlem, Zaanstad/waterland, Kop Noord Holland	ENW
GEB Rotterdam, GEB Den Haag and REB Dordrecht	ENECO
PNEM (Noord Brabant) and MEGA Limburg (Limburg)	PNEM/MEGA

In 1997 five companies dominated the distribution of electricity, and on a smaller scale the distribution of gas, and each developed and strengthened collaborative relations with still independent distribution companies in their local environment.[12] So five distribution companies succeeded in gaining substantial market share by merging, and each established strong regional positions in the electricity market. In 1998 PNEM and MEGA marked the beginning of a new area, when these two already large companies decided to merge, establishing one giant distribution company (at least according to Dutch standards). Consequently, the concentration of market power increased, since the distance among the top five players enlarged substantially by the PNEM/MEGA merger. PNEM/MEGA became the first Dutch company selling more then 20,000 GWh of electricity (see Fig. IV.5).

In gas sales, PNEM/MEGA also took a top position, but was less dominant over its rivals as in electricity sales (3.1 billion m^3 versus 2.4 billion m^3). The mergers in the top ranking of Dutch distributors also

---

[12] In 1997 PNEM and MEGA had not yet merged.

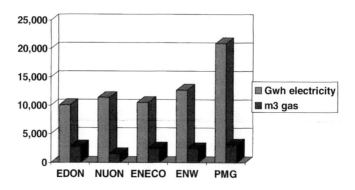

Fig. IV.5. 1997 Gas and electricity sales: top five distributors.

extended the distance between the top five and the rest of the Dutch distribution companies. Based on electricity sales in 1997, the Dutch distributors can be distinguished in three relatively separated groups: large, medium and small (see Table IV.7).

Table IV.7 summarises the result of the mergers between 1988 and 1998, reflecting a development towards three different types of integrated distribution companies: large, medium and small. In 1998 the restructuring of the Dutch distribution market continued by the announcement of

Table IV.7. Dutch distribution companies ranged along 1997 sales of electricity.

Large (> 10 million MWh sales)	Medium (>1 million<10 MWh)	Small (< 1 million MWh)
1. NV EDON	1. Energie Delfland NV	1. Cogas

2. NV ENECO	2. NV Delta
	   Nutsbedrijven
		2. Energiebedrijf Midden-
		   Holland NV (EMH)

3. Energie Noord West
   NV (ENW)
	3. NV Energie en
	   Watervoorziening
	   Rijnland (EWR)
		3. NV Energiebedrijf
		   Rijswijk Leidschendam
		   (ERL)

4. NV NUON	4. NV REMU	4. Energiebedrijf Zuid- Kennermerland (EZK)
5. PNEM/MEGA Groep NV		5. NV Frigem
		6. NV Nutsbedrijf Heerlen
		7. NV Nutsbedrijf Maastricht
		8. NV Nutsbedrijf Regio Eindhoven (NRE)

		9. NV Regionaal
		   Energiebedrijf Gooi en
		   Vechtstreek (REGEV)

		10. NV Rendo Holding
		11. NV Nutsbedrijf Westland

several new mergers, especially among the large distribution companies. By the end of 1998 the first move was made by a conglomerate of five distribution companies[13] announcing a merger that would establish the largest Dutch distribution company with an overall annual turnover of seven billion Dutch guilders. Soon this move of the five companies was responded to by the announcement that PNEM/MEGA was to merge with EDON. The effect of these latest mergers, completed in 1999, consolidates the Dutch distribution market into three parts, two of them dominated by one of the giant distribution companies (the NUON-group and the PNEM-MEGA-EDON group) and a third part left for a mixed group of small and still independent distribution companies.

IV.A.a. Mono-gas companies
Among the third group of small and independent distribution companies, 11 specialised in gas distribution and sales. These companies are locally based and all with municipal ownership structures (see Table IV.8).

The scale of the mono-gas companies is relatively small. Only Gamog,[14] operating in the mid-eastern part of the country, sells more than 1 billion m³ gas. The scale and reach of all the other companies is much more restricted. The prospects of the mono-gas companies seem to be hard, due to their limited reach and specialisation in gas sales. Actually, mono-gas companies are facing increased competition of integrated distributors and the interests of both mono-gas and integrated companies have diversified over the last couple of years, resulting in a detachment

Table IV.8. Dutch mono-gas companies 1997.

Name	$(10^6)M^3$ Gas (sales)	Number of gas connections	Employees (total)
Gamog	1168	329530	403
Obragas	757	178063	172
GCN	622	183593	200
GGR-gas	544	101902	163
Intergas	501	133314	138
Amstelland	421	61287	167
Haarlemmermeer	247	43594	81
GZO	207	56859	85
NO-Friesland	184	54352	94
Westergo	178	59063	80
GMK	126	48467	70

[13] These companies are NUON, ENW, Regev, EWR and Gamog (only gas).
[14] In 1999 Gamog merged with NUON.

of mono-gas companies from the national association of distributors, called *EnergieNed*. They established an independent organisation called *ENERcom*, advocating the interests of the gas companies and purchasing gas on behalf of its members. The erection of *ENERcom* reflects the increasing diversity of interest among electricity and gas. In facing competition, gas companies are supported by the Dutch national gas organisation called *Gasunie*. This organisation is highly dominant in the Dutch gas market and is able and willing to face competition with electricity. *Gasunie* is pushing new product development and increasingly offers a wider range of gas-based alternatives to customer's energy equipment. A recent, but promising development is the gas-fired heat pump and micro CHP, but it is highly uncertain whether these innovations are able to stand the increasing pressure and competition of the integrated distribution companies. The story of Gamog, the largest mono-gas company, may be illustrative. Within a year this company changed its corporate strategy by switching from an offensive mono-gas business profile into a merger with one of the giant integrated distribution companies. Other mono-gas companies will follow. One of these companies, Haarlemmermeer, had already a recover takeover bid from a foreign company in November 1999, but at that time the Minister for economic affairs blocked this transaction. The general expectation is that mono-gas companies will be sold as soon as the new Dutch gas legislation is accepted by Parliament.

IV.B.The game of scope: Integration across value chains

The merger process in distribution was not only driven by strategies to extend the company scale, but also to broaden the company scope. The large distributors in particular took over small, municipal owned gas companies, in this way extending their gas sales to develop strategies as integrated *energy* distribution companies. Some of the distributors also got involved in large-scale heat distribution, adding heat as the third energy commodity to their sales. Actually, the development of CHP facilities became a very serious business for distribution companies from 1989, as was illustrated in section II. The joint activities of distributors and industry in CHP development actually took two directions. In smaller projects, up to 1,500 kWe capacity, the distributor took the risk of the investments and bought electricity surpluses in the public grid. In the larger projects, mostly with industry, the risks and profits were shared by establishing a joint venture in combination with so-called off balance financing, providing considerable advantages to both partners. As a result, the share of decentralised cogenerating capacity has increased significantly from 2200 MWe in 1987 to 7000 MWe in 1997, now accounting for a market share of about 22%, currently bringing the Netherlands, after Finland, into second position in the European ranking of cogenerators. The increase of CHP based generation capacity in the Netherlands is illustrated in Fig. IV.6.

With a strong position in energy sales (gas, electricity and heat) the larger companies started to develop strategies across value chains, extending their business orientation to other utilities. Fig. IV.7 summarises the focus of these strategies.

In the 1990s, distributors seriously extended the range of products, while retaining the energy supply and distribution that had been and still was pivotal in their business. For the first time cable television distracted companies from their core (energy) business, increasing their awareness of the potential gains of integrating different utilities in the corporate business. By the end of the 1980s cable TV was expected to be a booming business and almost all distributors were infected by the idea that they had to enter that market. Companies started cable television activities on a limited scale by participation, takeovers and by establishing own business units. Table IV.9 illustrates the results of the attempts to integrate across value chains.

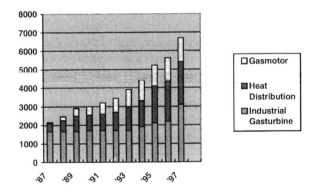

Fig. IV.6. Growth combined heat and power (in MW).
Source: COGEN Nederland.

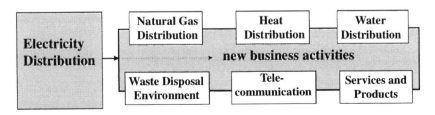

Fig. IV.7. The focus of business strategies across value chains among large cogenerators.

Table IV.9. Number of distributors in other than energy business in 1997.

Business type (in %)	Large	Medium	Small
Cable television	100	50	36
Telecom	80	0	0
Water	20	50	27
Waste management	40	25	0

Among all three types of distribution companies, cable television is most popular next to the core business of energy sales, but among the smaller companies, only about a third developed cable activities. In general, companies concentrated on hardware, offering broadcasting facilities to other companies. Only the larger companies developed additional activities in telecom, but as Table IV.9 illustrates, not all large companies are active in this field, and some of them only very briefly (see also below).

Table IV.9 also reflects the rather limited integration of energy supply and distribution with water distribution and waste management. Medium and small companies turn out to be relatively active in water distribution, in comparison to the large companies. Actually only one large distributor (NUON) developed significant water supply activities and has ambition to extend this utility next to the energy supply (see also below). Only large distributors developed waste management activities, which in general are restricted to a local scale. The waste management activities of two large distributors are rather extensive and they developed significant business units for waste management. One of them, EDON, developed a whole range of waste treatment activities, such as waste disposal, soil cleaning and waste incineration. In 1997 they opened a facility combining waste incineration and electricity generation.

Table IV.9 reflects the rather limited integration across value chains, releasing the significance of the concept of the multi-utility and the rather limited adaptation of this concept by the Dutch distributors until now. Only the large distributors actually have prospects to develop as multi-utilities in the Netherlands, and even among this group the prospects are rather differentiated and full of pitfalls and angles. A closer look at the business profiles of the top five distributors may illustrate this point.

Table IV.10 summarises some core elements of the business profiles, as expressed in the annual reports of the top five companies.

Three of the five companies adopted the multi-utility concept in business profile; only ENW currently concentrates on energy trade and supply. In 1997 ENW decided to sell its activities in cable television and telecom to concentrate on the energy business. NUON and ENW too sold

Table IV.10. Major company profile: top five distributors.

Company	Business profile
PNEM/MEGA	• Core business: Multi-utility • Gas and electricity trade and supply both national and European • Cable television, strong regional position • Waste management, strong regional position • 'Green profile'
ENW	• Core business: Energy trade and supply (electricity, gas and heat) • Electricity and gas trade and supply. Involved in European gas trade
NUON	• Core business: Energy trade and supply and water supply and management • Strong 'green profile' (national market leader green electricity) • Cable television/telecom as second core • Explicitly stated international ambitions
ENECO	• Core business: Energy and telecom • Strong regional and national position in electricity, gas and heat • Telecom, strong regional position
EDON	• Core business: Multi-utility • Electricity and gas, regional and national and international • Strong 'green' profile • Telecom, strong regional position • Waste management, strong regional position

their telecom business and ENECO is seriously considering selling its too. The telecom activities of ENW were already relatively restricted and the company decided to withdraw from the telecom business when it became clear that a further development of this business demanded huge investment, which would heavily burden the company's development in energy business. From 1998 on, ENW therefore concentrated on energy and its strategy became directed towards the establishment of a strong regional and national market position in energy.

None of the companies adopting the concept of multi-utility in its business strategy covers the whole spectrum of utilities, but, instead, until now, each concentrates on a specific portfolio. PNEM/MEGA and EDON have waste management units and cover the widest range of utilities. NUON is the only one supplying water and water services, and has withdrawn from cable television/telecom.

All companies share the ambition to enter the European market, but until now international activities are still rather limited. PNEM/MEGA is most explicit in expressing its international ambitions, and to date are the only company trading internationally by importing British gas. PNEM/MEGA currently invests in its own gas grid facilities to supply

British gas in its supply region,[15] directly competing with *Gasunie*. NUON developed another strategy to enter the international trade market. This company participated with in two foreign gas companies, one in Great Britain and one in the United States. NUON, most explicit in expressing a green business profile, also developed partnerships in Romania and China in the erection of wind turbines. So the actual steps taken by the large distributors to enter the international market are still rather limited. Until now, companies have only expressed their international ambitions, whereas the actual steps are still rather limited.

The *four medium-ranked companies* are all located in the urban western part of the country and basically operate on the residential market. They all take a middle position in the Dutch market: on the one hand in business development referring to the profiles of the 'big brothers', and on the other hand, sharing a local business orientation and municipal-based ownership structures with the group of small distributors. The medium distributors all sell both gas and electricity in combination with other services, like cable television, water and waste management, but the integration of these services is much less established in comparison with the large distributors.

Only half of the group developed cable television activities and none of them is really active in telecom. Only one company supplies water and water-related services (water treatment) and only two companies offer green electricity, some of which is generated by their own generation capacity. So, compared with the large distributors, the integration of utility services is rather heterogeneous and far less developed among the group of medium-ranked distributors. They basically operate in their own supply area, and, with one exception, they do not have national or international ambitions. Only DELTA, operating in the southern part of the country participates in the British gas contract and the grid-investment of PNEM/MEGA. The business profile of DELTA is most similar to the one of large distributors and DELTA is not afraid of expressing international ambitions. Actually, DELTA has a fairly strong background since it developed a good solvency position (about 60% in 1997)[16] in comparison to other distribution companies.

The activities of the small distribution companies across value chains is rather restricted. Companies combining energy distribution with cable television and other services are a small minority in the group of small distributors. None of the smaller distributors created completely new organisational structures, other than the organisational adjustments

---

[15] DELTA, heading the medium ranked distributors, participates in these international gas trade activities.
[16] DELTA, Annual report 1997, p. 75.

Table IV.11. Number of mono-gas companies in non-gas business in 1997.

Cable (in %)	18
Telecom (in %)	0
Water (in %)	9
Waste management (in %)	0

obliged by the new Electricity Act to separate between commercial and non-commercial activities.

The integration across value chains by mono-gas companies is even more restricted as is illustrated in Table IV.11.

Only two companies entered the cable television market and only one is distributing water. Until now, mono-gas companies have stuck to their core business by concentrating on the supply and distribution of gas and gas-related services. In general mono-gas companies operate as 'captive customer' of the mid-stream and rather dominant gas-operator *Gasunie*. They all have tied purchase contracts with *Gasunie* and the high margins on the domestic gas price is passed to the shareholders: this obligation keeps companies from entering other businesses and developing other than gas and gas-related activities.

IV.C. The game of costs: Efficiency improvements in distribution

The last game Dutch distributors had to play in facing the liberalised electricity market, the game of cost reduction and efficiency improvements, was almost forgotten in the political turbulence accompanying the design process of the new legal framework for the liberalised market. The process of accomplishing a market-oriented company structure and developing a market-oriented business focus started relatively late in the Netherlands. In 1994, the association of Dutch distributors *EnergieNed* initiated a first benchmark among Dutch distributors, showing significant differences among distributors in productivity, caused by differences in structure and processing of work activities. A repetition of this benchmark in 1996 among 19 Dutch distribution companies[17] concluded that an overall progress in productivity of 20% had been attained in comparison to 1994 (calculated as the ratio of number of connections and full time labour equivalents), and that a restricted innovative performance and potential existed.[18] In barely two years, distribution succeeded in increasing its overall

---

[17] The participating companies are unknown, but include both integrated and mono-gas companies.

[18] Anderson Consulting, *The Race for Results*, Arnhem 1997.

productivity by some 20%, only by adjusting work processes without any structural reorganisation or forced release of employees. See Fig. IV.8.

The efficiency improvements have been calculated for three different groups of companies (low, medium and high performers) and three different work processes (supportive, technical, and customer).[19] The calculation only accounted for gas and electricity distribution to industrial and household customers, other services were excluded. The remarkable progress in productivity becomes even more interesting if the causes are taken into account, since the efficiency improvement was only the gain of optimising work processes and work procedures. In general none of the distributors reorganised its geographically-based company structure, with locally-based, small-scale satellites in charge of the distribution of gas and electricity in specific geographic areas. The mergers and takeovers of the last couple of years did not really change

Productivity
Customers / FTE 1994 - 1996

company performance:
lowest 5 Cies / average / best 5 Cies

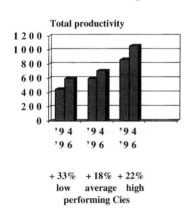

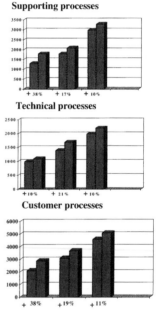

Fig. IV.8. Productivity improvement 1994–1996.
Source: Anderson Consulting, *The Race for Result*, Arnhem, 1997.

---

[19] The Anderson report only tentatively lists the content of these processes. Supportive processes include: management and strategy, human resource management, finance, purchase and logistics, information technology and facilities. Technical processes refer to planning and management, connections, technical maintenance and grid construction. Customer processes refer to metering, invoice services, information and advice.

Table IV.12. Productivity of distributors in 1996 and 1997.

Productivity	Large	Medium	Small
Average 1996	324	296	209
Std. deviation 1996	38	55	89
Average 1997	287	295	213
Std. deviation 1997	57	78	92

the highly-differentiated and locally-based company's structure of distributors. Between 1994 and 1996 the efficiency improvements were basically the result of adjusting work processes and the introduction of new information technologies. The surplus of labour resulting from this first organisational 'refreshment' was not released but put in charge in non-core activities, not included in the productivity-improvement calculations.[20] The benchmark also shows remarkable differences among companies. The overall average productivity in 1996 was 710 connections/FTE, but this average is highly flattered by one or two companies with a connection/FTE ratio of 1000 to 1100. So the conclusions of the benchmark in regard to productivity improvement should be taken with some care.

The productivity efforts of distribution companies are further put in perspective by own calculations for the whole group of distribution companies. Table IV.12[21] not only manifests differences among the three groups of distribution companies, but also a decrease in productivity between 1996 and 1997 in the group of large and medium-sized companies. Only the small companies succeeded in improving productivity, on a very limited scale. In the group of large companies the differences in productivity increased in one year, since the deviation from average increased in 1997. So the calculation of labour force developments of all companies supports the conclusion on the somewhat flattered picture showing up in the 1996 benchmark of the distribution companies.

Next to the productivity improvements, distribution companies are in the process of developing and strengthening a commercial orientation in business activities. Companies are searching for ways to satisfy customer needs by means of new products and services. Examples are billing and invoice services to allow for tailor-made contracts, composed multi-site invoicing, real time pricing and online billing. Some companies are developing technical services such as street lighting for local authorities and

---

[20] Between 1994 and 1996, companies still had employment commitments due to the social policy of shareholders.
[21] The table has been calculated as the ratio total connections of electricity/total number of employees, since the annual reports do not specify labor inputs, but only list total labor force.

all kinds of additional technical and utility services for industrial consumers, such as co-generation, energy audits, load management, utility management and remote energy control.

According to the 1996 benchmark, companies have problems adopting these kinds of commercial products and services and developing a more innovative business orientation. Companies were still rather reluctant in adapting new identities and missions to guide the business reorganisation and to develop new business strategies equipped for the competition ahead. Companies were facing information problems hindering the establishment of customer (market) driven strategies and new product development. The information technology in use turned out to be highly inadequate in providing for detailed customer information as a tool of new product development. Companies also severely lacked commercial skills, competence and knowledge, and employees, questioned for the benchmark, lacked optimism on the company's flexibility and potential in adopting and adjusting to the competitive market conditions: they observed a rather reluctant transition of the company.[22] Lack of commercial and marketing skills is also reflected by the negligence of branding by the companies. Several larger companies changed names three times over the last years. The continuous change of company names without a clear market brand does not contribute to the identity of the companies to customers.

This overall image, based on 19 distribution companies, showed up in the 1996 benchmark. Between 1996 and 1999 the reorganisation in distribution continued. Companies were not only forced to further the commercial performance, but also to adjust to the legal requirements of the new electricity law, forcing them to separate all commercial activities from non-commercial, regulated activities such as transport and distribution to captives. As a result, companies reorganised their business to unbundle commercial and non-commercial activities legally, administratively and financially. So between 1996 and 1999 companies had to adapt to a new, market-oriented business orientation and at the same time had to restructure their business according to legal obligations. As part of this, they had to establish different types of business units, each guided by a different set of parameters, and to further the efficiency of the business organisation.

One of the major problems Dutch distributors are facing is the lack of capital. In general the equity capital of the companies is rather restricted and exceeds the amount of one billion Dutch guilders only in three companies. Only PNEM/MEGA managed to build an equity capital of more than two billion Dutch guilders (see Fig. IV.9 and Table IV.13).

---

[22] Research conducted by Booz-Allen & Hamilton in 1998 draws similar conclusions.

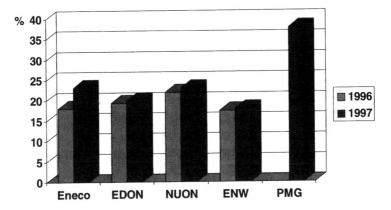

Fig. IV.9. Solvency: top five distributors.

Companies are currently developing stronger solvency positions by restricting annual dividends in favor of capital reserves, but only PNEM/MEGA succeeded in attaining the target of about 35% solvency. The other four large distributors still haven't met this target. As Fig. IV.10 illustrates, the annual return on sales[23] of the companies are rather diversified.

Internally, distribution companies adopted significant changes in company structure. This process of reorganisation was partly driven by the legal obligations of the new electricity law and partly by the need to adopt commercial orientation. The new electricity law obliged companies to split transport/distribution and trade/supply activities at the

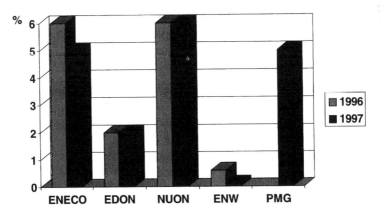

Fig. IV.10. Return on sales top five distributors (rounded figures).

---

[23] Returns on sales have been calculated as the ratio of net result and net turnover.

Table IV.13. 1996/1997 overview of basic financial data top five distributors.

All data in Dutch guilders

ENECO	1996	1997
Overall net turnover (including all surcharges)	2,809,344,000	2,853,460,000
Net turnover electricity	1,549,001,000	1,618,508,000
Net turnover gas	1,157,279,000	1,129,360,000
Net turnover heat	103,064,000	105,592,000
Energy purchase	1,978,927,000	2,006,939,000
Overall operation costs	903,504,000	868,643,000
Labour costs	295,169,000	264,594,000
Net profit	170,000,000	143,957,000
Equity capital	616,830,000	751,772,000

EDON	1996	1997
Overall net turnover (including all surcharges)	3,013,321,000	3,095,864,000
Net turnover electricity	1,479,000,000	1,564,000,000
Net turnover gas	1,314,000,000	1,246,000,000
Net turnover heat	—	—
Net turnover telecom	132,000,000	168,000,000
Net turnover waste management	58,000,000	84,000,000
Energy purchase	2,024,353,000	2,055,983,000
Overall operation costs	1,052,512,000	1,074,606,000
Labour costs	295,018,000	323,625,000
Net profit	70,208,000	72,422,000
Equity capital	938,532,000	975,573,000

NUON	1996	1997
Overall net turnover (including all surcharges)	2,700,546,000	2,808,170,000
Of which:		
Energy	2,520,419,000	2,606,642,000
Other products	180,127,000	201,528,000
Energy purchase	1,737,251,000	1,814,347,000
Overall operation costs	2,594,305,000	1,814,347,000
Labour costs	274,459,000	279,197,000
Net profit	182,177,000	189,252,000
Equity capital	1,248,201,000	1,425,453,000

ENW	1996	1997
Overall net turnover (including all surcharges)	2,975,500,000	2,975,800,000
Net turnover electricity	1,760,300,000	1,811,100,000
Net turnover gas	1,169,700,000	1,112,300,000
Net turnover heat	15,100,000	19,600,000
Net turnover telecom	8,700,000	11,200,000
Net turnover waste management	—	—
Energy purchase	2,975,500,000	2,975,800,000
Overall operation costs	930,000,000	916,800,000
Labour costs	363,300,000	388,600,000
Net profit	19,900,000	4,000,000
Equity capital	615,600,000	625,900,000

Table IV.13. 1996/1997 overview of basic financial data top five distributors
continued

All data in Dutch guilders

PNEM/MEGA	1996	1997
Overall net turnover* (including all surcharges)		4,945,155,000
Net turnover electricity		2,862,021,000
Net turnover gas		1,294,510,000
Net turnover heat		115,779,000
Net turnover telecom		124,037,000
Net turnover waste management		—
Hot water appliances		20,873,000
Energy purchase		3,520,979,000
Overall operation costs		1,272,859,000
Labour costs		408,607,000
Net profit		239,283,000
Equity capital		2,546,659,000

* Overall net turnover is taken from PNEM/MEGA joint annual report. The specification of turnover for electricity gas etc. is calculated as the sum of separate turnover of PNEM and MEGA in 1996 and 1997.

company level. As a result, almost all companies adopted an organisational model uniting different business units in a holding structure, in which transport and captive-supply is clearly separated from commercially oriented activities. The top five distributors reorganised their company structure along similar lines: a holding uniting business units for infrastructure/captives, energy trade and supply, water, telecom and waste, whereas the business unit energy trade and supply has been divided into sub-units for different groups of customers, like industry, services, etc. NUON and EDON also established separate business units for sustainable energy.

Similar to the large distributors, the *medium-ranked distribution companies* are in a process of organisational transition to adjust to the legal requirements of the new electricity law. They have all split their commercial activities from transport and distribution, but they have not yet consolidated completely new overall company structures. As table IV.12 illustrates, the medium-ranked companies started to improve efficiencies, but the slimming of the organisations was still rather restricted in 1997. Here the companies feel the presence of their municipal owners still stressing and supporting strong local interests, such as employment, low tariffs and profit maximisation. In general, the companies are facing rather conservative positions of their owners in regard to their commercial ambitions.

The *small integrated distribution* companies, all owned by municipalities, are in a rather backward position in comparison to the medium and large distributors. The small companies concentrated on gas and electricity distribution in their locally restricted supply areas. Their overall business reach is rather restricted, as is illustrated in Fig. IV.12.

The small companies started to increase productivity, basically by releasing some of the labour force. The release in 1997, illustrated in Fig. IV.13, was primarily the result of early retirements. As with the large and medium distributors, the small companies also made financial reserves to finance the productivity improvements.

As with the other distribution companies, the *mono-gas companies* also started to improve the productivity and efficiency of their organisations. As Fig. IV.14 illustrates, the results are still rather tentative, because the process to release employees has just started. So the 1997 picture is not really divergent to the one of the integrated companies.

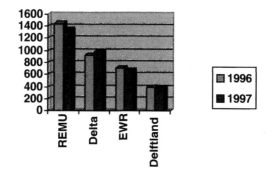

Fig. IV.11. Employment of medium ranked distribution companies in 1996 and 1997.

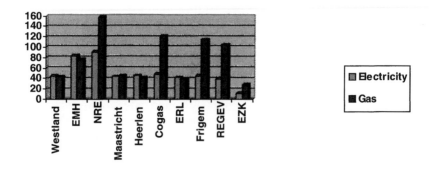

Fig. IV.12. Gas and electricity connections (x 1000) of small integrated companies in 1997.

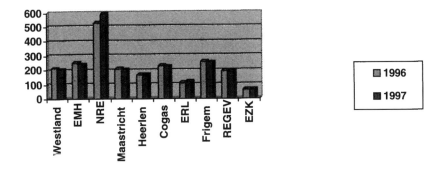

Fig. IV.13. Employment of small distributors in 1996 and 1997.

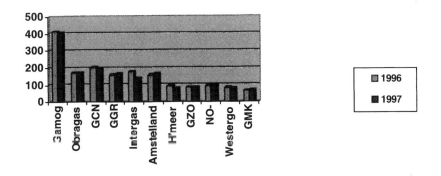

Fig. IV.14. Employment and release of mono-gas companies in 1997.

V. Public Service Obligations

The public service orientation and performance has dominated the Dutch electricity industry almost from the very beginning of its establishment, and has guided its historical development. Even the institutional adjustments of 1989 were basically motivated to maintain the high public service performance of the electricity industry and even in 1998, the institutional structure and the regulation of the electricity industry was dominantly inspired and motivated by public service obligations. Protection of customers by tariff control, security of supply in the short and long term and protection of the environment have been, and still are, dominant public standards in the electricity industry. Electricity supply was, and still is, of high quality in the Netherlands and malfunction or system fallout is rare, even under the worst weather conditions. Important tools to ascertain and to maintain the public service orientation and performance of the electricity industry have been a strong national energy policy (of which electricity policy is part), strict electricity regulation and full public ownership of the electricity industry (basically provincial and municipal). However, with liberalisation ahead, the significance and impact of public ownership is decreasing.

Until 1989, the ownership structure was an important tool in the strategic orientation and development of electricity companies, because, until then, shareholders were in commanding positions with substantial influence on corporate strategy. Employment and tariff structure were dominant in the strategic focus of the companies. After 1989, many energy companies altered their legal status and continued as limited companies, releasing the *legal* dominance of shareholders in corporate strategy. The changing legal status of corporations did not affect the public orientation in a company's performance, but was the first step in pushing back the influence of local and regional authorities in the electricity industry in favour of the central government. Now with liberalisation ahead, the significance of public shareholders on corporate strategy is further set back, because the new electricity act has blurred the *traditional* legitimisation of public ownership structures. The public service obligations have been integrated in the new national electricity act and electricity companies are obliged to separate commercial and public oriented activities at the company level. As a result, the impact of municipalities and provinces on corporate strategies has further diminished and many local authorities now start questioning the legitimacy of continuing shareholdership of distribution companies for other than financial reasons. Each year, shareholders get significant amounts of money (dividend) and municipalities and provinces, always in need for money, have integrated these purchases in their annual budgets. So financial purchase more and more surpasses public interest considerations as legitimate base for public ownership. A full privatisation of the electricity industry is not expected, because until 2002, only a minority of the shares may be sold to the private sector and only by approval of the Minister for Economic Affairs. From 2002, all company shares may be transferred to the private sector. These developments are illustrative of the changing orientation in and legitimacy of, public ownership structures in the electricity industry. For decades it was legitimised to support and to ascertain the public service performance, but this function now has been taken over by national electricity legislation and the central authorities. Public shareholders are left only with a financial legitimisation of shareholdership.

In the final decades of the 20th century, environmental obligations became a significant public service obligation of the electricity industry, an obligation continuing under liberalisation, but designed differently. Despite the significance of gas in electricity generation, the environmental impact of the electricity industry has been, and still is, a major issue domestically, and lately energy conservation and energy saving have been added due to climate change policy (reduction of CO_2 emissions). Between 1989 and 1998, central authorities and the electricity industry developed joint strategies to release the environmental impact of electricity generation and use.[24] Central to this was the 1990 acidification agreement (convenant) with generators and distributors committing them to release the environmental impact of electricity generation and consumption by investment in new generation technology and by energy-saving campaigns for end-users. Distributors initiated a long-term environmental action program aimed at energy savings in small industry and households and they were allowed to add an environmental surcharge to tariffs to raise finance for the environmental program. The program runs until 2001 and then stops. After 2001, the environmental obligations of the electricity industry have been designed in congruence with the liberalised electricity market. So liberalisation did not release the environmental obligations of the electricity industry, but only altered the regulatory means to meet the environmental targets.

The new approach in controlling the environmental impact of the electricity industry concentrates on green or sustainable electricity, an obligation explicitly stated in and part of the new Electricity Act, and next to liberalisation, the second major target of the act. The target is to increase the share of green electricity from the present 1.5% to 10% in 2020. The act defines the meaning of green electricity (hydropower up to 15 MW, wind, solar and bio-mass) and embodies legal provisions to develop coercive means to attain the green target in case companies fail to increase the share of green electricity on a voluntary basis. Central to this is the establishment of a system of green certificates referring to the amount of electricity generated with renewable resources. Each licensee is obliged to have a legally prescribed number of certificates representing the amount of green electricity he produces and/or supplies and all certificates represent the total share of green electricity in the system. Licensees are allowed to trade in green certificates enabling them to sell surpluses or, for those lacking green electricity, to meet the legal obligations by purchasing certificates. The trade of green certificates will be part of the Amsterdam Power Exchange.

---

[24] In section 2 above, it was already illustrated how distributors took advantage of environmental arguments by investing in CHP-based generation capacity to trigger the dominance of generators in electricity supply.

Table IV.14. Overview of distributors supplying green electricity.

Green electricity (in %)	Large	Medium	Small
Solar	100	50	63
Wind	60	50	27
R&D	100	50	18

Green electricity is available in the Netherlands for households, and on a limited scale also for industrial consumers, but tariffs still exceed those for fossil-based electricity. Table IV.14 gives an overview of companies supplying green electricity.

Despite the relatively large number of distributors active in and offering green electricity, the share of renewables in electricity generation is still rather limited in the Netherlands. Currently only 1.5% of the electricity stems from renewables. Only one distribution company, NUON, expresses an explicitly green company profile and is aiming at a company share of 10% green electricity by in 2010, instead of 2020 as is obliged by the new Dutch Electricity Act. Price differences between fossil and renewable-based electricity are decreasing, due to a rise in energy tax tariffs, leaving price differences of some three Dutch cents in 1998. Apart from the willingness of companies to increase their green activities, the further development of green electricity is severely hindered by legal restraints and bureaucratic obstacles of local and regional authorities. At the local and regional level, the sophisticated and highly detailed Dutch environmental regulation, in combination with open and highly responsive policy processes allowing for extensive public participation, not only increases the time needed to establish new green production facilities, but often blocks their construction. Suitable locations to erect, for instance, wind turbines, are already rather rare in the Netherlands, and on the few locations suitable for wind turbines the population often expresses a high NIMBY-consciousness.[25] Investment in large-scale wind turbines, a major green option in the Netherlands, is not only frustrated by a lack of locations with optimal physical conditions, but also by municipalities unwilling to facilitate investments. So apart from the willingness a motivation of industry, bureaucracy and citizens protest and resistance may become a major problem in the further sustaining of the electricity industry. In the Energy Report of November 1999, the Minister for Economic Affairs announced regulatory initiatives to overcome the problems in wind turbine investments.

---

[25] NIMBY refers to the contradictory attitude of many citizens pleading for sustainable energy on the one hand, but unwilling to accept production facilities in their backyard on the other (NIMBY is the acronym for 'Not In My BackYard').

But industry not only faces green electricity targets, but also finds its fossil-based production charged with environmental obligations put forward by climate change policy. As a result of the Kyoto agreements, the EU region takes a share of 8% in the global CO_2 reduction, committing the Netherlands to a 6% reduction in the overall EU reduction efforts. A tremendous challenge, according to industry, since the potential of cost-effective investments in a further emission reduction is rather limited. Apart from the option to hasten the introduction of green electricity, reduction targets may be met by investments in CO_2 storage, in combination with accelerated investments in new CHP-based, gas-fired generation capacity and the replacement of coal and oil by natural gas as basic fuel for electricity generation.

VI. Market in Operation

VI.A. The Amsterdam Power Exchange

One of the Dutch options in the emerging European electricity market was to take advantage of the geographic location and the extensive domestic high-voltage grid infrastructure (with international connections, see Fig. IV.15), by establishing an international power exchange.

Fig. IV.15. International connections Dutch grid.

Table IV.15. Expected trade volume Amsterdam Power Exchange.

Market arena scenario	Cumulative trade volume
+ Distribution companies and industry	3%
+ Generators (bid-restrictions) and Foreigners	19%
+ Generators (no bid-restrictions) plus traders	28%
+ PCO's (processing deals)	32%

A Dutch power exchange could be the third one in Europe (next to Scandinavia and England) and could position the Dutch trade right in between both other locations, bringing the Dutch power exchange into the centre of European trade. Public officials and representatives of generators, distributors and large customers started preparing the establishment of a Dutch power exchange labelled as the Amsterdam Power Exchange (APX) in 1997. By the end of 1997 the first simulations started and Table IV.15 lists the expected trade volume of the APX, based on these simulations.[26] The system was subsequently tested in a pilot trading volume without financial and physical equivalents. In 1999 the APX became operational.

The power exchange started with physical trade as a day ahead spot market. Non-physical (financial) trade (futures and options) will be introduced next to the physical trade, probably sometime in 2001/2. By the end of 1999 all four power companies, twelve distribution companies and seven industrial consumers participated in the APX. Foreign companies participating in APX are Electrabel, Gergen Energi, Southern Company, Grupo Endessa, Vattenfall, Kom-Strom, ENRON and Eastern. The trade-volume is sometimes relatively high (600 – 800 MW), but there are problems too, especially regarding import and export of electricity. These problems are caused by technical restrictions of the high-voltage grid. In general prices are relatively low, but in congruence with price-levels on power exchanges elsewhere in Europe (2.5 – 3.5 Euro per MW). In the future, the APX might also be involved in the trade of green certificates, the basic Dutch instrument to increase the share of green electricity.

VI.B. New entrants

The liberal electricity market has attracted several new actors to the Dutch market. Initiatives of different groups of new actors are expected, among others, foreign companies and private industry. They all have the interest and ambition to start activities on the Dutch market, but since no one is very explicit in stating strategy, it is hard to be more specific. New entrants will act unpredictably and will influence the Dutch scene.

---

[26] The software used by the APX was bought in Spain.

Several foreign companies participate in the Amsterdam Power Exchange, which can be taken as a clear sign of interest. These companies are expected to contribute to the trade volume of the power exchange. Norsk Hydro and Intergen were more explicit in expressing interest in the Dutch market by actually starting to prepare for the establishment of a CHP power plant. The crossroad of Dutch, Nordic and British gas has been chosen as the location of this new plant, which seems to be a rather good location to develop trade and supply of both gas and electricity. German companies show significant interest supply in the Dutch market from 1999 onwards. PreussenElektra, HEW, VEW and REW contracted sales for over 1,000 MW. Another clear manifestation of foreign interest in the Dutch market is the so-called 'lease-back' contract of the generation company EZH, UNA and EPON with US investors. Further signals of foreign interest in the Dutch electricity industry have been given by the foreign companies taking over three of the four Dutch power producers in 1999. Experienced electricity traders are entering the Dutch market, bringing in a lot of trading skills. The list of new entrants is large: Eastern, Vattenfall, Statkraft, VEW, PreussenElektra, ENRON, Bergen Energi, RWE and many more.

The second group of new entrants comes from private industry. Actually this group is already operating on the electricity market since 1989, when it took advantage of opportunities offered by the Electricity Act 1989 to develop own generation capacity in joint venture with distribution companies. Until 1999, electricity supply of this decentral generation capacity to the grid was actually discouraged by the tariff structure, which was not very satisfying for the private producer. The liberal market, featuring third-party access, ceases this type of barrier for decentral generation capacity, but will not ban it, since the Dutch transport tariff does not account for distance, only for use of the grid. This tariff structure disadvantages electricity transport over short distances. Joint investments in CHP power plants are no longer the privilege of distributors only, since generation companies take participation in this kind of joint venture.

VI.C. End user trade

In the warm-up to liberalisation, the 'race' for customers started already in 1998 before the new electricity law was in operation. Companies are increasingly aware of the need and importance of offering satisfying contracts, meaning offering reliability as in the old days but for lower prices. The ultimate challenge is to offer electricity as cheaply as possible and everybody wants to be the cheapest of all. In the attempts not only to keep present customers but also to get new contracts, Dutch companies not only have to account for domestic competitors, but also for foreign competition. The commercial danger of foreign companies is not only their ability to offer good prices, but the commercial skills and competence they bring to the Dutch market. Here the Dutch companies are in a backward position, because they are relatively inexperienced in commerce. Several foreign companies are already trading in the Netherlands, including some Norwegian, British and German companies. The hunt for large customers started in 1998 and the Dutch national railway company was one of the first to announce the hunting season had opened. The national railway company clearly challenged the Dutch energy companies by contracting a significant part of its electricity need (some 200 million Dutch guilders annually) from the German electricity company PreussenElektra.

Some electricity companies anticipate the release of captives after 2004. Their strategy concentrates on new residential areas, presently under design and construction in different regions of the country. The planning and construction of the energy facilities in these new residential areas has been exempted in the new Electricity Act, to achieve optimal energy facilities, meaning effective and efficient energy facilities, but at the same time as sustainable as possible. So gas and electricity connection is no longer obvious in these areas, because the energy planning process allows for deliberating the whole spectrum of possible conventional and/ or sustainable alternatives. The ultimate decision on energy infrastructure is no longer taken by the regional monopolist, but by the municipal authorities. This procedure already illustrated some of the new competition ahead between integrated and mono-gas companies. Companies are extremely motivated to win the energy supply for the new area and to implement energy options that might give them competitive advantages for all eligible customers.

VII. Towards Market Consolidation

The structural changes in the Dutch electricity industry have been rather significant over the last decade and in mid-1999 the Dutch market still seemed far from consolidated. The market is full of tensions, both in generation and in distribution and supply. It is hard to forecast precisely where this process will lead or end up. In this section we will draw some conclusions on the future prospects of the Dutch electricity market.

VII.A. The preoccupation with scale

One of the striking points of the market developments over the last decade is the strong focus on business scale of companies, both in generation and distribution. This drive for scale seems to be part of a historical process which dates back to the beginning of the 20th century when the Dutch electricity system was established. The development of the Dutch electricity system has been accompanied by a continued debate on scale of the system and the companies operating the system. Until 1989, the scale debate was basically driven by the need to increase the efficiency of the system as a whole and of the companies operating in the system, but this changed in the 1990s. The need for scale became the primary drive to ascertain the survival of the Dutch system in an open European market. The merger debate in generation was primarily driven by this motive. Dutch generators were too small to survive in a European market, but the only way to strengthen the conditions for an independent Dutch generation potential in the European market, by merging the four independent generation companies, failed. Generators were left with only one alternative: integrating with strong partners either horizontally or vertically. This seems to be the only alternative for the Dutch generators, and the developments to mid 1999 have shown the lack of alternatives for generation companies apart from integration. The most probable scenario for Dutch generation companies is being bought by other companies, both domestic and foreign. The generators have no potential to survive as independent power producers, basically because they severely lack capital to innovate both the quality and quantity of their capacity.

In distribution the scale issue has been tackled differently over the last ten years of the 20th century. Here the merger process succeeded and left the Dutch market split in three different parts at the end of 1998. The largest part, representing 80% of the Dutch distribution market, had become the domain of five large distribution companies; a second part left only a few medium-sized companies; and a third part comprising small, but still independent, distribution companies, some of them only distributing gas. As a result, the outlook of the distribution sector changed, increasing the heterogeneity in scale, scope and strategic orientations among companies. Interest cleavages have shown up, not only between generation and distribution, but also among distributors, as was illustrated by the establishment of *ENERcom*, the association of mono-gas companies, releasing the one dominant consensus model in the Dutch electricity industry. The probable future routes of the distribution companies will be explored in more detail for each of the three groups separately.

VII.B. The large distribution companies

The five large distribution companies, PNEM/MEGA, ENW, NUON, ENECO and EDON control about 80% of the electricity supply in the Netherlands and their geographical location is illustrated in Fig. IV.16.

The future challenge of the top five distributors is two-fold: on the one hand they have to further their commercial skills and competencies to adapt successfully to the new commercial oriented environment, and, on the other hand, they have to continue the process of improving the performance of the organisation by consolidating the internal transitions. In the discussion of the 1996 benchmark of distributors it was concluded that the companies still have a long way to go to improve their business performances. The same still holds for the top five distributors, as was explicitly concluded in the 1998 research of Booz-Allen & Hamilton on the prospects of Dutch distributors to develop in an European environment and to adapt to the concept of multi-utility.[27] The research concludes a rather limited adaptation of the concept of multi-utility by the present large distribution companies.[28] Companies did not succeed in sufficiently transforming their business organisation to allow them to enter the European market and their

Fig. IV.16. Geographic location top five distributors.

---

[27] Booz-Allen & Hamilton, 'The emergence of multi-utilities and the potential impact on the Dutch market'. The Hague, 1998.
[28] Thus far, for Dutch distributors the multi-utility concept resembles only a conglomerate of different products offered by different business units of the holding and not yet an integrated package of services offered by one organisation.

solvency position hindered a further development by merger or takeover. In general, companies are aware of the changes needed to adapt to the challenges of the liberalised market, but up to 1999 they had not succeeded in consolidating the necessary transformations. The report observes a rather fragmented Dutch distribution market, with too many companies, all missing the potential to develop as an European player. Furthermore, companies were operating in a highly fragmented legal environment which is highly obtrusive to the further development as multi-utility. The legal framework hinders the establishment of synergy among utility services at the company level. In general the research of Booz-Allen & Hamilton sketched a rather pessimistic future of Dutch distributors in the emerging European environment. Without significant public support and without releasing present legal barriers, Dutch distribution is bound to disintegrate, and may become an easy object for foreign takeover. This prospect frightened the Dutch government and by the end of 1998 the Dutch government responded by a statement of the Minister for Economic Affairs, saying the future reforms of other utility sectors next to electricity, such as gas and water, should advocate and not block the further development of Dutch distributors as multi-utilities.[29]

Early in 1999 the larger distributors had made up their minds and in a relatively short period of time, two new mergers were announced, reshuffling the market positions in the largest segment of the Dutch distribution market. The first merger was between NUON, ENW, EWR and Gamog. Regarding the type of activities of these companies, the newly established NUON group concentrates on energy and water supply and distribution. This strategy was confirmed by NUON when it sold its shares in telecom soon after the merger was announced. The company wanted to concentrate on energy (electricity, gas, heat and renewables) and water. The NUON group was the largest distribution company in the country only for a very short period of time, because soon after the announcement of the merger of the NUON group, PNEM/MEGA announced a merger with EDON, bringing PNEM/MEGA back to the first position among the larger distributors. The business profiles of PNEM/MEGA and EDON fit well, because both companies developed a rather wide multi-utility approach in business, including not only energy and water, but also telecom and waste treatment. ENECO announced a separate strategy by cooperation with Shell International, adding commercial and international experience to their scope.

---

[29] The source of this statement is a short announcement in a periodical of *EnergieNed*, called *Energie Nederland*, (Vol. 1 Nr. 9, p. 1). The Minister made the statement in response to questions from one of the members of Parliament.

Both latest mergers have brought giant companies to the Dutch market, at least according to Dutch standards, but the question still remains whether both have the potential to continue independently in an European environment. During 1999 this question was still open, but in case both companies will be taken over by foreign companies, the latest mergers contributed to the improvement of their position *vis á vis* foreigners interested in buying both companies.

VII.C. The medium-ranked distribution companies

The prospects of the medium-ranked companies to a large degree depend on their ability to develop and to maintain a strong local position in energy supply. However, in a couple of years, they will be challenged by competition of the large distributors, which all clearly expressed national ambitions, bringing them in the traditional supply areas of medium- and small-ranked distribution companies. It is still uncertain whether these companies can stand this challenge. Their future existence as independent suppliers depends on their ability to develop commercial skills and competence in congruence with the scale and scope of their business. In the short term they may concentrate on the supply of gas and electricity to captives, which ascertains turnover and financial profit as in the old days at least until 2004. However, their present purchase contract with SEP/generators ends in 2001, and this will bring the medium-ranked companies in search for new electricity purchases. At this moment it is not clear whether medium-ranked companies independently have the potential to attain new purchase contracts that are commercially attractive, or whether they have to join strategic alliances or to merge with others.

VII.D. Small integrated distribution

The short-term perspective of small integrated distribution companies is to concentrate on the distribution of energy to captives, a strategy which holds at least until 2004, the year in which all customers will have free choice of energy supplier. Private households are already dominant in the customer portfolio of the small companies, and concentrating on this niche not only matches best their skills and competence, but may also satisfy the expectations of their municipal owners, having basically financial interests in the continuation of ownership. For that reason small companies are rather restricted in developing commercial activities, since this may increase the financial risks of the owners. In the longer run the small companies may have problems to continue as independent suppliers. They basically have only two options: developing alliances with larger distributors or merging and disappearing as independent suppliers. Municipal owners may be decisive in this strategy. They may decide to continue the annual dividends, or they may go for a takeover offer of one of the larger distributors.

VII.E. Mono-gas companies

The future position of mono-gas companies is rather similar to the one of small integrated companies, meaning a rather restrictive relationship with municipal owners not willing to accept any commercial risks and a customer portfolio dominated by private households. But mono-gas companies are severely in danger if their ambition is to continue as independent gas suppliers. Firstly, these companies have to go beyond the present local reach of their supply activities, bringing them in direct competition with the larger integrated companies. It is far from clear whether the smaller mono-gas companies are capable of responding to this competition of integrated companies who can offer a more diversified package of energy and services than the mono-gas company. Secondly, the core business of mono-gas companies is of great importance for the further development of the multi-utility ambitions of large distributors. The large distributors can only satisfy these ambitions by takeovers of mono-gas and small and medium integrated distributors. For that reason the large companies will not allow the smaller companies to increase market share. Until 2004 mono-gas companies may concentrate on the gas supply of captives, but after 2004 their existence as independent supplier becomes highly uncertain. Probably these companies will face uncertainty by 2003 if the idea of eligibility, announced in the 1999 Energy Report, is implemented. The story of Gamog is illustrative in this regard. This company was one of the front runners in developing and implementing a mono-gas strategy to compete with electricity, but the company chose to merge with NUON.

VIII. Summary and Discussion

The recent moves to adapt to the new competitive market structure, makes it hard to forecast any real outcomes at the time of writing (mid 1999). The market hasn't consolidated yet. Electricity companies, used to the blessings of the Dutch corporatist model, are increasingly facing the boundaries of the conflict modulating potential of this model. Tensions and turbulence, resulting from market anticipation, diversification of positions and interests, increasingly subvert the old conventions of collaboration and coordination in the electricity industry. The emerging competitive forces urge for a revision of, or perhaps an alternative for, the Dutch consensus model, since the larger companies at least tend to develop separate strategies in search for market power. The findings clearly demonstrate the route ahead for Dutch companies. Already in 1998 before full implementation of the new Electricity Act, competition started and foreigners entered the Dutch market. The large companies were the first to anticipate the emerging transitions, firstly by the need to enlarge the scale of business and secondly by the need to improve efficiencies of internal work processes. Their anticipating behaviour has been taken as a reference by some of the smaller companies in adjusting to the changing environment, but not all companies have been successful. Many small companies have been taken over by the larger ones or joined together in alliances to increase their significance as a market player. Several foreign companies settled in the Netherlands and started to penetrate the market in search for contracts among the first group of customers to be released early 1999. Foreign companies may take competitive advantage of the commercial skills and competence they bring in, whereas Dutch companies are still in the process of swinging to competition and adopting a commercial orientation.

The Dutch route to adopt to the changing environment started already in the mid 1980s, by the debate on the scale of electricity supply and company performance (see Table IV.15).

In the run up to the new Electricity Act of 1989, distribution companies anticipated the proposed legislation by changing the legal status of their companies and by adapting efficiency and cost reduction programs. This period, represented by the second column in Table IV.15, basically reflected a process of emancipation of Dutch electricity companies in responding to the emerging changes in the electricity market. The legal change to limited company was a first prerequisite to release the tight relationship with public shareholders necessary to be able to broaden the

Table IV.16. Changing the structure of the Dutch electricity market.

1920-1986 Public oriented	1987-1998 Emancipation	1999-2002 Liberalisation
integral part of municipality	separate legal entity	stakeholders public sector
manages grid/ connection	manages grid/ connection	liberalisation business sector
social services (water heaters)	focus on efficiency and satisfied customer	separation grid and energy trade
	horizontal integration	access to buying markets
		market positioning

publicly oriented strategic focus which dominated from the 1920s on. As a result, between 1987 and 1998 the Dutch electricity market changed significantly in structure and outlook. The number of companies reduced drastically, generation and distribution disintegrated and introduced the first signs of competition on the Dutch market when distributors started to generate electricity. They successfully attacked the dominant position of the generators headed by *SEP*, in this way contributing to the need to restructure the market again relatively shortly after the 1989 revision. The new Electricity Act of 1998, reflecting the new liberalised conditions, was formulated in response to this need of restructuring. The first group of eligible customers, the giant industrial customers, may cause a serious market push which may bring the Dutch market into real competition. The state of the art in adopting this new liberalised era at the structural and the company level has been analysed in this chapter and column 3 of Table IV.15 summarises the basic challenge of energy companies.

It is far from clear if and how Dutch companies will manage to adopt to the changing environment. One of the problems companies are facing is their legally-driven positioning in the value chain, which may impede synergy in business development. This problem first appeared in 1989 when the Electricity Act 1989 forced the then integrated companies to disintegrate between generation and distribution. The problem continues; although the new Electricity Act of 1998 allowed for vertical integration it obliged companies to unbundle transport and trade. Dutch companies are in a backward position to foreign competitors who bring in their commercial skills and competence. Dutch companies lack the financial potential to decrease this disadvantage. Only by severe investment may they succeed, but the options are not overwhelming. Forward integration is difficult when knowledge and capital for new product and service development is scarce on the Dutch market. The same holds for a further horizontal integration of distribution companies to establish 'giant' companies of over two million customers, such as the merger of five distribution companies announced in December 1998. Actually, these kinds of merger initiatives are rather astonishing from a perspective of accelerating the swing towards commercial orientation and business development. These mergers do not add anything to the required commercial skills or to the improvement of the solvency position. Backward integration, as announced by the PNEM/MEGA group, may be an alternative as long as the generation part of the company meets competitive prices, because this will be the dominant commercial standard to meet in a market facing overcapacity in the short term. The present purchase pooling contract between generators and distributors, which runs until 2001, hides the most severe problem of distributors: their lack of knowledge of portfolio management, that is, managing supply and demand of the electricity commodity. In 1999 this is a non-item. But the question remains how distributors will react when the majority of generating capacity is sold to new entrants and generators address end users directly. What will be the potential influence of the large neighbouring generators like EDF, Electrabel and RWE? Inefficient generators will suffer severe competition in the Dutch market as soon as the present pooling contract with distributors ends in 2001. Until 1999 only the PNEM/MEGA group had developed a strategic option to establish a clearer position in the value chain in comparison with other Dutch distributors. Whether others will follow on the route of vertical integration is still unclear. Entrance to cheap, competitive supply sources will be the key to success. The survival game highly depends on matching cheap supply and managing the end-user market. In 1999 this game had just started and its outcome was still fully open.

References

Anderson Consulting, The race for Result, Arnhem, 1997.

Annual reports 1996 and 1997 of Dutch energy companies.

Arentsen, M.J., R.W. Künneke en H. Moll, The Dutch Electricity Reform. Reorganisation by Negotiation, in: Atle Midttun (ed.), *European Electricity Systems in Transition. A Comparative analysis of policy and regulation in Western Europe* Elsevier Science Ltd., Oxford, 1997, pp.167–197. ISBN 0 08 042994.

Booz-Allen & Hamilton, The emergence of multi-utilities and the potential impact on the Dutch market, The Hague, 1998.

Minister for Economic Affairs, Derde Energienota (Third White Paper on Energy), Dutch Parliament, 1995-1996, 24 525, nrs. 1–2, SDU Publishers, The Hague, 1995.

Minister for Economic Affairs, Energy Report 1999, The Hague 1999.

Chapter V
Corporate Strategies in the German Electricity Supply Industry: From Alliance Capitalism to Diversification

LUTZ MEZ

I. Introduction

The Electricity Supply Industry (ESI) is among the most powerful economic sectors in Germany, and constitutes an economic and political power cartel which has been able to resist all attempts at altering the framework conditions for German energy policy in recent decades. The legal and institutional framework has cemented this structure and secured the privileges of the large utilities as well as the small local monopolies, the *'Stadtwerke'*. In the last decade, issues such as deregulation, energy or CO_2 taxes, privatisation of public utilities, and the realisation of a single European market for energy have also affected Germany, bringing with them major changes and new risks for the electricity business (Mislees-Black *et al*, 1996).

The powerful ownership links between the ESI and major financial and industrial interests in Germany indicate that this industry is an integral part of what has been termed German Alliance Capitalism (Shonfield, 1968, 1971). In contrast to competitive capitalism, alliance capitalism is characterised by close ties and collaborative relationships between commercial entities, and the success of industries within this system relies on the concerted orchestration of large resources in pursuit of common goals. With its huge turnover and vast profits, protected by its monopoly, the ESI grew into the major cash cow of the German economy. The political status of this economic system was consolidated by links to state bodies at all levels and, through revenue-sharing, with German municipalities by way of generous concession fees.

As early as 1976, the German monopolies board criticised the ESI as one of the 'competition-free economic sectors' (Monopolkommission, 1976, p. 52). This was not always the case. Before World War II, there were more than 16,000 public electric utilities in Germany. In the 1950s there were still about 3,500 in the Federal Republic of Germany alone. Today there are only about 1,000. However, this concentration understates the actual power structure of the ESI. Six national grid operators now control most of the regional utilities and a considerable share of the local energy utilities. Within the next ten years the number of public electric utilities will shrink to probably 200–250.

Two main trends can be made out in the German ESI: (1) concentration and centralisation of capital in the two biggest companies, and (2) an opposing trend towards 're-municipalising' energy supply in the hands of '*Stadtwerke*' and other local utilities.

This chapter analyses the corporate strategies of the three ESI giants in Germany: RWE Energie AG, PreussenElektra AG and Bayernwerk AG. Their owning mother companies, RWE, VEBA and VIAG respectively, are diversified management holding companies, all still dominated by the energy business. Although not completed at the time of writing (end 1999), in fall 1999 VEBA and VIAG announced their intention to merger—the new company is called E.ON AG—and some weeks later RWE and VEW (one of the smaller grid operators) did the same.

RWE AG is Germany's number one electricity provider. It tops the list in turnover, workforce, investment, and in the generating capacity both of its own and of its contracted power stations. RWE was founded in 1898 as the local utility in Essen. Even before World War II, RWE had gained a leading position in the German ESI. In 1989, RWE was restructured as a holding company, with RWE Energie AG responsible for electricity and gas supply. Today, RWE Energie contributes only 30% of RWE's total revenue, but almost half of its profits.

PreussenElektra AG was founded in 1927, and belongs to VEBA. The company is the second largest with respect to electricity supply and power capacity. In 1985, the present company was created out of the fusion of Nordwestdeutsche Kraftwerke AG with Preußenelektra AG. The VEBA holding company also owns VEBA Kraftwerke Ruhr AG, Braunschweigische Kohlen-Bergwerke AG and Thüga AG. The PreussenElektra group consists of a number of regional utilities, including Schleswag AG, HASTRA AG, and PESAG AG, all controlled by majority ownership.

Bayernwerk AG has been part of the VIAG holding company since 1994. Among other energy companies, Contigas Deutsche Energie-AG and Isar-Amperwerke AG belong to the Bayernwerk group. Bayernwerk was the first of the three giants to react to the new situation, by restructuring the company's internal organisation.

As a result of German re-unification, VEAG AG, the national grid operator in the new *Länder*, became a joint subsidiary of the seven other national grid operators. The energy giants are also striving for control of the smaller national grid operators, VEW, HEW and Bewag. Since 1997, the number four on the German electricity market has been EnBW Energie Baden-Württemberg AG, created by the fusion of Badenwerk Holding AG and Energie-Versorgung Schwaben Holding AG.

Several attempts by American and other foreign energy companies to gain a foothold in Germany since the beginning of the 1990s have failed. This closed shop persisted until 1997, thanks to IPP activities and the stock holdings of the big German utilities. The situation changed when the Swedish power company Sydkraft AB—already a minor shareholder in VEBA AG—together with PreussenElektra, bought a share of HEW. RWE had also expressed an interest in the package, but lost out in the bidding. And when the Berlin government sold its majority holding in Bewag AG in May 1997, the deal was closed by a consortium of PreussenElektra, VIAG and the US company Southern Energy. In 1999, the Swedish State utility Vattenfall bought another share of HEW. And Electricité de France took over the 25% share of the state of Baden-Württemberg on EnBW.

Such changes in the ownership structure of the German ESI are the result of changing framework conditions, liberalisation of the electricity market and privatisation of ESI companies, and the new stockholders will certainly influence the corporate strategy of the companies in the future. In the case of Bewag AG, Southern Energy not only chairs the supervisory board, but is also represented on the board of directors.

This chapter starts with an overview of the background, structure, and history of the German ESI, describing the national resource base and technical makeup of the system. A short description of the electricity regulation system and recent changes in the regulatory framework follows. The development of the ESI's structure and strategy in Germany is explained in terms of scale and scope, and the horizontal and vertical configuration, the concentration process, as well as diversification into new business areas, are analysed. Special attention is given to patterns of and changes in ownership in the German ESI. One section examines in detail the organisation of RWE, Germany's largest electrical utility, comparing the organisational changes with those in other companies. The chapter concludes by summarising the principal paths of change and the impact of commercial strategies on society and the environment.

II. Background and History of the German ESI

II.A. National resource base and technological structure

The German electricity supply system is based on the indigenous fossil fuel energy sources hard coal and lignite, and imported nuclear fuel, and this is reflected in the structure of installed generating capacity. Coal-fired plants rank first with 33.4 GW. The capacity of the lignite power stations is 21.2 GW, while natural gas has 21.6 GW and nuclear power 23.5 GW.[1] Oil-fired plants can produce 8.8 GW, hydro-electric plants 8.9 GW. In 1997, German power stations had a total installed capacity of 119.8 GW (see Fig. V.1).

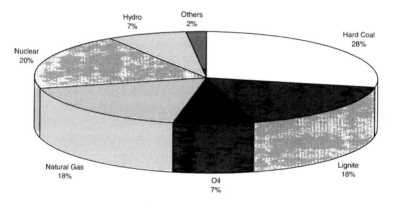

Fig. V.1. Installed and contracted capacity 1997 119.8 GW.

The structure of the power station industry corresponds to the distribution of the various energy sources, when one takes into account the fact that nuclear energy and lignite are used mainly in the base-load range, while coal and oil-fired plants operate in the medium-load range (see Fig. V.2). In 1998, nuclear electricity had a share of 30%, followed by hard coal and lignite with 27% and 25% respectively. The share for natural gas has been on the increase since 1994, while power generation from oil-fired plants has been declining. Hydro-electric power has, with 4%, a small but stable share in electricity generation. The rest is generated from a variety of renewable sources, such as waste and wind.

---

[1] According to the Bündesministerium für Wirkschaft report (BMWi) 20, nuclear power plants with a total capacity of 23,496 MW are in operation, including Mülheim-Kärlich (1,302 MW), which has been closed down by the courts. (cf. BMWi 1999, p. 42).

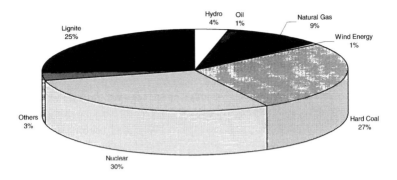

Fig. V.2. Electricity generation 1998 552 TWh.

A considerable number of wind turbines have been erected in recent years. With an installed wind turbine capacity of over 4,400 MW at the end of 1999, Germany became the leading user of wind power in the world (*Neue Energie*, 2/2000, p. 12).

The overwhelming share, 80 percent, of the power station industry is owned by the national grid operators. Moreover, thermal power stations are generally condensation plants, and the share of electricity generated by combined heat and power stations is 10%. This is due to the fact that CHP plants were for a long time constructed exclusively by HEW and Bewag, as well as by other *Stadtwerke* which had established large district heating systems. Since German reunification, there has been a slight shift back towards more use of CHP. The newly founded *Stadtwerke* in the new *Länder* have invested mainly in CHP technology, in order to maintain their relatively broad use of district heating and to gain a level of independence from pre-delivered electricity. Furthermore, the international trend towards decentralised CHP has reached German industry and utilities. At the end of 1996, a total of 3,300 small CHP stations (5,600 MW) were in operation, accounting for nearly 5% of electricity generation in Germany. 40% of these units are located at industrial sites and 35% in ESI.

II.B. The tradition of electricity regulation in Germany

German electricity regulation had traditionally consisted of a mix of public and private law. Basic energy law as embodied in the '*Energiewirtschaftsgesetz*', adopted in December 1935 and laying down the framework conditions for cheap and secure electricity supply, defined German state control of the sector for more than 60 years. The other important piece of public legislation for the sector is the Monopolies Act, which exempted electricity supply. However, contracts for concessions, demarcation, as well as supply to special customers, the technical conditions for feeding surplus electricity into the grid, reserve deliveries and other arrangements are all based on private law (Zängl, 1989).

There have been numerous attempts at reforming the ESI, but both bottom-up and top-down approaches have always failed. In the mid-1980s, a strategic about-turn in energy policy, as well as the re-municipalisation of electricity supply, was articulated and widely discussed in the wake of the Chernobyl disaster. This has remained the policy position of the SPD and the Green party, and is also supported by local activists.

In response to long-standing criticism of monopolistic practices in the electricity industry made by the deregulation commission, the CDU-led federal government attempted to push through more typically liberal reforms. A reform proposal drafted by the Ministry of Economics in October 1993 included a partial break-up of the industry, access for third parties and stricter controls on electricity prices. It was subsequently heavily modified and finally, in March 1994, retracted, because of open resistance from the municipalities and opposition signalled by the majority of the SPD-governed *Länder* in the *Bundesrat*.

The introduction of environmental concerns into the German system has been more successful than the initiatives towards liberalisation. The Ordinance on Large Combustion Plants (GFAVO) introduced strict limitations on all emissions such as SO_2, NO_x and particulate matter. With the restrictions it places on private property rights in favour of the environment, the GFAVO constitutes an exemplary top-down policy tool. The Technical Guidelines on Air Quality (TA-Luft) were similarly supplemented. The Electricity Feed-In Act, enacted in 1990 on the initiative of the German Parliament, provides another notable environmentally-oriented change in the framework conditions, fundamentally improving the economic viability of renewable energy. The act obliges public utilities to accept electricity generated from renewable energy sources (sun, wind, water, biomass, and waste treatment) and lays down predetermined rates for paying the producers. The act serves to support electricity generation from renewable energy sources.

II.C. Regulatory developments in the 1990s

In autumn 1996, the German government attempted once again to implement the European electricity market directive. The draft legislation was in the mould of earlier proposals, planning to remove both the demarcation treaties and the single supplier formulae in concession treaties. Proposals for state control of investment in new power stations and transmission lines were dropped without any substitute proposals. Access to the grid can be dealt with in two ways: by negotiated access or as an exemption through establishing a single buyer system. As regards transmission fees, government has the right to regulate them, and the associated terms and conditions, with legislation. However, instead of this draft, a functionally similar voluntary agreement was settled in May 1998 between the Association of German Electricity Supply Companies (VDEW) and the industrial associations BDI and VIK. The agreement contains a flat rate for transmission within an area up to 100 km from the national border. Transmission into other regions costs an additional ¢7.0/kW/km (approximately). Since January 2000 a second voluntary agreement makes third party access easier. Single buyer areas, mainly for *Stadtwerke*, are permitted until the year 2005. Within these areas, special customers can purchase electricity from third-party suppliers through the local utility.

The new act further intends to separate power generation and transport. Grid operators must keep their transmission grid business separate from generation, distribution and other activities. Electricity suppliers with tariff customers must also separate out their finances, that is manage separate accounts for generation, transport and distribution, recording profits and losses separately for each activity. Single buyers must also distinguish transport from generation and distribution.

As for access rights, exclusive clauses are prohibited, but concession fees may be paid. State control of the electricity sector is considerably reduced. In future, suppliers without tariff customers will require no licence for their activities, where they generate electricity as industrial producers, in CHP plants or using renewable sources. Nor does an industrial company's internal supply require a licence.

Crucial amendments were also made to the so-called Feed-in Act. Grid operators now have to accept up to 5% of their electricity supply from renewable sources, and biomass electricity must be accepted without any limit.

The German Parliament adopted these changes as a so-called article law, amending the basic Energy Act, the Monopolies Act and the Feed-in Act in November 1997. The new Energy Act came into force on April 29, 1998. Only a few days later, PreussenElektra began an appeal against the law before the constitutional court, as did the federal, Hessian, Saarland and Hamburg parliamentary parties of the SPD in June. The energy policy spokesman for the SPD announced that a review of the new energy act would be one of the first acts of the new (SPD-led) Federal government after the elections in September 1998.

The subsequent coalition agreement between the SPD and the Green party explicitly mentions support for renewable energy sources and energy conservation as vital components of a modern energy policy. Phasing out nuclear energy and removing the hurdles for renewable energy sources and CHP are key issues which this government has dealt with during its term of office.

II.D. Structure of the ESI in Germany

The German electricity supply industry comprises public suppliers, industrial power generators, and power stations owned by Deutsche Bahn (the national railway operator) and private producers. In 1999, public supply accounts for nearly 90% of the electricity market and takes place at three levels:

- national: eight national grid operators 'Verbundwirtschaft';
- regional: 80 regional companies; and
- local: approximately 900 city and town utilities.

The national grid operators are mainly wholesale producers, selling about 65% of their production on to other electricity companies. Only about 10% of production is sold to tariff customers. The regional and local companies are mainly distributors, purchasing 80% and 63% respectively of their sales from the *Verbundwirtschaft*.

The comparison of electricity supply and supplier companies clearly demonstrates the differences in size between the DVG member companies as shown in Table V.1. RWE alone sold 132.5 TWh in 1998, more than a third of all electricity, whereas Bewag, with 13.1 TWh, accounted for only 3.6%. The allocation across different consumer sectors shows the varying importance of special contractors, tariff customers and other utilities.

At regional level, electricity supply is provided by regional companies, working together in the Association of Regional Energy Supply Companies (ARE), which currently has 52 members. There are an additional 28 non-associated companies, taking the number of regional suppliers to 80. Of these companies, 56 are directly or indirectly governed or strongly influenced by the big utilities.

At the local level, municipal utilities (Stadt- und Gemeindewerke) become involved in the German electricity market. The Association of Local Companies (VKU) has more than 500 member companies engaged in electricity supply. The relatively large number of electricity companies in Germany, compared to other EC countries, should nonetheless be viewed in the context of a two-fold control by the energy giants, through powerful financial (capital) link-ups and electricity supply.

The grid operators of the Verbundwirtschaft are also the main electricity generators. The total electricity generated in Germany in 1998 came to 552.0 TWh; domestic consumption was 487.5 TWh and consumption

Table V.1. Profile of DVG 1998.

Members	Capital stock	Work force	Electricity sales	Customer's structure in %			Power stations and contracted capacity	Peak load	High voltage trans- mission
	(Mio. DM)		(TWh)	Special custo- mers	Tariff custo- mers	Other utilities	(MW)	(MW)	(km)
RWE Energie AG	2,300	19,817	132.5	34.9	11.7	53.4	26,543	21,831	21,000
PreussenElektra group	1,250	22,838	106.2	27.6	12.8	59.6	18,124	11,577	18,580
Bayernwerk group	1,461	17,683	72.6	28.5	22.2	49.3	11,355	11,120	15,000
EnBW group	1,250	12,605	51.3	25.5	22.2	52.3	10,478	8,130	9,680
VEAG AG	500	7,663	47.2	0.1	0	99.9	9,416	8,311	11,491
VEW AG	800	4,948	34.0	28.9	14.4	56.7	4,238	6,122	5,340
HEW AG	460	4,747	13.8	61.8	27.0	11.2	3,688	2,041	1,391
Bewag AG	560	9,038	13.1	52.8	47.0	0.2	3,116	2,666	892
Total DVG	8,581	99,339	470.7				86,958	71,798	83,374

Source: DVG Jahresbericht 1998, Annual Reports.

by power stations and transmission losses 65.3 TWh. Of this, about 492.7 TWh (89.3%) were produced by public utilities, of which 80% was generated by the Verbundwirtschaft. The regional utilities generated 9%, local utilities 11% (see Fig. V.3).

The Regional Supply Companies (only members of the ARE) supply 30.5 million customers directly, and a further 14.9 million indirectly. The electricity supplied in 1997 amounted to 198.2 TWh, which represented 36% of the total supplied by public utilities.

In this context, it should be pointed out that there are also major differences in scale. The smallest company delivers only 0.5 TWh, while OBAG AG, the largest regional company, delivers 11.9 TWh. While ARE member companies account for a major share of electricity supply, their role in energy generation is limited; only 18% of total supply is self-generated, the rest being contracted from the Verbundwirtschaft. Here, the dominance of the Verbundwirtschaft becomes apparent. The small share of the ARE corresponds to their own perception of themselves as being primarily responsible for energy distribution across the country. The limited role played by regional companies in electricity generation is further highlighted when electricity supplied is compared with generating capacity. The maximum capacity of ARE power plants was 8,796 MW in 1996. As 37.9 TWh were produced, the average utilisation time was 4,300 hours.

The regional utilities in turn dominate municipal companies with respect to electricity supply. They transport power to 615 local distribution

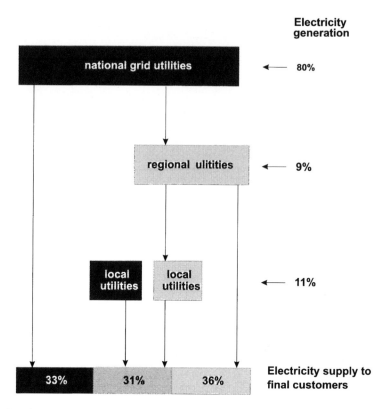

Fig. V.3. Structure of public electricity supply in Germany.
Source: Schiffer 1999.

companies and thereby provide the electricity for 14.9 million people
(ARE, 1998, p.33).

Local utilities are in a similar situation. They are primarily active in
distributing electricity generated by regional or national grid utilities.
Between 1961 and 1990, the share of self-generated power in Germany
dropped from 35% to only 20%. Member companies of the VKU in the
West German Länder supplied 148.3 TWh in 1996, which represents
about 31% of the total public electricity supply. Of the 538 VKU members active in the electricity market, 166 companies have no generation
facilities of their own. Most of the companies generate from no more than
30% of their power; some none at all. Only 51 local utilities generate more
than 30% of the power they distribute. At the same time, 75% of power
plant capacity is owned by only ten companies, such as Technische Werke
Stuttgart and the *Stadtwerke* of Hanover, Bremen, Kassel, and
Saarbrücken. The installed generation capacity of the local utilities
amounted to 14,400 MW in 1996, producing 45.4 TWh.

Another important sector in the electricity market is industrial production. Industrial producers are primarily responsible for meeting the energy needs of industry and the railways, although they feed surplus power into the grid. The maximum capacity of industrial power plants was 10,787 MW in 1998 (Schiffer, 1999, p. 168). Generation from the production sector amounted to 52.1 TWh in 1998, which means that industrial generation accounted for 9.4% of electricity generated in Germany.

The coal-mining companies play a special role in the German electricity market. STEAG (owned by Ruhrkohle AG, 71.08%, the Gesellschaft für Energiebeteiligung, 25%, and RWE-DEA AG, 1.62%) and Saarbergwerke (owned by the federal government, 74%, and the Saarland, 26%) possess a formidable combined capacity of about 6,000 MW. They supply electricity to the public grid, although they do not belong to the national grid utilities. In February 1998, the Federal Cartel Agency accepted Ruhrkohle's takeover of Saarbergwerke and Preussag Anthrazit GmbH. The new company operates under the name Deutsche Steinkohle AG.

In the statistics, the electricity activities of the mining and production sectors are often merged. The organisation of the industrial energy sector, the VIK Verband der Industriellen Energie- und Kraftwirtschaft e.V., represents about 90% of all participants. Although the share of independent industrial generation has risen in recent years, the volume of electricity produced is still far below its level in the early 1970s, when about 70% of industrial demand was supplied internally. According to the National Statistical Office, industrial utilities in 1996 had an installed capacity of 18,676 MW. Since 1970, the volume bought from public utili ties has grown faster than total demand. One reason is that a number of power stations came to belong statistically to the public utilities sector. Generation capacity at VEBA, Klöckner, Thyssen and Volkswagen was taken over by national utilities. The main reason for the fall in industrial capacity is thought to be the introduction of favourable private contracts, which convinced industry to close down its own generation facilities.

Additional generation capacity is owned by Deutsche Bahn AG, the national railway company. Its installed capacity in 1998 was 1,541 MW, with a generated volume of 7.2 TWh.

III. Development of ESI Structure and Strategy in the 1990s

III.A. Scale and scope in Germany

RWE was a key force in determining the scale and scope of the ESI in Germany (for more details see Mez/Osnowski, 1996). As the leading utility in the 1920s, RWE established an integrated grid system with a dispatching centre in Brauweiler. Furthermore, the company pioneered the use of lignite power stations. In the 1950s, block sizes of 100 and 150 MW were the largest in the world, as was the RWE power station Frimmersdorf in 1962, with a total capacity of 2,000 MW. Lignite-fired blocks of 300 MW and 600 MW also came onstream for the first time in RWE power stations.

RWE played a similar role in the commercial development of nuclear power: the 250 MW water-cooled reactor Gundremmingen A, built in 1962-66, was the first of this scale in the world. Some years later, another RWE project—the pressurised water reactor Biblis A (1,200 MW)—became the largest nuclear power plant outside the USA. In June 1969, RWE ordered the plant from Kraftwerk Union AG. Biblis A was connected to the grid in 1975, the second block Biblis B in 1976.

Together with leading banks, RWE invented a new model for financing power stations: leasing. In 1974, RWE sold the 600 MW gas-fired power station Meppen to a leasing company owned by several banks, and leased it back again. The idea was to avoid borrowing and maximise capital, sharing the costs and profits with the big banks.

Similar models were used for the nuclear power plants Mülheim-Kärlich and Gundremmingen B + C. In the case of Mülheim-Kärlich, RWE, together with Deutsche Bank, Dresdner Bank, and Schweizerische Kreditanstalt, founded a company in Luxembourg in 1975, mainly to spread the risk, but also to profit from favourable conditions for depreciation. This nuclear power station, ordered from BBC, turned out to be a technical disaster. Mülheim-Kärlich was in operation for 13 months between 1986 and 1988 before being shut down by a court order.

In the case of Gundremmingen B + C, a joint venture by RWE and Bayernwerk, the financial risk was transferred to a consortium of banks specialised in leasing.

Issues of scope have been important from very early on in RWE history. The company is famous for controlling every step in the electricity value chain, 'from the first piece of coal to the last light bulb'. In fact, the founding idea of the company was to take advantage of buying the steam from a coal mine for the power station located at a nearby site, thus avoiding charges by the coal syndicate. This model was able to generate electricity more cheaply than other utilities. Even at the turn of the century, RWE secured the fuel base for its power stations, hard coal and lignite, by buying shares in mining companies. In the 1920s, it broadened its scope in the direction of the Alps, combining hydro-electric power with coal-generated electricity from the Ruhr district. Electricity-based innovation for industry and for private households expanded RWE's corporate activities.

In 1969, RWE bought a large holding in Gelsenberg AG, signalling RWE's entry into the petroleum business. This deal was described at the time as Germany's 'largest capital transaction since the end of the war' (Radkau, 1998, p. 226), but the turmoil leading up to the oil crisis led to a decision to sell the shares to VEBA in November 1973—at a huge profit. RWE's next foray into the petroleum business came in 1988, when it bought Deutsche Texaco from Texaco for approximately $1.2 billion.

The diversification and restructuring of RWE began in 1989, when the present holding structure was created and the core business of electricity was hived off to the legally independent RWE Energie AG.

As German industrial power producers were able to challenge the ESI by starting up their own gas-fired CHP stations, this became the arena for strategic action. The ESI's solution for the industrial sector is to contract out not only small-scale power stations, but also large CHP plants. The chemicals company BASF, the largest single energy customer in Germany, has been contracting a 390 MW combined-cycle power plant from RWE which started operation in 1997. A similar contract for combined-cycle plants with a total capacity of 800 MW was signed in 1995 between RWE and the chemicals company Hoechst. Additional contracting projects are to be realised with Bayer AG and Opel AG. RWE predicts 2,000 MW of newly-installed CHP capacity at industrial sites in the next four to five years.

III.B. Horizontal and vertical configuration of the ESI

III.B.a. The concentration process

The German electricity supply industry exhibits a close vertical integration, as power trade in the past was primarily a nationwide business. Generation, transport, wholesale, and retail supplies are still dominated by the national grid operators (EWI, 1998).

In 1994, about 54% of total power was generated by the three largest utilities, 70% by the six largest. Concentration of generation capacity increased remarkably in the period 1970 to 1994, due to the construction of large power station units. Of public electricity supply, 61% was generated by the three largest energy groups (RWE, VEBA/PreussenElektra, VIAG/Bayernwerk) in 1994. At European level, RWE ranked third behind EDF and ENEL, followed by National Power (UK), VEBA as number five and VIAG as number ten (ibid.)

High-voltage transportation is dominated, at 80%, by the national grid operators, while the three largest alone account for more than 60%. Wholesale cycling to regional and local utilities shows even a higher concentration. In 1994, about 90% was conducted by six national grid operators and their groups. The two mainly local utilities HEW and Bewag have, as yet, virtually no wholesale business.

Before German re-unification, concentration and centralisation of capital in the ESI developed slowly compared to other sectors. At the level of the national grid operators, the merger of Preußenelektra AG (PREAG) and Nordwestdeutsche Kraftwerke AG (NWK) to form PreussenElektra AG was the only significant event. With a holding of 69%, PREAG had a controlling share in NWK. As part of VEBA, both companies merged in 1985 to form the second largest German national grid utility.

In the mid-1970s, the German Monopolies Commission (Monopolkommission) was established. In its first report, it criticised the high concentration and lack of competition within the ESI (Monopolkommission 1976). In this context, an analysis of concentration within the ESI was carried out by the Institute of Energy Economics in Cologne (Mönig et al., 1977). Although the big utilities continued to broaden their horizontal control via capital holdings in regional and local utilities, the political climate was against more concentration in the ESI, and the monopoly agency prevented several deals and takeovers (for example, Stadtwerke Bremen).

Beginning in the mid-1980s, the re-municipalisation campaign in local utilities demonstrates an opposing trend. Quite a large number of municipalities decided to intensify their energy activities, and tried to buy back power stations and/or local grids from national grid operators or regional utilities.

The re-unification of Germany marks both a turnaround at the levels of the national grid and the regions and an intensification of the opposing trend at local level. When the Treuhand Anstalt sold the national grid operator Vereinigte Energiewerke AG (VEAG) and the lignite mining company Lausitzer Braunkohle AG (LAUBAG) to two nearly identical consortia of the seven West German utilities, a period of conflict and transformation in the energy sector in Eastern Germany came to an end. The deal cost approximately $5.7 billion, the largest deal managed by Treuhand during its operations. The sales contract was signed in September 1994 and in autumn 1995 all stocks were handed out. Furthermore, all 14 East German regional utilities came to be dominated by the West German utilities as majority shareholders. In one exception, West Berlin's Bewag merged with the East Berlin utility. As a result of the conflicting positions of municipalities, East German Länder and the West German ESI, about 140 local utilities have been founded in the New Länder and come into operation since re-unification. Some of them soon became subsidiaries of the national grid operators. In the case of Stadtwerke Leipzig, RWE Energie became a 40% shareholder. This investment was paid back in 1995, when the city of Leipzig realised that VEAG and the regional utility WESAG had priority for RWE.

When VIAG was founded 75 years ago, the holding consisted of 40 companies, including the predecessors of VAW Aluminium and SKW Trostberg. The VIAG energy subsidiary Elektrowerke AG was active in Eastern Germany, operated five major power stations and held participating interests in a number of smaller utilities. Elektrowerke became power supplier to the German railways, and in 1931 participated in founding Bewag. In 1939, VIAG acquired 50% of Bayernwerk AG from the State of Bavaria. During World War II, VIAG's interest was reduced to 40% when Bayernwerk's stock capital was increased. In the course of VIAG's privatisation in 1986–1988 Bayernwerk acquired a 25% stake in VIAG. In 1994 VIAG was able to increase its equity interest in Bayernwerk AG (Pohl, 1996).

In 1994, VIAG accomplished one of its long-held goals by increasing its interest in Bayernwerk AG from 38.9% to 95.2%. This was made possible by the privatisation policies of the Bavarian government. The State of Bavaria held 58.3% of Bayernwerk and reduced its interest in VIAG to 25.2% in return for a payment of approximately $1.3 billion. In addition, a majority interest of 82.2% in Isar-Amperwerke AG was resolved by a share exchange with RWE. Bayernwerk offered 50% of Thyssengas GmbH in return for 25.01% of Isarwerke GmbH.

The actual restructuring of the ESI was triggered primarily by the liberalisation of the European power market. In Germany, the privatisation efforts of some Länder and municipalities have provided additional impetus to the concentration process. In 1997, the most important example of privatisation efforts in Germany was the sale of a majority interest in Bewag. A consortium of PreussenElektra, VIAG and Southern Energy paid approximately $1.8 billion to the Land of Berlin.

There have been several other acquisitions and mergers in this area, including those of Vattenfall into HEW, EdF into EnBW, and the merger of VEBA/Viag and RWE/VEW.

III.B.b. Diversification and new business areas (gas, waste, telecommunications etc.)

All three of the German energy giants have expanded and diversified into a variety of subsidiary activities. While VEBA and VIAG, as the parent companies of PreussenElektra and Bayernwerk, were set up as holding companies and have been active in areas such as chemicals, non-ferrous metals, transportation and glass for decades, RWE has transformed itself, mainly over the past ten years, expanding its activities into other areas.

At a local level, gas supply has been a core activity of the Stadtwerke since the 19th century. National utilities also developed gas distribution as an additional activity: VEW, for example, became one of Germany's largest gas suppliers. In the second stage of the privatisation of the Berlin gas utility Gasag, Bewag won the bidding in conjunction with Gaz de France and was able to increase its stake in the company significantly.

In many cases, waste management and telecommunications became important ESI activities in the beginning of the 1990s.

III.B.c. Patterns and changes in ownership (including foreign investors)

The German ESI is positioned somewhere between public and private ownership (see Fig. V.4). In 1997, 468 utilities or 60.8% of a total of 770 members of the Association of German Power Stations (VDEW) were still publicly owned, which means that over 95% of the capital was owned by the federal state, the Länder or municipalities. 206 utilities of 26.7% were so-called public–private utilities, with less than 75% private and less than 95% public capital. Finally, 96 companies or 12.5% of the utilities were private, with over 75% private ownership. This structure is due to the large number of small local utilities owned by municipalities.

At the level of the national grid, the structure is different and the trend is quite unambiguous. Since the conservative–liberal government took office in 1982, the tendency has clearly been towards privatisation or reduction of public ownership. VEBA and VIAG, with their respective

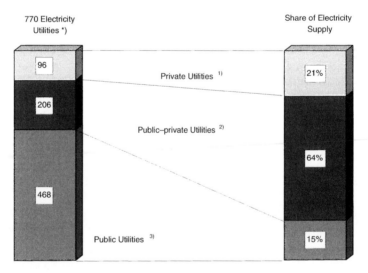

1) >75% private capital
2) <95% public and <75% private capital
3) >95% public capital (Federal government, Länder, municipalities etc.)
*) VDEW members

Fig. V.4. Ownership structure of public utilities in Germany 1997.
Source: VDEW.

electricity subsidiaries, were transformed from state enterprises to business groups of international standing.

The Federal government owned 43.75% of VEBA until 1984/85, when the investment was reduced to 25.55%. In March 1987, the Federal government sold all of its remaining shares. VEBA today has more then 400,000 stockholders. A major stockholder is the Allianz financial services group, with 10.2%.

The VIAG privatisation was also conducted in two stages. The first took place in 1986, when 40% of the capital was issued at a price of approximately ¢94 per share. The final tranche followed in 1988. VIAG held 40% of Bayernwerk's stock, and to avoid influence from undesirable third parties, the utility decided, in agreement with the VIAG management, to purchase VIAG shares on the open market. Bayernwerk acquired a 25% stake in VIAG, and in light of these cross-holdings, the two companies formed a strategic unit as the VIAG/Bayernwerk group.

RWE did not remove the multiple voting rights of municipal stockholders until April 1998. Since the hyperinflation of the 1920s, most of the municipal shares had been registered shares with a twenty-fold vote, and this had secured the voting majorities for municipal stockholders until this time. A certain proportion of RWE stocks were preferred shares, giving entitlement to preferential profit distribution but no voting rights. By transforming preferred to common shares, RWE was able to pay out approximately $0.8 billion in compensation to the cities and municipalities.

Foreign investors have tried to gain a foothold in German ESI, starting with attempts in the new Länder after re-unification. Several attempts have failed, but in the case of East Germany's second largest lignite mining company MIBRAG, an international consortium of Morrison Knudsen (USA), NRG Energy (USA) and PowerGen (UK) was able to acquire the company for approximately $1.15 billion in 1994. The lignite is contracted for use in power generation in the newly-built power stations Schkopau and Lippendorf. The 900 MW Schkopau power station is also partly owned by two of the foreign investors. VEBA Kraftwerke Ruhr AG holds 58.9% and Saale Energie GmbH 41.1%. Saale Energie GmbH is owned by PowerGen and NRG Energy with 50% each. With this deal, foreign investors broke into the German ESI for the first time. However, without a stake in any of the national grid operators, no foreign investor had a chance to win industrial customers for IPP or succeed in outsourcing projects.

A kind of breakthrough occurred in 1997, when foreign investors, together with German national grid operators, were able to purchase holdings in the two smallest national grid operators, HEW and Bewag.

The State of Hamburg reduced its interest in HEW to 50.2%. PreussenElektra and Swedish Sydkraft A/S acquired 15.4% and 21.8% of HEW respectively, while HEW invested approximately $0.7 billion to gain a cross-holding of 15.7% in Sydkraft. Until then, the Swedish utility had been a minor shareholder in VEBA with 3%, and it reduced this stake to finance the HEW investment. Moreover, PreussenElektra holds 17.6% of Sydkraft. The State of Hamburg reduced its interest in HEW to 25.1% in 1998 by selling stocks to Vattenfall.

The State of Berlin sold its majority share of Bewag to a consortium of PreussenElektra, VIAG and Southern Energy. Each of the two German companies had already held 10% of the shares (or 14.1% of voting capital). Through the deal, VIAG was able to increase its holding to 26%, while PreussenElektra had to make do with 23%, after intervention from the Federal Cartel Agency. With 26% of Bewag's capital stock, Southern Energy Holding Beteiligungsgesellschaft mbH, a subsidiary of Southern Energy Corp. (USA) was the first foreign investor to make a strategic inroad into the core business of German ESI.

VEW has ownership links to RWE and VIAG/Bayernwerk. RWE, through the subsidiary Energie-Verwaltungs-GmbH, holds 25.3% of VEW's stock shares, and Bayernwerk holds 12%, 5% of which are through Isar-Amperwerke AG. In October 1998, close co-operation was agreed between RWE and VEW, the merger was announced in 1999 and completed in 2000.

EnBW is the only national grid operator that continues to have no controlling capital links with the three large utilities. Since the merger of EVS and Badenwerk to form the EnBW, the majority interest has been owned by municipal shareholders. The major shareholder is the Zweckverband Oberschwäbische Elektrizitätswerke (OEW) with 34.8%. The Land of Baden-Württemberg owns 25.2%. Regional utilities such as Neckarwerke Stuttgart AG (8.7%) and Kraftwerkübertragungswerke Rheinfelden AG of the Elektrowatt group (2.8%) have minor stakes in EnBW.

In 1999, French EdF competed with RWE for the share of 25.01% of EnBW's stocks, owned by the Land of Baden-Württemberg. The Land sold its stocks in January 2000 for DM 4.7 bn. to EdF. The main shareholder of EnBW remains still the 'Zweckverband Oberschwäbischer Elektrizitätswerke (OEW)'.

A cross-holding between EnBW and Swiss Watt AG was established when the consortium of Nordostschweizerische Kraftwerke AG (31%), Bayernwerk (24.5%), EnBW (24.5%), and the Credit Suisse Group (20%) acquired a majority interest in Watt AG. At the end of December 1997, Elektrowatt's energy division was transferred to Watt AG.

III.B.d. Financial issues, investment patterns and relations with the stock market (profitability vs responsibility)

In the 1990s, the electricity business was crucial to the profitability of RWE, VEBA and VIAG. The major share of the holdings' profits derived from their energy subsidiaries (see Figs. IV.5 and IV.6).

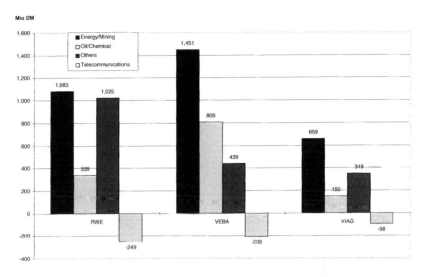

Fig. V.5. Profits of market sectors 1996.
Sources:
RWE Annual Report 1996/97, p. 95.
VEBA Annual Report 1996.
VIAG Annual Report 1996, p. 24 (AG), p. 72.

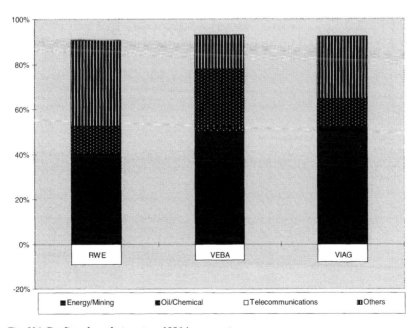

Fig. V.6. Profits of market sectors 1996 in percent.

Table V.2. Sales and cash flow of VIAG, RWE, and VEBA (in bn. DM).

	1990/91	1991/92	1992/93	1993/94	1995	1996	1997	1998
Bayernwerk Group	6.250	6.434	6.377	8.127	9.175	9.548	10.332	11.074
Bayernwerk AG	4.397	4.348	4.300	4.377	4.505	4.515	4.458	4.351

Source: Bayernwerk Annual Report 1998, pp. 76–77.

VIAG	1990	1991	1992	1993	1994	1995	1996	1997	1998
Sales	19.423	23.587	24.311	23.734	28.957	41.932	42.452		
Cash flow	1.953	2.402	2.301	2.084	3.982	4.422	4.502		

Source: VIAG Annual Report 1996, p. 78.

RWE Energie AG	1991/92	1992/93	1993/94	1994/95	1995/96	1996/97	1997/98	1998/99
Sales	16.549	16.617	16.710	16.407	16.312			
Cash flow	3.643	4.195	3.101	3.428	3.749			

Source: RWE Energie AG Annual Report 1996/97.

RWE Group	1991/92	1992/93	1993/94	1994/95	1995/96	1996/97	1997/98	1998/99
Sales	51.737	53.094	55.750	63.585	65.436	72.136		
Cash flow	7.525	7.349	8.102	8.643	8.695	8.986		

Source: RWE Annual Report 1996/97, RWE in Zahlen.

PreussenElektra Group	1991	1992	1993	1994	1995	1996	1997	1998
Sales	9.563	12.080	12.400	15.753,6	15.854,3	15.398		
Profit		890	968	1.028	1.060	1.859		

Source: PreussenElektra Annual Report 1996, p. 2.

VEBA AG	1991	1992	1993	1994	1995	1996	1997	1998
Sales		65.419	66.349	71.292	72.372	74.541		
Cash flow		6.706	7.014	7.337	8.570	8.538		

Source: VEBA Annual Report 1996.

Oil and chemicals make up the second largest block of profits, while telecommunications is still producing losses. The telecommunications divisions were sold in 2000 and gave cash for each group.

Turning to sales development, cash flow, earnings and profits, the three big utilities and their holding companies show remarkable results (see Table V.2). Between 1993 and 1996, sales by the VIAG/Bayernwerk group jumped from approximately $13.7 billion to over $24 billion.

The cash flows of the three holding companies show the independence of credit financing. In general cash flow has been greater than total investment.

PreussenElektra was able increase its profits from approximately $508 million (1992) to over $1 billion (1996).

III.C. Overview of the ESI structure and changes

Before the mergers of VEBA/Viag and RWE/VEW in 2000, the structure of the ESI in Germany was dominated by eight national grid companies—all interlinked through mutual capital holdings (see fig. V.7).

Afer the creation of E.ON and the new RWE, the core of German ESI consists of only six national grid companies. According to national and European antitrust clearance decisions, E.ON and RWE have to sell all stakes in other national grid companies (see fig. V.8).

The restructuring of the German ESI is still going on. E.ON and Sydkraft sold their shares in HEW to Vattenfall. Further, E.ON will sell the 49 percent share of Bewag to HEW, bringing this company in a favourable position to take over the majority of VEAG.

IV. Organisation of The ESI At Company Level—The Case of RWE

IV.A. Organisational model

The RWE group is a corporate group with 100 years of history. RWE's corporate strategy can be characterised as one of steadily widening and building up a gigantic power structure by way of diversification. RWE still means electricity to many consumers, and is the number one on the German electricity market. But the energy sector today makes up just one third of the group's total revenues. Other activities by the RWE holding company are mining, petroleum and chemicals, construction and civil engineering, waste management, mechanical and plant engineering, and telecommunications (Fig. V.9).

In the business year 1996/97 the RWE group, with net sales in the region of $41.2 billion, figured as the sixth largest German company. An additional $2.3 billion (approximate) was traded within the group, which employs a workforce of 137,000. The figures for the energy division were

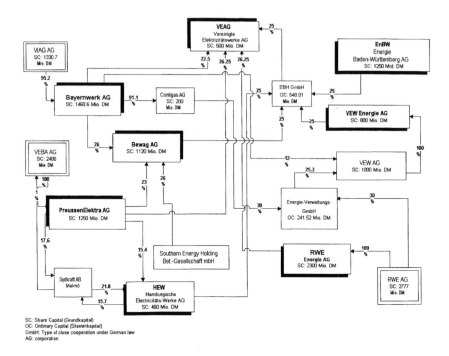

Fig. V.7. The national grid operators in Germany before the mergers.

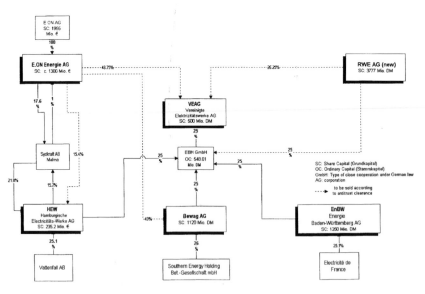

Fig. V.8. The national grid operators in Germany after the mergers.

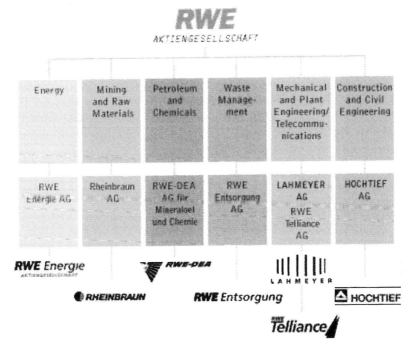

Fig. V.9. The RWE group: organisational model.

as follows (all figures approximate) total revenues $12.17 billion, cash flow $2.14 billion, and profit on ordinary activities $1.17 billion. The workforce was 20,521.

RWE had already started to diversify into other areas in the 1920s, when the Essen electricity utility acquired a minority share in the construction company Hochtief AG. In the late 1920s, RWE became stockholder in Ruhrgas AG and Frankfurter Gaswerke AG. In 1937, RWE expanded into mechanical and plant engineering, gaining a majority holding in Rheinelektra AG, which in turn had a stake in Stierlen-Werke AG (since 1974 Stierlen-MAQUET AG). And in 1940, RWE acquired a majority share of the famous manufacturer of printing presses, Heidelberger Druckmaschinen AG.

After World War II, RWE concentrated on the mining and raw materials sector, and mainly on its core activity of power generation, by founding the network power syndicate, the Deutsche Verbundgesellschaft, and by broadening its scope in the nuclear business.

Its transformation into a multi-national corporation started in the second half of the 1980s. In 1988, RWE took a decisive step towards diversification with the acquisition of Deutsche Texaco AG. A new RWE group organisation along the lines of a holding company was devised.

Friedhelm Gieske became RWE's first chairman of the board of management. Gieske and Günther Klätte, who opposed restructuring, became spokesmen of RWE's board of management in 1988. The new structure as the holding company RWE AG was adopted on 18th January 1990 at the shareholders' meeting. Five—and subsequently six—group divisions were created. The core businesses of electricity production and distribution were put together in the newly founded RWE Energie AG, and this company started operation on 1st March 1990, also taking on gas and water supply, as well as district heating.

Mining and raw materials were already concentrated within the subsidiary Rheinbraun AG. The oil business, exploration and production of petroleum and natural gas and chemicals were housed in RWE-DEA Aktiengesellschaft für Mineralöl und Chemie. A new company, RWE Entsorgung AG was founded for waste management and recycling activities.

For an intermediate period, all activities in mechanical and plant engineering were taken over by Lahmeyer AG für Energiewirtschaft and Rheinelektra AG, which in 1997 merged to become LAHMEYER AG.

The sixth division, for construction and civil engineering, was added in 1990 with the adoption of Hochtief as a subsidiary.

In September 1994, RWE grouped all of its telecommunications activities into RWE Unitel AG, later renamed as RWE Telliance AG, a part of RWE Energie AG. In 1997, RWE Telliance AG was transformed into an independent unit, and today this company, together with LAHMEYER AG and the Nukem group, is responsible for RWE's activities in mechanical and plant engineering and in telecommunications.

The new concept 'Challenge 2000'—adopted in early 1999—stands for a reversal in the corporate strategy of RWE. As a multi-utility/multi-energy corporation, RWE will concentrate in the future on energy and energy-related services. Aiming to be at the top of European energy utilities, RWE had to find a quick answer when VEBA and VIAG announced a merger of their companies on 27th September 1999. RWE tried to buy a 25% share of EnBW, but the Land of Baden-Württemberg sold its stocks to French EdF. In October 1999, the merger of RWE and VEW was announced. The new RWE views itself as an international company for energy and energy-related services at every level of the valve chain

IV.B. Organisation of new activities and new alliances

Electricity supply has been become more flexible, with increasingly individual responses to the demands of electricity customers.

Since the beginning of 1998, RWE Energie offers a bonus for special contractors. Customers with electricity bills exceeding $1.7 million receive a 5% rebate upon signing a new five-year contract. About 50% of RWE Energie's sales to special contractors goes to large customers. To keep ahead of the competition, RWE reduced its electricity prices for major electricity consumers (by international standards) in 1997. 60% of the electricity supply for Germany's ten largest electricity consumers was supplied by RWE. The company's response to liberalisation is to reduce prices and offer contracting solutions for industrial heat and power supply. Further contracts and tariffs for multi-sites and chainstore customers were developed and introduced in the beginning of 1998 (Stromthemen, 4/98, p. 2).

Since 1996, RWE has been offering customers a green tariff to promote renewable energy. In April 1998, a total of 15,000 RWE customers voluntarily paid an additional premium of approximately ¢11.5 per kWh. The company has set aside approximately $11.5 million for this program, and up to April 1998, it is estimated that 2.6 million kWh have been sold (RWE press release 29.04.1998).

EnBW kicked off the competition in the market for tariff customers in summer 1999 when the new electricity brand 'Yello' was introduced. With the formula 19/19—which stands for 19 Pfg/kWh and a monthly fee of 19 DM—Yello obtained 100,000 private households as new customers throughout Germany within several months.

The response from RWE and PreussenElektra was not long in coming; in September 1999 PreussenElektra offered the brand 'Elektra Direkt', and RWE's brand 'Avanza' was introduced in November of the same year. All national grid companies followed with branded electricity, even the niche product green electricity was paid very high attention by companies obtaining certificates for new green or ecologically-produced electricity.

Bayernwerk's hydro affiliate offers take-or-pay contracts for 'Aquastrom', where private households can use up to 4,000 kWh within one year.

IV.C. Overview of organisational changes

Most of the major electricity utilities have recently undergone far-reaching organisational change, triggered primarily by the EU-led liberalisation of the European power market. Aside from core functions such as load dispatching, power distribution and power trading, which will be handled either by the operational holding company or by service companies, generation activities at nuclear, fossil and hydro-electric plants have been consolidated in special companies.

RWE is not in favour of legally independent units within the energy group. The responsibilities of different managing directors for production, transmission and distribution were laid down in 1997. RWE chairman,

Kuhnt, argued against further changes, warning of possible problems in coordination. After the merger, the new RWE set up:

- RWE Power
- RWE Rheinbraun
- RWE Trading
- RWE Systems.

PreussenElektra concluded its organisational changes by mid-1998. The board of supervisors accepted the restructuring on March 12th 1998 (Stromthemen, 4/98, p. 2). PreussenElektra set up the following legally independent companies:

- PreussenElektra Kraftwerke AG & Co. KG, made up of Veba Kraftwerke Ruhr AG, the conventional power stations of PreussenElektra, and Braunschweigische Kohlenbergwerke AG. The installed capacity will be of the order of 12,000 MW.
- PreussenElektra Kernkraftwerke GmbH & Co. KG, holding all nuclear power stations owned by PreussenElektra and affiliates in the nuclear business.
- PreussenElektra Netz GmbH & Co. KG, responsible for the high-voltage grid.
- PreussenElektra Engineering GmbH, an engineering services company.

Bayernwerk, as first of the three giants, started operating independent companies in its electricity business on 1st January 1998.

- Bayernwerk Kernenergie GmbH (BKE) has assembled all the group's nuclear power stations (4,400 MW)
- Bayernwerk Konventionelle Kraftwerke GmbH (BKW) operates all conventional fossil-fuelled power stations (5,500 MW) in Bavaria and partially owned coal-fired power stations in Bexbach, Rostock and Lippendorf.
- Bayernwerk Hochspannungsnetz GmbH (BHN) operates the high-voltage grid.

Since 1996, all hydro-electric power stations have been gathered together under Bayernwerk Wasserkraft AG. Regional utilities affiliated to the Bayernwerk group, such as EBO, Isar-Amperwerke, OBAG, TEAG and ÜWU, will in future be solely responsible for regional distribution and marketing.

The number four of the German ESI, Energie Baden-Württemberg AG (EnBW), which was created by the merger of EVS and Badenwerk in 1997, is actively entering the competitive arena. EnBW created a business group of companies in the sectors:

- Energy and energy-related services;
- Waste disposal;
- Telecommunications;
- Land management; and
- Real estate management.

The structure of the EnBW business group tries to combine existing forces and systematic expansion by adding important partners. The following affiliates are creating the core of the business group:

- EnBW Kraftwerke AG;
- EnBW Transportnetze AG;
- EnBW Gesellschaft für Stromhandel mbH;
- EnBW Energie-Vertriebsgesellschaft mbH; and
- EnBW Regional GmbH.

EVS and Badenwerk have become regional utilities, responsible for tariff customers and distribution. EnBW has international activities in Thailand, Switzerland, Hungary, and the Czech Republic.

V. Conclusion

The liberalisation of the electricity market is favouring the expansion strategies of the energy giants. The trend towards internationalisation and globalisation of the energy business can be seen in the world-wide trading of electricity, international investment and partnership, and the higher yields. The German ESI is scarcely present at all in the strongest growth regions, such as South America and south-east Asia, and holds back from IPP activities or forging new alliances. The era of closed supply areas with a guaranteed development is over, and the future is characterised by risk and insecurity. Deregulation followed by re-regulation, and the privatisation of the ESI, will create more competition and a change in attitude towards the electricity market.

V.A. Principal patterns in Germany

The big three in the German ESI have transformed from state enterprises into company groups with international stature. Furthermore, since the early 1990s, all groups have devoted themselves to selective expansion and diversification. While the core business lines are still focused on energy supply, new business areas such as waste management and telecommunications have been built up. To keep the custom of special contractors, this group has offered new contracts with better conditions and rebates of up to 25%, and outsourcing solutions have outflanked the construction of industry-owned power stations and/or replaced outdated capacity in this sector.

The German electricity supply market is stagnating, and will continue to do so in the long run. This has led to a wave of concentration and centralisation of capital. Additional capital ownership linkages have appeared among the national grid operators. In consortia with foreign investors, PreussenElektra and VIAG/Bayernwerk have increased their interests in HEW and Bewag. RWE and VEW have initiated closer co-operation. After the announcement of the planned mergers of VEBA/VIAG and RWE/VEW, centralisation and concentration of the German ESI reached a new stage. It is predicted that the number of local electricity utilities will decrease from 900 to 200–250 by 2010.

The arrival of foreign energy companies such as NRG Energy, PowerGen, Sydkraft and Southern Energy in Germany marks a new stage in the organisation of the ESI. In 1999, Vattenfall and EdF became major stockholders of German national grid companies. The Swedish–German Vasa Energy and the Finnish Fortum group are planning to construct several gas-fired power stations at the former nuclear site Lubmin, ready for operation in 2003, and Enron was the first foreign energy company to receive a licence to supply electricity and gas in Germany after the new energy law came into force.

Using negotiated TPA, the first voluntary agreement on tariffs for third-party access slowed down many efforts to enter the market and made life difficult for new competitors. The European Commission criticised the distance price component and the comparatively high transmission fee. Since January 2000 a second voluntary agreement has been in operation, which makes third-party access easier.

Since German re-unification, an increase in activities abroad can also be observed. RWE, Bayernwerk and PreussenElektra have signed contracts with utilities, power stations and mining companies in Central and Eastern Europe. Additional activities have started in neighbouring countries such as the Netherlands, Switzerland, Austria and Scandinavia, or within the UCTE (Spain, Portugal, and Croatia). It is interesting to note that no major German utility bid was made during the privatisation process in England and Wales, while several offers have been made for an interest in Electricité de France.

V.B. Impact of commercial strategies on society and the environment

Since the restructuring of the German ESI is in progress, its impact cannot yet be determined exactly. Within the German ESI, expectations are that the strong position of the largest utilities will increase over time.

Organisational changes will be used to achieve substantial cost reductions by exploiting the opportunities offered in the liberalised electricity market. This will not only produce synergy effects but also reduce the workforce. New jobs will be created in areas where the old workforce had no competence.

To avoid loss of market share among special industrial contractors, rebates and new contracts were already on offer in late 1997, and the tariff structure has been changed to meet industrial customers' demands for transparency and flexibility. Further contracting solutions using state-of-the-art gas-fired CHP plants at industrial sites will mark a new commercial strategy in the German ESI.

If an increasing proportion of new capacity is added in the form of gas-fired power stations, the environmental impact will be positive, as the fuel is cleaner and such power stations are more efficient than condensed type plants. To date, the ESI has not been able to meet the national carbon dioxide reduction target.

Integrated resource planning and demand-side management schemes still play a subordinate role within the German ESI. After the new energy law was set in power, initiatives for energy-efficiency programmes by municipalities and for households were stopped by most utilities. Green electricity as brand found some attention, but the extent of such programmes is generally rather small.

Literature

ARE (1998) Regionale Energieversorgung 1996–1997, Hanover.

Bayernwerk AG (1999) *Geschäftsbericht 1998*, Munich.

Bundesministerium für Wirtschaft (BMWi) (1999) *Energie Daten 1999. Nationale und internationale Entwicklung*, Bonn.

Deutsche Verbundgesellschaft (1999) *Jahresbericht 1998*, Heidelberg.

EWI (1998) *Konzentration und Wettbewerb in der deutschen Energiewirtschaft. Gutachten im Auftrag des Bundesministeriums für Wirtschaft. Forschungsauftrag Nr. 46/95. Kurzfassung*, Cologne.

Energie Baden-Württemberg AG (1999) *Annual report 1998*, Karlsruhe.

Mez, Lutz & Rainer Osnowski (1996) *RWE—Ein Riese mit Ausstrahlung*, Kiepenheuer & Witsch, Cologne.

Mirrlees-Black *et al.* (1996) *Das neue deutsche Stromgeschäft. Kunden tanken Energie*, Dresdner Kleinwort Benson Research, Frankfurt am Main.

Mönig, W. *et al.* (1977) *Konzentration und Wettbewerb in der Energiewirtschaft. Aktuelle Fragen der Energiewirtschaft*, Band 10, Munich.

Monopolkommission (1976) *Mehr Wettbewerb ist möglich. Hauptgutachten 1973/1975*, Nomos, Baden-Baden. For the electricity industry see p. 382 ff.

Neue Energie, 2/2000.

Pohl, Manfred (1996) *Das Bayernwerk 1921 bis 1996*, Piper, Munich.

PreussenElektra AG (1998) *Geschäftsbericht 1997*, Hanover.

Radkau, Joachim (1998) *Das RWE zwischen Kernenergie und Diversifizierung 1968-1988*, in Schweer & Thieme (eds.), pp. 221–244.

RWE AG (1998) *Geschäftsbericht 1997/98*, Essen.

RWE Energie AG (1999) *Annual report 1998/99*, Essen.

Schiffer, Hans-Wilhelm (1999) *Energiemarkt Deutschland, 7. völlig neu bearbeitete Auflage*, TÜV Verlag, Cologne.

Schweer, Dieter & Wolf Thieme (eds.) (1998) *Der gläserne Riese: RWE - ein Konzern wird transparent*, Gabler, Wiesbaden.

Shonfield, A. (1968) *Geplanter Kapitalismus. Wirtschaftspolitik in Westeuropa und USA*, Kiepenheuer und Witsch, Cologne.

Shonfield, A. (1971) *North American and Western European Economic Policies: Proceedings Conference held by the International Economic Association*, McMillan, London.

Stromthemen, 4/1998.

VDEW (1997) *VDEW-Statistik 1996, Leistung und Arbeit*, Frankfurt am Main.

VEBA AG (1998) *Geschäftsbericht 1997*, Düsseldorf.

VIAG AG (1998) *Das Geschäftsjahr 1997*, Munich.

VKU (1997) *Geschäftsbericht 1996/97*, Cologne.

Zängl, Wolfgang (1989) *Deutschlands Strom. Die Politik der Elektrifizierung von 1866 bis heute*, Campus, Frankfurt, New York.

Chapter VI
Change and Sustainability in the French Power System: New Business Strategies and Interests versus the New *Relaxed Status Quo*

LIONEL CAURET

I. Introduction

The European Directive on electricity was adopted on the 20th June 1996, after six years of negotiation. Two different interpretations of the directive can be identified. The first one is directly determined by Article 7A of the European Union Treaty and advocates the establishment of a free market for electricity: the common market must be a space without any barrier for the circulation of persons, products and services, including electricity. The second interpretation is a direct consequence of Article 90–2 of the Treaty and enhances the defence of existing 'public services'. The French position is largely based on the second approach. But even such a restricted interpretation disturbs the national system and assumes strategic adaptations by all parties involved.

In order to reach a global consensus, the French State launched, early in 1998, a national meeting process with all the main operators, based on the following documents published in 1998: the Directive itself, the official *'livre blanc'* (the 'white book', a baseline for national negotiations), the *Dumont Report* based on interviews of main parties involved and which defends a particular future organisation, and a first Law project announcing the main positions of the State. In November 1999, after a long delay, the transcription of the Directive in the French law was still being discussed but in the final negotiations: its submission to a special Commission Mixte Paritaire (CMP) was planned for 18th November 1999. This date was decisive. The Law was finally voted in February 2000.

In order to clarify the future practical organisation as well as main adaptations induced by the Law, the author analyses these debates, the negotiating process, the new demands and emerging strategies of main parties involved in the French electric system, including EDF, self-sustaining industrials, trade unions, State and potential competitors. It details how the future competitive market and the EDF position are presently and variously perceived in France: EDF as 'the wolf in the sheepfold', as 'a dog kept on the leash among a new pack of wolves', or 'among big and small mammals living in a world in harmony'.[1] The author tries to define and to comment on the future French balance between the status quo and new claims in the power system. He questions the reality of the market opening and its mid-term sustainability, even if a large short-term uncertainty necessitates caution and the avoidance of any definitive conclusions and predictions.[2]

II. Short Overview of The Present French System

Since 1946 and the Nationalisation Law, the French electricity system has been based on the state-owned utility *Electricité de France*, which continues to be a vertically integrated public service. It is organised as a pure monopoly for transmission (over 63 kV) and importation/exportation, a quasi-monopoly for production (90%) and distribution (95%).[3] In 1998, the EDF main indicators were:

- turnover: 28.2 billion Euro
- net result: 0.32 billion Euro[4]
- production: 459.8 THw
- 82% from nuclear plants
- sales in France: 383.8 TWh
- present debt (1997): 19.4 billion Euro

---

[1] These metaphors were used by some speakers at the International conference 'Electricité, service public et concurrence: des enjeux aux solutions pour la France'—Ecole des Ponts et Chaussées, Paris—May 6–7, 1998.

[2] All monetary figures in the text are given in Euro. The exchange rates used are: 1 Euro = FF 6.55 and US$ 1 = FF 5.5.

[3] With 98 GW installed, EDF represents 94% of the total capacity and 95% of the electricity sales. There are 140 independent distributors representing between 5% and 10% of the total consumption, mainly based in rural areas, but also in a few towns such as Belfort, Strasbourg and Grenoble.

[4] Compared to 0.9 billion Euro in 1996. This decrease was the result of the tariff reduction by 4.6% in April 1997 and by a warm winter which limited the power consumption for heating. The 1998 results could be low, partly because some nuclear plants have been switched off for technical reasons and replaced by classical thermal plants.

- customers in France: 29.8 million
- customers abroad: 15 million
- employees (1997): 116.462

Concerning power generation and according to the 1946 Law, four types of power stations could be owned by producers other than EDF:

1. industrial self-generation units, integrated in the industrial process (steam, gas and heating systems), without any power limitation;
2. urban-waste power plants without any power limitation (since 1949) and district heating plants owned by local authorities (since 1980);
3. small independent power units with an annual output lower than 12 GWh or an installed capacity lower than 8 MW; and
4. some large units, owned by local authorities or industries before 1946 and mainly used to satisfy their own needs (if they did not disturb the public network).

Because the nationalisation law made EDF the only operator allowed to sell electricity to customers, EDF has since been obliged by Law to purchase the power in excess from other producers. The 1955 Law defined these purchase conditions, which applied until 1995. Such purchase prices are indirectly based on EDF tariffs for customers minus the distribution costs,

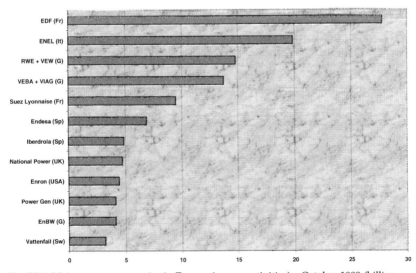

Fig. VI.1. Main power companies in Europe (power activities)—October 1999 (billion FF).

i.e. on long term avoided costs,[5] as the article 27 of the convention of 27th November 1958 explains.

Since 1946, the French power system (and some other public services) has also been based on a series of principles which defines the notion of public service in France. Some of them appear irrevocable as social tools for equity, others are questioned in the present debate:

1. Obligation of supply: whatever his location, a person or entity must be supplied with power as soon as he wants.
2. Continuity of supply.
3. Tariff equalisation: for a given type of customer, tariffs are uniform throughout the country.
4. Supply at least cost: the utility must supply the cheapest kWh possible.
5. *'Spécialité'*: the utility, mainly the distributor, is not authorised to develop activities which are not directly relevant to its power activities. It must maintain its development in a limited number of activities defined by the State.[6] As a consequence, the sector is composed of EDF as the quasi-unique power supplier and by more than 35,000 atomized firms for installation, maintenance etc.
6. *'Mutabilité'*: this principle obliges a public service company to continuously adapt its service supply to the changing needs of customers.

Table VI.1. Production/consumption of electricity in France, 1995.

Net Production 1995 (TWh)		Consumption 1995 (TWh)	
EDF	427.0		
CNR	17.4	Total low voltage:	145.5
Charbonnage de France	8.6	Supplied by EDF: 137.1	
SNCF	1.4	Total high voltage:	222.6
Other producers supplying to the grid	6.3	Supplied by EDF: 203.8	
		Export:	72.7
Chemicals	2.9	Import:	2.8
Steel	1.3	Losses:	29.4
Other industrials	6.3	Pumping:	4.2
Total	471.2	Total	477.2

Source: DGEMP, 1997.

---

[5] I.e. what the firm should have invested by its own for new plants and supply power.
[6] I.e. EDF is not yet allowed to compete in some markets such as cabling or cartography, but is allowed to take on part of the waste management in France.

We will see that the principle of *'spécialité'* and the defence of the least cost planning based on a long-term approach are two of the most questioned points the debate: upholding these points in the face of implementation of deregulation creates several regulatory dilemmas for the State.

Another main feature of the French system is the assumed existence of a societal convention sustaining its development for more than five decades. This supposed convention results from an efficient interplay and common objectives between the three main institutional parties involved in the power field over the period: the State, the utility and the trade unions, complemented by a general acceptance by the French people. It is the reason why the technical and economical analysis are not sufficient to understand some features of the national power system (Poppe & Cauret, 1997). Firstly, the French State has a long tradition of direct involvement in the economy, supported by an historical trust in its role. Secondly, dominated by the engineers' thought and deeply rooted in the elitist system of 'State Corps',[7] the decision-making process for energy is highly centralised, closed, naturally more inclined to implement cost-effective large power facilities within a long-term view under monopoly (dams, then nuclear) than to manage small power plants under competition. Reconstruction of the country after World War II, security of supply, energy planning and social transfers such as price equalisation have been the main priorities imposed by the State and were successfully implemented by the State-owned utility EDF. At the same time, the utility remains a symbol of the social gains of the 1950s and 1960s, with the development of new models of employment, wage policies, and retirement plans. Trade unions have been very active in these evolutions They now increasingly defend this concept of public service for customers and for employees since EDF–GDF is one of the last strongholds within the working class and the economy. All these reasons explain why electricity in France is not perceived just as a simple commodity, but also as an economic tool, a social symbol and a source of national pride.

III. From the Pure Single Buyer to Regulated Third-Party Access

In 1991, the first European project proposed pure Third-Party Access (TPA), with an unbundling of operations and the creation of a pool. The 'transporter' should become just a service provider outside the market, neither a buyer nor a seller. Producers were free to plan their investments and allowed to negotiate directly with consumers. France advocated at first another model, the principle of the pure 'single buyer/single supplier'.

---

[7] The *Corps des Mines* and *X-Mines* engineers are notably leading the Ministry of Industry, EDF and the French nuclear industry.

This alternative imposes an unique entity for managing the grid. This entity is also the unique buyer in its zone of activities. That means that even if a large customer can sign direct contracts with suppliers of its choice, the grid manager of the region buys this contractual electricity and integrates it in its own generation system. The main arguments given by French authorities to defend this position were:

1. the defense of the long-term planning for the supply side (nuclear plants are cost-effective with a long pay-back period);
2. the fact that theory legitimises the monopoly for efficiently balancing supply and demand, and optimising dispatch;
3. the necessity to maintain the mission of public service.

Finally, France relaxed its position and agreed to adopt the regulated TPA, under which a supplier can use the grid for transporting its power to its customers in exchange of the payment of a fee publicly announced to the grid manager. The European Directive for electricity, signed in June 1996 included these alternatives and enlarged the initial range of options for each country:

1. The possibility of imposing the missions of public service such as supply security, quality, regularity, tariffs and environmental criteria (Art. 3.2).
2. The possibility of imposing the long-term planning (Art. 3.2), eventually coupled with a bidding system (Art. 6) or an administrative system of authorisation for new plants (Art. 5).
3. The possibility for each country to choose between the regulated TPA, which gives a fixed transmission price for each supplier (Art. 17), the case-by-case TPA (or negotiated TPA) which allows a negotiated transmission price for each supplier (Art. 18), and the 'single buyer' (Art. 16).
4. The possibility of enlarging the initial range of customers eligible to choose their supplier (Art. 19).
5. The possibility of integrating environmental constraints and criteria (Art. 8.3).
6. A safety clause concerning countries that open their market more than obliged by the Directive, in order to limit the potential importation of kWh (Art. 19.5).

The range of combinations can be large from one country to another (principle of subsidiarity). Note that there is no obligation to set up a new entity for managing the grid. But other items must be implemented whatever the country: the unbundling or separating of activities of an integrated utility in order to avoid cross-subsidies and other potential advantages given by its dominant position (Art. 14); the right for large customers over 100 GWh to choose suppliers; the clear identification of the grid manager and the progressive implementation of competition (Art. 19 and 25).

IV. Potential Impacts of the Directive in France

IV.A. Distribution: no change

French municipalities are the franchising authorities for electricity distribution. They delegated this activity for fifty years mainly to EDF or to small local distributors (municipal power corporations in a few rural areas and towns). This horizontally-integrated organisation of the distribution with local monopolies will not change, mainly to prevent any rush to profitable industrial and urban areas and any desertion of rural locations.

IV.B. Transmission: a reinforced but controlled role for EDF

With the 'regulated TPA' option, a fully vertically-integrated utility (P-T-D)[8] can be maintained. In France's case, it means that EDF keeps all its activities, notably transmission: the high-voltage grid remains a pure monopoly managed by the state-owned utility via the GRTE (Gestionnaire Réseau Transport Electricité), the new EDF's entity in charge of the grid management, and supposed to be independent of other EDF's activities. This grid management means more than just the role of service supplier. It also implicates the short-term management of the national and regional dispatching and the utility participation to the long-term energy planning of the country. On the other hand, the utility will be obliged to transport electricity from a producer to its own customers, for a transmission fee that is fixed in advance and which represents the real transmission cost. That assumes an effective unbundling and clarity to fix this price.

IV.C. Production: a new competition for some eligible customers

Article 19 of the Directive fixes minimal conditions for eligibility. In France, their implementation concerns 400 eligible industrial customers in the first step (> 40 Gwh/yr), plus 400 in the second step (> 20 GWh), and then another 1700 in 2003 (> 9 GWh). About 30% of the French electricity market is potentially affected by the competition imposed by the European Directive.

The Directive has, in principle, the following major consequences in France: larger customers can choose their suppliers; private and/or

---

[8] Production, Transmission and Distribution.

Table VI.2. Eligibility for competition in France.

	Consumption level imposed by Art. 19 for eligibility	France's eligible customers	Cumulative share in EDF turnover
1st January 1999	> 40 GWh	~ 400 customers Iron, steel, cement and mechanical industries	25%
1st January 2000	> 20 GWh	~ 400 customers Food industries, electronics, chemical companies	30%
1st January 2003	> 9 GWh	~ 1700 customers Biggest medium-sized firms, airports, some hospitals and stores	33%

foreign IPPs are allowed to sell electricity to eligible customers and to use the grid for transmission under declared fees; such authorisations and eventually the bidding process will be integrated into the national supply planning managed by the regulator; the unbundling imposes the accounting separation of the EDF activities. The obligation for EDF to buy excess power generated by auto-producers from renewable, urban-waste power plants and combined heat power units is maintained, under conditions.

V. Existing Competition in the French Power Sector

Competition is not totally new in the French electricity market but does not directly concern the power supply. Its forms in some niches (final energies, self generation, exports) are unique compared to those existing in other countries.

V.A. Competition between every types for some end-uses

On one side, the national policy of energy independence has reduced oil usage and pushed the consumption of nuclear kWh. On the other side, the nuclear overcapacity since the 1980s obliged EDF to sell more kWh and to adopt a strategy for boosting demand. Competition between energies (gas, electricity and fuel) for competitive end-uses (heating, water heating, air-conditioning and for some processes in industry) increased significantly for two decades. The market success of gas and fuel heating over the five last years has forced EDF to reinforce its strategy (see below).

As defined in Cauret (1997), the EDF strategies have always been adapted to demand variations. Until 1974, EDF just followed supply-side objectives by sizing grid and plants in order to answer to the natural growth of the demand. This growth was lead by the captive markets of electricity. Between 1974 and 1982 (Fig. VI.2.a), two new priorities appeared for the utility: the nuclear program for national energy independence and, as a direct consequence, the management of the overcapacity generated by this program.[9] EDF needed to reduce this gap between demand and supply and developed new markets for electricity such as space heating, water-heating and new industrial uses. Between 1982 and 1987 (Fig. VI.2.b), the national energy demand (including electricity) slowed significantly as a consequence of the economic crisis. The competition became stronger in this saturated energy market. EDF needed to change its strategy from a simple supply logic to policy focused on the technical. The network was improved over the period, permitting a better supply (less power cuts and lower voltage variations). Between 1987 and 1996 (Fig. VI.2.c), the EDF environment definitely changed. The end of the nuclear program showed a high debt level. Electricity export then became an efficient way for starting to clear the debt and for managing

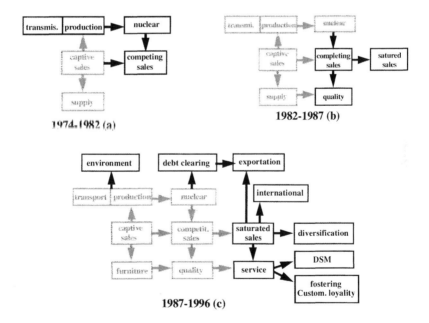

Fig. VI.2. Evolution of EDF priorities and strategies.
Source: Cauret (1997).

[9] For Hourcade (1991), this overcapacity was the combined consequence of at least two events: the failure of the demand prediction by EDF and the necessity to impose a rhythm of plant implementation higher than that of real needs in order to meet scale effects.

the power surplus. They were also a new challenge for employees joining new EDF activities abroad and diversification in the country. In the electricity saturated market, the technical improvements of the previous period were followed by the development of new services including DSM programs. We can now summarise all these periods: to supply kWh only until 1974; to reduce overcapacity by conquering market shares with competing uses of electricity (1974–1987); to react to the saturated market (1987–1996); to prepare the market opening (1996–1999). In the following figures, objectives shown in bold are the priorities of each period, those in grey are the priorities of the previous periods.

If the expected freer market pushes EDF to reinforce its efforts for supplying new services to industry, these efforts have been already developed previously for competitive end-uses. Figures also remind us that whatever the power system you manage, you must take into account previous choices to implement future strategies.

V.B. Self generation[10]

Independently of the Directive, the self-generation by industrials and private-owned distributors is expected to increase due to the lower gas prices. Furthermore, the current threshold of 8 MW imposed on self-generation has been increased by the State for power generation from renewable, urban-waste power plants and combined heat and power units. EDF is obliged by the 1946 Law to buy the power produced in excess by self-sustaining industrials.[11] These enforced purchases were based on tariffs defined each year by the State. As allowed by the May 1955 decree on electricity in case of overcapacity, this obligation was temporarily suspended on 23rd January 1995 for new projects of self-generation units, except for self-generated power from renewable, waste-fired plants and combined heat and power units (decree of 20th May 1994).

The case of CHP units is exemplary, even if its development in France is still very low compared to other countries. In 1994, only 570 CHP units (3,000 MW) were operated, mainly in industry. CHP potential is estimated by officials to be between 5,000 and 10,000 MW, over 15,000 MW by equipment suppliers.

Until 1997, when EDF purchased power in excess by self-sustaining producers, the tariffs used were calculated without taking into account real avoided costs.

A collaborative process between the French Ministry of Industry, EDF, GDF, CHP suppliers and other experts was launched in the mid 1990s.

---

[10] Industrials generating by themselves the power they need.
[11] The other distributors have the same obligation in their area.

It allowed producers to fix in March 1997 new temporary conditions (over 1997 and 1998) concerning tariffs, more favourable to CHP development (Batail, 1997b). These new conditions were based on a long-term view integrating technical alternatives such as gas turbine with combined cycle. This new calculation allowed a more attractive financial assessment of CHP projects. Furthermore, the purchase prices proposed by EDF to each supplier were determined by contract over the first 12 years. This allowed better assessment of the competitiveness of each CHP project than before. Finally, a CHP generator was authorised to sell to EDF 100% of its generation, and not just its power in excess. Some other advantages for CHP projects were introduced; including no tax on oil or gas over the five first years and a bonus for energy efficiency.[12] These new conditions for CHP were so attractive that the objectives fixed for the first five years (2000 MW of new CHP units) have been realised during the first year, *via* an aggressive policy of equipment suppliers such as Vivendi and Suez-Lyonnaise. Strongly criticised by EDF, these temporary conditions were suspended in December 1998, and just a few of them were implemented again on mid-March 1999. Large uncertainties exist for 2000 and 2001 concerning tax, power threshold for the purchase obligation of EDF (presently 8 MW; 12 or 20 MW in the future). Whatever the reason, we affirm that such a stop-and-go policy is not favourable to any smooth industrial development.

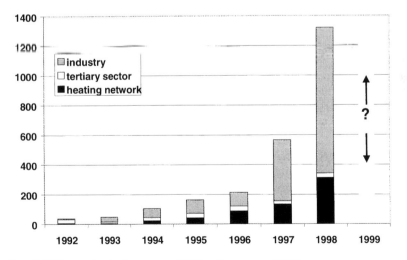

Fig. VI.3. New authorized projects of CHP units per year (MW).

---

[12] 0.02 FF/kWh when energy efficiency is over 65%, with a maximum 600,000 FF per year; 0.01 FF between 55% and 65%, with a maximum 300,000 FF per year. Note that the same evolutions were expected for developing self-generated power from renewable sources.

V.C. Competition abroad with imports/exports of electricity

A kind of competition exists for electricity exportation. EDF exports around 65 TWh per year for a turnover of 2.5 billion Euro, with various impacts depending on the different level of competition from one country to another: spot activities in Great Britain; semi-spot activities in Italy; long-term contracts in Germany and Switzerland (most of them ended between 2005 and 2010). An unresolved question exists concerning the EDF export: what is the real profitability of these power exports? What is the relation between the kWh price proposed and the real supply cost? In 1996, following the pessimistic estimations of INESTENE (1996) on this gap, this question was asked by representatives at the Parliament, but they received no answer from the power sector.

VI. New Role of The Eligible Industrial Customers: Influencing Buyers, Self-generators or Sellers

Usually, the main stake for industrial customers is the improvement of their competitiveness. Concerning their power needs, three different alternatives exist for the industrial customers:

1.   they purchase electricity;
2.   they invest to guarantee self-sustainability (power and/or heat);
3.   they sell the excess power and/or heat produced to the grid or to other close industrials.

Note that choices 2 and 3 can sometimes be compatible with the utility strategy when self-generation is a method for reducing electricity demand during the high-peak periods. For instance, with the French 'EJP' tariffs, large customers happily switch off some appliances during peak days when requested by the utility, in exchange for cheaper off-peak kWh.

But for industry, the energy decisions don't mean just a reduction of the energy bill. They implicate a global industrial optimisation. The case of Air Liquide, the world leader for industrial gases such as hydrogen and oxygen (40 billion Euro in 1998), is a good example. It consumes 5.5 TWh per year in Europe and 80 of its sites could be directly eligible. It produces on its own 4.8 TWh per year (combined heat and power units) and sells excess power to the grids or directly to customers when it is allowed by law. It is clear that its competitiveness and decisions do not depend just on the electricity bill, but on its strategies, which implicate important industrial choices such as:

- locating the new production sites;
- transporting electrons or molecules;
- choosing between gas and electricity;
- buying electricity or developing self-generation; and
- selling heat, power and/or energy services and/or utilities.

As Chevalier (1997b) writes, competition can make the energy decision contagious. Elf Atochem renegotiated its electricity bill with EDF as soon as the competing Teesside project was operational. The new industrial expectations enlarge the range of services they want to receive from the same supplier: multi-site tariffs, energy audit and optimisation, process efficiency, project financing, industrial waste management, externalisation of maintenance. With the Directive, their energy needs and demands become more influential. They have indirectly conditioned the national debates and changes in the suppliers' strategies.[13] In the French case, the industrial goals quickly generated different demands concerning the future organisation of the power market:

1. Which would be eligible, an industrial factory or an industrial firm as a whole? In some cases, such as Air Liquide, each site of the company is eligible. But what will happen for large industrial customers without any are site eligible by itself?
2. The traditional power sector must be able to answer to the new industrial expectations (quality, more flexible contracts, multi-services etc.), otherwise industrials will change their suppliers or their location.
3. An institution should be precisely identified for clarified accounting control of the transmission price announced by EDF, but also for regulating contracts between suppliers and eligible customers.
4. The transmission cost should not integrate expenses which are not directly linked to the power transmission. It also means the disappearance of 'tax at the frontier' and of the tariff depending on distance.
5. With the development of the European gas network, the competition between energies will be reinforced. Better rules concerning the link between natural gas, power generation and competition should be defined. This point invites EDF and GDF to transform the present competition into a future alliance for supplying multi-utilities.

---

[13] In February 1999, one site of the major French iron & steel maker Usinor, with an annual energy bill around 300 M ECU, announced its decision to buy power henceforth from Air Liquide instead of EDF. In March, the Principality of Andorra gave up EDF and signed a new contract with Endesa. Also in March, three eligible sites of Shell asked EDF for details of its price for power transportation.

VII. Strategies of Electricité de France (EDF) in Facing the European Market

As the President of EDF declared on 23rd October 1998 (Gallois, 1998), EDF has defined high objectives for its future: keep its competitiveness high and become a real industrial firm, the first *energetic firm* in Europe with a larger range of activities in order to counteract new potential competitors. But in such a large firm, points of view are not uniform between departments. Each department interprets the Directive with its own vision and interests. Not all of them are covered in this chapter. For instance, financial and juridical issues concerning future trading or contracts are not analysed. Instead we look at the main changes which are particular to the French system. Hence, we have identified, maybe subjectively, the following themes:

1. the new industrial project including the defence of the long-term planning, the new relationships with equipment industries and the diversification in France and abroad;
2. the new commercial objectives including tariff reductions, new services for fostering customers' loyalty and enlarged partnerships with local authorities; and
3. the firm's organisation, including the new internal management, the achievement of its total autonomy and the sharing of particular social costs. The integrated company is becoming an industrial group.

VII.A. A new industrial project

VII.A.a. Defence of long-term planning

The cost-effectiveness officially claimed by the French system supplied is the result of long-term planning, based on a constant industrial partnership between the main parties involved and supported by a clear State policy. Concerning the nuclear program, EDF maintains that the partnership over a long-period with the same suppliers (Framatome and Alsthom) has allowed the global nuclear competitiveness. Such a long term appreciation is still defended by the utility while potential bidding system and authorisations as predicted by the Directive could favour the short-term evaluation and smaller plants. The Dumont report (1998) gave the same analysis. The objective of Art. 3 of the Directive allows this approach. It is clear that EDF and the State will defend the same global long-term view for avoiding any heterogeneous group of nuclear plants and the cancellation of economy of scale. Furthermore, as Hourcade (1991) and Boisson *et al.* (1998) explain, the cost efficiency of a new type of nuclear plant is highly dependent on the national program implemented (number of plants and speed of building). That is a particularity of the nuclear line, the other types of plants being more dependent on the international market and so more flexible. And we have seen previously that it induced the French overcapacity. Concerning the official cost-effectiveness, let us add that independent experts have never had real access to central data for a complete independent evaluation. Announced values are just produced by the State and EDF. But some alternative surveys have tried progressively to qualify this affirmation (Finon, 1989) on surgeneration; INESTENE, 1998 on indirect subsidies). They suggest a lower cost-effectiveness than that officially claimed.

But the most important change in the future could be the increased use of gas instead of the quasi-unique nuclear line.[14] The present and future technical and cost efficiencies of the gas and coal lines are major arguments for EDF to implement in the future a new balance between kWh from nuclear, gas and coal units in order to maintain its competitiveness. In 1999, estimations of the future kWh cost from gas and nuclear generations, calculated by the DIGEC (Ministry of Industry), were equal in several scenarios. In this case, we can surely forecast a growing temptation by EDF for a closer partnership with GDF (see below). Whatever these economical issues, most experts expect a lower share of nuclear power in the future than at present. Note that EDF does not want to become in the future just a nuclear operator and to give up the small plants to the other operators. This situation would be financially unsustainable.

VII.A.b. New relationships with equipment industries

The long-term view is also applied with all the equipment suppliers. EDF spends an average of 8 billion Euro per year on equipment and maintenance services concerning production, transmission and distribution. Its technical and commercial abilities are absolutely necessary to allow at the end cheap kWh and high quality of supply. Vagneux (1996) explains that until now, EDF used to negotiate long-run contracts with French industrial partners. Almost all its equipment suppliers were French but we can wonder if they were numerous enough to permit an effective competition between them. Whatever the answer, EDF had organised a close control of their technical options and of their R&D. In counterpart, the growth of electricity demand allowed a high level of orders by EDF. Today, the opening of such equipment/service markets and the international merging of

---

[14] The present nuclear plant give to EDF a strong advantage with low costs. But with the future replacements, gas alternatives could be cheaper. Potential competitors are yet totally involved in these alternatives and could take advantages in the future if EDF remained only in the nuclear field (Boisson *et al.*, 1998).

businesses in the equipment sector are changing the market rules (Salaün, 1994).[15] EDF is now obliged to find new suppliers worldwide in order to preserve competition between suppliers and also to respect new European rules. Some new risks for the utility appear: less control on R&D; less technical cooperation with suppliers and more opportunities for them to impose equipment developed in-house; potential alliances among suppliers to conquer new markets with dumping strategies to the detriment of quality. Facing the new force of the equipment suppliers which have more power to impose their conditions, EDF is obliged to reorganise its relationships with industry. That is why the utility has implemented in the mid-90s new evaluating processes such as the *'programmes d'examen d'aptitude'* (PEA) in order to better evaluate the abilities of each potential supplier to conceive and to provide equipment in total accordance with its needs. But because of inertia, the utility advocates a progressive implementation of the new rules imposed by the Directive.

VII.A.c. Diversification of activities

The temptation of diversification appeared early in the 1990s as a potential way to pose new challenges and to motivate the employees facing the national slowing of electricity demand. Later, as for internationalisation, this temptation became a necessity for counteracting the building of multi-utility firms. Since 1991, EDF has wanted to use its knowledge and abilities in derived fields such as engineering, HVAC engineering, energy services, cartography, telecommunication, cabling and waste management. But EDF is presently an *EPIC*:[16] its missions are strictly defined by the State and it is obliged to respect the principle of *spécialité* which limits its activities irrelevant to the power sector. The utility keeps advocating its suspension, or at least its relaxation. But in 1995, the Council of State has not allowed EDF to develop activities in cartography, household automation and cabling. The main argument was and remains that the sudden arrival of a so large a company could develop unfair competition in such markets composed presently by small-sized private companies and craftsmen. Diversification remains thus limited: EDF is obliged to create subsidiaries to pursue such activities, in order to avoid any internal cross-subsidies; and its derived activities are authorised just for public lighting (*via* CITELUM), water distribution and urban waste management (*via* TIRU), and some other subsidiaries mainly for engineering (*via* SDS, Gogétherm, Charth, Seychaux & Metz, Game, etc.).

---

[15] See the European Directive 'excluded sectors' 93–38, 14th June 1993 and the WTO Agreement of 15th April 1994 concerning the state-owned firms.

[16] *Etablissement Public à caractère Industriel et Commercial.* Consequently, EDF has a low capitalisation without any concordance with its real value.

Officially, authorised diversified activities are defined as those which improve the EDF power services. But they also coincide with markets where powerful competitors such as Vivendi and Suez-Lyonnaise are present.[17] The purchase of the French equipment/service firm Clémessy by EDF/Cogéma/Siemens (vs GTIE/Vivendi) is a good example of this diversification.[18] However, Clémessy created a (political) problem: 30% of its turnover is turned to customers which are non-eligible in the first and second phases of the Law. The principle of *spécialité* is then questioned once again.

VII.B. *New commercial objectives*

VII.B.a. *Fostering of small and large customers' loyalty with new multi-utility services beyond the meter*

As a direct consequence of the previous point, EDF wants to become a multi-service supplier and be allowed *to go beyond the meter* (which is forbidden at the present time), for supplying all services supplied by other emerging suppliers. In the residential sector, it is also a way to re-capture market share lost during the last few years for heating and water heating (EDF, 1998c). As Boîteux (1996) says,[19] *'our utility [EDF] will resist the destructive pressures only if the customers will side with it'*. That requires EDF to keep loyal existing customers for competitive uses and attract new customers with new direct services.

Hence, since 1987, the improvement of the supply quality for low-voltage customers is a priority (see Fig. VI.4). More recently, new services have been proposed: improved real-time pricing, a few DSM actions, advisory services for energy efficiency, packaged services, labels as *Vivrélec* for residential heating, commitment for higher service quality, extended opening time for offices. But the domestic customers' satisfaction grows too slowly (EDF, 1998a) and the electrical space heating loses market shares for several years: the policy of *market recovery by quality* will be reinforced with a focus on heating (EDF, 1998c).[20] In fact, the EDF strategy remains strictly focused on space heating (EDF, 1999).[21]

---

[17] In January 1999 EDF sold its subsidiary Videopole, working in TV cabling.

[18] Clémessy supplied power equipment and services to 17% of the French eligible industrials and to 500 large customers in Germany.

[19] Marcel Boîteux was the EDF President in the early 1980s. He is also considered as the *father* of the French tariffs based on marginal costs.

[20] In the *firm project* (EDF, 1998c), the demand-side management for small customers is not mentioned. The development of the competing uses of electricity (heating and cooling) is the unique objective. The development of electric heating in France was criticised for a long time (it meant low investment, very high power bills and social problems of unpaid bills).

[21] Space heating adds in 1998 4.3 billion Euros into the total EDF turnover, the same amount than that of the total eligible industrials.

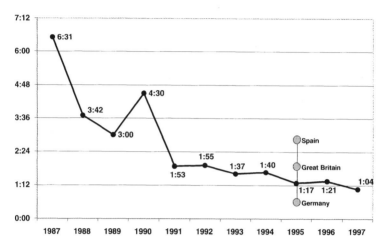

Fig. VI.4. Average duration (hours) of power cut for EDF low-voltage customers. *Source*: EDF, 1997a & 1998a.

Concerning the commercial sector, a service supply adapted to each type of customer is developed, such as *Offres Amplitudes Tertiaires* for schools and *Accès Professionnel* for craftsmen and retail merchants. New services are also available for industrial customers such as *Emeraude* (quality), 100% PME-PMI and the club *Partenariat France*[22] for medium-sized firms and *Emeraude* contracts for the larger customers. New tariffs for industrial customers, including multi-site tariffs, are also implemented.

One of the main changes could be the supply of new services combining power and gas utilities for industrial customers. EDF will supply multi-site tariffs to some of these. As the President of EDF declared on 23rd October 1998, EDF is inclined to develop closer synergies with Gaz de France (GDF).[23] Combined heat and power units and decentralised units, both using gas as combustible, shall be cost-efficient alternatives in some cases for large industrial consumers and EDF wants to be able to supply such alternatives. A better control on gas trading and gas/power prices would be a strong advantage in the future market. Hence, EDF could gain a public image no longer based on atomic power but on multi-energies. Another way is to keep developing partnerships with

---

[22] 50 larger French firms, including EDF, are involved in this club in order to advise medium-sized firms that want to develop their activities abroad.

[23] EDF and GDF have some common administrative departments such as the management of human resources and commercial offices in direct contact with small and medium customers (a customer receives a single bill for power and gas). But the two state-owned firms are strictly separate and are strongly and aggressively competing, each of them being managed by its own staff and following its own strategies.

industrial manufacturers and installers for a common promotion of the electricity alternatives and the improvement of the equipment and service supplies. Local partnership with industry for developing new processes can be another way to foster the industrial customer's loyalty. As an example, EDF, Péchiney and Alcatel are involved in a common research project for developing a new technology of 400 kV cabling, able to be installed on existing transmission infrastructures without any adaptation and allowing a 10% reduction of Joule losses.[24]

VII.B.b. Closer partnerships with local authorities
The utility tries to reinforce its relationships with local authorities, which are discreet but central parties involved in the power sector while also being large customers themselves, franchising authorities for distribution and sometimes self-sustaining producers (micro-hydraulics notably). The definition of the new concession contract (1992) between local authorities and distributors—which reactivated municipalities' responsibilities and included higher quality of service and local environmental goals—the multi-service expectation (public lighting, waste management etc.) and the agreement for progressively underlying HV lines confirm their central role. They expect new services, which must be respected. EDF also implemented actions for social measures concerning low-income families and young unemployed persons, and involved itself with a series of local programmes for developing economic activities in poorer areas. Why such a strategy targeting the local authorities? Several reasons explain this effort:

1. Closer relationships with local authorities can certainly offer powerful local allies to EDF which allow the counterbalancing of some State expectations.
2. Each project for the implementation of new HV transmission lines is increasingly questioned and faces the amplified reluctance of local people as well as the local politicians. As a consequence, EDF must clearly justify today the function and the necessity of such projects, which was not necessary for a long time. This could be a major problem in the future for the grid manager.
3. Furthermore, the water companies Suez-Lyonnaise and Vivendi are very familiar with local issues in other competing markets (water, waste etc.) and could convince municipalities to lobby for becoming eligible customers, then choosing their power suppliers. Hence, closer relationships with local authorities is the best way for EDF to guarantee the *status quo* in the distribution pole.

---

[24] The overcost is balanced by the reduction of losses.

VII.B.c. Tariff reduction

Even if price reduction was for a long time a strategic goal for EDF and an obligation imposed by the mission of public service, this reduction is accelerated,[25] with the agreement of the State. These reductions at first benefit the larger customers, next medium-sized ones, and finally smaller ones.[26] It looks like the usual strategy of a monopoly faced with a new market contestability. Another point concerns the structural evolution of tariffs. French tariffs are based on the marginal development cost of new power units. Because of the future gas alternative (semi-base) and lower oil prices, the gap between summer and winter tariffs, and between off-peak tariffs and peak period tariffs will be reduced.[27] Finally, the tariff structure would be simplified in order to become a new commercial tool easier to understand by customers (EDF, 1998c).

VII.C. New internal organisation and sharing of social issues

VII.C.a. Reaching a growing autonomy

EDF wants to be autonomous in order to achieve a real industrial strategy in France and abroad. All four-year contract plans since 1984 and company contracts since 1996 between the utility and the State have improved this situation step by step. The last contract gives the utility a real autonomous management in exchange for negotiated performance goals oriented by the European expectations. It clarifies medium-term objectives for the utility: development of a method for calculating transmission price, tariff reduction; implementation of the unbundling; improvement of services to customers; international development; new clarified financial rules between the State and the utility; additional environmental criteria and social policies. In order to avoid rivalry between the EDF's president and the general director, who were until 1998 appointed by the Council of Ministers, the 1946 Law was modified in November 1998: the EDF's president is allowed to appoint by himself the members of his board. But a growing autonomy also means financial autonomy. In January 1998, the State allowed the increase of EDF owned capital from 3.7 billion Euro

---

[25] In current Francs: −4.6% in 1997, −2.8% in 1998; in constant Francs: −6% in 1997, −14% between 1997 and 2000.

[26] The last tariff reduction since 1st May 1998: −1.9% for small customers, −4.3% for medium-size customers and −2.2% for industrials.

[27] This gap reduction, requested by the State, has already started. For instance, the price ratio between most expensive hours and cheapest hours was reduced by 30% in 1997 for *'tarifs verts'* (tariffs charged to larger customers).

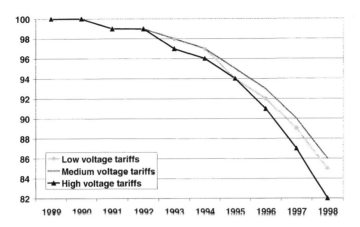

Fig. VI.5. Evolution of EDF tariffs.
Source: EDF, 1998b.

to 12.6 billion Euro in order to be closer to the real financial power of the state-owned firm. The obligation for EDF to purchase self-generated power in excess from IPPs is another point: the conditions have been strongly varied for several years and remain highly questioned. The utility would like to remove this obligation.

VII.C.b. Restructuring of the firm

The utility organisation keeps being improved to be closer to customers than before and more reactive to market evolutions in France and abroad. The Department for Strategic and Commercial Development, created in 1988, was dismantled in 1996 and replaced by the Department of Development. Its commercial expertise was shared between different departments. But these changes were just superficial. The global strategic policy of the firm remained divided between departments, which defended their respective prerogatives. And main decisions were sometimes imposed by the most influent directors, not by the most pertinent ones. The firm structure did not fit the new environment. Internal inertia, partly caused by the rivalry between the EDF president Alphandery and the executive staff during Alphandery's period in office (1995–1997), have significantly delayed the necessary reorganisation of the utility.

In 1998, the new staff launched a reform in order to correct this (EDF, 1998c). The new frame is henceforth based on two main blocks: one in charge of all the activities concerning customers (in France and abroad, small and large customers, strategy, service supply etc.), and one regrouping all the industrial activities (building, maintenance and operation for equipment, generation, transmission, distribution, R&D, engineering).[28] The global organisation is then expected to move from management by means to management by aims. An homogeneous and more efficient commercial strategy could appear from such a simplified organisation. It will be more easily diffused throughout the firm. For instance, all the existing subsidiaries (see below) were managed independently until now, without any real synergy and common projects. They are now regrouped into the EDF frame in order to create a global supply (*Pôle Services*): engineering with Seychaud & Metz; operation and maintenance with Clémessy; investments and services with Cogétherm. As a direct result, EDF has signed in 1999 its first multi-service multi-energy contract (with the car maker Renault). And 50% of existing contracts with eligible customers have been prolonged because of these combined supplies. But such structural changes are very difficult to implement, because of strong internal barriers and ancient rivalries which could appear as soon as a department's staff could lose a part of its traditional independence and prerogatives. CFDT Energie (1999) notably criticised the fact that main current changes were decided by a few members of staff, without any real dialogue with other managers. The creation *ex-nihilo* of EDF Trading, considered by some employees as 'an artificial transplant', was an example of this atmosphere.

VII.C.c. Implementation of a new internal management

Internal debates have been organised for some years in order to define the global Firm Strategic Plan (PSE). This process has partly allowed the negotiation of a common project for the firm and the definition of more precise objectives, accepted at once by managers, employees and trade unions. The PSE was supposed to be used as the settlement for the new contract between the utility and the State, but also to define technical or commercial objectives of each local entity. It included an effective decentralisation of decision processes, which is necessary in the new power environment. Another increasing necessity for EDF is the internal flexibility of labour. EDF provides a high level of in-house training, but the geographic mobility of employees remains limited and insufficient. In order to solve this problem, an agreement was signed between EDF and the minority trade unions CFDT, CFTC and CGC on 31st January 1997.

---

[28] In the new staff organisation, besides the President, two new posts are created: a General Director 'Customers' and a General Director 'Industries'. Note that restructuration of the industrial activities would include a downsizing policy: –7% in R&D, –9% in engineering, –13% in classical generation and –6.5% in nuclear generation. Note finally that the new Director for Customers, Mr Caperan, was not as usual a man from the firm: he was previously the Commercial Director of the Italian car maker Fiat.

It mainly concerned the reduction for voluntary employees of their working week from 38 to 32 hours, paid as 35 hours, and a plan for the hiring of 11,000 young persons for 32 hour-per-week jobs. But in September 1998, this agreement was cancelled by the Court of Paris, after the majority trade unions CGT and FO had lodged a complaint about its supposed incompatibility with the agent status: this program created in fact two kinds of employee, which was judged incompatible with the existing status. But a new agreement was discussed and signed in January 1999 (see section IX on trade unions). At the same time, the existing status has been partly changed by decree to allow such a part-time program.

VII.C.d. Sharing of the costs of national solidarity

As a public service, EDF is obliged to support some solidarity costs or *'charges d'intérêt général'* (for example, tax on hydraulics, growing financial losses in some regions such as the French overseas territories, etc.). These charges represented one billion Euro in 1997. In the future competitive market, EDF does not want to solely support all these charges, and advocates their division between all the operators. Another point concerns the tariff equalisation throughout the country, which supposes a unlimited kWh supply everywhere with equalised prices. But private suppliers can't accept all these constraints. It is the reason why EDF officials such as Boîteux (1996) claim that private competing firms will be unable to offer such a large public service. The problem is still discussed and could be solved by the definition of an obligatory minimum universal supply and by the creation of a fund for financing some public obligation, provided by all operators involved in the power sector. But negotiations will be very difficult between EDF and potential competitors to define the complete fund mechanism, which could easily appear as a market barrier to potential IPPs.

VII.C.e. Adapting mechanisms for particular internal costs

In the future, some social EDF features could have impacts on its competitiveness. A internal survey in 1997, published by the previous chairman, showed that the labour cost in EDF was 50% higher than that of its potential competitors.[29] A more recent survey, cited by the new EDF President in mid-October 1998 at the EDF meeting on management in Nantes, claimed another estimate with lower overcost (from 5 to 15%). For Orange (1998), this gap is not due to higher wages of EDF employees (they are almost equal to those earned in foreign private companies), but to the EDF

---

[29] Elyo (1998) announces the same wage overcost if it should implement the present EDF–GDF status for its own employees.

social policy for its employees: significantly higher contributions by EDF to pension funds (50%, compared with the usual 25% in France); the financing of social activities, equal to 8% of the wage bill (compared with the average 2.5% in France); a particular calculation of the overtime remuneration; the quasi-free electricity and gas for employees, etc. EDF, trade unions and State are negotiating in order to modify some of these points. In order to motivate the employees, the system of worker participation in the firm profits shall be maintained. Furthermore, each employee can convert his share profits of free time. In these negotiations, a subtle game can be identified between the Presidency and the main trade unions. The reorganisation of these internal costs appears central to the evolution of the EDF productivity, even if we do not yet know exactly how to qualify it. Has EDF important potential gains elsewhere or shall it dramatically cut these costs? Whatever the answer, EDF chairman Roussely declared in summer 1999 that he wanted to reduce the production costs by 30% in three years (these gains should come partly from EDF and partly from industrial partners Cogéma, Framatome).

An important point concerns the public service missions: they are sometimes considered as constraints by the utility. But EDF successively achieved these goals for a long time. This success gives the French people a good image of the power company, reinforced by strong advertising campaigns as TV, radio, and newspapers) supported by EDF. Because of that, the danger of displaying two-tier services, one for eligible customers with lower prices and efficient services, the other for captive customers, must be avoided. EDF needs a global integrity for keeping its good image, the professional quality of its agents and large economies of scale.

VIII. EDF Strategy Abroad and Industrial Partnerships

Since 1992, as with all the larger power companies, EDF via EDF International has followed a strong strategy world-wide. For five years, its total investments abroad reached two billion Euro, representing 13 GW and 13 million customers. These are expected to continue growing in the future. The 1997–2000 contract between the utility and the State plans another two billion Euro for new international projects.

EDF goals are clearly identified:

1. maintain its world leadership and defend its position of 'largest company in the world', as a reaction to the rapid growth of new multi-energy firms such as Enron (US);
2. enhance the value of its natural know-how for conquering shares in deregulated markets;

3. enlarge its technical and commercial know-how, mainly for medium-sized plants, new services to customers and negotiation process with authorities;
4. improve its global efficiency; and
5. propose new attractive challenges abroad to its employees who face a saturated national market.

EDF seems to forecast the building-up of a few dominant firms in the future power market world-wide and plans to be one of them by conquering part of growing markets abroad as an alternative to the French saturated market.

The EDF international activities are based on strict criteria and objectives:

1. long-run investments in generation, transmission and/or distribution;
2. high return on investments;
3. partnership with international and local operators for sharing risks;
4. priorities for Europe, Latin America and Asia.

This large range of geographic targets is peculiar to EDF. Other European companies usually focus on one privileged region: Endesa (Spain), Iberdrola (Spain) and EDP (Portugal) in Latin America; German companies in Eastern and Central Europe; British companies in Pacific Asia, etc. In Europe, EDF is involved in Switzerland (Atel *via* Motor Columbus AG) and Sweden (Sydkraft,[30] Graninge) for distribution; Portugal, Spain, Italy and Hungary for generation; and in Russia, Ukraine and Slovakia for nuclear safety.

In China, EDF has been a major partner for building the nuclear plant at Daya Bay and, in partnership with GEC–Alsthom, for building a 2*350MW coal-fired plant in 1996. It also signed the first BOT contract in China totally financed by foreign investors for building the 2*1000 MW nuclear plant at Ling Ao. In Latin America, EDF has been one of the first foreign investors in the privatisation process. It won some major bidding processes: Edenor (Argentina, 1992) with Endesa (Spain); Edemsa (Argentina, 1998) with Saur; Light (Brazil, 1996) then Eletropaulo (Brazil, 1998), both with AES (US) and Houston Energy (US).

The most important operation for EDF remains its purchase of the distribution utility London Electric (GB) in November 1998 (2.7 billion

---

[30] EDF sold its shares in Sydkraft early in 1998 (benefit: 130 million Euro).

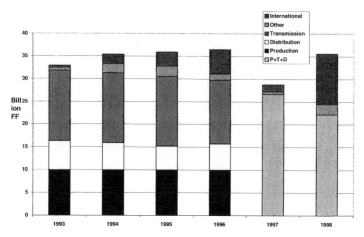

Fig. VI.6. Evolutions of EDF investments.
Source: EDF (1997) & Energie Plus (1999).

Euro).[31] This large involvement of EDF in Great Britain[32] reveals a new strategy abroad: until now, the French utility didn't or couldn't participate in the numerous bidding processes in deregulated markets (GB, USA, NZ) while the French power system was totally protected and under monopolistic rules. This operation in Great Britain also appears as a major strategic opportunity to acquire new know-how: with LE, EDF manages for the first time a utility in a totally deregulated market and supplies to customers who are all allowed to choose their suppliers; it is also the opportunity to supply services to multi-site industrial customers throughout Europe; furthermore, LE manages some CHP units and activities in gas distribution;[33] finally, LE appears as a kind of life-sized test bench for new services which are not yet authorised in France. That is why, for the first time, EDF presented a candidature without any minority or majority partners whereas until that time, it had maintained a minority presence in consortiums. But this British bidding makes us point out another important event: some voices from the British Government started to defend the principle of reciprocity. If such a position were adopted, it could mean a pressure on the opening of the distribution system in France or a slowdown of the EDF development throughout Europe. All these comments are similarly applicable to the current purchase of the German utility EnBW.

---

[31] The North–American company Entergy bought London Electricity for 2 billion Euro late in 1996.

[32] In July 1999, EDF via London Electricity purchased the supply business of SWEB, based in the south-west of England.

[33] In 1999, LE lost some residential power customers but attracted new gas customers.

It is also clear that there are different types of alliance. In some cases, EDF implements industrial cooperation for achieving new technical knowledge. For instance, in August 1998, EDF and the French oil company Total announced the launching of a project to build a gassification unit coupled with a 365 MW combined-cycle power plant (690 million Euros) at Gonfreville (Fr). EDF and AlliedSignal (USA, turnover of US$ 15.3 billion in 1998) signed in March 1999 an alliance to sell microturbines (60–90 kW) throughout Europe, the Eastern Countries and Maghreb. EDF has also developed its expertise for gas and power trading (purchase of Atel, creation of EDF Trading in partnership with Louis Dreyfus for power, gas, fuel in February 1999). Participation in consortiums for purchasing foreign companies are sometimes justified for sharing risk (Argentina, Brazil) and/or overcoming some financial limits. Let us add that EDF funds its own international development while competitors such as Enron and AES directly finance just a small part of their activities (*via* capital increase and/or sophisticated financial mechanisms). That is why EDF is sometimes perceived abroad as a 'shy' investor (Cauret *et al.*, 1998).

Investments overseas are not always a complete success. Some partnerships with other investors (shared management) are sometimes highly difficult. In the case of Light (Brazil), the shared management between EDF, AES, Houston (USA) and the Brazilian industrial CSN has created conflicts (Tolmasquim, 1998, Cauret *et al.*, 1998). The Light Director of Administration is appointed by CSN, the Director for Distribution by EDF, the Director for Generation by AES and the Financial Director by Houston. They defended opposite strategies, interests and management styles, reflecting those of their own firm. When the Brazilian regulator (ANEEL) gave penalties to Light for its bad 1997 results, EDF was criticised for more than its partners in newspapers, as a consequence of its 'public service' fame. This image of public service utility has been weakened throughout the continent. This last point is not anecdotal. In France, the compatibility between the EDF policy abroad as a private firm and its traditional national activities as a public-service oriented firm is debated. We can also wonder about the EDF autonomy abroad. In the case of London Electricity, the State-owned utility received the agreement of the French State. But in the case of Gerasul (Brazil, September 1998), the French State finally obliged EDF to withdraw its offer because of the highly risky business it suddenly meant at this time (financial crisis in Asia and Russia).

IX. Strategies of Trade Unions and EDF Employees

Above all, the French power system is organised by three main parties: the State, EDF and the trade unions (Poppe & Cauret, 1997). Trade unions, notably CGT and CFDT, but also FO, CFTC and CGC, are strongly involved and unavoidable in each decision process of the power company. They have been included as natural participants in the national debate to reform the French power system. Trade unions and employees confirm the EDF arguments to encourage a competition under balanced rules. They are allied to EDF to defend the notion of public service. Their reasons can be different, but their demand remains the same. Two of the main fears claimed by trade unions concern the long-term sustainability of the firm and the potential progressive disappearance of the special EDF–GDF status providing some significant social advantages to each EDF–GDF employee (quasi-free electricity and gas; the social 1% based on the distribution receipts of the utility and not on its profit as is usual in France, etc.). It also concerns the arrival of powerful industrial firms able to compete with the French nuclear industry. Their fears have been summarised thus:[34]

1. the possible risk of a technological waste if EDF is obliged to reduce its market shares;
2. the possible risk to make the energy diversification disappear (this energy diversification was possible in the past because of the long-term planning partly insured by EDF);
3. the fear of industrial alliances abroad which create bigger industrial firms and, on the opposite side, the limitation of the EDF activities by the principle of *spécialité*.

The main demands from trade unions advocate the agents' status, the growing autonomy for the utility and the more or less partial maintenance of the French nuclear line. If the defence of the status is a pure trade union's attitude, the other arguments mainly concern the utility strategy and remind us that trade unions are largely involved in the main decisions:

1. The extension of the EDF–GDF employees' status for all employees working in the power sector. This includes 8,000 persons presently working in EDF subsidiaries or subcontractors and, in the future, employees working for competitors. These positions are argued by the need to guarantee competition between suppliers by imposing the same social constraints and the need to maintain the quality of the public service.

---

[34] Speech by D. Cohen (trade union CGT): 'The point of view of Trade Union'—International conference *'Electricité, service public et concurrence: des enjeux aux solutions pour la France'*— Ecole des Ponts et Chaussées, Paris, May 6–7, 1998.

2. The withdrawal of the principle of *spécialité* imposed to EDF which prevents the utility from enlarging its service supply to multi-utilities; it should be applied not just to eligible customers but to all customers.
3. The withdrawal of the frontier at the counter presently imposed on EDF and GDF which limits their service supply to customers. This demand is a consequence of the previous one but appears very symbolic in France.
4. The development of synergies between EDF (electricity) and GDF (gas), allowing at the same time better opportunities for developing activities and a reinforced position to avoid the dislocation of the EDF–GDF structure and to maintain the agent status.
5. The upholding of a homogeneous nuclear system in order to maintain economies of scale.

But the union analysis is not totally uniform and CGT remains reluctant to any change. In November 1998, the CGT published a survey on the generation abilities of EDF. Its extreme pro-nuclear position criticised the weak investment planning over the ten next years, which would be able to cover only 50% of the future needs and which *'gives private suppliers the opportunity to become unavoidable'*.[35] This extreme claim is not defended by other trade unions, which are more inclined to implement a new gas/nuclear balance in the future.

The arguments of EDF and of the trade unions are sometimes the same (relaxation of the principle of *spécialité*, extension of the status to all parties involved, closer partnership with GDF), sometimes different or opposite (reform vs *status quo* for the status, nuclear planning vs new energy mix). The problem of status seems central. It could be questioned in the new power market. Boîteux (1996) explains that such a status reinforces the cohesion between EDF–GDF employees but at the same time creates inflexibility for the utility. For the EDF staff, new rules and new activities in France and abroad combined with the saturated national market could oblige EDF and GDF to adopt a more flexible management, inducing increased hiring under private work law. Furthermore, we can not imagine competitors such as Vivendi and Suez-Lyonnaise simply agreeing to implement these rules in their own organisation (see below). But the debate on the status is fundamental for the utility, not just for itself but because it conditions the internal relationships between the Board and employees. As Lesourne says (in Stoffaës, 1998, p. 103), the close internal partnerships, the main element of the success in the past, were partly the result of the consensus about status. It must remain a key point of

---

[35] David Cohen, Secretary of the CGT Federation on Energy, 10th November 1998.

the internal consensus in the future, and not become a source of internal crisis. This condition is unavoidable because EDF as a State-owned company is a 'political company' which needs a consensual strategy. Let us finally mention a paradox: even if it is crucial, there is no official definition of the status. A text exists which gives a restricted juridical definition of it. But there are also a lot of advantages progressively cumulated over fifty years which are not in this text but which are now considered as unavoidable elements of the status. Let us finally conclude that in the future, all these social negotiations need the creation of an employers' association in France representing the interests of the power suppliers. Until now, such representation did not exist because of the position of EDF as the unique significant supplier.

X. Strategies of New Suppliers

X.A. Pressure from French multi-utilities

If EDF is the biggest electricity utility worldwide, relatively this size is not so large compared to some leading industrial firms which also have power activities for example Suez-Lyonnaise, SIEMENS. If such firms want to conquer market share, they can use their strong financial and technical abilities. On the French market, a few private companies, such as the powerful water-distribution firms Vivendi (ex-Compagnie Générale des Eaux) via its subsidiaries Compagnie Générale de Chauffe (CGC) and Esys-Montenay, and Suez-Lyonnaise (ex-Lyonnaise des Eaux) via its subsidiary Elyo,[36] started to challenge the EDF monopoly position late in the 1980s, occupying all the free spaces allowed by law—power units lower than 8 MW—by implementing a lot of these little units.

These companies are traditionally involved in the management of local public services. As a matter of fact, if local authorities usually control public services, such as water or electricity distribution, they frequently delegate management to public service (Vivendi and Suez-Lyonnaise for water, EDF for electricity) by signing long-term contractual agreements. From water distribution, these two companies have progressively enlarged their activities to waste management, public works, telecommunication and other public services in France and abroad such as private hospitals, collective catering, and the property business. They are leading the world market in water distribution, the European market in waste management and the French market in energy services. Vivendi increased its turnover from 22 billion Euro in 1993 to 31 billion Euro forecast in 1998,

---

[36] Others suppliers exist (municipalities, some industries) but their electrical role remains small and limited compared to those of water companies.

and Lyonnaise from 14.6 billion Euro in 1993 to 31 billion Euro in 1997. Both of them now concentrate their activities around three main poles: energy, telecommunication and water. They have given up some of their diversified activities such as catering, property business and financial affairs. Furthermore, they implement strategies based on mergers. Their financial potential remains high: Suez-Lyonnaise announced in April 1999 it could invest 30 billion Euro within 2002 (in *Les Echos*, April 2, 1999).

Concerning the energy activities, the strategy of both firms is based on the management of a wide range of energy technologies, which are usually not developed inside the companies but rather under license, and also on the development of services for the rational use of energy. This diversified set of techniques makes them able to fit local demand. It also contrasts with the French electric system as a whole, which is strongly based on large nuclear power plants. Both companies are developing generation activities, combined heat and power, wastes-to-energy, natural gas and hydroelectric facilities. The electricity share is still low but dramatically growing. Their energy supply includes energy services (management and maintenance) for municipal equipment, public and private buildings and district heating.[37] In 1993, the energy activities represented 5 billion Euro for Vivendi and 1.6 billion Euro for Suez-Lyonnaise. Note that energy activities of Lyonnaise increased by 61% from 1993 to 1996, mainly because of the merging of Tractebel (see below). In 1999, the energy activities raise 10.5 billion Euro for Suez-Lyonnaise which is already the second largest independent producer in Europe, and 4 billion Euro for Vivendi. But the bases of electricity business of the two companies are different, even if both companies dramatically develop experiences abroad partly in order to be ready for a possible deregulation of the French electricity market.

Lyonnaise was largely involved in electricity production and distribution before 1946. Up to now, it has operated local power generation and distributed power and gas in a few French towns (Strasbourg, Monaco, Grenoble, Bordeaux). But the merger–absorption operation of the financial holding Compagnie de Suez by the technical firm Lyonnaise in June 1996, which created Suez-Lyonnaise, is the main event. The justification of such an operation was the total alignment of their activities and the creation of financial strength. Suez, by controlling the Compagnie Générale de Belgique (CGB) since 1988, gave Lyonnaise the control of 50.3% of Tractebel (Belgium) and the benefit of its high

---

[37] In 1998, Vivendi managed 243 district heating networks in Europe, including 165 in France.

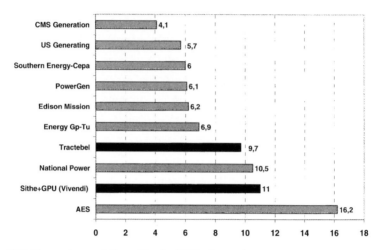

Fig. VI.7. The ten largest IPP worldwide (GW)—September 1998.
Source: Tractebel, 1998.

technical knowledge in industrial services and public utilities.[38] It is a powerful advantage for penetrating power and gas markets world-wide. The close proximity to the French border and to the very industrialised North of France could be decisive. But the integration of such a large subsidiary was at first difficult, even if activities of Tractebel and Elyo are apparently complementary (power/gas transmission and generation in the first case; energy efficiency, CHP and heat/refrigeration nets in the second). In fact, the Tractebel turnover in energy activities reached 8 billion Euro in 1997, compared to the 2 billion Euro of Elyo. That is why Elyo was sold to CGB in April 1999 to create a unique energy pole. Suez-Lyonnaise increased in September 1999 its participation in Tractebel capital from 50.3% to 100% and implemented the merging of Electrabel and Distrigaz to set up a complete multi-energies company. Note finally that Suez-Lyonnaise is the world leader of water management (via its subsidiaries Calgon, Narco and US Filter) and has already 60,000 industrial customers, a powerful opportunity for implementing a multi-services supply.

---

[38] Tractebel manages 30 GW for power generation including five nuclear plants in Belgium. It transmits 100 billion m³ of gas worldwide, mainly via its two subsidiaries in Belgium: Electrabel (15 GW, 74,000 km of HV lines) and Distrigaz. It participates into Interconnector, the future gas dispatching centre in Netherlands and Belgium. Tractebel also develops its activities overseas. On 15th September 1998, it won a major bidding for acquiring Gerasul, a large producer in Brazil ($947 million).

Without any history in the electricity field, Vivendi has developed its experience abroad within ten years. Because it was a new entrant in the power sector, it was not obliged to follow any traditional 'energy line': it was free to develop different types of energy (gas, renewable and decentralised units). Its subsidiaries, Compagnie Générale de Chauffe (which mnages 55 GW of thermal installations) and Esys Montenay, have been restructured through a new entity, Energie Services. Two new entities have been set up, Sithe (11 GW of power plants in the USA) and Dalkia (energy services). In November 1998, Sithe acquired the North American GPU (6.5 GW) for US$ 1.7 billion and increased its installations by 60%. It was, in 1998, the largest IPP in the USA. But Vivendi is also among the world leaders for water management, environment and communication. Hence, the financial markets have obliged Vivendi to clarify its activities and then to give up its energy branch. In September 1999, the firm announced that it sold Sithe. The service entity Dalkia is expected to be sold to EDF.

It is clear that such firms are influential parties in the reform process in France. Their demands during the negotiations were: the creation of an independent entity (i.e. not controlled by EDF) for managing the grid and all industrial activities linked to its operation; the development of a real independent expertise for this entity; the spinning off of the EDF activities in order to limit any temptation for crosse-subsidies and to guarantee a total transparency of the system; the rejection of the status for activities under competition; and a limited sharing out of the cost for national solidarity. Because of the present uncertainties, they implement in France today a case-by-case policy on local industrial sites.

X.B. Foreign and national multi-energy companies

Vivendi and Suez-Lyonnaise are cautious but traditionally present in France. Foreign players are presently more sceptical. Abroad, a lot of energy companies are adapting a multi-energy strategy (Brochu, 1997) when EDF is obliged at the present time to be just an electricity supplier. World-wide, oil and gas companies are looking for new activities. They naturally appear as dominant participants in the short-term wholesale market for electricity or as independent producers (Exxon, Shell, Total, Enron). In September 1997, Shell declared new goals and adopted a '*fuel to power strategy*'. Early in 1998, it was involved in several power projects representing 10 GW throughout the world. See also the case of the oil, gas and power company Enron, which claims to have become '*the world's leading energy company, creating energy solutions world-wide for a better environment*'. It manages independent production and trading in each continent, notably in Europe where it expects to rapidly become one of the most important gas and power operators and marketers.[39] But if it has already opened offices in main European towns,[40] it excludes France as one of its present priorities (EDF, 1998b). Foreign investors, except for a few local industrial CHP projects, are waiting for the definitive Law before implementing or not a more global strategy in France. Furthermore, it is not impossible that such potential entrants wait for the second and third phases of the Law in 2001 and 2003: potential profits are maybe larger with medium-sized customers than with large industrials.

The particularities of the French oil and gas market (notably the particular links between GDF and EDF) presently limit such evolutions in the French sector.[41] But some experts, (including Percebois, 1997) expect unavoidable strategic alliances of GDF with an oil and gas company to avoid the emergence of competition for gas transmission and gas distribution (possibly Elf or Suez-Lyonnaise). In this environment, relationships between GDF and the French oil companies Elf and Total changed in 1997, with two new agreements allowing closer partnerships between them. That was an opportunity for GDF to improve its activities in gas production and to reinforce its positions in distribution. For Elf and Total, that was a chance to be more present in the gas distribution segment. The evolution in the power sector can partly explain these alliances. GDF manages its own gas units and could become a significant potential competitor. But this balance changed again during the 1999 summer and the merger between TotalFina and Elf Aquitaine which created the fourth largest oil company.[42] On one side, EDF; on the other side, TotalFina–Elf. What is the future for GDF? In October 1999, the official report Bricq argued to a partial privatisation of GDF, with its capital opened notably to EDF and TotalFina–Elf plus foreign investors. At the same time, the Minister of Energy, Mr Pierret, declared that an EDF–GDF merger would not be possible.

---

[39] Enron is a multi-utility firm. See its current 13 billion FF takeover bid for the English water distributor Wessex Water. In *Les Echos*, 27th July 1998.

[40] In November 1998, Enron offices existed in Frankfurt (Ger), Madrid (Spa), Milano (Ita), Oslo (Nor), Moscow (Rus) and London (UK). In March 1999, Eastern has opened a luxurious Parisian office but officially only for developping trading (which not yet authorised in France).

[41] The gas production is managed by Elf Aquitaine; the gas importation by GDF; the gas transmission by GDF, SNGSO (70% Elf and 30% GDF) and CFM (50% GDF, 40% Elf and 10% Total); the gas distribution by GDF and 17 small local companies. Competition is emerging: Elf wants to develop a gas transmission activity and Suez-Lyonnaise and Vivendi to create their own gas distribution activities where gas is not yet distributed. Note that in the 1960's, in order to break the stranglehold of American and British oil companies, France built two strong oil companies, Elf Aquitaine and Total. The first one is now the largest privately owned French firm.

[42] EDF owns 2.4% of the TotalFina–Elf capital.

The future relationships between EDF and GDF will be decisive for determining a new national energy mix based on nuclear and gas (and no longer just on nuclear), and to supply common and complete power and gas services to customers. Such a closer partnership, *'a reinforced partnership'* (EDF, 1998c), is discussed between the two firms. It is announced unavoidable by EDF to counteract the arrival of multi-energy and multi-utility firms. It is supported by trade unions. But GDF wants to keep its autonomy and remains totally reluctant. Hence, we don't know at the present time which kind of partnership will be implemented. There is a large range of possibilities from the simple case-by-case partnership for conquering new markets abroad to a strategic alliance or even the total integration of activities. The unique evidence is that this partnership shall be commercial with a long term stability, and not just financial.[43] But on the other side, commercial teams in EDF–GDF regional centers, which were traditionally combined, were strictly split in 1999.

Other existing French entities, such as CDF[44] and CNR[45] are also potential power competitors with existing plants and high technical knowledge. The case of CNR is interesting. As the CNR chairman announced in Destot (1998) and as DGEMP (1999) confirms, CNR will be considered as an IPP. That would imply new relationships with EDF which are not yet clarified but already crucial. As a power generator, it could then sell electricity in the Rhône region, attracting such low prices (hydraulics) that municipalities could be more inclined to become eligible customers and to question the franchising contracts for distribution. We wonder if, as the domino effect, the CNR could disturb the stability of the distribution.

XI. Strategies of The French Nuclear Industry

XI.A. The industrial system between development and awareness

The main consideration in the nuclear field in France is the overcapacity of the power system. The older French nuclear plants are just 20 years old and their life expectancy has been increased from 20 to 40 years. Hence, the first replacement of nuclear plants is not planned before 2015.

---

[43] The European Union could interfere in such an alliance if it considers that a dominant market position could be created.

[44] Charbonnages de France (CDF) is in charge of the coal sector in France. It has managed the closing of French mines in the 1970s and the 1980s. The power generation is an opportunity to restart its development, notably with the new highly efficient coal-burning plants. In 1994, CDF set up a subsidiary, SNET, in charge of its power plants.

[45] Compagnie National du Rhône (CNR) was set up in the 1920s in order to build and operate dams along the Rhône river. It operates 25% of the French hydroelectric units and sells its power to EDF (who part-own CNR).

This is a radical change in the nuclear industry. Until early in the 1990s, the French nuclear overcapacity was supposedly transitional and the continuous development of the supply side was accepted. In late 1990s, we know that the situation dramatically changed. For Falgaronne (1997), *'the problem is now stated in industrial terms'*. Faced with a change in the French power system, the French nuclear industry, dominated by Framatome, Alsthom, Cogéma and the State-owned Center for Atomic Energy (CEA), defends the maintenance of the link between nuclear power, long-term planning, cheap kWh and French global competitiveness. But they are under a series of uncertainties concerning their future: how can they keep their technical leadership just through maintenance of operated plants, without any new projects for at least 15 years? What will be the share of gas in the future national energy mix? How to overcome the current German withdrawal?

In order to maintain an international leadership position in nuclear technology, partnerships have been created between French industrials and EDF.[46] See for example the research project N4+, launched by Framatome and EDF in 1989, enlarged in 1992 to increase the German company Siemens in order to develop the European Pressurised Reactor (EPR), the nuclear reactor of the future. But some reluctance appears in other countries. The first negative event was the choice by Siemens of an alliance with British Nuclear Fuels rather than with Framatome.[47] The later decision by Schröder's Government to give up the German nuclear program was the second decisive event and a serious setback to the attempt for establishing an international safety standard. The German Ministry for Environment, Mr Trittin, claimed in January 1999 that the EPR would not be implemented in Germany. Finally, the sudden German willingness to cancel contracts concerning the treatment of German nuclear wastes by Cogéma (La Hague, F) and BNFL (Sellafield, GB) is another drastic event, even if the cancellation of such contracts will take some time.[48] The official share price of CEA–Industries, the owner of Cogéma, decreased by 37% in one month. The building of Daya Bay and Ling Ao in China and the French involvement in the eastern countries

---

[46] The EDF involvement in this project is maybe justified by its fear of seeing the French nuclear line becoming less efficient and less competitive, which could make its prices increase. In the long term, the technical leadership of the line can be maintained just by maintenance activities.

[47] Mr. Cl. Birraux, the French representative of Haute Savoie, wrote a report published in 1998 which reveals the French lack of convenience concerning the EPR project. See Birraux (1998).

[48] Late in January 1999, experts predicted that treatment of German waste could continue for five or six years.

operating nuclear plants are the last few opportunities to maintain the French knowledge.[49]

Furthermore, the competition with foreign nuclear industries is strong. Tractebel (Belgium) has chosen Mitsubishi (Japan) rather than Framatome–Siemens to replace main pieces of the Tihange nuclear plant. On its side, EDF wants to retain its freedom to choose in the future the most competitive energy mix, including gas, coal and nuclear alternatives. It then maintains a technological awareness on foreign nuclear lines directly competing with the EPR project: PWR reactors, BWR reactors such as the Japanese efficient ABWR etc.

Because of all these facts, the main stake for the French nuclear industry concerns its R&D efforts, which have been financed by the State for a long time. Will they be maintained? The White Book in 1998 did not clearly answer this question. The official Birraux Report of 1998 revealed a lack of goals clearly announced by the Government and by EDF concerning the nuclear future. Another challenge for the nuclear industry is its ability to adapt its structures and its activities in order to face an uncertain future and to wait for an eventual restarting of nuclear programs. It means a change in their organisation. The chairman of Framatome advocated a new logic of specialisation between the operator–designer EDF and the equipment suppliers (Destot, 1998).

In fact, the reorganisation of the sector is still undertaken differently from one firm to another. As producer of the nuclear fuel and manager of the nuclear wastes, Cogéma, owned by CEA–Industries, could be weakened the most by the current sudden events. Concerning EDF, we have seen how it has deeply participated in the design of its nuclear plants and how it now changes its organisation, including the reduction of manpower affected by the nuclear services.[50] Framatome has quickly anticipated the slowdown of its nuclear activities. Now its non-nuclear activities account for half of its turnover and the number of its employees working for nuclear projects has been regularly reduced since 1992. Framatome also negotiates with Siemens for an eventual closer partnership. But Alcatel, which owned 44% of the Framatome capital, announced in 1998 its willingness to give up this share. In July 1999, it sold its participation in Framatome to Cogéma. What will be the future role of EDF in the nuclear industry?

The nuclear choice is not just an industrial perspective. It also generates political debates which could have global impacts. For instance, it is clear that the present Government, based on a coalition including the majority Socialist Party, the pro-nuclear communist party and the

---

[49] Some talk of alliances with a Russian firm have been also reported.

[50] This manpower had been sized in the past for the building of six new nuclear plants per year—in Les Echos—21st January 1999, p. 54.

nuclear-opposed green party, could be checked by the parliamentary debate on electricity. The opposition between the pro-nuclear CGT and the balanced opinion of the CFDT could also stress inter-union relationships during the negotiations on the status and on the Law.

XI.B. The 'unique thought', the nuclear line and the environmental issues: a hidden ambiguity

Another French peculiarity is the link claimed in official speeches between nuclear power and environmental issues. DGEMP (1998b) describes *'the sustainable development of the nuclear energy'* as *'a resource quasi-unlimited, non-polluting and very competitive'* (p. 21). The Ministry of Industry affirms in Destot (1998) that *'our electro-nuclear system is not polluting'*. This reasoning is based on the following argument: with 75% of its power generated from nuclear plants, France is not a major CO_2-pollutant and leads by example in limiting the Greenhouse impacts and aiming to reach Kyoto targets. French officials advocate the extension of nuclear power world-wide under strict safety rules, a good way to defend the industrials of the sector. But this position totally eclipses the controversy on nuclear waste transportation and management, an issue which is neither solved nor publicly discussed in France.

Nevertheless, nuclear safety meets more global problems even in France. The French global reality of the *'unique thought'*, i.e. the fact that all decisions are made by a few persons without any societal debates, is evident in the nuclear field and remains true for the energy sectors as a whole. As the MP Bataille said about the right for citizens to be informed on nuclear issues, the members of Parliament have almost never fulfilled this informing mission (Bataille, 1996). Bauby emphasises the lack of independent expertise, *'the weak autonomy of the Civic Society, plus the quasi-absence of opposition force and of experts out of the system, particularities of the French Society'* (Bauby, 1996, p. 64). An event revealed in summer 1998 is a good example of the gap between the French nuclear world and society. The two reactors of the nuclear plant at Belleville had been suddenly stopped for over a year: their 'confining walls' no longer satisfied the safety rules.[51] Because this stop was not planned, the power generation from alternative plants could cost EDF 230 million Euro during winter 1998. Hence, EDF and the Board for nuclear safety (DSIN) declared that there was no danger, advocated the restarting and criticised what they considered excessively strict rules,[52] while the Institute for Nuclear Safety—the official technical expert of the DSIN—and the

---

[51] The problem was due to the aging of the structures.
[52] *'Un dilemme qui vaut un milliard'*, Libération, 25th August 25 1998, p. 14.

Ministry of Environment restated their positions. With no independent judgement of each point of view, this difference of reasoning has to be clearly pointed out. Other news items have shown a stronger mobilisation of local people: opposition to the project of power HV line Boutre-Carros in the region of Nice; controversy about the choice of the municipality Bure as a new site for nuclear waste storage.

Alternative voices criticise this general opaqueness of the nuclear sector. In the 1980s, theoretical debates were launched on the cost-effectiveness of the nuclear line, but they had no impact. A new step is maybe taken now, with the slow but effective development of an independent new form of expertise beside the traditional one usually shared by EDF, nuclear industry and ministries (INESTENE, 1994). More globally, the independent expertise develops and uses more and more operational tools and methods. As a consequence, opponents can henceforth use a more technical language than before, closer to that of nuclear officials. Then they can be more effectively present in the decision process.

XII. Strategies of Independent Distributors

The case of the 215 non-state-owned distributors (NSOD) is unique. They manage 5% of the total distribution and are directly in contact with customers in their own areas (mainly rural zones and a few towns). Note that EDF is a minority auctioneer of some of them and owns 74% of Electricité de Strasbourg. Facing the European Directive, they defend their interests by confirming some basic principles:

1. Contrary to EDF, they are not under a strict principle of *spécialité*. They developed an innovative strategy and are closely adapted to the local demand requirements. Some of the them, like Electricité de Strasbourg, supply combined services (power, gas, telecommunication). The quality of their electricity supply is improved year after year and some of them are significantly involved in a real DSM strategy, to defer reinforcement investments or to reduce their bill to EDF. They will accept the reduction of kWh prices only if it does not mean a decrease in quality and a reduction in security. Note that there is an indirect yardstick competition between distributors (including EDF), because each one is obliged to compare the efficiency of its activities to that of the other.
2. The French system is partly based on cross-subsidises from urban areas to rural zones (principle of equalisation). The FACE manages this subsidising system. Created in 1928, it is a fund allowing the development and the reinforcement of the network in rural zones. This national solidarity is paid by customers and by distributors. But

industrial customers and urban distributors are reluctant to contribute to this fund. Another uncertainty concerns measures for low-income families. 170,000 poor families received social funds for paying their bill in 1999. But who shall pay for this social policy in the future, the customer or the taxpayer?

3. The 177 *régies* (distributing power to 5% of the customers) buy electricity from EDF and sell it with services to their customers. At the present time, they are considered as buyers and not as customers. Hence, they are not eligible in the new system. In fact, this non-eligibility would be officially a way to protect the principle of tariff equalisation. Note that in this case, there is no argument allowing EDF to conquer such markets abroad. Note that at the present time, a partial eligibility has been adopted for the amount of power sold by a *régie* to its eligible customers.

In Boisson *et al.* (1998), the national federation FNCCR, which represents the independent distributors, explains its fear of their disappearance in an environment allowing competition. Its demands and recommendations for avoiding this event are notably:

1. The definition of a special wholesale tariff for acquiring electricity. In this case, who will pay for it? EDF alone or all the suppliers?
2. The definition of *régies* as eligible customers, with the argument that the Directive and its objective of free market are incompatible with any discrimination between parties involved.

Let us conclude on this subject with the following point: even if the *régies*, located mainly in rural zones, don't represent a large part of the power market in France, they directly concern the local political game which is very powerful and influential at the Parliament. Their positions will surely be strongly defended during the debate on the Law in Chambers.

XIII. Position of The State Versus The National Energy Policy

XIII. A. From a defending attitude to an adapting strategy

We have seen in Section III the main priorities of the French State in inducing an adapted Directive. Note that the French position has changed in the past. Prior to June 1996, the French State held a defensive attitude: Paris which defended the notion of public service '*à la française*' vs Brussels, which just wanted to promote competition. As described by Poppe & Cauret (1997), this attitude was the result of the large consensus existing in France to preserve the public-service orientation of the power sector. Furthermore, Henry (1997) notes that in France, the State was traditionally free to define what a mission of public service was, to choose the operator for managing it and to fix its rules. As a consequence, a special administrative law has been developed, as an autonomous branch in the French law, and perfectly fitted to public service companies. This juridical harmony has been disturbed by the European decisions and as induced a defensive reaction.

The French black-and-white view should have been given up in 1996 for being more offensive and more reactive, to face the unavoidable European changes: *'the* [French] *public services must take the counteroffensive: not against Europe—[...]—but by supporting the common market project'* (Stoffaës, 1997). The French position changed when its principle of pure 'single buyer' was accepted by Brussels as an alternative to the third-party access. Furthermore, Bauby (1998) points out the compromise negotiated at this time between French and German officials who were previously opposed on the degree of market opening.[53] Beyond the usual State priorities—energy independence, long-term energy planning, defense of public principles as pricing equalisation and continuous tariff reduction for all customers—and its willingness to implement a freer market, the State and EDF want to avoid a two-tier utility, i.e., a competitive one tuned to eligible customers with low prices and efficient services, and a non efficient one for captive customers.[54]

XIII.B. Between opening the market and defending the existing system

Public authorities prepared the future market by balancing *status quo* and new claims: by controlling the ratio of real cost/price for each supplier and the transmission cost announced by EDF; by fixing new purchase tariffs for EDF, which is obliged to purchase power in excess of some independent producers (a public service mission); by sharing some social costs between all the producers; and by organising the authorization system for new plants between EDF and independent producers. Note that, because of the present overcapacity, the first significant bidding will

---

[53] Concerning the German position, Bauby (1998) gives two arguments in favor of the free market: the improvement of the German industrial competitiveness by reducing power costs; the reduction of the role of local municipalities in the power sector (they managed via the Stadtwerke at this time 30% of power supplied to German final customers).

[54] Let us add that some European representatives proposed the inclusion of social criteria into the European Directive on the power market. It was rejected notably by the French politicians.

not be launched before 2010. This new regulation will support both the competition rules (by limiting dominant positions and by solving conflicts) and national priorities. We can add that the State attitude reflects the national consensus concerning the power system. French people are proud of its system devoted to the notion of public service. They are highly reluctant to consider any competition. Some experts remind us that the same attitude existed concerning the telecommunications field before competition, and that now, French customers enjoy the significant tariff reductions caused by competition in the sector. But, contrary to France Telecom, the power system represented by EDF is the result of a particular national consensus existing for more than five decades.

As a consequence of all these issues and perspectives, the 1997–2000 *'contrat d'entreprise'*,[55] which was negotiated between the State and EDF and signed in April 1997, shows the main French priorities for facing the Directive impacts.[56] It also shows how the State both prepared the market opening and defended the existing structures. The contract includes:

1. The improvement of services to customers: customers must be satisfied, everywhere in France in items of punctuality, an enlarged range of services supplied (including for EDF the right to propose CHP services) etc.
2. The reduction of EDF tariffs to customers: −13.3% in constant Ff over the period. But this reduction will be more or less significant depending on the type of customer. The non State-owned distributors are also under this objective. The global frame of tariffs will also be changed in order to be closer to the real cost. For instance, peak-load tariffs in winter will be reduced and off-peak tariffs in summer will increase.
3. The reinforcement of international development (13 billion FF over the four years).
4. The clarification of the financial links between the State and the utility.
5. The participation maintained into the social policy and a constant involvement for safety and environment awareness.

---

[55] Each 'contrat de plan' (1983, 1989 and 1993) and the current 'contrat d'entreprise' (1997) fixed the objectives for EDF for four years. These economical, social and commercial objectives are negotiated with the State.

[56] At the same time, a similar contract between the State and Gaz de France (GDF) was signed with the same objectives.

XIV. Final evolutions, Perspectives and Comments

XIV.A. Step-by-step evolutions of the Law project as partial answers to parties involved

The meeting process launched early in 1998 has been effective but long-winded. The main parties involved strongly criticised the first Law project. Mid-September 1998, a new Law project was published. It took into account the main critics claimed by the Council for Competition and some proposals from Dumont Report (1998). In this new version, the Government agreed to relax its position compared with the first one. The most important change was the future creation of a Commission for Electricity as an independent regulator, composed of five members. Its President and two members would be appointed directly by the Government, another by the Senate and the last one by the Parliament. Another relaxed position concerned EDF: like other competing producers, the public utility could build new plants after authorisation from authorities. The bidding process previously envisaged for generation could be maintained just for the type of plants (nuclear, gas etc.).[57]

But in this version of the Law, the Government did not make all the concessions expected by other parties involved. For instance, the Commission would be in charge simply for solving conflicts concerning the access to the grid (transmission and distribution), with no power for penalties. Its missions seemed to exclude problems such as EDF power purchases or the control of crossed-subsidies. Furthermore, EDF remained the transmission operator, while the Dumont Report (1998) advised the creation of an independent entity. EDF would appoint the president of the transmission entity for six years. The unique change was that this person should be accepted by the Minister of Energy. Finally, EDF was allowed to enlarge its supplies to eligible customers from the strict energy supply to energy service supplies, in order to be able to react strongly against competition from multi-services/multi-energy companies as defined before. On the other side, the law also defined the types of eligible customer: an industrial site eligible by itself; some multi-site customers; a few delimited geographical areas composed of different firms. Independent distributors would not be eligible. Finally, the social status of EDF–GDF employees was maintained and could be extended to all new competitors although it was not so clear in the case of cogenerators. This Law version did not satisfy potential competitors. For

---

[57] 'Electricité: le gouvernement accepte la création d'un régulateur autonome', D.CO. Les Echos, 16th September 1998.

instance, the Chairman of Vivendi rejected this project which, he said, *'cumulate*[d] *all the conservatism'.*[58]

XIV.B. The Law project: the official opening and the non-attracting relaxed status quo

In November 1998, a new version was transmitted to the State Council. Compared to the previous one, some arrangements were included. Notably, the Commission for Electricity became allowed to investigate and give penalties[59] if rules concerning the grid access and the accounting unbundling were not respected. Furthermore, the Commission was now composed of six members, three being appointed by the government, one by the Senate, one by the Parliament and one by the Council for Economic and Social Issues. The local authorities also received new powers, such as the obligatory consultation with the regional authorities for any new project of generation and transmission. But even such new changes did not hide the global stability of the French power system. It appeared more like a quasi *status quo* than like a disruption: the Commission is just an adviser (not a decider) concerning tariff evolutions, planning and license for generation; its independence and neutrality are not guaranteed by the project; its real means of expertise are not clarified; EDF remains the central dominant operator defended by the State for generation, transmission and distribution, with a decisive advantage of information access. The Commission for Electricity symbolises in fact the reluctance of authorities to totally open the market, their willingness to remain the regulating authority and to maintain a strategic size for EDF. As a symbol, the 1946 Law will not be abrogated and replaced by the new Law, but just corrected and completed by it.

Regarding supply, the State remains a centralised regulating authority. As a result, it could favour one generation line compared to another *'in accordance with considerations of public service and long-term planning'.* That means that:

1. units of IPPs shall be authorised;
2. each IPP project will be integrated into the national supply planning defined by the State each five years and so should be compatible with the main orientations of this planning;

---

[58] *'Electricité: l'autorité de régulation pourra prendre des sanctions'*, Les Echos, 6th & 7th November 1998, p. 10.
[59] A temporary suspension of the access to the grid and/or financial penalties in the limitation of 3% out of the turnover of the firm charged, 5% in the case of a second offence.

3. if spontaneous projects would not be sufficient for reaching targets fixed by the national planning, notably the target mix between primary energies, the public authorities could launch a bidding process.

But ambiguity exists concerning the role of EDF. Furthermore, in the Law project, there is in fact no place for real power trading in France: the traded power must be generated in France; the trader must be a producer; the power traded by a producer must not exceed 20% of its production; the trading contracts must exceed three years.

The enforcement of competition rules should be at least partly controlled by another institution. Some general French laws still exist in order to control competition whatever the sector and in accordance with European Directives. The edict 86-1243 of 1st December 1986 instituted the Council for Competition as responsible for verifying whether free market rules are respected. This Council can be called in by the Ministry of Economy, by firms or by itself. But its effectiveness seems limited: although its article 10-1 proposes the notion of *'price excessively low compared to costs'* to legitimise its actions, it doesn't precisely define which costs must be studied and what *'excessively low'* means. The opening of the power sector should impose a better operating definition concerning EDF tariffs, taking into account the distinction between regulated activities and activities in competition. The existing price-cap regulation, compatible with an integrated system and based on marginal costs of future development, should be maintained for captive customers. The financial unbundling and the creation of subsidiaries for each activity (generation, transmission, distribution, energy services) are announced as the best way to guarantee transparency.

But the unbundling is not imposed between medium-voltage distribution and the activities of commercialisation. That could be a problem for some eligible customers. Hence, another question is how to pay the fixed costs of production from EDF and to whom; how to share out costs (fixed costs for production, human resources and transactions) between regulated and non-regulated subsidiaries. In an integrated company, the fine line between assets for regulated activities and non-regulated activities is very hard to identify. There is no problem if EDF is able to significantly increase its productivity and then, to reduce its tariffs. But if not, the temptation to transfer some costs to captive customers would be strong. As a consequence, whatever the quality of the control, potential competitors will never trust the neutrality and the confidentiality of EDF as the grid manager: it is linked to EDF as the main producer and EDF as the traditional service supplier, which knows its customers very well. That is a crucial barrier for potential entrants. Of course, the Law project obliges each power company to adopt the unbundling and to clarify each year the rules used to allocate costs/receipts and assets/liabilities to each activity. But the National Council of Competition and/or the Commission for Electricity shall be able to develop a convincing expertise and to calculate costs with such a distinction, which is very uncertain when we remember the information asymmetry. Furthermore, the co-existence of so many regulating entities (Ministry of Industry, Commission for Electricity, Commission for Competition, local authorities) raises questions about the global effectiveness of the system. Remember that the State remains the regulator, the national planner, the main shareholder *via* EDF and becomes the guarantor for competition.

XIV.C. Uncertainties concerning the future real operational criteria

Because of the imposed European deadline, France had to open its market for the first range of larger customers on 19th February 1999. On 20th February, the large industrial consumer Usinor announced that for one of its sites in France, its new power supplier would be Air Liquid,[60] and not EDF anymore. In August, the paper-maker Svenska Cellulosa signed a supply contract with RWE. Some other French industrial consumers were entering into negotiations with foreign suppliers. At the same time, the State decided to accelerate the process for voting through the final Law. Early in November 1999, the Senate accepted the project with a few amendments.[61] But the system remains strongly protected. A special meeting (*Commission Mixte Paritaire*) with all the parties involved was planned for 18th November: if it succeeded, the Law would be voted in December by the Parliament; but it did not, the Law was not yet voted and deferred for some months, and the French power system faced important problems, penalising EDF: limitating its activities in Spain, causing problems for EDF Trading, and raising criticism from Brussels on its activities abroad. The Law was voted in Feb. 2000.

In 1999, the debate on the operational criteria really decided the concrete degree of opening of the French market. What is the sustainability of such a system? Trading remains highly limited (contracts over three years at least) and we can expect a powerful pressure from

---

[60] It seems that Air Liquide was able to supply both power and a rare industrial gas needed by Usinor; a multi-utility supply.

[61] 1/ power plants below 15 MW (3 MW in the previous project) need just an authorization; 2/ some measures are proposed for guaranteeing the independency of the grid manager (GRT). It temporarily remains into EDF but in one year, a new Law will have to define the new GRT, maybe out of EDF; 3/ rules on trading activities are partially relaxed: trading is now allowed for a producer without any limitation linked to its total production; trading is now authorized for entities which do not produce electricity themselves.

eligible customers and potential suppliers for extending conditions. Even the question of the eligible customers is not yet totally answered. If the current restrictive definition is retained, less than 5,000 large industrial customers will be allowed to choose their suppliers. But if eligibility is extended to multi-site companies, 150,000 customers could become eligible. There will be the same debate with the municipalities over 70,000 inhabitants who claim willingness to become eligible. Managed by the mayors of Montpellier, Grenoble and Douai, the political lobby of mayors (who are also often representatives or senators), could refuse to adopt the Law if such towns are not eligible. Another crucial discussion will concern the degree of relaxation (a partial suspension?) of the principle of *spécialité* imposed on EDF. A first step was made early in December 1998: the Council of State decided to partly relax the principle and to allow EDF to enlarge its service supplies for larger industrials, under the condition that the electricity supply represents more than 50% of the complete bill in each case. Will this threshold be effective? How will it be controlled? Furthermore, the Law project authorises EDF to enlarge its service supply to eligible customers with new 'technical or commercial activities as soon as they complete directly or indirectly its missions of public service'. This definition seems ambiguous

We can predict that all these fuzzy but central themes will be vigorously discussed again. Lobbying will stress debates on the real degree of extension of the employees' status, on the future conditions for CHP and on the reality of the fund for national solidarity (sharing out of social costs, i.e. rural areas, tariffs for low-income families etc.). The competing game will not be the same according to the final combination of these operational criteria. The future French organisation will also depend on EDF's ability to restructure itself, to find new partners and markets in France and abroad, and to develop new know-how. Let us finally evoke different scenarios for the state-owned utility combining various levels of geographical expansion, of enlarged supply and of partnerships: EDF as a company just focused on power services just in France, or in Europe or world-wide, with majority or minority in partnerships; EDF as a company supplying multi-utility (multi-energy?) services in France, or in Europe or world-wide, with majority or minority in partnerships. Note that in all the French scenarios, nuclear power in France and elsewhere is assumed to run smoothly and not be disturbed by any major technical trouble or important incident. Hence, the range of possibilities is large and influenced by the combination of endogenous decisions and of exogenous events. The future of EDF could be conditioned by its abilities to manage gas-and-power trading and transmission), new generating sets and new services supplies. Finally, if the transcription of the Directive means opportunities for geographical, functional and technological diversification, the French case presently retains the geographical extension, discusses the technological dimension, and questions the functional opening of the competitive market.

Beneath the obvious protection of the French market, several significant and symbolic changes appeared in the French power system in 1999:

1. Some basic principles, irremovable since 1946, have been questioned: the temporary conditions for CHP units since 1997 insert a *conceptual progress* by cutting for the first time the links between tariffs imposed for purchasing power in excess and EDF tariffs for sale; the question of the principle of *spécialité* has also been raised.
2. A few large French customers (Usinor, Cellulosa Swenska) have effectively already chosen other power suppliers. EDF is implementing a new industrial project for maintaining and reinforcing its position.
3. In April 1999 Standard & Poor's reduced, for the first time, its grading of EDF by decreasing its mark from AAA to AA+, basing its decision on the prediction of the future withdrawal of the State as guarantor and by the low profitability of the French utility.
4. A fundamental industrial reorganisation was implemented in the national energy sector, which had been unchanged for several decades: the mergor between TotalFina and Elf; the withdrawal of Alcatel from the nuclear line and of Vivendi from energy activities; and the debate on the future of Gaz de France.

All these events will surely have an impact on the French power system. They unquestionably prove that changes are irrevocable even in France. Two other significant changes must be mentioned: the appearance of different interests among the decision-makers traditionally united, even if their common 'sprit de corps' still exists; and the development of an independent expertise which slowly introduces a new voice able to block or at least delay any non-justified power project.

XV. Conclusion

The translation of the European Directive into French Law was submitted to Parliament on 19th February 1999. But the debate was dramatically delayed and the new Law voted in Feb. 2000 only. The European principle of sudsidiarity allowed French authorities to adapt the Directive to the unique French market. We have explained why electricity in France is not seen just as a simple commodity, but also as an economic tool, a social symbol and a national pride. Hence, French decision-makers have chosen an unbalanced equilibrium defending the existing system. We have noted that there has not been any complete debate on competition in France, but just a focus on the potential risks and disadvantages of such a competition. What is the sustainability of the system announced by the Law project? We think that there is a three-step answer: the dominant philosophy of the Law, its concrete operational criteria, and the expected growing pressures.

The dominant philosophy of the Law and its definitive orientations were published in mid-November 1998. If the Law project officially opens a part of the supply side and then respects the strict *minimum of the minimum* imposed by the Directive, it will definitely maintain the integrated EDF, its dominant position and the willingness shared by politicians and trade unions to preserve national long-term planning and an internal stability. Added to the uncertainties concerning the abilities of the new regulator, these premises indirectly but strongly limit competition by dissuading most potential entrants. That is why we have named the Law project as a *'relaxed status quo'* which just permits IPPs to implement a very few local projects on a case-by-case policy rather than a global strategy.

During the final debates in 1999, the powerful lobbying from local authorities and from multi-utility companies aimed to enlarge free niches and tried to make the system change more significantly. Operational criteria are negotiated (level of relaxation for *spécialité*, for extension of status etc.). Each combination of operational answers may respect the main spirit of the Law. But at the same time, it can establish an operational system different to that of other combinations. That is why there are a lot of submitted amendments to the Law and a long parliamentary debate, because of the number of parties involved and opposed, despite the implementation of a special accelerated process.

In the medium term, whatever the definitive Law, exogenous or endogenous pressures will be decisive. Firstly, the reduction of the eligibility threshold will truly reveal the objectives of potential entrants. Hence, the ability of EDF to keep its medium-sized customers will be decisive. Secondly, the unavoidable pressure from the benchmarking with other European power markets will be strong. Remember how aggressive the EDF policy is abroad and on the contrary, how reluctant EDF and the State are to a freer national market. Some voices in Europe are still inclined to impose the principle of reciprocation to EDF, which could disturb its international development or the distribution in France. The success or failure of new major partnerships by EDF (possibly with GDF) will be also a key point, if it turns EDF into a multi-utility firm satisfying eligible customers. The future electricity consumption (saturation or increase) will be crucial for motivating new competitors in France. Strictly political choices, such as the future planing share for nuclear generation, will be fundamental for the implementation of the competition into power generation.

Finally, we think that the French way will last only if the traditional parties involved remain (EDF staff, trade unions and State) close partners. That is why the negotiating process on the employees' status is fundamental, not in itself but by its ability to maintain a coalition sharing the same project. Hence, uncertainty on the regulator's ability to verify prices and to impose sanctions will not be the unique decisive point that will guarantee the long-run sustainability. The fact that the state-owned utility is globally favoured will be acceptable only if it proves in the future its ability to maintain a high efficiency for services and costs compared to other countries and other companies. If the system fails to maintain these two objectives (efficiency and internal stability), the French uniqueness could no longer be defended when the next Directive is discussed in 2006. And at this point, all the scenarios could be possible, from system stability to its break-up.

Finally, the Directive translation confirms the existence of various national styles and languages when talking about power from one country to another. It makes us wonder about the reality of the future European market as an homogeneous market or as a compilation of heterogeneous systems. In France, it also echoes the dichotomy between the technical and elitist language which still controls the decision process in the energy sector and the societal language which is still largely excluded from the debate by keeping citizens outside the decision-making process. That is another challenge for the future, a challenge for democracy.

Literature

Batail, J. (1998a)/DIGEC Les contrats d'entreprises conclus entre l'Etat, EDF et GDF: ce qui va changer pour les clients. *Revue de l'Energie*, No. 494, January 1998, pp. 5–8.

Batail, J. (1997b)/DIGEC Les nouvelles conditions d'achat de l'électricité produite par cogénération: des avancées majeures pour la tarification, *Revue de l'Energie* No. 487, May 1997.

Batail, J. (1997c)/DIGEC Le marché intérieur de l'électricité: la négociation de la directive et l'organisation du futur système français. In *Economies et Sociétés, Economie de l'énergie*, Série EN No. 7, May/June 1997, pp. 117–135.

Bataille, C. (1996)/Member of Parliament, *Rapport sur la gestion des déchets nucléaires de haute activité*, Report ordered by the Parliamentary Office for scientific and technical choices, 1996.

Bauby, P. (1998), Points de repère sur le modèle EDF, Draft paper for discussion presented at the Seminar SIGEM, University of Paris VIII, 26th October 1998.

Bauby, P. (1994), Electricité et société, *Cahiers de Prospective*, Inter Editions 1994.

Baudru, D. & Rigamonti, E. (1998), Stratégie des acteurs et dérégulation des marchés du gaz et de l'électricité en Europe, *Revue de l'Energie*, No. 499, July/August/September 1998, pp. 439–450.

Birraux, Cl. (1998), Rapport sur la sécurité des installations nucléaires, Office parlementaire d'évaluation des choix scientifiques et technologiques, published 14th May 1998.

Boisson, P. *et al.* (1998), *Energie 2010–2020: les chemins d'une croissance sobre,* Commissariat auPlan, report coordinated by P. Boisson, *La Documentation Française,* September 1998.

Boîteux, M. (1996), *Electricité de France existera-t-elle encore dans cinquante ans?,* 1997 Management Institute of EDF and GDF.

Bonduelle, A. (1998) & Fenet, S./INESTENE, *La libéralisation du marché européen de l'électricité,* Les Echos Etudes, Novembre 1998.

Brochu, S. (1997), La déréglementation et la création d'entreprises multiénergétiques, *Revue de l'Energie,* No. 486, March–April 1997, pp. 271–275.

Cauret, L., De Gouvello, Ch. & Defeuilley, Ch. (1998), *Comportements stratégiques des entreprises sur les marchés de l'électricité en Amérique Latine; premières conclusions sur les stratégies des investisseurs étrangers,* Report CIRED/CNRS to EDF/DER, 17th December 1998.

Cauret, L. (1997), *Dynamiques de la Maîtrise de la Demande d'Electricité; jeux d'acteurs et outils en métropole et en outre mer,* Doctorate in Economics, CIRED/EHESS and CENERG/Ecole des Mines de Paris, 11th December 1997.

Cauret, L., Adnot, J. (1996), *Why optimise an already efficient system? Overview of the French DSM approach,* 19th International IAEE Conference, Budapest, May 27–30, 1996.

CFDT Energie (1999), *EDF: la méthode Roussely à l'épreuve du temps,* in *La Tribune,* 6th July 1999.

CFDT Energie (1998a), CFTD comments on *'Le projet d'entreprise: vers le client, le compte-à-rebours européen'* announced by EDF, 23rd October 1998.

Chevalier, J.M. (1997a), Contestabilité des marchés et nouvelle dynamique concurentielle: une nouvelle problématique économique de l'énergie, *Revue de l'Energie,* No. 486, March/April 1997, pp. 209–216.

Chevalier, Cl. (1997b), La stratégie des acteurs: la montée des arbitrages interénergétiques, *Economies et Sociétés, Economie de l'énergie,* Série EN No. 7, May/June 1997, pp. 295–311.

Conseil (1998) *La future organisation électrique française,* Conseil Economique et Social, Editions des Journaux Officiels, 18th May 1998.

Destot, M. (1998), *Les défis internationaux de la politique énergétique française,* Proceedings of the Parliamentary Meetings on Energy, Conference of June 1998 organised by the Representative Mr. Destot, June 1998.

DGEMP (1999), *Regards sur 1998: énergies et matières premières,* Ministry of Industry, 1999.

DGEMP (1998a)/Ministère de l'Economie, des Finances et de l'Industrie (1998), *Vers la future organisation électrique française; textes clés,* February 1998.

DGEMP (1998b)/Ministère de l'Economie, des Finances et de l'Industrie (1998), *Rapport annuel 1997: Energies et Matières Premières,* 1998.

Dumont, J.L. (1998) *Réussir la future organisation électrique française,* Report to the Prime Minister, 2nd July 1998.

EDF (1999), *'Vers le clien',* February 1999.

EDF (1998a)/Department of Strategy, *'Faits Marquants 1997',* June 1998.

EDF (1998b)/Research Department, *'Enron: un acteur global de l'énergie à la recherche d'atouts supplémentaires',* Limited diffusion, April 1998.

EDF (1998c), *'Le projet d'entreprise: vers le client, le compte-à-rebours européen',* 23rd October 1998.

EDF (1997a), *1996: une année charnière dans l'évolution d'EDF avec de bons résultats financiers,* EDF Conference, March 1997.

EDF (1997b), *Electricité de France,* internal document by the RHCOM/EDF, April 1997.

EFE (1999) *Le nouveau cadre juridique de l'électricité en France,* EFE professional seminar, Paris, 28th January 1999.

EFE (1998), *La libéralisation des marchés gaz et électricité: comment être prêt?*, EFE professional seminar, Paris, 22–23 October 1998.

Elyo (1998), '*Avant-projet de loi sur la modernisation et le développement du service public de l'électricité: contribution au débat du groupe Suez-Lyonnaise des Eaux*', Internal paper, 27th October 1998.

Etat (1998), *Avant-projet de loi sur la modernisation et le développement du service public de l'électricité*, 16th September 1998.

Falgaronne, F. & Bruel, P. (1997): EDF, Department of Strategy, Le renouvellement du parc nucléaire: problématique et enjeux, *Annales des Mines*, August 1997.

Finon, D. (1998)/IEPE, *Electricity reform in France*, International Conference on Electricity in Europe in the 21st century: what performance and what game rules?, Panthéon Sorbonne, Paris, France, 13–14 November 1998.

Finon, D. (1997)/IEPE, Le contrôle public des industries électriques libéralisées: les leçons des expériences européennes de libéralisation, *Revue de l'Energie*, No. 486, March/April 1997, pp. 244–247.

Finon, D. (1989), *L'échec des surgénérateurs: autopsie d'un grand programme*, Presses Universitaires de Grenoble, 1989.

Gallois, D. (1998), EDF veut diversifier sa palette d'énergies et de services, *Le Monde*, 24th October 1998, p. 21.

Glachant, J.M. & Finon, D. (1998), *Why is there diversity in the European Union's electricity industries? A neo-institutional analysis*, (preliminary version) International Society for New Economics 1998 international Conference, Paris, September 17–19, 1998.

Henry, Cl. (1997), Concurrence et services publics dans l'Union Européenne, *Revue de l'Energie*, No. 486, March/April 1997, pp. 187–198.

Hourcade, J.Ch. (1991)/CNRS EHESS, Calcul économique et construction sociale des irréversibilités: leçons de l'histoire énergétique récente, in *Les figures de l'irréversibilité en Economie*, EHESS 1991, pp. 279–309.

INESTENE (1998), *Soutiens et subventions de l'Etat aux énergies en France*, December 1998.

INESTENE (1996), *The electricity trade in Europe: the case of France*, Report financed by Greenpeace, 1996.

INESTENE (1994), Diminution des émissions et des tensions induites par les transformations énergétiques, 1994.

Krause, F. et al. (1994), Nuclear power: the cost and potential conventional and low-carbon electricity options, *Energy Policy in the Greenhouse vol. II, part 3E*, International Project for Sustainable Energy Paths (IPSEP), 1994.

Lambinon, C. (1997), Les stratégies d'approvisionnement des clients industriels, consommateurs intensifs en électricité, *Economies et Sociétés, Economie de l'énergie*, Série EN No. 7, May/June 1997, pp. 289–293.

Lucenet, G. (1997)/UNIPEDE, Le secteur électrique européen en 1997: situation, évolution et perspectives, *Revue de l'Energie*, No. 486, March/April 1997, pp. 223–231.

Mandil, Cl. (1997)/DGEMP, Electricité: une directive européenne à transposer, in *Annales des Mines*, August 1997, pp. 14–18.

North, D.C. (1991), *Institutions, institutional change and economic performance*, Cambridge University Press, 1991.

Orange, M. (1998), L'ouverture à la concurrence remet en cause les spécificités sociales d'EDF, *Le Monde*, 2nd May 1998, p. 15.

Percebois, J. (1997), La déréglementation du secteur gazier en Europe: leçons et perspectives, *Revue de l'Energie*, No. 486, March/April 1997, pp. 256–269.

Poppe, M. & Cauret, L. (1997), *The French electricity regime*, in *European Electricity Systems in Transition*, Editions Elsevier 1997.

Salaün, F. (1994)/EDF, *Stratégies et nouvelles formes de concurrence: prospective de l'industrie électrotechnique*, Mission Prospective/EDF, 1994.

Souviron, J.P. (1994), *Final Report on the First National Energy Debate in France*, December 1994.

Stoffaës, Ch. (1998) & Saab, A.E./EDF, *Potentiels 2010–2025: EDF dans le monde à venir*, EDF/ Cahiers de Prospective, 1998.

Stoffaës, Ch. (1997), EDF, Réconcilier les services publics et la construction européenne: le cas du secteur électrique, *Revue de l'Energie*, No. 486, March/April 1997, pp. 237–240.

Tolmasquim, M. *et al.* (1998), *European and North business strategies abroad: the Brazilian case*, (draft paper), Salzburg Meeting at Leopoldskron, Austria, 19–20 May 1998.

Vagneux, J.P. (1996), EDF General Department, *Les achats d'EDF dans l'environnement européen et mondial*, EDF GDF Management Institute 1997.

Chapter VII
Business Strategies Evolving in Response to Regulatory Changes in the US Electric Power Industry

JOHN L. JUREWITZ

I. Introduction

The US electric power industry is currently undergoing huge structural changes at unprecedented speed. For the most part, these revolutionary changes are the result of strategic business decisions responding to radical shifts in the industry's regulation. The main drivers of these changes are the increase in competition in wholesale power markets following passage of the Energy Policy Act of 1992 and the adoption of retail competition in a rapidly expanding number of state jurisdictions (currently 24). This chapter reviews these institutional changes and their impacts on the business strategies being pursued by both traditional utilities and new independent players in the US power market.

The electric power industry is a major sector of the United States economy. It accounts for over $210 billion in annual sales, $40 billion in annual investment, and 35% of primary energy use. For the past 90 years, this industry has been treated as a natural monopoly. Vertically-integrated utilities have operated within designated local geographic retail franchises, subject to pervasive regulation of prices, service quality, investment, and protection from entry by competitive rivals. These local monopolies typically owned or contractually controlled sufficient generation to serve the full demands of their franchised retail customers. For their part, retail customers had little choice but to purchase all their electricity from the local monopoly utility.

This vertically-integrated monolithic structure began to unravel in 1978 with the passage of the Public Utility Regulatory Policies Act (PURPA). PURPA created a special class of wholesale generators known as Qualifying Facilities (QFs) and required utilities to purchase at regulated prices all the power these QFs produced. This requirement overcame the monopsony power of utilities to exclude these generation competitors by simply refusing to purchase their power. However the ensuing experience with state-regulated QF pricing was largely an economic failure, especially in certain states where excessive amounts of QF power were contracted at exorbitant prices. Disillusionment with this regulated pricing regime quickly led many state regulatory commissions to adopt competitive auctions for soliciting new generation capacity. But these centralised procurement processes were also an imperfect format for introducing generation competition. The local utility remained the sole procurement agent acting on behalf of its franchised retail customers so that individual customers still had no ability to choose their own suppliers. Moreover, supply-side business interests rapidly became adept at politically influencing the key decision of how much new generation was solicited through these competitive auctions. The result was solicitation of excess capacity in some states. By the early 1990s, the political economy of the electricity industry was becoming increasingly intolerable in several states where retail electricity prices had increased to levels 50% above the national average (including California and many New England states).

On 20 April 1994, California broke from this traditional industry structure and became the first state to adopt *retail access*—the ability of end-use customers to "shop" the electricity grid and choose their own retail suppliers. Other states quickly followed California's lead, especially the high-cost states in the US Northeast. By June 1999, 24 US states had adopted policies to phase in retail access over relatively brief transition periods. Thus the US joined an emerging international trend toward liberalisation of electricity markets.

The purpose of this chapter is to explore the many ways in which US companies are responding strategically to these changing regulations and radically reshaping the US and international electric power industries. In doing so, it is important to keep in mind that business strategies manifest themselves in two basic ways. First, economic interest groups pursue rent-seeking strategies to shape the regulatory "rules of the game" in their own favour. Second, within the framework of these established rules, business people realign their asset portfolios and devise new business strategies to maximise value for their shareholders. For the most part, this chapter focuses on the second of these two dimensions of corporate strategy.

II. The Organisation and Regulation of the US Power Industry

To understand corporate strategies in the US power industry, it is first necessary to understand certain basic features of the structure and regulation of the industry. To begin with, the industry is huge. It is composed of more than 3,000 utilities with about 800,000 MW of generating capacity, delivering more than 3 trillion kWh, and generating revenues over $210 billion annually (see Hyman, 1997). More than 75% of retail electricity sales are made by investor-owned utilities (IOUs). These institutions are the main focus of the restructuring reforms taking place in the US and are the primary subject of the discussion here. But it is important to recognise that the ownership structure of the electric power industry is among the most peculiar of any US industry. In addition to the approximately 200 IOUs and the numerous investor-owned independent generators, wholesale brokers, marketers and retailers, there are numerous publicly-owned power entities. These include about 2,000 local municipal utilities, about 1,000 rural electric cooperatives, six federal power marketing authorities, and numerous public power districts and state-owned power projects. These public power entities are usually not regulated by either the state public utility commissions (PUCs) or the Federal Energy Regulatory Commission (FERC). Nonetheless, they are an important part of the competitive landscape and their separate regulatory and tax treatment is a source of competitive anxiety for IOUs.

II.A. Historical foundations of regulation

Beginning in the first decade of this century, state PUCs began imposing economic regulation on IOUs. By 1916, 33 states had formed utility regulatory commissions. The scope of state regulation was very broad and generally governed retail prices, quality of service, obligation to provide service within designated geographic franchise areas, protection against entry of competitive suppliers, and approval of major new investments. During the 1920s, two significant developments took place: first, utilities began becoming more interconnected with one another, including interconnections across state boundaries; second, holding company structures began to dominate the industry. Both of these trends created an industry structure which could not be satisfactorily regulated by individual state PUCs, largely because of the US Constitutional prohibition of the regulation of interstate commerce by individual states.

These events led to the passage in 1935 of both the Federal Power Act (FPA) and the Public Utility Holding Company Act (PUHCA). Under the FPA, the federal government asserted jurisdiction over the regulatory gap that had developed between state PUCs due to their inability to regulate the prices at which power was transacted in interstate commerce. The FPA conferred this task upon the Federal Power Commission (which in the mid-1970s was restructured as the Federal Energy Regulatory Commission). Under PUHCA, Congress attempted to curb holding company abuses by essentially prohibiting companies from owning electric facilities in more than one state unless these facilities are directly interconnected.

To adequately understand the US power industry it is essential to appreciate that federal regulation by the FERC does not have the same pervasive scope as regulation by the state PUCs. Instead, under the US structure of regulatory federalism, state PUCs have traditionally exercised the primary regulatory control over utilities while the FERC has simply plugged the regulatory gaps between states by regulating interstate electricity commerce (although this traditional model of state-federal jurisdiction seems to be rapidly eroding under the current industry restructuring). Specifically, the FERC regulates the pricing, terms and conditions of both power sales for resale (i.e., wholesale power sales) and the provision of transmission services in interstate commerce. Because the US power industry (with the exception of Texas, Alaska, and Hawaii) operates as two huge synchronous grids—the Western Interconnection and the Eastern Interconnection—all wholesale power sales and transmission services offered by IOUs (except those in Texas, Alaska, and Hawaii) are regulated by the FERC. The FERC also has authority to approve power pooling arrangements and mergers. However, unlike state PUCs, the FERC does not establish exclusive geographic service franchises, control entry of competitors, impose an obligation to serve, or license any electrical facilities (other than hydroelectric dams).

II.B. Emerging competition

For the first 30 years following World War II, the dominant trend in the electricity industry was the growth and consolidation of most IOUs into vertically-integrated enterprises, owning or controlling the generation resources needed to satisfy their retail customers' demands and becoming continually more interconnected with one another. This structure of regional, vertically-integrated monoliths began to change with the passage of PURPA in 1978. Under PURPA, utilities were obligated to purchase power from QFs and pay them PUC-regulated prices equal to the purchasing utility's avoided cost—i.e., the cost the utility would otherwise have incurred to produce or purchase a similar amount of power in the absence of QFs. QFs were exempted from any additional economic regulation by state PUCs and also exempted from PUHCA, thereby allowing private companies to own non-interconnected QFs in multiple states. Significantly, IOUs were allowed to own up to 50% of a QF. Some state PUCs were quite aggressive in establishing liberal pricing terms for QF power and, as a result, strong QF industries developed in these states; the large number of QFs clearly demonstrating the physical feasibility of maintaining reliability while integrating large numbers of independent generators into power systems. It also created a strong political-economic constituency favouring further pro-competitive restructuring.

By the mid-1980s, some businesses became interested in developing stand-alone, merchant generation facilities that did not meet the narrow technical qualifications of a QF. But development of these facilities faced several impediments. Among these impediments was the fact that these facilities would be subject to utility price regulation by the FERC under the FPA. Based in part on the demonstrated success of QF development, the FERC wanted to encourage the development of these stand-alone, merchant non-QF generators. Therefore, it launched its market-based price regulation initiative. Rather than regulating prices based on traditional cost-of-service principles, the FERC began approving wholesale prices as "just and reasonable" under the FPA, based upon a demonstration that these prices were negotiated at arms-length in a competitive environment in which the buyer had a reasonable number of alternative suppliers and the seller had no substantial market power, especially vertical market power due to control of wholesale transmission access.

Despite the FERC's successful market-based pricing initiative, there remained several barriers to the further development of merchant generation and more competitively-structured wholesale power markets. First, provision of transmission service by a utility was entirely voluntary. This gave utilities a degree of monopsony power over independent generators as well as the potential to use their transmission strategically to favour their own generation and power sales. Second, independent developers of non-QF generation still faced the PUHCA prohibition against owning non-interconnected facilities in multiple states.

In 1992, the federal government removed both of these competitive impediments by enacting the Energy Policy Act (EPAct). EPAct mandated that utilities provide wholesale (not retail) transmission access under FERC regulatory oversight. EPAct also created Exempt Wholesale Generators (EWGs), by exempting from the PUHCA prohibition of scattered multi-state facilities any stand-alone generator selling its power entirely to a utility for resale. EWGs were specifically forbidden from selling their power to end-use retail customers. But EWGs were not exempted from FERC price regulation under the FPA and the FERC must still determine that the wholesale prices they charge are just and reasonable.

Instead of mandating any particular direction for industry reform, EPAct simply removed these two very significant impediments to wholesale competition. EPAct did nothing to directly mandate electric industry restructuring. Indeed, it strengthened existing barriers to the introduction of retail competition by expressly prohibiting the FERC from ordering transmission access for retail customers and prohibiting EWGs from selling their power directly to retail customers. Nonetheless, by removing the discretion of utilities over wholesale transmission access and introducing substantial new business opportunities for EWGs, the passage of EPAct propelled the industry headlong toward a new structural equilibrium.

Immediately following the passage of EPAct, the main FERC agenda was to use its newly expanded authority to further encourage wholesale competition. This meant establishing a simple ministerial process for certifying EWGs, implementing open wholesale transmission access rules, resolving the wholesale stranded cost issues created by open wholesale access, and continuing its market-based pricing initiative. By far the greatest new challenge was to implement the transmission access provisions of EPAct in such a way as to maximise wholesale competition by thoroughly removing the vertical market power that utilities held over transmission. Ultimately, in Orders 888 and 889, the FERC chose to accomplish this by ordering all utilities to internally separate their transmission service from their power marketing functions, implement strict codes of conduct for transmission service personnel, establish internet databases with real-time posting of transmission availability and pricing, and file highly prescriptive pro-forma open-access transmission tariffs with the FERC. Order 888 also established 11 principles for the formation of Independent System Operators (ISOs) but did not mandate their formation. Although Orders 888 and 889 have been very successful in improving non-discriminatory access to transmission, complaints still persist about alleged anti-competitive and discriminatory practices. This has led some parties to advocate mandatory participation of utilities in independently governed Regional Transmission Organisations (RTOs) such as ISOs. In April 1999, the FERC issued a Notice of Proposed Rulemaking to explore these issues with the intention of possibly adopting further rules.

II.C. The retail access revolution

Following the passage of EPAct in 1992, the California PUC initiated a proceeding to decide what, if anything, the PUC should do in response to this federal legislation. It was not clear that any action was necessary, but California's regulatory structure was in crisis. Electricity prices were 50% above the national average, the state was in a major recession, and businesses were leaving to locate in adjacent states. Most parties seemed to agree that California's central planning process for procuring new generation resources had become dysfunctional and too costly, but there was no consensus on a solution. Large customers wanted retail access, but utilities, small consumers, QFs, environmentalists and labour unions were all opposed. Ultimately, free market philosophy and lack of an appealing alternative won the day. On 20 April 1994, the PUC issued its landmark decision adopting retail access.[1] Other states quickly followed, especially those in the Northeast which generally had comparably dismal histories of expensive and politicised resource procurement processes and high retail prices.

As shown in Fig. VII.1 and VII.2, by June 1999, 24 states had adopted retail access policies. Not surprisingly, these policy initiatives were concentrated in those states where previous institutions had failed to assure inexpensive power. Sixteen of the states have average retail prices exceeding 6.5¢/kWh and virtually every state in this price range has adopted retail access, while only 8 of 31 states with prices below 6.5¢ have adopted retail access. Moreover, several of these remaining low-cost states are quite vocal in their reluctance to adopt retail access, fearing it will raise their retail prices. In view of this bipolar division among the states and the general political philosophy favoring deferring to state

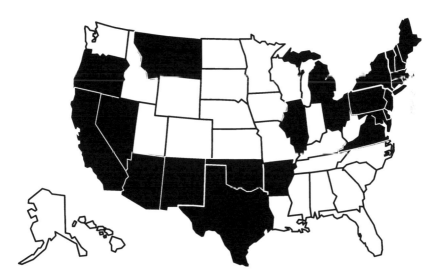

Fig. VII.1. 24 states have adopted retail access (September 1999).
Source: U.S. Energy Information Administration.   Retail access law or regulatory order adopted.

---

[1] See California PUC (1994).

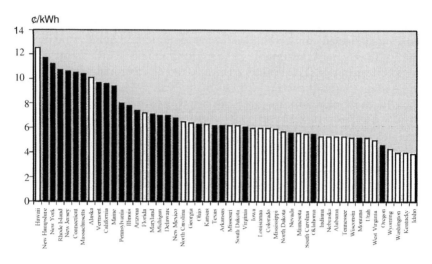

Fig. VII.2. Average revenues in states adopting retail access (1997).
Source: U.S. Energy Information Administration.

decision-making on matters of mainly local concern, it does not seem likely that the federal government will act any time soon to mandate retail access nationwide. In fact, a coalition of 23 state PUCs was formed in late 1998 for the purpose of lobbying the US Congress not to adopt a federal mandate ordering retail access, but instead to allow states to proceed on their own initiative. Thus, although it is certainly possible that federal legislation could be enacted to further clarify state-federal jurisdictional authorities, establish new reliability institutions, or further facilitate competition, it does not seem likely there will be a federal mandate ordering nationwide retail access in the near future. Without such a federal mandate, it seems likely that the number of new states adopting retail access will slow during the next few years pending an evaluation of its success in other states.

This patchwork of state-by-state retail access produces a mixed strategic picture for US utilities. Several major national and international players such as Edison International, PG&E, GPU, CMS, and PSE&G are operating from local bases in states where retail access has already been adopted. Some large holding companies such as AEP and Entergy are straddling states in both worlds. Still other companies—especially significant players based in the Southeast such as Southern, Duke, and FPL—are operating from local fortresses still structured as vertically-integrated monopolies. These differences undoubtedly have an effect on corporate strategies.

II.D. The impacts of regulatory changes on corporate strategies

Electric utilities and independent companies are developing business strategies to pursue promising business opportunities within the changing structure of utility regulation. Corporate strategies are heavily influenced by the regulatory rules of the game and, in many cases, it is essential to understand these rules in order to makes sense of strategic choices. Within the US structure of regulatory federalism, there is a single set of federal rules (although not necessarily clear and unambiguous) plus a patchwork of state rules. Utilities operating in states with retail access will generally pursue different corporate strategies from those in other states.

Regardless of whether a utility operates in a state with retail access, its strategies will be affected by changes in federal regulations. The following are the most important of these federal changes and their respective impacts on business strategies:

- *Open wholesale transmission access:* With the adoption of mandatory wholesale transmission access in EPAct, ownership of transmission has lost much of its strategic value. Implementation of EPAct through FERC Orders 888 and 889 and, more recently, the voluntary formation of ISOs and the prospect of possible mandatory participation in RTOs have gone even further to eliminate the strategic value of utility transmission ownership. At the same time, these initiatives have tremendously strengthened the structure of wholesale markets by broadening their geographic scope and increasing investor confidence by reducing the potential for discriminatory abuses by transmission owners. This has fostered tremendous growth in the number of players in wholesale markets.

- *Creation of EWGs:* By creating EWGs, Congress enabled generation developers to own stand-alone, non-QF generation throughout the US It also allowed these generators to freely buy and sell power at wholesale. Together with the FERC's market-based pricing initiative, these provisions have facilitated the development of large numbers of new merchant plants, encouraged the stunning growth of independent marketers, and enabled utilities to expand their ownership of non-QF generation into other states, thereby reducing their resistance to divesting major portions of their traditional vertically-integrated local generation portfolios as part of comprehensive state-mandated retail access plans.

- *Market-based pricing:* Major credit for the progress toward competitive wholesale markets must be assigned to the FERC's market-based pricing initiative. Market-based price regulation was absolutely necessary in making wholesale marketing and merchant development of EWGs attractive enterprises. This initiative was enabled by the fact that the FPA fortunately does not prescribe the application of cost-of-service regulation, but instead merely directs the FERC to assure that wholesale prices are just and reasonable. Without the FERC's bold market-based pricing initiative, none of the competitive wholesale market revolution of the last decade could have taken place except through Congressional legislation amending the FPA—a rather unlikely event.

Thus, even in the absence of individual state actions to adopt retail access, federal initiatives would be creating competitive wholesale electricity markets and having major influences on utility business strategies. In particular, the strategic value of owning transmission would still be substantially reduced, the geographic scope of wholesale markets would be substantially expanded, numerous wholesale marketers would be entering the market, entrepreneurs would be developing merchant non-QF generation, and utilities would likely be undertaking at least modest generation divestitures to reduce their local generation market shares sufficient to receive market-based wholesale pricing authority from the FERC.

The adoption of retail access by many states has created regulatory structures that, for the most part, complement and extend the changes taking place in wholesale markets essentially by making these wholesale markets accessible to competing retailers and their customers. Moreover, largely due to the structure of past institutional boundaries, the move toward retail access has resulted in the regulatory jurisdiction over large segments of the industry being inadvertently shifted from state PUCs to the FERC. This massive shift includes authority over the pricing of power sold by the new owners of divested generation, services provided by ISOs including ancillary services and transmission services, and even low-voltage wire services supplied to a retail access customer or wholesale generator. Essentially, state PUCs are left with regulatory jurisdiction primarily over local distribution networks (and even then, somewhat ambiguously), independent retailers (whom, in general, the PUCs are trying not to heavily regulate), and the terms under which the local distribution utility continues to offer retail services such as basic energy supply, metering and billing to end-use customers not choosing to purchase these services from competitive retailers. The following are the most important elements of state retail access initiatives and their broad impacts on business strategies:

- *Stranded cost recovery:* At the inception of retail access initiatives, various credible independent researchers estimated the level of utility stranded costs at $100–$200 billion nationwide. Moreover, as previously discussed, these stranded costs were concentrated in the states with the highest retail rates—those most inclined to adopt retail access. Not surprisingly, for most utilities in these states every other dimension of corporate strategy paled in comparison to assuring recovery of these stranded costs. Subsequently, most states adopting retail access allowed utilities to recover almost all stranded costs in exchange for other political concessions. While the precise mechanisms for recovery of stranded costs vary considerably from state to state, most of these mechanisms create incentives for utilities to divest major portions of their traditional non-nuclear generation. Moreover, to the extent that utilities are allowed to retain ownership of non-nuclear generation, they are encouraged or directed to place this generation in a separate "unregulated" subsidiary (where FERC market-based price regulation still applies).

- *Generation divestiture:* Although only Texas and Maine have directly ordered utilities to divest generation, all states have to some extent encouraged utilities to divest at least partially. The main public policy reason for divestiture is to reduce the concentration of local generation ownership in order to create more competitive wholesale power markets. In most states, divestiture is proceeding on a "voluntary" basis in exchange for favourable treatment of stranded cost recovery. Moreover, divestiture itself facilitates stranded cost recovery by serving to unambiguously establish the level of stranded costs up front as the difference between a facility's sale price and its remaining book value. This avoids the need to determine the level of stranded costs through some contentious administrative determination of future profitability based on an energy price forecast. Utilities may also see some regulatory benefits in divesting their vertically-integrated generation from their local distribution utility and replacing it with a similar amount of out-of-state generation to fill out their asset portfolios. Under this structure, utilities may be hoping that the state regulator of their local distribution business may feel less justified in reducing allowed returns on the local distribution business in response to higher profits earned in the out-of-state generation business. It remains to be seen whether this hope will be realised. If it is not, many utilities may be inclined to divest their distribution businesses.

- *Functional separation of business units:* In general, utilities are being encouraged or directed to place their competitive activities in separate subsidiaries and retain only their monopoly utility functions within the regulated utility. Specifically, they are being encouraged to divest some or all of their non-nuclear generation and place the remainder into "unregulated" subsidiaries. Likewise, to the extent they wish to offer competitive retailing services, they are being required to develop these businesses as strictly separated subsidiaries. These reorganisations are generally being pursued through holding companies structured to qualify for exempt status under PUHCA. Beginning in the late 1980s, most large utilities began restructuring into exempt holding companies to pursue new diversification ventures as their internal cash generation began to exceed their need for internal financing of new electric plant. However, only one new entity (UNITIL) has organised as a registered holding company in the past 25 years. Altogether there are only 12 registered electric utility holding companies in the US

- *Utility role in competitive energy retailing:* While rules vary by state, most states adopting retail access have required utilities to establish separate retailing subsidiaries if they wish to offer competitive retailing services such as electricity price hedging, etc. Utilities themselves are restricted to offering only regulated, tariffed services and there are political pressures to confine these services to "plain vanilla" services rather than specialised products designed to compete actively with third-party retailers. No state except Maine has yet to adopt a plan that would somehow involuntarily re-assign customers to competitive retailers at the outset of restructuring. Instead, the local utility is designated as the default provider: if a customer does not make an explicit choice to be served by another retailer, the local utility remains his retail supplier. But any advantage that this may create for the incumbent utility in retaining retail market share typically creates no profit opportunity because default service prices are generally set on a cost pass-through basis with no profit margin. This zero-profit structure serves no retailer's commercial interest—neither utility nor independent retailer and may not be stable in the long term. In several states, the long-run role of the local utility in default service has been explicitly reserved as an issue to be revisited after several years of experience.

- *Unbundling of metering and billing:* It is difficult to generalise about metering and billing rules across states. Most states have opened billing to competition, but many have been reluctant to open metering to competition, at least initially. Key questions are whether the local utility should be the default provider of metering and billing, and if so, whether the utility should provide a cost-credit to retailers providing their own metering and billing; or whether metering and billing should simply be deregulated altogether, either on a sudden or gradual basis. Strategic developments in this area will likely take a few years to become clearer as regulatory rules develop further. Given the advantages of scale economies in these activities, it seems likely that the long-term victors will be large information processing enterprises doing business on a regional or national scale.

- *Restrictive Affiliate Rules:* Most states have adopted very strict rules designed to erect firewalls between monopoly functions (e.g., transmission, distribution and default retailing) and new competitive ventures affiliated with the utility. For instance, in most states the utility is precluded from making referrals of customers preferentially to affiliated competitive businesses or from giving affiliates preferential access to competitively sensitive information of any kind. These rules substantially constrain the range of business strategies that utilities might otherwise find attractive in a less restrictive regulatory environment. As a matter of public policy, these structured mandates appear in many instances to eliminate certain efficiencies of scale and scope. The implicit judgment by regulators appears to be: (1) that this potential loss of static efficiencies is more than offset by the greater dynamic efficiencies of increased competition, (2) that there are populist benefits in reducing the utilities' political-economic power, or (3) that there are political benefits in building a constituent base of competitive enterprises beholden to regulators for their existence and economic protection.

II.E. Environmental impacts of restructuring

Beginning in the 1970s, environmentalists had become sophisticated and effective participants in utility regulatory proceedings before state PUCs. The main focus of their attention was on retail electricity rate structures, conservation and demand-side management programmes, and new generation resource selection. Early in the policy debate over retail access, many environmentalists aligned themselves with utilities in opposition to retail access. Under retail access, centralised resource procurement would cease and market forces would assume control over new generation resource selection. Environmentalists apparently feared the prospect of shifting electricity environmental policy making away from state PUC central procurement decisions—a forum they were confident they could influence—and toward state legislative tax and subsidy policies, a forum where they felt less confident. As the retail access bandwagon gained momentum and its adoption seemed inevitable, environmentalists generally exchanged their support of utility stranded cost recovery for utility support of so-called "public goods changes" to fund demand-side management and renewables development. These charges were essentially a kind of tax levied on all customers interconnected to the grid and controlled and disbursed by designated public authorities.

The likely future environmental impacts of retail access are speculative. Changes will derive mainly from three underlying impacts: effects on emissions from existing power plants, impacts on conservation and demand-side management, and the environmental characteristics of new generation resources. Beginning with the first of these impacts, there are several cross-cutting forces that will affect emissions from existing powerplants. There will be increased pressure to implement rate structures with two separate components: a fixed charge reflecting grid infrastructure costs, and a time-differentiated commodity charge reflecting the hourly market price of power. Compared to the current average-cost rate structure, separate and lower commodity charges will stimulate electricity consumption generally and thereby tend to increase air emissions. The spread of time-differentiated pricing will reduce the growth of peaking facilities but also tend to increase off-peak production from base-load generation such as coal plants. This may also increase air emissions but also raise other environmental concerns. Emissions may also be increased if restructuring leads to increased shutdown of nuclear plants. However, as discussed further below, a trend seems to be developing toward consolidation of nuclear plant ownership. This could lead to more efficient operations, greater confidence in nuclear economics, and an extension of plant lives, thereby reducing air emissions but raising other environmental concerns. Finally, with the separation of commodity prices at retail, customers may increase their adoption of end-user electrotechnologies and reduce their use of other end-use fuels (such as fuel oil and natural gas) thereby reducing air emissions, especially local air emissions.

The expected impact of restructuring on demand-side management is also ambiguous. In most states adopting retail access, demand-side management programs are continuing to be funded through public goods charges levied on all interconnected customers. With the separation of electricity commodity prices, customers will see lower incremental prices and thereby be inclined to adopt fewer conservation measures. On the other hand, incentives toward peak-load management should increase as more customers are exposed to real-time price signals. This should also lead to increased interest in demand-side bidding of interruptible customer loads and development of the institutions necessary to facilitate this.

The expected impact of restructuring on development of new renewable generation is also ambiguous. On the negative side, the choice of new generation is no longer made through centralized resource procurement processes and subject to political pressures from environmentalists. On the positive side, retailing efforts at "green pricing" seem to be having some success, although it is yet unclear how successful these efforts will be. Many states have adopted mandatory labelling laws requiring retailers to tell consumers what generation technologies are being used to produce their power, especially if they are making any green marketing claims. Other states are collecting renewables funding revenues through public goods charges and subsidising development of new renewable generation. Several states are imposing a renewables portfolio standard requiring all retailers to purchase specified and gradually increasing minimum percentages of their supply portfolios from renewable generators. Several bills introduced in the federal Congress have also proposed the adoption of a national renewables portfolio standard.

II.F. The technological foundations of restructuring

In the causal chain driving institutional change, current technological boundaries shape the bases of relative economic scarcity and, therefore, relative market prices. These prices, in turn, direct incremental technological innovations toward breakthroughs having the greatest economic payoffs. Meanwhile, social institutions tend to evolve to support the social organisation of production most compatible with the most economical production technologies. Thus, technological change and its associated economies are key drivers of institutional change.

Ironically, the current retail restructuring of electricity markets is not being driven primarily by technological changes internal to the power industry itself, but rather by external changes, especially in information processing and communication technologies. Many observers like to point to the recent progress in gas turbine development that has dramatically improved thermal efficiencies and reduced optimal generator scale. (Many even predict that large central-station generation will soon be a thing of the past). These changes undoubtedly fanned the fires of wholesale competition by creating favourable economics for cogeneration, on-site self-generation and small-scale EWGs. They also ultimately fanned the fires of retail competition by creating incremental generation economics that were considerably below the embedded cost of generation for utilities in many states (although falling gas prices would have been sufficient by themselves to achieve this result). This created a strong constituency for attempting to bypass the sunk costs embedded in utilities' existing generation portfolios. But it is important to recognise that these forces would not have resulted in retail access without the enabling technologies of the information revolution. Only in the 1990s did it become realistic to implement the huge information exchanges necessary to coordinate the electric system in the absence of vertical integration, conduct the necessary myriad market transactions, and figure out who owed what to whom at the end of the day. Without the information processing revolution, broad retail access would be impossible.

As we move forward, further technological changes are expected. Advancements will continue to occur in information and communications systems creating intelligent real-time load management and other retail services. These will complement the current structures implementing retail access. However, advancements in small-scale distributed generation can also be expected. While such advancements should be welcomed, their impacts on current and evolving institutions are difficult to predict. To a large extent, current institutions are based on simplistic distinctions between wholesale and retail market activities that would be challenged by the widespread development of distributed generation. Surely, to the extent further technological change favours large-scale development of distributed generation, further major institutional adjustments are likely to occur.

III. Recent Business Strategies In Response To Structural Change

The US power industry is huge and diverse. The remainder of this chapter attempts to summarise the major changes taking place in the industry as private business strategies respond to changes in the regulatory environment. The main focus is on the business strategies being pursued by traditional IOUs and major independent power players. The broad dimensions of restructuring are now reasonably clear. The once tightly-integrated vertical structure of the industry is being restructured into four horizontal strata of yet undetermined geographic scope. The top and bottom competitive strata, generation and retailing, are being functionally or structurally separated from the middle two natural monopoly strata, transmission and local distribution. Prices in the two competitive segments are being deregulated and open access to the monopoly elements is being mandated subject to regulated prices, terms and conditions. Traditional IOUs are repositioning their assets by attempting to transfer their valuable assets from regulated to non-regulated activities with the consent of regulators and other stakeholders, while also attempting to develop valuable expertise in the emerging new competitive service markets. It is unlikely these incumbent IOUs will be able to succeed on a competitive basis in all the areas they have traditionally pursued as protected monopolists. For those who choose wisely, there should be many opportunities to capture value. The strategic trends reviewed below include:

- the explosion of competitive wholesale marketing,
- the consolidation of IOUs through mergers and acquisitions,

- the huge divestitures and repurchasing of generation by IOUs,
- the consolidation of nuclear generation ownership,
- the emergence of retail energy services,
- the diversification of IOUs into telecommunications,
- the possible evolution of independent transmission companies,
- the branching out of most large players into foreign electricity investments.

III.A. Wholesale power marketing

Wholesale power marketers are simply entities who own power and sell it for resale typically under FERC market-based price regulation. They acquire ownership over power by either producing it themselves or purchasing it from another party. By 1998, the FERC had granted market-based pricing to well over 500 marketers including 337 entities that are entirely independent of IOUs, 123 entities affiliated with traditional IOUs, and 73 IOUs.[2] In creating EWGs, EPAct specifically provided that they be allowed to buy and sell power at wholesale. Thus, EPAct created a potentially huge number of additional power marketers. Later, the FERC further broadened the field by ruling that contracts, books and records were not "facilities" under the meaning of PUHCA.[3] As a result, a power marketer owning no physical production facilities does not fall under the restrictions of PUHCA and, therefore, does not need to apply for exemption as an EWG. More importantly, since not required to apply for status as an EWG, these entities are not governed by the prohibition against retail sales applicable to EWGs and can, therefore, make sales in both wholesale and retail markets.

The volume of sales by power marketers is probably the best single index of the growth of competitive wholesale electricity markets in the US The growth since the beginning of 1995 has been nothing less than dramatic. In the first quarter of 1995, there were only eight active marketers and their total sales were only 1.8 million MWh. By the end of 1998, there were over 120 active wholesale power marketers with annual sales totaling 2,283 million MWh.

Fig. VII.3 shows the top ten marketers of 1998 by sales volume. Although these statistics are national and fail to indicate anything about concentration in regional markets, they suggest very active, competitive markets. Together, the top ten marketers account for slightly less than 60% of all sales. Moreover, this percentage has declined from almost 75%

---

[2] See FERC (1998).
[3] Louis Dreyfus Electric Power Inc., 62 FERC 61,524 (1993).

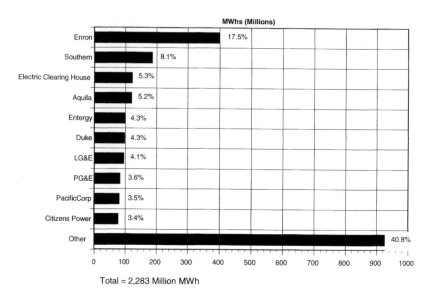

Fig. VII.3. Top ten wholesale power marketers (1998).
Source: Edison Electric Institute, *1999 Power Marketers.*

in 1996. While Enron is the clear leader and likely to remain so for some time, its relative market share has steadily slipped as new players have developed. (For instance, Enron's market share was 35.7% in the first quarter of 1996.)

It is impossible to associate the phenomenal growth of wholesale power marketing with a particular business strategy; rather, it is the manifestation of several strategies. Traditionally, utilities would use wholesale power markets on an opportunistic basis to sell power from the remaining available capacity of their facilities not being immediately used to serve their retail franchise customers, or to buy power from other utilities when it was cheaper than generating the power from their own facilities. Virtually all utilities engaged in these activities, but the efficiency of these markets was inhibited by the uncertain availability of transmission. Moreover, the urgency of pursuing these transactions was somewhat muted because most utilities controlled sufficient physical facilities to meet their retail customers' power needs and the utilities' power supply costs could be passed through to captive retail customers, albeit subject to reasonableness reviews by regulators.

In the newly restructured industry, new factors are driving the increased activity in wholesale power markets. New independent generators rely on power marketing expertise to maximise the value of their assets. Likewise, even traditional utilities are under greater pressure to increase the performance and utilisation of their generation and transmission assets. Furthermore, as retail access proceeds, many utilities have come under pressure to divest a portion of their generation assets. This has left them in a situation in which they no longer own generation adequate to serve the demands of all those retail customers who have not yet chosen alternative suppliers. Therefore, these utilities now have an urgent need for power marketer services to help them handle these suddenly exposed market risks. Likewise, newly-emerging retailers have similar needs for the risk management services of power marketers. Additionally, retail access has exposed the previously unsatisfied demands of customers for customised energy-related services.

In general, three different strategies have emerged in the power marketing business:

- The generation approach is the most traditional and focuses on selling generation output into the highest value markets.
- The retail approach focuses on working closely with end-users to identify needs and then going into the power market to satisfy these needs.
- The intermediary approach aggregates power from various sources, separates these portfolios into individual risk components, and then repackages these components into various physical and financial products to meet both individual customer and retailer needs.

Along with the new demands for power marketing services come greater abilities to satisfy them, due largely to open wholesale transmission access. Wholesale trading hubs and marketing centres are beginning to emerge for electricity similar to those in the gas industry. These hubs provide for price discovery for standard products traded at physical transfer points. This fosters the development of market liquidity. When the trade press began publishing wholesale power prices in 1994, prices were available for only seven locations: now they are available for approximately 24 locations. Development of these spot markets has also been helped by the emergence of new for-profit market makers such as Automated Power Exchange (APX), now operating private exchanges in California, New York, Ohio, and Illinois.

Growth in electricity futures trading is another significant development. Trading in electricity futures began on the New York Mercantile Exchange (NYMEX) in 1997. NYMEX now has trading in four futures contracts – two in the Western Interconnection and two in the Eastern Interconnection. NYMEX reported that in 1998 more than 80 million futures contracts were traded, an increase of nearly 10 million over 1997. Options trading also increased to more than 15 million in 1998, an increase of nearly 2 million over 1997.[4] The Chicago Board of Trade (CBOT) offers trading in two contracts – one delivered at Unicom and another at TVA. The Minneapolis Grain Exchange offers a contract for delivery at Minneapolis. Furthermore, both NYMEX and CBOT are pursuing the expansion of futures trading to additional delivery points.[5] As the geographic scope of markets expands and trading becomes more regular and liquid, new option and hedging contracts will emerge to assist market players in managing risks. Furthermore, especially because gas is the boiler fuel used in power plants operating at the price-setting margin during most hours of the day, electricity and gas markets are converging. Transmission of electricity has become a substitute for transporting gas, and *vice versa*. Considerable locational and temporal arbitrage opportunities will continue to develop. This is already in evidence in the list of top ten marketers in Fig. VII.1. Most have considerable gas trading interests and expertise.

Traditional utilities have all had internal power marketing functions and many will be tempted to expand these functions as a business strategy. Therefore, the field is likely to remain crowded with low profit margins. But even in the long term, most observers expect wholesale power marketing will remain a high-volume, low-margin, high-risk business. Episodes like the 1998 Midwest price spike will lead periodically to sober reassessments of business strategies such as the total withdrawal from the futures market of major players like LG&E, who recently announced it was leaving the speculative side of the power trading business to focus on the development of its physical generation portfolio. New Century Energies and Columbia have also recently announced their withdrawal. Cinergy, which defaulted on some major transactions during the Midwest price spike event in the summer of 1998, reported losses of $73 million. It has pledged to fix its trading problems or withdraw from the business.

III.B.   Utility mergers and acquisitions

Probably the most publicly visible sign of emerging corporate strategies is the large number of recent utility merger announcements. Table VII.1 shows a list of the largest of these mergers. Even though merger activity had increased from historical levels during the years immediately preceding EPAct, it has accelerated enormously in subsequent years, especially since 1997.

---

[4] See Kukart (1999).
[5] See FERC (1998).

Table VII.1. Selected major utility mergers and acquisitions in the last ten years.

Partners	New name	Completion
Pacific Power & Light	PacifiCorp	1989
Utah Power & Light		
Midwest Energy	Midwest Resources	1990
Iowa Resources		
IES Industries	IES Industries	1991
Iowa Southern Utilities		
UtiliCorp United	WestPlains Energy	1991
Centel Corp.		
Indiana Michigan Power		1992
Michigan Power		
Iowa Power	Midwest Power System	1992
Iowa Public Service		
Kansas Power & Light	Western Resources	1992
Kansas Gas & Electric		
Northeast Utilities		1992
Public Service of New Hampshire		
Entergy	Entergy	1993
Gulf States Utilities		
Texas Utilities	Texas Utilities	1993
Southwestern Electric Service		
PSI Resources	Cinergy	1994
Cincinnati Gas & Electric		
Midwest Resources	MidAmerican Energy	1995
Iowa-Illinois Gas & Electric		
Duke Power	Duke Energy	1997
PanEnergy		
Enron	Enron Portland General	1997
Portland General Electric	Electric	
Houston Industries	Houston Industries	1997
NorAm Energy	(Renamed Reliant)	
Ohio Edison	FirstEnergy	1997
Centerior Energy		
Texas Utilities	Texas Utilities	1997
ENSERCH		
Public Service of Colorado	New Century Energies	1997
Southwestern Public Service		
Puget Sound Power & Light	Puget Sound Energy	1997
Washington Energy		
Southern Company	Southern Company	1997
Vastor Resources		
Union Electric	Ameren	1997
CIPSCO		
WPL Holdings	Alliant Energy	1997
IES Industries		
Interstate Power Co.		
LG&E Energy	LG&E Energy	1998
KU Energy		

Table VII.1. Selected major utility mergers and acquisitions in the last ten years
continued

Partners	New name	Completion
Delmarva Power & Light	Conectiv	1998
Atlantic Energy		
Long Island Lighting	KeySpan Energy	1998
Brooklyn Union Gas		
Enova	Sempra Energy	1998
Pacific Enterprises		
Boston Edison Company (BEC)	NSTAR	1998
Commonwealth Energy		
AEP		1998
Louisiana Interstate Gas		
NiSource		1998
Bay State Gas		
CalEnergy	MidAmerican Energy	1999
MidAmerican Energy		
Duke Energy	Duke Energy	1999
UP Fuels		
Carolina Power & Light		1999
North Carolina Natural Gas		
Dominion Resources	Dominion Resources	Pending
Consolidated Natural Gas		
Energy East (NYSEG)		Pending
Connecticut Energy		
Northern States Power (NSP)	Xcel Energy	Pending
New Century Energies		
National Grid Group		Pending
New England Electric (NEES)		
UtiliCorp United		Pending
St. Joseph Power & Light		
New England Electric (NEES)		Pending
Eastern Utilities Associates (EUA)		
SCANA	SCANA	Pending
Public Service of North Carolina		
AES		Pending
CILCORP		
Consolidated Edison	Consolidated Edison	Pending
Orange and Rockland		
Sierra Pacific Resources	Sierra Pacific Resources	Pending
Nevada Power		
Scottish Power		Pending
Pacificorp		
American Electric Power	American Electric Power	Pending
Central and South West		
Western Resources	Westar Energy	Pending
Kansas City Power & Light		
Dynegy	Dynegy	Pending
Illinova		
Energy East (NYSE&G)		Pending
Central Maine Power		

Table VII.1. Selected major utility mergers and acquisitions in the last ten years
continued

Partners	New name	Completion
Northeast Utilities		Pending
Yankee Energy System		
Indiana Energy	Vectren	Pending
Southern Indiana Gas &		
Electric (SIGCORP)		
UtiliCorp United		Pending
Empire District Electric		
S.W. Acquisition		Pending
TNP Enterprises		
Energy East (NYSE&G)		Pending
CTG Resources		
Wisconsin Energy Corp.		Pending
WICOR Inc.		
Carolina Power and Light		Pending
Florida Progress Corp.		
Unicom		Pending
PECO		
Consolidated Edison		Pending
Northeast Utilities		
Detroit Edison (DTE)		Pending
Michigan Consolidated Gas (MCN)		
Allegheny Energy		Pending
West Virginia Power		
Berkshire Hathaway		Pending
MidAmerican Energy		
KeySpan Energy		Pending
Eastern Enterprises		
Sierra Pacific Resources		Pending
Portland General Electric		

* *Source:* Edison Electric Institute, *Electric Utility Restructuring Activity* and *Utility Merger Status Update*, October 1999.

In reviewing utility merger activity, it is important to keep in mind that the market for corporate control of utilities in the US is unusually constrained by PUHCA. There may well be many potential suitors for utilities who have no desire to become PUHCA-registered holding companies. Therefore, until PUHCA is either substantially amended or repealed, eligible suitors appear to be practically restricted to either other domestic utilities or foreign companies.

The potential explanations for utility mergers are diverse. Public announcements generally emphasise two rationale: achieving efficiency savings through combined operations, and creating a larger and more diverse organisation better able to survive competitively. Less-public explanations might include an expectation of increasing the ability to exercise market power as well as simple satisfaction of management egos. In truth, it is not so obvious that simple horizontal mergers of neighboring electric utilities will produce strategic benefits. The publicly claimed cost efficiency improvements are usually no more than 2–3% of revenue (and largely unverifiable in any event). Moreover, in view of open transmission access, it is questionable whether the merged entities would have any greater ability to exercise vertical market power. The FERC is likely to order the merged entity to join an RTO, thereby virtually eliminating its ability to exercise greater vertical market power through control of transmission access. The FERC will also scrutinise any increase in horizontal market power and may order some amount of generation divestiture as a precondition of merger approval.

Setting aside satisfaction of management egos, this leaves the increased ability to survive competitively as the best hypothesised motivation for mergers. Such a rationale must be based on increased economies of scale and scope. No doubt many of the almost 200 IOUs in the US are too small to achieve sufficient scale economies to survive in a competitive market and many of the mergers may be warranted on this basis. However, in the new market there will be many niches and becoming a giant may not be the best survival strategy for many of these niches. In energy trading, for instance, profits depend on speed of response. Mega-mergers may simply create large bureaucracies unable to respond profitably in such a fast-paced environment. To the extent that mergers are a substitute for a more imaginative competitive strategy, they may prove worse than doing nothing at all.

In addition to horizontal mergers which may or may not achieve significant scale economies, the list in Table VII.1 also contains many mergers apparently based on achieving increased economies of scope—especially so-called "convergence" mergers between electricity and gas companies. One rationale for these mega-mergers is to form a full-service energy company capable of supplying integrated energy solutions to medium and large customers over a wide geographic area. A separate but complementary motive is to capture efficiencies in the wholesale gas and power markets. Most observers believe that nearly all new large power plants built in the next few decades will be gas-fired. Moreover, combining gas and electric businesses provides electric companies with a strategic hedge on the unknown future of distributed generation and its possible impact on the economic viability of the electric grid. Thus the competitive futures of large-scale combined-cycle plants as well as small-scale gas-fired fuel cells, cogeneration, microturbines, and aeroderivative turbine technologies may all be the kinds of commercial speculation driving interest in convergence mergers. These convergence mergers are clearly evident in Table VII.1. Among the most notable are:

- Enron – Portland General Electric
- Duke – PanEnergy and UP Fuels
- TXU – ENSERCH
- Southern Company – Vastor
- AEP – Louisiana Interstate Gas
- NiSource – Bay State Gas
- LILCO – Brooklyn Union Gas
- Enova – Pacific Enterprises
- Dominion – Consolidated Natural Gas
- CP&L – North Carolina Natural Gas
- EnergyEast – CMP, Connecticut Energy, and CTG Resources
- SCANA – Public Service of North Carolina
- Northeast Utilities – Yankee Energy System
- Indiana Energy – SIGCORP
- Wisconsin Energy – WICOR
- DTE – Michigan Consolidated Gas
- KeySpan – Eastern Enterprises

Many more convergence mergers between electric and gas utilities can be expected in the future.

Another phenomenon worth noting in Table VII.1 is that major acquisitions of traditional electric utilities have not been limited to purchases by other US utilities and foreign companies (as discussed later). For instance, independent marketer Enron purchased Portland General Electric in 1997.[6] More recently, two large independent developers of power plants, CalEnergy and AES, have each moved to acquire major utilities— MidAmerican and CILCORP (pending)—paying $2.42 billion and $885 million respectively. Another large generation developer, Dynegy, has recently announced its plan to acquire Illinova in a $7.5 billion merger. Some observers speculate that these acquisitions of traditional utilities by large independent power producers are motivated primarily by interests in acquiring retail customers and that these companies may later sell the associated distribution wires businesses.

One final thing worthy of note is that moves were made in 1999 by small groups of investors to turn two publicly traded utilities into privately held corporations. In May 1999, an investor group headed by a former chairman and CEO of LILCO announced an agreement to acquire TNP Enterprises, parent of Texas–New Mexico Power, for approximately $1 billion including assumed debt. In October 1999, billionaire Warren Buffet of Berkshire Hathaway announced his intention to purchase

---

[6] Enron has recently announced the sale of PGE to Sierra Pacific Resources.

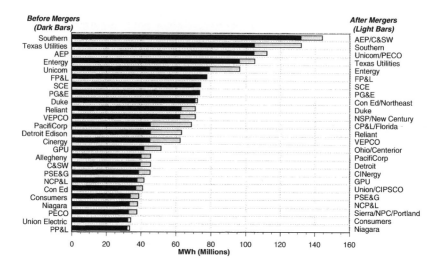

Fig. VII.4. Changes in the size distribution of the twenty largest 20 U.S. utilities (1996 Retail Sales).

MidAmerican Energy (recently merged with CalEnergy) for approximately $2 billion of equity and $7 billion of assumed debt.

Fig. VII.4 shows the impact of recently completed or announced mergers on the change from 1996 to 1999 in the size distribution of the largest 20 US utilities (as measured by total retail kilowatthour sales in 1996) assuming all announced mergers are completed. Despite the long list of mergers in Table VII.1, the impact on the size distribution of the largest 20 utilities is not especially visually impressive even though 8 mergers impact this size distribution. In addition to the creation of some giant utilities (e.g., AEP/CSW, Unicom/PECO, and ConEd/Northeast) within the top 20, mergers are also having a significant effect on the consolidation and absorption of smaller utilities toward the bottom end of the size distribution. This may be the more impressive structural change taking place.

III.C.   Sales and purchases of existing generation

Many US electric utilities are now divesting substantial portions of their traditional generation portfolios. For the most part, this is being done voluntarily in exchange for FERC approval of market-based pricing authority or mergers, or as part of a state-approved retail access package that provides the utility with recovery of its stranded costs in exchange for its support of retail access. Only the states of Maine and Texas have directly ordered utilities to divest generation. Most generation sales have been at prices considerably exceeding book values, allowing utilities to reduce their stranded cost exposure and pay down debt. According to Moody's Investors Service, virtually all of the more than 20 utilities that have sold generating assets in the past two years have improved their credit ratings by doing so.

Table VII.2 shows the amounts of generation being sold or offered in these restructuring-related divestitures. The total realignment of generation portfolios is dramatic. Almost 100,000 MW of capacity have been offered for sale, with about 60,000 MW already sold. According to the Electric Power Supply Association, this has brought the total capacity of operating merchant power plants in the US (plants not owned by local utilities or operating as QFs) to over 120,000 MW in October 1999.

Fig. VII.5 shows the top dozen purchasers of this divested generation. Buyers and sellers seem to fall into several broad categories. Some utilities clearly have business strategies to remain players in the US generation market (e.g., Edison Mission Energy and PG&E Generating). Even though their parent utilities are divesting generation, their generation affiliates are buying large amounts of generation elsewhere. Essentially, these utilities are simply rearranging the geographic location of their domestic generation portfolios in response to public policy desires that they reduce their generation market shares in their traditional local market areas to mitigate market power concerns. Other utilities appear to be exiting generation altogether with no intention of returning (e.g., NEES, Montana Power—not shown in the table). Some purchasers are independent generators taking advantage of utility divestitures to expand their generation holdings (e.g., Sithe, AES), while several buyers are utilities in the Southeast where state PUCs have generally shown little inclination to adopt retail access (e.g., Duke, Southern, FPL). These utilities may harbour hopes of remaining vertically-integrated generation owners at home while also owning competitive generation in other utilities' service territories. Alternatively, they may believe that adoption of direct access in their home states is inevitable and will eventually compel them to divest portions of their local generation. Therefore, they need to buy generation in other states now when it is for sale or risk losing their share of the national generation market.

Utilities are accustomed to owning and operating generation. Many undoubtedly believe that they are reasonably competent in doing so and will pursue a strategy of trying to remain in this business. But it is rapidly becoming a far different business than these traditional utilities are used to. The new game has no captive retail customers to absorb the risks of inefficient generator operations. Instead, the new generation business must efficiently manage an asset in a competitive wholesale market. This

Table VII.2. Restructuring-related generation divestiture (MW sold and offered).

Company	Fossil and Hydro (MWs)	Nuclear and Power Contracts (MWs)
Bangor Hydro	166	282
BEC Energy	1,983	670
Central Hudson	972	
Central and South West	1,904	
CMP Group	1,233	574
Con Ed	6,293	
Conectiv	1,732	710
Commonwealth Energy	984	675
DQE	3,311	
Edison International	9,562	
Energy East	2,366	210
EUA	543	522
GPU	5,346	1,522
Green Mountain Power	118	
Illinova	950	
KeySpan	206	
Maine Public Service	92	18
Montana Power	1,556	104
NEES	3,960	1,100
Nevada Power	1,964	
Niagara Mohawk	3,917	1,080
Northeast Utilities	3,772	435
Orange & Rockland	962	
PacifiCorp	1,049	
PEPCO	6,120	680
PP&L Resources	467	
PG&E Corp.	10,924	
Portland General	2,485	
Puget Sound Energy	829	
Sempra Energy	1,976	800
Sierra Pacific	1,085	
UGI	70	
Unicom	11,570	
UniSource	1,992	
United Illuminating	1,133	129
UNITIL	24	267
Vermont Yankee	560	
Total	92,048	11,494

Source: Edison Electric Institute, *Divestiture Action and Analysis*, Sept. 1999.

will involve not only traditional physical operational competencies but also new power marketing expertise or alliances with marketers. Key strategies for success will include risk sharing with fuel providers, redesigning operation and maintenance practices, taking a much more disciplined approach to incremental capital additions, and building a

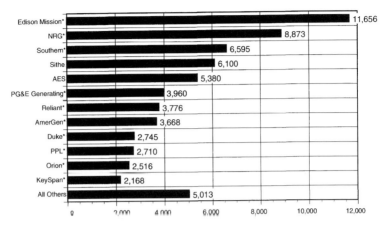

Fig. VII.5. Top twelve purchasers of recently-divested utility generation (September 1999)
* Affiliates of traditional utilities.
Source: Edison Electric Institute, *Divestiture Action and Analysis,* September 1999.

portfolio of regional generating assets to capture economies of operations and integrated bidding. It seems reasonable to expect that the core of survivors will be considerably smaller than the number of past utility incumbents and that the US generation industry will become substantially more concentrated in the hands of a few large national generating companies.

III.D. Consolidation of nuclear generation ownership

As shown in Table VII.2, many utilities are also divesting nuclear plants. Over the past year, there has been clear evidence of significant consolidation of nuclear generation ownership. Recent transactions are summarised in Table VII.3. AmerGen, a partnership of PECO and British Energy,[7] has been the front runner, purchasing Three Mile Island 1 from GPU, Clinton from Illinova and Soyland, Oyster Creek from Jersey Central, and Nine Mile Point from Niagara Mohawk. Entergy Nuclear recently entered into an agreement to purchase Pilgrim from Boston Edison. It is also rumored that either AmerGen or Entergy is likely to be the successful purchaser of the Vermont Yankee plant. AmerGen's parent, PECO, has recently announced its intention to merge with Unicom and consolidate generation operations. Both PECO and Unicom have huge nuclear generation portfolios totalling 13,279 MW, about 18% of total US nuclear

---

[7] British Energy's core business is nuclear power generation in the UK where it operates eight nuclear stations totalling 7,300 MW.

Table VII.3. Recent major nuclear plant sales (All 100% interests except as indicated).

Plant	Size (MW)	Seller(s)	Buyer
Pilgrim	670	Boston Edison	Entergy Nuclear
	73	Commonwealth Energy	Entergy Nuclear
	73	EUA	Entergy Nuclear
Three Mile Island 1	872	GPU	AmerGen
Clinton	950	Illinova & Soyland	AmerGen
Oyster Creek	619	Jersey Central	AmerGen
Nine Mile Point 1 & 2*	1,081	Niagara Mohawk	AmerGen
	205	NYSEG	AmerGen
Peach Bottom**	164	Conectiv	PECO
	164	Conectiv	PSE&G
Salem**	328	Conectiv	PSE&G
Hope Creek**	52	Conectiv	PSE&G

* Sale involved 59% of Unit 2.
** Sale involved fractional shares of plant.

generation. One of the supposed business strategies underlying this merger is the consolidation of these nuclear operations.

Many nuclear plants are openly for sale on the market: Vermont Yankee, Seabrook, Millstone 2&3, San Onofre 2&3 (SDG&E's share), James A. Fitzpatrick, and Indian Point 3. Furthermore, it can be safely assumed that many other nuclear owners are actively testing the divestiture waters and that the only real issue is an acceptable sales price. Moreover, in nearby Ontario, Canada, Ontario Power Generation recently put the eight Candu reactors at its Bruce nuclear power complex up for sale. Totalling over 6,000 MW, the Bruce facilities are the largest nuclear complex in the world. Both Entergy and Amergen are reportedly interested buyers of Bruce. Entergy has announced its intention to buy an additional 5,000 MW of nuclear capacity within the next five years, bringing its total to 10,000 MW.

Sellers of nuclear plants fall into three broad categories. First, some plants are being divested as a result of direct divestiture commitments or incentives to divest contained in political settlements adopting retail access. (For instance, Massachusetts provides stranded cost recovery only if the seller divests *all* generation.) The sales of Nine Mile Point, Pilgrim, and Vermont Yankee seem to fall into this first category. Second, for business strategic reasons, a seller may elect simply to exit *all* generation. The sale of Clinton by Illinova seems to fall into this category. Third, an owner may be experiencing difficulty operating a plant profitably and may simply believe that the plant is worth significantly more to another owner who considers it can operate the plant more profitably. The sale of Oyster Creek by Jersey Central may fall in this third category.

So far, all recent sales of nuclear plants in the US have been distressed sales, in the sense that the past owner had previously announced a nuclear exit strategy and appeared eager to sell the plant. All sales have been sweetened by 3–5 year power purchase contracts providing a time cushion with positive net cash flows while the new owner attempts to reduce operating costs. All plant sales prices have been minimal ($10–80 million per unit) reflecting little more than the value of the near-term power purchase contract. All sellers have received stranded cost recovery for the shortfall between book value and sales price. Sellers have transferred all decommissioning liabilities to new owners and have attempted to assure that they retain no residual liability whatsoever. All transferred decommissioning trust funds have been topped off using ratepayer funds to bring trust fund amounts up to levels consistent with Nuclear Regulatory Commission (NRC) funding formulae.

Counterbalancing these transactional sweeteners, it should be acknowledged that there are also certain regulatory and business barriers to consummating nuclear transactions. The NRC must approve all license transfers and the licensee must meet the test of being an "electric utility." The NRC has been moving toward a liberalised functional test of this "electric utility" qualification based on technical competence, financial security, domestic ownership, security of access to off-grid and on-grid power, and lack of anti-competitive concerns. A foreign-owned business may not be a majority owner of a US nuclear plant. Tax ambiguities are also inhibiting transactions. These can be removed by a federal law clarifying that the transfer of a nuclear plant and its associated decommissioning trust fund is not a taxable event and that any new owner will retain the current tax-advantaged treatment of annual trust fund earnings.

Roughly half the nuclear plants in the US are owned by multiple parties through co-tenancy agreements. Plant governance in these agreements is usually by consensus. The plant license cannot be transferred without the agreement of all co-tenancy partners and, in the newly restructured environment, they will generally have conflicting competitive interests. Potential purchasers will generally be interested in purchasing 100% of the plant shares, but not all owners may be interested in selling and some owners will usually see benefits in strategically holding back to extract a greater share of the sales price.

Nuclear plant buyers apparently believe they can extract values exceeding the purchase prices paid. These values are likely based on five potential strategies:

- improving operating and investment efficiencies,
- extracting greater market revenues by combining these plants within large regional generation portfolios,

- extracting locational values through ancillary services markets,
- extending plant lives and deferring decommissioning by extending NRC operating licenses, and
- eventually decommissioning the plant for less than the amount accrued in the decommissioning trust fund.

An important question is whether the transition to a more competitive environment will improve the economic future for nuclear generation in the US or hasten its demise. There is no clear answer to this key question. In recent years, the conventional wisdom has been that no utility chief financial officer would approve investment in a new nuclear plant and that no PUC would approve accepting the financial risks on behalf of retail franchise customers. On the other hand, under traditional utility regulation, utility management had an uneconomic incentive to continue to operate existing nuclear plants because plant closure would threaten the recovery of sunk costs from ratepayers. In the new competitive environment, these regulatory distortions are removed. A confident chief financial officer of a nuclear generation consolidation company with a large nuclear portfolio may see little or no incremental financial risk in initiating construction of a new nuclear plant. On the other hand, a poorly operating nuclear plant may be more likely to be shut down in the new environment because the decision to do so will not be distorted by a regulatory framework that makes recovery of sunk costs a part of this decision calculus. On balance, it seems likely that restructuring may improve the economic future of nuclear power in the US by consolidating operations in more professional hands, forcing more economic decision-making, and consolidating nuclear portfolios into a few companies who view nuclear power as a solid business platform.

III.E. New merchant power plants

Regardless of the further spread of retail access, it is doubtful that any new generation plant will ever again be constructed under the traditional cost-of-service framework. Instead, it is the market that will be relied upon to bring forth adequate new generation. There are clear signs that the market is responding enthusiastically to this challenge. In its March 1999 survey of the electric utility industry, Goldman Sachs compiled an extensive (though not necessarily comprehensive) list of new merchant generation facilities planned or under construction in the US The list totals 85,030 MW, with more than 30,000 MW in the Northeast, roughly 10,000 MW each in the Southeast, Midwest, and Southwest, and over 20,000 MW in the Far West.

The list of companies in all areas is extremely diverse. PG&E

Generating is a big player in the Northeast with plans for over 9,000 MW, almost one-third of the planned additions in the region. Sithe is the largest of the independents in the Northeast in terms of planned additions with 4,300 MW. In California, the California Energy Commission lists 20 projects totalling 13,464 MW as current, expected or approved licensing cases. These projects are spread among 13 separate developers: Calpine is the largest with 2,380 MW; PG&E Generating second largest with 2,098 MW; Duke is third with 1,736 MW.

III.F. Energy services retailing

As each successive state adopts retail access, its native utilities have had to decide the course of their retailing strategies. The result has been a cultural shock for utility management. All utilities have been engaged for years in marketing energy services to captive customers. Most believe they have some amount of retailing experience and expertise, and certainly all have a large number of retailing employees with a vested interest in pursuing a retailing strategy. Moreover, years of thinking like vertically-integrated monopolies have conditioned management erroneously to regard the financial security of all their upstream investments as being critically dependent on their retaining a base of retail customers. In short, every traditional utility has a knee-jerk corporate reflex to want to retain as many of its current retail customers as possible and the more aggressive utilities have ambitions to expand their local retailing bases into regional or national retailing businesses.

But following a more deliberate and sober strategic assessment, internal sceptics usually arise to challenge this conventional reflex. First, a large part of the retailing business is a pure commodity business in which the primary service is the provision of various risk hedges, especially to large customers. While this business is familiar to wholesale power marketers, it is almost totally foreign to the traditional utility's retailing employees. Moreover, it is a risky, low-margin business likely to draw a good deal of concern from the utility's chief financial officer. Second, being a successful retailer to large customers with nationwide accounts may require a national, or at least broad regional, retailing operation. It may not be possible to be successful with large customers while operating only on a local basis. Third, it is not at all obvious that successful retailing is required to achieve success in any other upstream production and delivery activity. Fourth, all states adopting retail access have also adopted very strict retailing affiliate rules designed to neutralise the incumbent advantages of the utility and its affiliates in retailing. Utilities are frequently prohibited from offering anything but the simplest of tariffs to customers. More attractive competitive products can be offered only through a retailing affiliate and the utility is prohibited from preferentially referring its customers to this affiliate or giving the affiliate preferential access to any customer information.

Thus far in the US, development of competitive retailing in those states adopting retail access has been slow to develop, especially for smaller customers. This is primarily due to the narrow retail margins available to competitors under the rules governing restructuring. For instance, in Massachusetts and Rhode Island, during the first seven years following retail access, customers have a choice of buying their power from a competitive retailer (including utility affiliates) or purchasing it from the local utility under a "standard offer." The problem for competitive retailers is that, as part of a complex deal to allow utilities to recover stranded costs while encouraging them to divest their generation, the pricing in these standard offers was set below prevailing wholesale prices during the first several years of transition. The result is negative retail margins for utilities and, therefore, an almost impossible market environment for independent retailers to attract customers.

The market environment is more favourable but still very challenging for competitive retailers in California. During an initial four-year transition, all customers' rates are frozen. All customers have the option of continuing to purchase power from their local utility. The utility is obligated to purchase all such power from the official spot-market Power Exchange (PX) and pass it along to customers at cost without any extra profit mark-up. Customers purchasing power from competitive retailers pay the frozen price minus these cost-based energy charges. Thus, to be attractive on a purely commodity basis, a retailer must offer to sell retail power below the PX wholesale power cost. Needless to say, retailers find it difficult to purchase energy at prices below the PX spot market and this makes it difficult for competitive retailers to win market share. Moreover, the retail price freeze essentially offers all customers a hedge against spot-market volatility. Once the four-year transition ends, this volatility in the utilities' basic service product will be uncovered and presumably competitive retailers can be considerably more successful by offering customers price-hedging services. Despite these transition conditions and the much-publicised temporary withdrawal of Enron from the small consumer market in California during 1998, the California market is nonetheless very active. Companies marketing to residential and small commercial customers in California must register with the State. There are 32 registered retailers. Ten of these retailers are affiliates of traditional utilities, including regional utilities such as Arizona Public Service and Salt River Project as well as large national players such as Duke, Southern, New England Electric and Green Mountain Power. After the first 18 months of market operation, 13.5% of all California IOU loads were being served by competitive retailers.

To date, the market in Pennsylvania has provided the most favourable environment for competitive retailers. Unlike Massachusetts, Rhode Island, and California, when a customer in Pennsylvania purchases power from a competitive retailer, the customer receives a reduction in his utility bill that exceeds the wholesale price of electricity by a considerable margin. This is essentially achieved by making a portion of the utilities' stranded cost avoidable by customers switching to competitive retailers. This creates a potential near-term profit margin for competitive retailers. But this pricing mechanism cannot be sustained in the long run. It is not clear what sustainable competitive structure will be introduced to succeed it after the transitional period of stranded cost recovery has ended.

Successful retail business strategies generally involve one or more of the following:

- branding,
- financial hedges,
- related energy services,
- "green" power marketing,
- metering and billing services, and
- simultaneous provision of multiple utility services.

Efforts at branding are immediately apparent in Table VII.1. Utilities with distinctive regional names such as Public Service of Indiana, Kentucky Utilities, Louisville Gas and Electric, Baltimore Gas & Electric, San Diego Gas and Electric, Tucson Electric Power, Middle South Utilities, and Houston Power and Light have become respectively PSI, KU Energy, LG&E Energy, Constellation, Enova, UniSource, Entergy, and Reliant. Moreover, mergers have created further opportunities to introduce new names such as Western Resources, Cinergy, FirstEnergy, Ameren, Conectiv, New Century Energies, Alliant, and Sempra.

But jettisoning a well-regarded regional name in pursuit of a national brand can be a double-edged sword. Incumbent energy providers have proven to have stronger brand equity than many critics believed. It appears that most residential customers will remain with their incumbent utility provider assuming the name stays approximately the same and prices remain roughly steady. Consequently, several attempts at national branding using obscure names have been dismal failures and quickly retracted in favour of names that are more recognisable at home while toning down their traditional regionalism. Thus, Pacific Gas and Electric initially created Vantus as its retailer but shortly thereafter renamed it PG&E Energy Services. Similarly, Public Service Electric and Gas launched Energis before renaming it PSE&G Energy Technologies. Southern California Edison spent a brief time under the obscure identity of SCECorp before renaming itself Edison International—a name with both national and international meaning as well as local recognition. A few other utilities such as Southern and Green Mountain Power are fortunate to have names that just seem to play well nationally while also retaining long-established local brand loyalties.

Some companies have spent large sums of money to establish brand names. For instance, Enron spent $75 million in 1998 to establish its brand nationally. In one of the most well-publicised failures, UtiliCorp United spent $20 million launching its EnergyOne brand in 1995. EnergyOne was to combine the services of UtiliCorp and PECO Energy with AT&T and electric security giant ADT Security Services.[8] In 1998, UtiliCorp shut down this multi-utility franchise branding program with not a single other utility having subscribed to use the EnergyOne brand. It seems likely that most potential franchisees had been working diligently to strengthen their own brand identity and viewed the prospective use of EnergyOne as a dilution of their own identity.

Retailing to large customers generally involves some mixture of providing commodity hedges along with various energy services. Hedging by itself is best viewed as essentially a commodities market service. Risks are high and margins are slim. But provision of energy services is a far different business. Energy service companies (ESCOs) provide a wide range of services including energy-efficient design services, computerised energy use modelling, equipment acquisition and installation, performance contracting, shared-savings programs, energy monitoring, facilities management, etc. ESCOs frequently specialise in developing, installing, and financing comprehensive, performance-based projects, typically five to ten years in duration, aimed at improving the energy efficiency or demand profile of customer facilities. Projects tend to be performance-based with the ESCO's compensation tied to the amount of energy actually saved. About 30–40 major ESCOs are currently active in the US. A few large super-ESCOs (such as Duke Solutions, Edison Source, Enron Energy Services, PG&E Energy Services, and Xenergy) account for most of the revenues.

Large customers are also pursuing retail strategies, but from the demand side of the market. For instance, the Illinois Chamber of Commerce recently established the Chamber Energy Alliance to act as a buying alliance for potentially thousands of small businesses in Illinois. The Alliance has entered into a ten-year agreement with MidAmerican Energy

---

[8] See Brew and Phelps (1998), p. 23–29.

to be its exclusive supplier of electricity, gas and energy services. Recently in Michigan, a group of ten medium-sized customers formed a joint purchasing alliance called Michigan Industrial Energy Cooperative (MIEC). MIEC has issued an RFP soliciting proposals from power suppliers for approximately 47 MW of power beginning in the year 2000.

Another important dimension of retail strategy involves metering and billing services. In most states adopting retail access, competitive retailers have a choice of billing customers directly or having the local utility bill customers on their behalf. In a few states, such as California, the competitive retailer can also elect to collect the bill on behalf of the local utility distribution company, thereby depriving the local utility of any billing contact with the customer. Many states, at least for the time being, have chosen to leave metering as an exclusive function of the local utility. However, a few states allow competitive retailers to own, maintain, and read meters. Competition in metering and billing is a potentially significant market that is only beginning to take shape. The future of this market will depend a great deal on precisely what regulations govern it, especially the pricing of these services and the ability of customers to avoid these charges by purchasing their metering and billing services from another provider.

A final retail strategy involves the simultaneous provision of multiple utility services. This is likely to be a significant component of the business strategies underlying many convergence mergers between electric and gas companies. For instance, this is likely a major motivation underlying the previously discussed convergence mergers of Enova and Pacific Enterprises, Dominion Resources and Consolidated Natural Gas, Indiana Energy and SIGCORP, and Northeast Utilities and Yankee Energy System. NEES has also recently announced the acquisition of Texas-Ohio Gas, one of the largest providers of unregulated retail natural gas service in the Northeast. In addition to combining gas and electricity, most large utilities are also pursuing telecom ventures to complement their electricity distribution or retailing businesses and create the potential for their offering multiple retail utility services.

III.G. Green power development and retailing

Retailing of "green power" has also become a significant niche business. A relatively large percentage of customers typically indicate in marketing surveys that they would be willing to purchase power produced by renewable generation even if they have to pay a modest price premium. In practice, green retailers have found the public more reluctant to buy green power than these surveys seem to indicate. Nonetheless, a few retailers are successfully pursuing the green retail market. For the time

Table VII.4. Green power retailers and products.

California		Pennsylvania	
Commonwealth Energy -	GreenSmart	Conectiv*	- Nature's Power
New West Energy*	- Green Value	Green Mountain*	- Nature's Choice
Edison Source*	- Earth Source		- Enviro Blend
Green Mountain*	- Wind for the Future		
	- EarthCare		
	- Renewables Electricity		
Keystone Energy	- Earth Choice		
PG&E Energy Services* -	Clean Choice		
APX	- Green Power Market		
PacifiCorp*	- Green Power		
Foresight Energy	- Ecopower		
Enron	- Earthsmart		

* Affiliates of traditional utilities.
Source: Center for Resource Solutions website, June 1999.

being in California, this market is supplemented by a 1.5¢ per kWh credit to green retailers funded through a public goods charge paid by all interconnected retail customers. Table VII.4 shows the green power retailers in California and Pennsylvania who have been certified by the independent non-profit Green-e program sponsored by the Center for Resource Solutions located in San Francisco.

It is also worth noting that APX (Automated Power Exchange), a private for-profit market operator, has begun operating a green spot-market in California. The APX market is based on buying and selling renewables certificates, or "green tickets". Each ticket represents the value of delivering renewable power separate from the commodity value of the energy itself. This allows a retailer to combine tickets with energy produced from any source and legitimately claim it is thereby paying for the production of a corresponding amount of green power. From May to September 1999, APX has handled about 175,000 MWh or green transactions and the ticket premiums have been recently selling at about half a cent per kWh (roughly a 15% premium over the commodity energy value).

To support their green marketing efforts, green retailers are pursuing partnerships with renewable generators or developing their own. For instance, recently Green Mountain announced the construction of 2.1 MW of new wind turbines in California and a small solar photovoltaic facility in Pennsylvania. GPU has recently completed a small solar photovoltaic facility in California and Green Mountain has contracted with GPU to purchase all the power from this facility for its green marketing program. Much larger projects are also on the drawing board. For instance,

Composite Power, a consortium of numerous parties, hopes to complete during the next two to three years the Nevada Green Energy Project, a project near Las Vegas consisting of 50–150 MW of several renewable technologies including wind, solar, geothermal, and biomass projects. Their long-term goal is to develop up to 1,000 MW of renewable power for retailing in deregulated markets in the western states.

III.H. Diversification into telecommunications

During the 1980s, several US utilities ventured far from their traditional expertise and attempted diversifications into far-ranging businesses such as real estate, financial services, even retail sporting goods and drug stores. For the most part, these diversifications proved to be miserable failures and engendered long-lasting negative reactions from the US financial community. Consequently, utility diversifications in the 1990s have generally involved closely-related businesses with reasonably clear prospects for business complementarity. Among the most frequently pursued diversifications are those into various telecommunications ventures. Indeed, deregulation in both the telecommunications and electric power industries is engendering business strategies likely to produce greater convergence in these two mega-industries.

For years, US electric utilities have had ample legal authority to build telecommunication facilities for internal use and most utilities own extensive telecom facilities for managing their power systems. Even before the advent of retail access, electric utilities began recognising they could use broadband, switched telecommunications to retail customers to enable substantial efficiency gains in the operation of their utility systems. With the spread of retail access, far more voluminous flows of information will be valuable to inform customers or their retailing agents of real-time prices as well as to drive demand-side management software and smart meters. Indeed, without the widespread development of two-way communications, much of the potential benefits of retail access will fail to be realised. Without such two-way communications, real-time demands may be so price-inelastic that the resulting price volatility in energy spot-markets may create a political backlash sufficient to slow down or arrest the spread of current retail access initiatives.

The Telecommunications Act of 1996 opened the telecom door for electric utilities by removing restrictions on use of their existing telecom networks and enabling them to compete broadly in telecom businesses. As a result, many utilities have begun leasing their excess capacity ("dark fibre") to telecom service providers. Some electric utilities have even begun operating as telecom service providers themselves or through partnerships and acquisitions. As summarised in Table VII.5, utilities are

Table VII.5. Selected ventures by electric companies into telecommunications.

Companies	Wholesale	Wireline	Wireless
American Electric Power (AEP)	x		x
Boston Edison	x		
Carolina Power and Light	x		
Central and Southwest	x	x	
Conectiv	x	x	x
Duke	x		
Edison International	x		
Enron	x		
Entergy	x		
MidAmerican	x		
Montana Power	x		
PacifiCorp	x	x	
SCANA	x	x	
Texas Utilities	x	x	
Virginia Power (VEPCO)	x	x	

Source: McGraw-Hill, *Electric Utility Week,* 1996-1999.

generally offering wholesale services, wireline services including voice and data, and even beginning to expand to wireless services.

The expansion of electric utilities into telecom is driven by various forces: their desire to compete in changing electric power markets, consumer demand for bundling multiple utility services, and the simple attractiveness of growth opportunities in telecom. While annual growth in electric revenues is forecast to be only about 2%, annual growth in telecom revenues is expected to be around 7%. In entering the telecom market, utilities are competing directly with incumbent telecom companies and numerous aspiring new entrants. This competition includes the regional Bell Operating Companies, interchange carriers, internet service providers, cable television providers, competitive access providers, and competitive local exchange carriers. In this competition, electric utilities can expect to be disadvantaged by their general lack of expertise in telecom technologies and retail marketing. However, they also enter the field with certain important advantages, including an extensive customer base, usually a reputation for reliable high-quality service, ownership of valuable rights-of-way and telecom infrastructure, widespread name recognition and a functioning billing engine capable of processing high volumes of monthly bills.

Electric utilities can generally take one of three courses in venturing further into the telecom industry: form strategic partnerships with existing telecom companies, acquire telecom companies, or branch out on their own. The partnering strategy allows a utility to gain many of the strengths that it traditionally lacks. For instance, PG&E has partnered with Microsoft and cable giant TCI; TECO with IBM; PSE&G, ConEd and Entergy with AT&T; UtiliCorp with Novell; AEP with Sprint; Boston Edison with RCN; CP&L and Duke with Bell South; PEPCO with RCN and Metricom; and VEPCO with Cox Cable and Nortel.

There are also numerous examples of purchases of telecom companies by electric utilities. AEP has recently purchased personal communication service (PCS) companies in Virginia and West Virginia to provide improved energy information products and services to its electric customers. SCANA is acquiring major equity interests in companies such as InterCel, providing PCS in the wireless communications market. Texas Utilities has acquired Lufkin–Conroe, the fourth largest telephone provider in Texas, to provide a full range of local and long-distance telecom services. The Williams Company has formed a joint venture (WilTel) with Nortel which offers a variety of data, multimedia, voice and video interconnect products; WilTel has, in turn, acquired Bell South's customer premise equipment sales and service operations in 29 states as well as two network system integrators, Comlink and SoftIron. MidAmerican and Alliant together have purchased a 35% interest in McLeod USA and have an agreement to invest $1 billion in McLeod to provide diverse telecom services throughout the Midwest and Rocky Mountain states.

Several utilities are undertaking major internal expansions either individually or jointly with other energy utilities. AEP, FirstEnergy, Allegheny Energy and GPU recently announced a partnership to link their systems across nine states from New York to Illinois to provide voice and digital services on a wholesale basis to retail service providers. Conectiv has transferred its fibreoptic assets to a subsidiary and plans to provide local telephone and long distance services in Delaware, Maryland, southeastern Pennsylvania and southern New Jersey. Through DukeNet, Duke Power will provide PCS in the Charlotte area in partnership with BellSouth, CP&L, and 31 Carolina-based independent telephone companies. DukeNet is currently leasing its dark fibre to carriers and is building a fibre-coax hybrid network to eventually deliver internet access, home security and automation services to homes. Edison International, the owner of the largest internal system of fibreoptic and microwave infrastructure in California (50,000 route-miles), recently launched a business venture to lease its excess capacity to retail service providers. Enron owns a 55 mile fibreoptic network surrounding the Portland area and plans to provide wholesale services and high-speed video, data, and multimedia services. In conjunction with Williams and Montana Power, Enron is building a 1,620 mile fibre optic network from Portland to Los Angeles. Montana Power, through Touch America, provides interconnection services in all of Montana's major cities as well as long distance services in the northwestern US Touch America now has over 15,000 miles of fibre installed in thirteen Western and Midwestern states. Idaho Power is a founding partner in Allied Utility Network which hopes to serve 20 million users with diverse retail services within five years. PacifiCorp and KN Energy have teamed up to offer an integrated package of energy, long distance telephone, cellular paging, internet and satellite television services under the Simple Choice brand. PacifiCorp owns 87% of telecom subsidiary Pacific Telecom which provides local telephone service in the West and Upper Midwest and aspires to become a leading provider of local exchange services in rural markets. SCANA offers telecom services over its 900 mile fibreoptic network (Gulf States FiberNet) running through Alabama, Georgia, Mississippi, Louisiana, and the Carolinas. Southern Company developed an extensive wireless network, called Southern LINC, to respond to its customer's emergency needs. Southern is now offering a variety of wireless telecom services. Finally, Williams, through Vyvx, offers broadcast-quality television and multimedia transmission services nationwide using its 17,000 mile fibreoptic and satellite systems.

III.I. Independent transmission companies

High-voltage transmission continues to be regulated by the FERC (except for the separate intrastate system in Texas). At least for now, high-voltage transmission continues to be owned by the same incumbent utilities owning the local distribution facilities. This produces a patchwork of transmission ownership broadly corresponding to current utilities' local retail franchise areas. As the industry undergoes restructuring from vertical columns to horizontal strata, the question naturally arises as to whether these separate local transmission companies will be separated eventually from their traditional distribution affiliates and rebundled over broad geographic areas to form so-called "transcos" through mergers, acquisitions, or joint ventures.

Although it is appealing to draw direct analogies to interstate gas pipelines, certain differences must be acknowledged. Gas pipelines generally provide unidirectional flow from distant gas fields to city gates. By contrast, electric transmission lines integrate regional generation resources and customers in a fabric of multiple, redundant paths with constantly varying line flows. The network interdependencies caused by parallel electric flows provide considerable justification for the regional consolidation of electric grid control. This integration could be achieved either through ISOs or regional transcos, and there is a debate currently raging over which of these institutional forms should ultimately prevail.

Utilities in states adopting retail access originally embraced ISOs as a means for shedding their vertical market power so that they could receive market-based pricing approval while also retaining a large portion of their generation. Ultimately, to placate regulators and facilitate recovery of their stranded costs, many of these utilities saw more wisdom in divesting larger amounts of their generation than originally contemplated. The FERC embraced ISOs as a superior way to eliminate vertical market power compared to the policing provisions of Orders 888 and 889. Therefore, the FERC began requiring participation in regional RTOs as a condition for approving mergers.

Integrating regional control over the grid through a not-for-profit ISO has certain advantages. It can be accomplished rather quickly over wide areas and accommodates participation by both IOUs and public power entities. Its degree of independence is more credible to a wider variety of stakeholders, and the FERC seems more comfortable affording ISOs light-handed regulation and delegating to them an active market oversight role. Yet there are also potentially serious drawbacks to ISOs. They are no more independent than the composition of their governing boards, and the separation of transmission ownership from control raises serious concerns about incentives for efficient operations and investments.

The term "transco" is usually used to refer to an independent transmission company that also performs the customary functions of an ISO. In this sense, ISOs and transcos are mutually exclusive choices. But an independent broad regional transmission company could also exist underneath the control of an ISO. The term "gridco" is sometimes used to distinguish this situation. Sometimes it is suggested that an ISO might serve as an interim institution until a gridco of sufficient size can be formed. Then, the gridco would assume the ISO's responsibilities and become a transco. But there are good reasons to be sceptical of the political feasibility of such a path. Proponents of integrating regional grid control under a transco emphasise the alignment of ownership and control, and the greater incentives for efficiency. Critics emphasise the difficulties of policing transco independence, structuring efficient operating and investment incentives, quickly achieving broad geographic scope, and attracting the participation of public power entities.

There are various entities which own extensive transmission systems in the US. These include large holding companies such as AEP, Southern and Entergy, as well as large federal entities such as Bonneville Power Administration, TVA, and WAPA. The UK's National Grid Group recently acquired NEES and EUA, both of which have divested most of their generation and retain largely wires assets only. In essence, the National Grid Company owns a gridco under the New England ISO. Recently, a new business venture, Atlantic Transco Inc. of Augusta, Maine, has offered to purchase the transmission systems of all New England utilities. The result would be a single gridco operating in conjunction with the New England ISO. Not surprisingly, NEES has stated it is not interested in the deal. Many observers speculate that soon-to-be NEES parent, National Grid, likely has similar and competing business plans for forming a New England transco or gridco.

Elsewhere, certain IOUs are attempting to press the transco issue with the FERC. For instance, in April 1999, Entergy filed the general structure of a transco proposal with the FERC and asked for an expedited declaratory order that its proposal met the FERC's requirements for an RTO so that Entergy could attract additional regional participants to its transco as soon as possible. The FERC has since issued such an order. In June 1999, the Alliance transco applied for approval by the FERC. Its members include AEP, CMS, Detroit Edison, FirstEnergy, and VEPCO. The Alliance transco would be larger than any of the previously approved ISOs and as such is currently the primary test case for FERC approval of a transco.

Seemingly stripped by regulators of its strategic value to assist commercial affiliates, the business value of owning transmission becomes an unresolved question. Price regulation by the FERC will be key. To the extent that the FERC imposes low rates of equity return and low depreciation rates on transmission investments, many will view transmission as an unattractive business. But sooner or later, the FERC will have to adopt reasonable policies to encourage grid investments. Expert transmission companies with world-class skills in grid expansion, operation and investment will eventually find it attractive to consolidate ownership of the US grid. To be successful, they will have to negotiate favourable regulation (presumably, performance-based), control costs, and correctly anticipate and accommodate the economics of distributed generation.

III.J. Foreign investment in the US

With a few notable exceptions, international firms other than British companies have not been major investors in the US market. One exception is Tractebel (Belgium) which has over 1,200 MW of generation in operation and over 1,100 MW planned or under development. Several other foreign firms also have small positions in the US generation market. Sithe Energies, a firm incorporated in the US and sometimes thought to be a domestic firm even though it is controlled by French (Vivendi) and Japanese (Marubeni) investors, has one of the largest portfolios of independent generation projects in the US totalling about 11,200 MW in operation with about 4,500 MW more planned or under construction. In October 1999, Sithe's owners indicated they are interested in selling all of Sithe's US and international generation.

The highly visible exception to the general lack of activity in the US by foreign electricity companies is the very active interest by British companies. As previously noted, Scottish Power is acquiring PacifiCorp, the National Grid Group is buying New England Electric System and Eastern Utilities, and British Energy as a partner with PECO in AmerGen is purchasing nuclear power plants.

In mid-1999, National Power announced plans to build 4,000 MW of new generation in the US by the end of 2001 to comprise half of its near-term plan to spend an additional $4 billion internationally, mostly in the US, Europe and Australia, to bring its generation portfolio outside the UK to 22,500 MW. National Power is currently building a 1,100 MW plant in Texas and has four other gas-fired plants and a windfarm totaling 1,441 MW elsewhere in the US It also has plans to construct two new plants in Texas and Massachusetts that would add another 1,650 MW to its US portfolio, bringing the total to over 4,000 MW. In 1999, National Power sold its 3,960 MW coal-fired Drax power station in the UK to AES for $3 billion.[9] In August 1999, National Power announced its goal to use the proceeds from its Drax sale to increase its US generation portfolio to 8,000 MW within five years. National Power is reportedly currently looking for either a significant acquisition or a joint venture agreement with a major US partner.

PowerGen is another UK firm with stated intentions to invest substantially more in the US market. In 1998, PowerGen was involved in serious acquisition negotiations with Reliant but the talks collapsed at the last moment. Meanwhile, in mid-1999, flush with $2.1 billion from the recent sale of 4,000 MW of its U.K. powerplants to Edison Mission Energy, PowerGen announced a strategic priority to buy a mid-sized vertically integrated US utility for up to $7 billion. Recently, PowerGen reputedly bid to acquire Florida Progress, but lost out to Carolina Power and Light.

III.K. US investment abroad

In recent years, US companies have begun making extensive investments in electricity production and distribution facilities in foreign countries. Although some of these investments have come from traditional overseas investors like US oil companies, most have come from traditional IOUs and unaffiliated US generation developers. Several related forces are behind this sudden explosion of US foreign investment. First, when EPAct amended PUHCA, it defined the legal concept of a Foreign Utility Company and categorically exempted such enterprises from the general

---

[9] The sale of Drax had been ordered by the UK Department of Trade and Industry as a condition of National Power's acquisition of the retailing business of Midlands Electricity.

PUHCA requirement that electric facilities owned by US companies must be physically interconnected. Thereafter, US companies investing overseas in electric facilities were freed from the administrative burden and uncertainty of having to seek a PUHCA exemption from the Security and Exchange Commission. The second important force was the growing privatisation and liberalisation of electricity markets throughout the world. Without these changes, there would have been far fewer opportunities for US foreign investment. The U.K., Norway, Argentina, Chile, New Zealand, the European Union and Australia have all adopted the principles of competition and retail access. A third important force has been the general slowdown of the expansion of the US electricity sector in the past 20 years compared to the growth prospects for electricity demand abroad. While US demand growth has slowed below 2%, electricity demand in some foreign countries is forecast to grow at an annual rate of 7% in the next decade. At home, US companies experience fierce competition with other US firms to build the new generation necessary to satisfy the limited growth in the domestic market. While competition abroad is also active, many companies are betting that bidding successes and larger profit margins will be easier to achieve.

The emerging international power business is dominated by companies from the US and U.K. Large markets developed most quickly in Asia and Latin America, with markets in Eastern Europe and the Middle East following later. The major US companies that appear most committed to an international power business include CMS, Central and South West, Duke, Edison International, Entergy, GPU, PSE&G, Reliant, NRG, Southern, Texas Utilities, UtiliCorp, AES, and Enron. US companies appear to be following a variety of business strategies overseas. Some seem to be specialising in the acquisition and management of transmission and distribution infrastructure; others largely in the development of generation facilities. Still others seem to be interested in pursuing a mixed portfolio of distribution and generation, either separately or as integrated systems.

Risk management is one of the most important success factors in the international power business. There are plenty of risks to be managed including ordinary investment and fuel risks, but also political, sovereignty, contractual, and foreign exchange risks. Risk management favours larger enterprises, and joint projects with other international developers, fuel suppliers, and banks as well as local strategic partners. Another reason size and partnering are important is access to capital: larger firms are generally able to use their superior access to capital markets to move more quickly and avoid project financing delays that may hamper smaller firms. To develop a generation portfolio in today's market requires an initial capital contribution of at least $500 million. It takes about $5–$10 million to assemble a viable project proposal. This means that with a success rate of one-in-ten, it would take an outlay of about $500 million to develop a portfolio of ten successful projects. A few independents such as AES and CalEnergy have been able to build impressive scale from rather meagre beginnings just 15 years ago. Other developers such as Edison Mission Energy have built scale gradually over the same timeframe, although with the assistance of a sizable parent. However, most developers are utility affiliates and relative newcomers. Some have been able to acquire scale instantaneously through acquisition, such as Southern Company's purchase of well-established international generation developer CEPA.

To the extent US companies are creating value through their international investments, they are either creating new assets through their dealmaking skills or enhancing the value of existing assets. Owning and operating these facilities for their full lifespan may not be the best strategy. Indeed, for some host countries, foreign financing of too large a portion of the domestic energy sector may cause balance-of-payment problems, thereby necessitating greater sharing of energy project ownership with local investors in the long term. Also, in order to develop a project, sponsors often must assume greater equity than they would like to hold in the long term. Ideally, many would prefer to have smaller equity amounts in a larger number of projects, thereby obtaining both risk diversity and greater leverage from their capital. To obtain this balance, project developers frequently sell off a portion of their equity at a later stage of project development.

Over the long term, US companies will need to decide the balance they wish to achieve between entrepreneurial project development and long-term portfolio investment in operating energy facilities. Therefore, it can be expected that these emerging global power companies will be active traders in these assets, buying and selling assets to take capital gains, raise capital for new project opportunities, and rebalance portfolios. They will maintain management control over many of their assets, although not necessarily through majority ownership. They will use their dealmaking skills, access to capital markets, and knowledge of local markets and politics as their main competitive advantages in acquiring both new and existing assets.

Although the international business strategies of US companies do not fall neatly into any clearly distinct boxes, there appear to be three broad categories. Some companies appear to be primarily interested in acquiring and operating transmission and distribution infrastructure; others are concentrating mostly on developing generation; while those in a third category seem interested in acquiring vertically-integrated systems. In the first category, several US companies appear to be interested in the acquisition and management of transmission and distribution infrastructure.

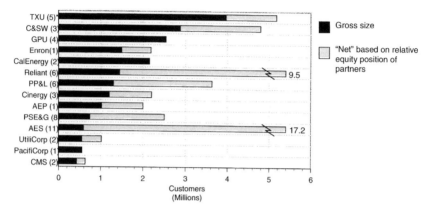

Fig. VII.6. U.S. companies with international distribution holdings (Excluding original utilities owned by parent).
* Numbers following names indicate number of separate distribution companies owned.
Source: McGraw-Hill, *Electric Utility Week.*

Fig. VII.6 shows the 14 US companies with the largest holdings of overseas distribution companies (as measured by distribution customers). Distribution, in particular, offers opportunities for substantial profits in some host countries because this is where many of the inefficiencies are to be found. Also, by purchasing distribution companies already in retail-access markets, US companies hope to more quickly develop the corporate culture and expertise necessary to succeed in the emerging retail-access markets at home. But international distribution investments may also have their downsides. Entrenched excess labour forces may be politically protected and difficult to reduce. Consumers may also feel socially entitled to large amounts of energy theft. Finally, once in foreign hands, distribution companies may be "sitting ducks" ripe for regulatory opportunism in the form of substantially reduced allowed returns.

As shown in Table VII.6, over half the UK regional electricity companies, by value, are now owned by US firms. Likewise, US firms also own over three-quarters of the distribution and retailing companies in Victoria, Australia. For instance, in early 1997, giant AEP joined with Public Service Colorado in paying $2.44 billion to acquire Yorkshire Electricity, a UK regional electric company. In late 1998, AEP announced an agreement with Entergy to purchase CitiPower, an electric distribution and retail sales company serving part of Melbourne, Australia. In late 1995, Central and South West acquired the SEEBoard regional electric company in the UK for $2.52 billion. Since 1996, CSW has also purchased multiple small distribution companies in Brazil. CSW is also developing generation resources in both Brazil and the UK CalEnergy, a US independent

Table VII.6. U.S. ownership of UK regional electric companies (October 1999).

UK REC	US Owners
Northern Electric	CalEnergy
Yorkshire	AEP and New Century Energies
Eastern	TXU
SEEBoard	Central and South West
SWEB	Southern and PP&L
Midlands	GPU

power producer owns Northern Electric, a U.K. regional electric company. GPU has been especially active in acquiring overseas transmission and distribution infrastructure. In 1996, GPU joined with Cinergy in paying $2.59 billion for Midlands Electricity, a U.K. regional electric company. In 1998, these partners sold the Midlands retailing business to National Power. In 1999, Cinergy sold its share of the Midlands "wires" business to GPU stating that it wished to pursue a strategy of non-regulated domestic and international growth initiatives. In 1998, GPU paid $1.9 billion to acquire PowerNet, the transmission system of the state of Victoria, Australia. In 1999, GPU announced the purchase of Transmissions Pipelines Australia, a gas transmission company that it will rename GasNet. GPU has also been bidding on New Zealand distribution companies. In addition, GPU owns interests in nearly 7,000 MW of generation at 21 sites in eight countries overseas. In 1995, Texas Utilities (TXU) won a bid for $1.6 billion to purchase Eastern Energy, a power distributor carved out of the former State Electricity Commission of Victoria. In 1998, TXU expanded its distribution companies to the U.K. and the Czech Republic when it purchased The Energy Group, which owned Eastern Electricity, the largest of the U.K. regional electric companies. Eastern Generation also owns, operates, or has an interest in eight power stations in the U.K. making TXU a significant generation player as well. In mid-1999, TXU also purchased a 36% share in the seventh-largest regional electric company in Finland. In 1995, Southern purchased U.K. regional electric company South Western Electricity (SWEB). Later Southern sold half of SWEB to PP&L, but retained management control. In 1999, Southern and PP&L sold the retailing arm of SWEB to London Electricity, now owned by Electricite de France. At the same time, PP&L moved to purchase controlling interest in Empress Emel, one of the largest electricity distribution companies in Chile.

UtiliCorp United has also followed a strategy of purchasing systems in English-speaking countries. In 1987, UtiliCorp acquired West Kootenay Power in Canada. Through a series of acquisitions beginning in 1993, UtiliCorp has assembled UnitedNetworks Limited, the largest wires operator in New Zealand. In 1995, a three-company consortium led by UtiliCorp purchased United Energy, serving parts of Melbourne, Australia, for $1.15 billion. In early 1999, UtiliCorp and an Australian partner acquired Multinet/Ikon, the largest gas distribution and retail company in Victoria, Australia.

On the other side of the strategic spectrum are US companies that have largely avoided investing in transmission and distribution infrastructure, instead choosing to specialise in generation development and acquisition. Among the traditional utilities doing so are Duke, Edison Mission Energy, and NRG (Northern States Power). All three companies were early domestic developers of independent power producers. Duke has developed projects mainly in Latin America. Recently, Duke purchased all of Dominion's (VEPCO) Latin American generation (shares in five projects grossing 1200 MW) after Dominion apparently decided to redirect its business strategy toward domestic markets. Duke has also purchased a major generation company in Brazil. Duke recently announced plans to move aggressively into the European generation market and is looking to make major acquisitions in the U.K., Germany, Poland and the Czech Republic. Edison Mission Energy is currently one of the two largest owners of independent power projects worldwide with major holdings in the U.K., Australia, New Zealand, Indonesia, Spain, Thailand, and Italy. NRG is also a large player internationally, with major generation plants in Australia, Germany, Latin America, and the Czech Republic. Entergy has joined the move toward international generation development after brief ventures into distribution companies. In 1996, Entergy purchased CitiPower, a distribution company in Melbourne. In 1997, it purchased London Electricity, a major U.K. regional electric company. Subsequently, Entergy sold both CitiPower and London Electricity, and now specialises largely in generation in the U.K., Argentina, Pakistan, Peru, and Chile.

US independents have also become major generation developers abroad. The largest among these are AES, CalEnergy, Enron and Dynegy. As discussed below, AES, CalEnergy, and Enron all have major investments in distribution companies as well. Only Dynegy continues to specialise overseas mainly in generation development. In 1996, Dynegy divested to AES its plants in Australia, the Netherlands, U.K., Canada and the Dominican Republic. In the future, Dynegy plans to concentrate its overseas efforts on Europe, where it has major affiliated natural gas facilities. In June 1999, Dynegy and Illinova, a traditional US utility, announced plans to merge, thereby forming a $7.5 billion combined company.

Finally, many US companies are pursuing both generation as well as separate distribution or integrated utilities overseas. Fig. VII.7 shows the world-wide independent generation holdings of the top 15 affiliated and independent US generators. Among the traditional utilities pursuing this course are CMS, Reliant, PacifiCorp, PSE&G, Sempra and Southern. CMS was a relative latecomer to independent power development, but it has rapidly acquired both greenfield and privatised plants in Argentina, Australia, Brazil, India, Jamaica, Morocco and the Philippines. In Argentina, Chile and the Philippines, CMS has developed and acquired clusters of assets including generation, distribution, transmission, and natural gas pipelines. Reliant owns major distribution facilities in Brazil and El Salvador as well as major generation plants in Colombia, Brazil and Argentina. In 1999, Reliant purchased UNA, a major owner of Dutch generation. In conjunction with this acquisition, Reliant has begun building a major energy trading and marketing operation based in the Netherlands. In 1995, PacifiCorp acquired Powercor, an Australian power distributor, for $1.6 billion. In 1996, PacifiCorp was a partner in a consortium purchasing a major Australian power plant. In 1998, PacifiCorp opened an office in Istanbul and is focusing on generation projects in Turkey, the Middle East and Eastern Europe. PSE&G is another relative latecomer to international development although is now has distribution companies in Brazil, Argentina, and Chile, as well as major generation plants in Argentina, China, India and Venezuela. Sempra is also very

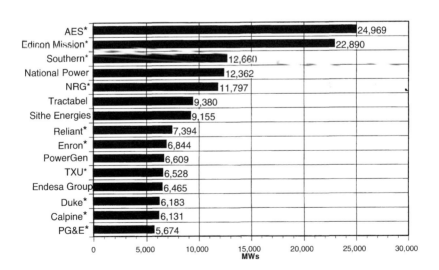

Fig. VII.7. Worldwide independent generation holdings of top 15 affiliated and independent generators (By net project ownership**) (October 1999).
* U.S. firms.
** Does not include portions of company portfolios with a preponderance of in-house generation, state funding or inherited capacity.

active in Latin America, sometimes teaming with PSE&G. Sempra has invested $800 million in Mexico, Peru, Chile, Argentina and Uruguay. Outside of Mexico, Sempra plays a management role only in Chile, where it recently acquired Chilquinta Energia, an electric distribution company with 1.1 million customers.

Southern Company is also a latecomer, but a giant. In the US Southern is a huge holding company with a still vertically-integrated utility system of 31,000 MW spread across five major operating companies in the Southeast. In 1997, Southern purchased Consolidated Electric Power Asia (CEPA) the largest independent power producer in Asia, for $3.4 billion. In 1995, Southern made a successful hostile takeover of South Western Electricity (SWEB), a U.K. regional electric company. Southern now owns SWEB in partnership with PP&L, as previously described. Southern has also purchased a significant share of CEMIG, a large integrated Brazilian utility with over 5,000 MW of generation, and has increased generation and gas pipeline investments in Chile. Southern also purchased a 26% share in BEWAG, a large integrated utility serving Berlin, Germany and having over 3,000 MW of generation. Southern also has purchased significant generation and distribution interests in Argentina, Chile, Trinidad and the Bahamas. However, in early 1999, Southern was forced to take a $200 million writedown to its 1998 earnings to reflect poor performance in Argentina and Chile. In September 1999, a Brazilian governor asserted control over Southern's CEMIG assets and the issue is currently in litigation. In the wake of these setbacks, Southern has announced its withdrawal from Argentina and Chile.

Even though US independents generally began solely as developers of generation within the US, the major independents have all pursued distribution in addition to generation investments abroad. These large independents include AES, CalEnergy, and Enron. AES is the largest of the independents and a giant by any standard, with active generation projects in about 20 foreign countries. AES is also a partner with Southern in CEMIG, the large integrated Brazilian utility with over 5,000 MW of generation. It also participates in seven other distribution companies, all in Latin America. CalEnergy focuses on generation development in Europe, Indonesia, the Philippines and Latin America. However, in 1996, it succeeded in a hostile takeover of Northern Electric, a U.K. regional electric company. Enron is another huge independent operating internationally. In its overseas activities, Enron is mainly a developer of generation with projects in about 20 foreign countries. In 1998, Enron purchased a major distribution company in Sao Paulo, Brazil, for $1.272 billion. Enron also owns interest in eight state gas distributors in Brazil.

IV. Synthesis and Speculations

This chapter has addressed the rapidly evolving business strategies of US electricity companies in response to the opening of both wholesale and retail competition at home as well as the privatisation of public electricity enterprises and liberalisation of electricity markets abroad. Much of what is happening can only be adequately understood against the background of the dual federal-state regulatory framework in the US Although the federal government has done much to facilitate and encourage competition in wholesale markets, these markets are still technically regulated and likely to remain so for sometime further. Retail competition has been introduced in nearly half the states in the US, comprising well over half the national population. Although a federal Congressional mandate for retail access is possible, most observers do not believe it is imminent. Nonetheless, retail access can be expected to continue to spread steadily on a state-by-state basis over the next decade.

Although retail competition has been adopted in 24 states, these restructurings are generally being phased in over several years and markets are currently open in only a handful of states. While the changes in corporate structures and strategies have already been dramatic, still further huge changes can be expected. Domestically, US business strategies are heavily influenced by the emerging changes in regulation. In the short term, corporate strategies have been understandably obsessed with the recovery of stranded generation costs. This has generally led to one of the most visible signs of corporate restructuring – the massive divestiture of roughly 100,000 MW of generation in order to determine the market value of these assets for establishing the levels of stranded cost recovery. For the most part, this generation has simply been purchased by other large US utilities and placed in their "unregulated" generation subsidiaries. In the long term, it seems likely that US generation markets will be dominated by about a dozen major players and many smaller ones. Some traditional utilities seem likely to specialise in generation, both domestically and internationally, and may even eventually quit their transmission and distribution businesses entirely. Generators may find it beneficial to vertically integrate into retailing, but this is for far from obvious: the two activities are very different businesses. Nonetheless, generators may find it beneficial to vertically integrate into at least wholesale marketing or form close alliances with wholesale marketers and perhaps even retailers in order to hedge their power market risks.

Another highly visible hallmark of restructuring has been the large number of mergers and major acquisitions. In many cases, these mergers have been motivated by the general belief that, up to a point, bigger will be better in the new competitive world. Many mergers have been "convergence mergers" between electric and gas companies pursuing the belief that unifying these two energy sources enables a company to offer customers preferred integrated energy services and also allows the company to better manage its electric generation fuel risks. Following passage of the Telecommunications Act of 1996, many electric utilities have also become aggressive in diversifying into various telecommunications businesses. In the long term it seems likely that the 200 IOU distribution utilities in the US will consolidate to 30 or fewer regional distribution companies. This number would likely be sufficient to capture most distribution scale economies. Economies of scope involving natural gas and telecom might even motivate still further consolidation down to a dozen large companies.

Ironically, the one competitive area whose future remains most unclear under retail access is retailing itself. Many companies are attempting to achieve national branding successes, but so far the evidence of success is mixed. Green marketing is one area where limited successes have been achieved, but the size of this niche remains uncertain. In most regions, except for large customers, retail competition has been slow to develop and incumbent utilities still retain the predominant share of smaller customers. In some states, retail customers are being subsidised to switch to new competitive retailers. But this policy cannot be sustained in the long run and it is not clear what public policy will supersede it. For mass retailing to smaller customers to become a viable business in the long term, there must be a real basis for a sustainable profit margin.

It is also not at all clear what the future of the US transmission grid will be. For the most part, the grid has been constructed historically through interconnections among autonomous local utilities. It seems almost certain that this structure is not a stable equilibrium in the new restructured environment and will evolve in the direction of consolidated ownership. However, it is not clear what institutions will be the catalyst for consolidation. Presumably, consolidators will be independent, stand-alone for-profit transmission companies. But development of such institutions will likely require increased financial encouragement from the FERC. Some regional grids could evolve into publicly-owned non-profit, or jointly-owned for-profit, institutions.

One of the most dramatic trends in recent years has been the interest by US utilities in investment abroad. Some US players have been developing this business steadily over the last decade or longer (e.g., Edison Mission Energy, AES). Others have burst on the scene only recently with huge acquisitions of generation (e.g., Southern's purchase of CEPA) or distribution systems (e.g., acquisitions of the UK and Australian regional electric companies). It remains to be seen how many of these ventures are truly value-creating and based on solid business expertise and how many are simply the latest manifestations of traditionally ill-fated utility diversifications. No doubt the specialised skills needed for international investment success will elude many current contenders.

In conclusion, although many trends are taking shape, it is too early in the game to accurately describe the various playing fields, let alone predict the victors. Indeed, trial and error seems certain to be the rule of the day. But the stakes are high and the game should be fascinating for participants and spectators alike.

Appendix

Guide to selected utility abbreviations and newly adopted names

Abbreviation or New Name	Affiliated Traditional Utility
AEP	American Electric Power (a registered holding company owning Ohio Power, Appalachian Power, Indiana Michigan Power, Columbus Southern, Kentucky Power, Kingsport Power and Wheeling Power)
Allegheny	Allegheny Power System (a registered holding company owning West Penn Power, Potomac Edison and Monongahela Power)
Alliant Energy	Merger of Wisconsin Power & Light, IES Industries and Interstate Power
Ameren	Merger of Union Electric and CIPSCO
Aquila	UtiliCorp Limited
BEC	Boston Edison Co.
C&SW	Central & South West (a registered holding company owning Central Power & Light, Public Service Company of Oklahoma, Southwestern Electric Power and West Texas Utilities)
Centerior	Merger of Cleveland Electric Illuminating and Toledo Edison
CILCORP	Central Illinois Lighting Co.
Cinergy	A registered holding company owning PSI, Cincinnati Gas & Electric and Union Light & Power
CIPSCO	Central Illinois Public Service Co.
CMP	Central Maine Power
CMS	Consumers Power
Conectiv	Merger of Delmarva Power & Light and Atlantic Energy
ConEd	Consolidated Edison
CP&L	Carolina Power & Light
DQE	Duquesne Light Co.
DTE	Detroit Edison
Edison International	Southern California Edison
Edison Mission Energy	Southern California Edison
Energy East	New York State Electricity & Gas
Enova	New name of San Diego Gas & Electric (superseded by Sempra after merger with Pacific Enterprises)

Abbreviation or New Name	Affiliated Traditional Utility
Entergy	Formerly Middle South Utilities (a registered holding company owning Entergy Louisiana, Entergy Gulf States, Entergy Arkansas, Entergy Mississippi and Entergy New Orleans)
EUA	Eastern Utilities Associates (a registered holding company owning Eastern Edison Company, Blackstone Valley Electric and Newport Electric)
FirstEnergy	Merger of Ohio Edison and Centerior Energy
FPL	Florida Power & Light
GPU	General Public Utilities (a registered holding company owning Jersey Central Power & Light, Metropolitan Edison and Pennsylvania Electric)
Illinova	Illinois Power Co.
IPALCO	Indianapolis Power & Light
Keyspan Energy	Merger of Long Island Lighting and Brooklyn Union Gas
KU Energy	Kentucky Utilities
LG&E	Louisville Gas & Electric
LILCO	Long Island Lighting Company
MidAmerican	Merger of Midwest Resources and Iowa-Illinois Gas & Electric
NEES	New England Electric Systems (a registered holding company owning Massachusetts Electric and Narrangansett Electric)
New Century Energies	Merger of Public Service of Colorado and Southwestern Public Service
NEU	Northeast Utilities (a registered holding company owning Connecticut Light & Power, Public Service of New Hampshire and Western Massachusetts Electric)
NIPSCO	Northern Indiana Public Service Co.
NiSource	Northern Indiana Public Service Co.
NRG	Northern States Power
NSP	Northern States Power
NSTAR	Merger of Iowa Power and Iowa Public Service
NYSEG	New York State Electricity & Gas
Orion Power	Baltimore Gas & Electric (Joint venture with Goldman Sachs)
PacifiCorp	Merger of Pacific Power & Light and Utah Power & Light
PECO	Philadelphia Electric Co.
PEPCO	Potomac Electric Power Co.
PG&E	Pacific Gas & Electric
PP&L	Pennsylvania Power & Light
PSE&G	Public Service Electricity and Gas
PSI	Public Service of Indiana
Reliant	New name of Houston Power & Light
SCANA	South Carolina Electricity & Gas
Sempra	Merger of Enova (San Diego Gas & Electric) and Pacific Enterprises (parent on Southern California Gas Company)
SIGCORP	Southern Indiana Gas & Electric
Southern	The Southern Company (a registered holding company owning Alabama Power, Georgia Power, Gulf Power, Mississippi Power and Savannah Electric & Power)

Abbreviation or New Name	Affiliated Traditional Utility
TECO	Tampa Electric Co.
TXU	Texas Utilities (a registered holding company owning Texas Utilities Electric and Southwestern Electric Service)
Unicom	Commonwealth Edison
UNITIL	UNITIL Corporation (a small registered holding company)
Western Resources	Merger of Kansas Power & Light and Kansas Gas & Electric
Xcel Energy	Merger of Northern States Power and New Century Energies
UniSource	Tucson Electric Power
Vectren	Merger of Indiana Energy and SIGCORP
VEPCO	Virginia Electric Power Co.
Westar	Merger of Western Resources and Kansas City Power & Light
Western Resources	Merger of Kansas Power and Light and Kansas Gas & Electric
Xcel	Merger of NSP and New Century Energies

Literature

Brew, A. and Phelps, L. (1998) "Has branding failed the electricity industry?", *Electricity Journal*, November issue.

California Public Utility Commission (1994) *Proposed Policy Statement on Electric Industry Restructuring and Regulatory Reform*, R.94-04-031 and 1.94-04-032.

Edison Electric Institute (1999) *Divestiture Action and Analysis*, (September).

Edison Electric Institute (1999) *Electric Utility Restructuring Activity and Utility Merger Status Update*, (October).

FERC (1998) *Staff report to the FERC on the causes of wholesale electric pricing abnormalities in the Midwest during June 1998*, FERC: 22 September.

Hyman, Leonard S. (1997) *America's electric utilities: past, present and future*, 6th edn., Public Utilities Reports, Inc.

Kukart, James R. (1999) "Utility stocks in the spotlight", *Utility Business*, April 1999, p 54.

Chapter VIII
New Strategies for Power Companies in Brazil

MAURÍCIO TIOMMO TOLMASQUIM,
JOSÉ CLAUDIO LINHARES PIRES and
LUIS PINGUELLI ROSA

I. Introduction

The main objective of this chapter is to analyse the new strategies of power companies in Brazil. Many are now being taken over by international utilities expanding their spheres of action throughout the power market in Latin America, where Brazil plays a leading role.

This chapter is divided into three parts, starting with the introduction. The second section discusses the principal motives fuelling the globalisation process in the Latin American power market, describing the strategies of the principal international players taking part in this process. This is followed by an analysis of new strategies being deployed by Brazilian power companies, stressing the institutional context shaping them. The chapter concludes with a few final remarks and observations.

II. Globalisation of the Latin American Power Market: Principal Foreign Players and their Strategies

II.A. Aspects prompting the global strategies of foreign utility companies

From the 1970s onwards, the power sector was affected by the interactions of a series of factors altering the structure of the market for this industry, traditionally a state-run monopoly,[1] introducing new players and competition that pressured traditional participants.

---

[1] Opportunities for fine-tuning economies of scale and scope with the vertical and horizontal integration of the power industry led to the incorporation of government monopolies in most of the developed nations.

From the economic standpoint, supply-side pressures—including rising fuel prices pumped up by oil crises, higher environmental costs and the appearance of dis-economies of scale with the phase-out of market interconnection—and demand-side constraints, imposed by a slowdown in consumption growth rates, all challenged traditional institutional models. Additionally, the dissemination of new micro-electronic technologies resulted in energy savings and more efficient ways of generating power (combined-cycle and fluidised bed).

Higher operating costs in the electrical sector prompted protests from consumers and strengthened liberal political platforms calling for a reduction in the role of the state in productive economic activities. Most of the developed countries introduced deregulation programs (at times accompanied by privatisation of assets) for their power markets, which weakened or even replaced the presence of government-run power utilities. Historically sheltered from competition by institutional barriers, they found their markets threatened through either the presence of new generation options (cogeneration and independent power production) or by the arrival of new players in the power distribution sector that were also involved in the supply of other network systems (sanitation, heating, fibre-optic cables and telecommunications). [2]

In a study of the strategies of power sector operators, Chevalier & Salaün (1995) indicate that this process is imposing a new institutional framework. This scenario will be shaped by internationalisation and diversification of the activities of current sectoral agents, with the arrival of new players in all segments of the electricity sector. These processes will result in new types of vertical/horizontal integration for companies that are traditionally monopolistic and state-run.

Faced with rising internationalisation throughout the world's economies, and threatened with losing their monopolies to potential competitors, companies began to use their networks to diversify their activities, moving into telecommunications and basic sanitation, for instance. This resulted in a movement running counter to the efforts of operators in other infrastructure segments. These trends resulted in the formation of informal horizontalisation on several occasions, based on joint ventures and strategic alliances between potential competitors and current operators. These associations are designed to make better use of opportunities for economies of scope, together with the competitive

---

[2] The case of Iberdrola, one of Spain's leading power companies, clearly illustrates the limitations encountered in mature markets by power companies. In 1997, the operating profits of Iberdrola reached US$ 1.25 billion, down 19.7% over the previous year. This was due to largely to a 6.8% cut in the average price per kWh, prompted by deregulation of the Spanish power market. (Gazeta Mercantil; 22 April 1998).

advantages inherent in the specialties of each of the participant companies. (Chevalier & Salaün, op.cit.).

The logic shaping power company diversification is based on a tandem trend. At the national level, the utilities are striving to firm up their positions as multi-service companies by acquiring a horizontal institutional configuration designed to withstand competition for services where technological convergence paves the way for other public utility operators. Particularly noteworthy are inter-capital networked operations set up to exploit telecommunications services, making good use of the prospects for profitability in this sector as deregulation progresses.

In contrast, at the international level, traditional operators are seeking possibilities for making good use of their specialties in the emerging markets of developing countries, where sweeping privatisation and deregulation programmes are currently under way. These investments are designed to offset possible losses in revenues caused by keener competition in their home markets. As a way of dealing with macro-economic uncertainties in these countries, these acquisitions are generally handled through consortia linking local and international operators.

II.B. The importance of Latin America's power market

Within this context, the Latin American market plays a strategic role in the expansion plans of major global power operators, thanks to its growth potential (see Table VIII.1), the context of liberalisation, opportunities for acquiring energy-based assets, and finally the energy integration process under way among the nations of Latin America.

Energy integration among the Southern Cone nations and other countries in Latin America falls within the context of the globalisation of these economies, with decisive effects on the strategy of existing operators, as well as stakeholders eager to enter the Brazilian and Latin American markets.

Despite the uncertainties caused by financial crises in the peripheral countries,[3] a boom is under way throughout Latin America, attracting investment by power companies in the developed countries, particularly through the acquisition of the assets of utilities up for privatisation. This is particularly clear in the construction of inter-country energy integration infrastructure such as gas and oil pipelines, power lines in border regions, etc. [4]

---

[3] This region is finding it hard to attract fresh investments, due to the financial crises in Asia and Russia, which caused economic agents to lok askance at the emerging economies.
[4] An example of this trend is the privatisation process of Brazil's power sector, which has generated some US$ 32 billion so far, selling off 22 utilities by October 2000, with over half the inward investment being foreign capital, invested in 17 of these utilities. (BNDES, 2000)

Table VIII.1. Power demand profile of selected countries.

Indicator Country	Argentina	Brazil	Chile	Colombia	Mexico	Peru	Venezuela
Consumption p/cap kWh (1998)	1,937	1,868	2,232	883	1,422	651	2,738
% Annual growth (1990–1998)	6,4	4,9	4,1	2,9	5,5	4,1	2,5

Source: Olade, Electricity International, US Department of Energy 1999.

In general terms, all countries in Latin America are developing bilateral or multilateral projects to build infrastructure networks, particularly gas pipelines for energy integration. Good examples of these are the Bolivia-Brazil pipeline and the Southern Gas Pipeline. The former carries gas from Santa Cruz (Bolivia) to Brazil, running 3.150 km across 5 Brazilian states and 135 Brazilian cities. The later running 210 km between Buenos Aires and Montevideo, carrying gas from Argentina. Projects are currently under study for the export of power from Chile to Peru, electrical inter-connections between Santiago (Chile) and Mendoza (Argentina), the Northern Andes Gas Pipeline linking Chile and Bolivia, and the Atacama and Trangás Gas Pipelines (Argentina–Chile), among others.

The developmental dynamics of the Latin American market indicate the formation of a single energy market over the long term. For the near future, the links of networks among the Southern Cone governments will play an important role in fostering and shaping an integrated energy policy for the Mercosur Southern Cone Market.[5] These efforts have warranted special attention in harmonising the regulatory framework for these various countries in order to expand energy markets in this region.

II.C. Principal companies in the Latin American market

Latin America's power market is drawing increasing interest from major utility corporations, due mainly to the investment opportunities opened up by privatisation processes under way, in parallel with energy interconnection projects. The main international players so far are Endesa and Iberdrola (Spain)—that have announced a merger between them[*]— EDP (Portugal), Tractebel (Belgium), EDF (France) and AES, Reliant (ex. Houston), Enron and Duke Energy (USA).

---

[5] The Mercosul Southern Cone Market is composed of Brazil, Argentina, Uruguay and Paraguay. Chile and Bolivia are in the process of joining.

[*] In October/2000, Endesa and Iberdrola groups had decided to start a process leading to the friendly merger of both companies. The conclusion of process, that it will create one of the largest utility of the world, it is subject to approval of Spanish and Euopean Regulatory Authorities.

The Endesa Group—which ranks fourth by size among North American and European utilities—is a holding company controlling some ten corporations which constitute an industrial group that is integrated both horizontally and vertically along seven basic lines of business. Each has a specific function: power generation and distribution, marketing, mining, international projects, diversification and services. Outstanding among these activities is power generation and distribution, and, more recently, the mobile and fixed telecommunication sectors.

For power distribution, the dizzying growth of the Endesa Group on the Spanish market—fifth largest in the European Union—brought its share up from 13% in 1990 to 44% in 1999. In terms of power generation, the Endesa Group accounted for 44% of all power produced in Spain in 1999.

The Iberdrola Group is the result of a merger completed six years ago between Iberduero and Hidrola, with its core competencies focused on the electricity business. This group generates, transmits and supplies these services to a market of over eight million customers in 14 autonomous communities (40.8% of the Spanish power distribution market). It recently moved into the telecommunications sector through investments in Brazil and established a partnership with EDP (*Electricidade de Portugal*) for strategic investments in Latin America.[6]

Portugal's largest corporation, EDP is a vertically-integrated state-owned enterprise that has recently passed through a structural unbundling process that has also internationalised its investments, driven by its strategic partnership with Iberdrola, mentioned above. Considered Portugal's leading multinational, its corporate strategy is centred on business and market diversification. At the international level, its targets include operations in telecommunications, sanitation (water distribution systems network), power generation and natural gas. Its operations outside Portugal are based on stakes in companies in Brazil, Morocco, Macao and Guatemala.

A company in the Suez Group (Lyonnaise Des Eaux S/A), Société Générale de Belgique specialises in independent power production, with revenues over the past two years of US$ 12 billion and a 1996 headcount of 63,000. It operates in over 100 countries and controls projects in nineteen others, through Electricity and Gas International (EGI), its international business unit. In Latin America, Tractebel Electricity & Gas International operates in Brazil, Chile, Peru and Argentina. Operating in Brazil since 1996 through Tractebel Brasil Ltda, this Belgian company has already invested US$ 1 billion, with US$ 800 million earmarked for the acquisition of the Gerasul power generation utility.

The final player in the list of European power companies currently most active

---

[6] This partnership was consolidated through cross-holdings: Iberdrola acquired 2.25% of the capital of EDP, which in turn took up 2.25% of the capital of its Spanish counterpart, in addition to non-executive seats on each other's Boards (www.edp.pt; 12 November 1998).

in Latin America is Electricité de France, a state-run corporation set up under the aegis of the law nationalising the French power sector after World War II. Since then, EDF has been responsible for ensuring French independence in terms of energy, guaranteeing universal power supplies through its vertically-integrated monopoly and playing an important macro-economic role in the nation's balance of payments, thanks to sizable exports throughout Europe.

Set up 15 years ago, the American-based AES Group specialises in power generation. With a staff of 27,000 and total installed capacity of 23 GW scattered throughout 35 countries including the USA, China, Germany, India, Pakistan and the UK, it is currently ranked the world's largest independent power producer, operating a total of 94 power plants. Latin America already brings in some 20% of its profits.[7]

The Reliant (ex. Houston…) Industries Incorporated Group operates in various segments of the energy sector production chain. With annual revenues of some US$ 9 billion, and assets hovering around US$ 18.4 billion, it is staffed by some 13,000 employees. Among other activities, this group handles the distribution of power and natural gas, power generation and energy services to over four million consumers in six US states, with 3.5 million consumers internationally level.

Based in Houston, the Enron Group is the leading gas distribution utility in the USA, and one of the largest in the world, with assets of US$ 19 billion and over US$ 4 billion in investment projects in various countries. In addition to operating, producing, transporting and retailing natural gas, this major independent power producer has 3.6 GW in operation, 3.5 GW under construction and 3.57 GW under development. It first moved into Latin America in the mid-1990s, focused firmly on Brazil. This group has shown interest in bidding in privatisation auctions of government-run power distributors in Brazil, making good use of experience gained through its power distribution activities in Oregon (USA).[8]

Operating in 50 countries, Duke Energy Corporation is the latest company to enter the Brazilian energy market, through the purchase of Cesp Paranapanema, one of the three generation utilities established through the split-up of CESP. With head offices in North Carolina (USA), Duke is the second-largest power generation, transportation and distribution utility in the USA, fuelled by an aggressive asset acquisition policy in Latin America. In addition to its Brazilian acquisition—its largest investment outside the USA—and other existing investments in Latin America, Duke

---

[7] *América Economia* (December 1997).

[8] In July 1998, Enron purchased control of Elektro, Brazil's sixth-largest power distribution utility, and is also building a gas-fired power plant at Cuiabá (MT). The purchase of Elektro was a vital part of its corporate strategy for the Southern Cone, which in fact mirrors its global strategy: building up an integrated operating system ranging from power production through to transportation and distribution.

also purchased the Latin American assets of Dominion Resources Inc (Virginia, USA), including power plants and other energy assets in Belize, Peru, Bolivia and Argentina.

In addition to these eight corporate groups, the CMS, CSW, Southern, PSEG and Entergy Power Groups (USA) all belong to a cluster of companies operating on the Latin American market whose presence is still discreet, although expanding.

With investments of over US$ 1 billion in the Southern Cone, the CMS Energy Corporation group is the holding company for international power and natural gas distribution operations, as well as independent power production, energy services and oil exploration and refining. With assets of some US$ 9 billion, its gross annual revenues top US$ 5 billion in 18 countries. Its principal subsidiary is the Consumers Power Company (CPC), based in Michigan, which is the fourth-largest power and gas distribution utility in the USA.[9]

The CSW Group is the holding company linking corporations owning power generation assets and other businesses. At the international level, CSW operates in the energy and telecommunications fields, as well as correlated services, often through partnerships, as is the case with its investments in Brazil's Rede and Inepar power distribution groups.[10]

The Southern Group is the main power supplier in the USA, with operations in ten other countries in four continents. In addition to the power business, Southern also offers wireless telecommunication services, although it still plays only a minor role in Latin America.

Concentrating its somewhat diversified activities in the gas and electricity areas, the PSEG Group recently began to expand into the international market. Similar to its operations in the US market, this group works as an independent power producer and distributor in Europe, Asia and Africa. Particularly outstanding in Latin America are its investments in distribution utilities in Argentina and its partnership in Brazil with Brazilian groups in a power distribution utility in Rio Grande do Sul State.

The Entergy Power Group works with power generation and distribution, with 98 distribution utilities scattered throughout North and South America, Europe and Asia, posting revenues of US$ 11.5 billion in 1998. Its activities in Brazil consists of its stake in the construction and operation of the Bom Jardim thermo power plant in São Paulo (800 MW).

---

[9] In addition to CPC, CMS has a further six subsidiaries handling the following projects: independent power production; natural gas processing, storage and transmission; engineering; marketing services; oil and gas production and refining.

[10] In 1997, the CSW Group merged with the American Power Group (AEP), which is one of the largest utilities in the USA, in order to reduce risk exposure and extend international expansion capacity through diversifying power generation input materials.

II.D. Principal strategies of Latin American utilities

Utility operations in Latin America are shaped by a series of strategic motivations, many of which are complementary. For the purposes of analysis, it is possible to identify three basic strategies:

- diversification of activities in the country of origin and abroad;
- acquisition of assets through privatisation auctions; and
- strategic partnerships.

II.D.a. Diversification of activities in country of origin and abroad

It is clear from the above analysis that these companies feature a common diversification strategy for their activities. However, pushed by their competitive markets, the European companies have taken the lead and developed aggressive diversification strategies both in their own countries and Europe-wide, while their US counterparts have lagged behind in this process. Nevertheless, some US companies—particularly Enron and AES—have also expanded their activities into other segments than the power business.

Endesa is implementing a global strategy with a marked presence in related sectors such as gas, telecommunications, basic sanitation and cogeneration. To do so, the group is implementing two concomitant measures: On the European market it is striving to diversify its activities through the acquisition of companies operating network services. On the international market, acting through Endesa International, its activities are centred on investments in the electricity business.

In terms of the diversification of activities, the most outstanding accomplishment of the Endesa strategy was the acquisition of Retevision (21.67% holding), the second-largest fixed telephony operator in Spain, in partnership with Telecom Italia and Spanish investment funds. This venture was firmly supported by the Spanish government, as a launch pad for the liberalisation process introducing competition into the public telecommunications network. To do so, it made good use of the entry of the Endesa group, deploying its lengthy experience and power line assets to encroach on the market of Telefónica de España, the newly-privatised dominant player on the Spanish telecommunications market.[11]

Like Endesa, the Iberdrola Group has been diversifying its activities and expanding its international activities, striving to firm up its position in sectors where its business capacities and experience endow it with competitive advantages. In addition to power, the group operates in the

---

[11] The partnership with Telecom Italia also resulted in the incorporation of Supercable Andalucia, set up to implement telecommunications services in Andalucia and Madrid.

engineering and consulting fields, as well as real estate and telecommunications.[12]

The international activities of the Iberdrola Group basically target the energy sector with regard to both services and investments in generation/distribution assets, particularly in Latin America. In parallel, Iberdrola has a strategy of penetrating the services market in various countries in Europe. The international activities of Iberdrola in Latin America are becoming increasingly strategic (Table VIII.2). In 1996, its Latin American subsidiaries contributed over 25% (more than US$ 1.5 million) of the total revenues of the group, servicing a market of over 4.5 million consumers (30 million inhabitants).

A multi-service company, Portugal's power distribution utility EDP is also a partner of Optimus, a cellular telephony operator, and is analysing its entry into the fixed telephony segment. It also recently established an association with Thames Water, a major UK basic sanitation utility.

Encouraged by the possible reformulation of the French power sector, the EDF group has diversified its domestic activities and boosted its export drive at competitive prices. Its share of the international market has expanded in terms of both consulting and other services, as well as through the acquisition of public utility assets (Hau, 1993 in Bajay, 1994).

On the domestic market, EDF has reacted to saturated power demands and the prospect for the arrival of new agents with two parallel measures. The first is the development of demand management programs, particularly for major consumers, which is still at the experimental stage. The second step—similar to the Spanish companies described above—is the deployment of a pro-active diversification strategy in other segments of the domestic market. Despite limited earnings from these activities— only 2% for 1993—the company's share of markets such as engineering, street lighting, cartography, cable television and garbage recycling is expanding.

Regulatory constraints hamper the range of diversification of the EDF group, based on the argument that it could use its monopoly in the power market to usher in predatory competition in other sectors. Nevertheless the EDF group already ranks third in the urban garbage management segment, through its TIRU subsidiary, which is also relatively active in garbage management markets in the USA, Austria, Canada and Spain. It also heads the cable TV market in the Alsace region.

Overall, in addition to ventures linked to its core competencies, EDF is launching an international investment process targeting other segments, particularly in Austria and Central Europe. On the international scene,

---

[12] These activities are under the responsibility of subsidiaries Iberdrola Energia (Iberener), Iberdrola Ingenieria y Consultoria (Iberinco) and Sociedad Uipicsa. Through Iberdrola Energia, Iberdrola recently expanded the scope of its activities by acquiring full stock control of Ondagua, a basic sanitation company in Malaga, Spain.

Table VIII.2. Investments in utilities in Latin America.

Country	ENDESA	IBERDROLA	EDP	TRACTEBEL	EDF	AES	RELIANT	ENRON	DUKE
ARG	Dock Sud (1a), Edersur (2)	Güemes (1a), Litoral Gas (5)		Litoral Gas (5), Gassoouto Andino (5)	L. Nihuiles (1b), Diamante (1b), Distrocuyo (3), Edenor (2)	Eden (2), Edes (2), S. Nicôlas (1a), C. Corral (1a), Parana (1b)	Edelap (2), Edese (2), Argener (4), Opco (1b)	Gas del Sur (4)	Neuquen (1b), Cerros Colorados (1a)
BOL		Electropaz (2), Elfeo (2), Cade (7)						Transredes (5)	Corani (1b)
BRA Bandeirante (16)	Cerj (2), Coelce (2), Electrobras (3), Sinapsis (8), C. Dourada (1b)	Ceg (5), Riogas (5), Coelba (2), Angra I (8), Cosern (2), Embraer (8), Telesp (7)	Bandeirante (2), Cerj (2), Coelce (2), Lajeado (8), Escelsa (2), Enersol (2)	Gerasul (1), Cana Brava (16)	Metropolitana (2), Light (2)	Light (2), Metropolitana (2), CCODEE (2), Cemig (1/2/3), Uruguaian (1a)		Ceg (5), RioGas (5), Cuiabá (1a), Gaspart (5), Elektro (2)	Parana-panema
CHI	Enersis (1/2), Sinapsis (7), Esval (6)	Tocopilla (1a), R. Duqueco (1b), Colbún (1/3), ESP (5)	Essel (6)	Gasoduto Andino (5)					
COL	Codensa (2), Emgesa (1b), Corelca (2), Barranquilla (6)						Valle Cauca (5), EPSA (1b/2), Salvajina (1b)	Centragas (5)	
DOM REP.									
GUA			Eegsa (2)					P. Quetzal (1a), P. Quetzal (1a)	
PER	Etevensa (1a), Piura (1a)			ILO Power (1a)					Aguaytia (5a), Egenor (1b)
POR								Ecoelectrica (1a)	
MEX				Diagapro (5)		Merida III (1a)	C.do Golfo (5)	Cancun (6)	Acasatta (1a)

Notes:

(1a)	Thermopower generation	
(1b)	Hydropower generation	
(2)	Power distribution	
(3)	Power retailing and transmission	
(4)	Cogeneration	
(5)	Gas distribution	
(6)	Basic sanitation	
(7)	Telecommunications	
(8)	Other (electrical and engineering services, generator construction or equipment fabrication).	

the EDF strategy is centred on acquiring the assets of power generation, transmission and distribution companies in emerging markets, while also diversifying its activities in Europe, free of domestic regulatory constraints in telecommunications, urban garbage disposal, etc.

Although the businesses of the Enron Group are concentrated in the energy segment, it has recently begun to expand into other infrastructure areas. In addition to the gas and electricity sectors, Enron intends to integrate its distribution networks into a fibreoptic system that will turn this company into a communications service provider working with long-distance telephony, handled through a fibreoptic communications grid being built in North America. In August 1998, Enron announced its purchase of Wessex Water plc, a water and sewage utility in the UK, as well as the incorporation of a subsidiary—Azurix—seeking opportunities in the water and sanitation market. In 1999, it acquired 100% of the capital of Acqua Management (AMX)[13] in Brazil, looking ahead to the expected privatisation of the country's sanitation sector. In this same segment in Argentina, Enron has acquired 30-year and 95-year concessions, operated respectively by Azurix Buenos Aires and Azurix Mendoza. In March 1999 it was awarded the concession to operate these services in Cancún (Mexico). In the natural gas sector, in addition to its stake in the Bolivia–Brazil Gas Pipeline as a partner of Petrobras and YPFB, Enron also operates in Brazil through Gaspart, which holds stakes in five gas distribution utilities in the north-east and two in the south.

The AES group—which is the most aggressive agent in the expansion process of utility companies in Latin America,[14] and whose original field of play has always been power generation—acquired various electricity distributors in this region: Eden and Edes (Argentina) and important holdings in Light, Cemig, CEEE-CO and Metropolitana (Brazil). In 1999, it took over stock control of the CESP Tietê generation utility, the second of three companies established through the dissolution of the state-run CESP, which was privatised in that year. By August 1999, it had already acquired control of Eletronet, the Eletrobras data transmission company. Its job will be to carry long-distance signals for access providers with operations in Brazil already planned or under way. Through these

---

[13] Owned by Brazilian mining magnate Eike Batista, AMX is endowed with the know-how required for drilling artesian bore holes (based on technology developed for gold mining) in order to sell this water. It also develops solutions in the drinking water area. This entrepreneur was appointed the CEO of Azurix in Brazil, receiving shares in the company in payment of the AMX sales price.

[14] For instance, through the AES Corporation, this group is currently the most aggressive foreign player on the Brazilian market, with investments that already top US$ 3 billion.

investments, AES intends to take over 10–11% of the long-distance data transmission market over the next three years.

In contrast to European utilities and the Enron and AES conglomerates, the other US groups have not yet started to diversify into other types of business, although operating in a wide variety of electrical sectors, both upstream and downstream. A typical example is Reliant. Through its subsidiary, Reliant Industries Energy, it has channelled investments into power generation, cogeneration and distribution projects, as well as laying gas pipelines and distributing natural gas.

II.D.b. Acquisition of assets in privatisation auctions

All these groups have played leading roles in the privatisation of assets in Latin America. For instance, the Enron Group—which operates in a globalised manner throughout all segments of the power sector—launched its activities in Latin America in the mid-1990s through the projects listed in Table VIII.2, with a marked stress on Brazil. To date, the group has focused on acquiring the assets of piped gas distributors in Argentina, Brazil, Bolivia and Colombia, as well as the construction of thermopower and cogeneration plants in Central America. More recently, the Enron Group took a vital strategic step in the Southern Cone through its partnership with international companies, Bolivian distributors and Petrobras, established to lay the Brazil–Bolivia gas pipeline.

EDF International has acquired the assets of various companies undergoing privatisation. The dynamics of this process are reflected in rising investment volumes: FF 300 million in 1993, FF 3 billion in 1995 and FF 5 billion in 1996.

Additionally, Endesa, Iberdrola and Reliant have made their presence felt at auctions in Argentina, Brazil, Colombia and Mexico, particularly those selling off companies which could provide short-term returns on investments in assets, making good use of the expertise built up through their activities in their home countries. This has focused largely on companies with ample potential for a rapid return on investment, thanks to rising demands for power and the elimination of losses caused by obsolete systems.

II.D.c. Strategic partnerships

All the utility groups studied here work frequently through strategic partnerships set up to channel investments or acquire assets in Latin America.

Illustrating this, the acquisition by Endesa of 29% of stock control of Enersis (Chile) warrants attention. Endesa also set up a strategic alliance with the Chilean group in order to bid in privatisation processes selling off utilities throughout Latin America. Prior to the takeover of Enersis[15] through the acquisition of shares in the parent companies of this Chilean group, this strategic alliance acquired Cerj (Brazil), as well as Emgesa and Codemsa (Colombia)[16]. Endesa Group holdings in these three companies are 20%, 49% and 49% respectively. The objective of this alliance is to take over 20% of the power market in Latin America.[17]

In the natural gas segment, Iberdrola set up a strategic alliance with two other natural gas companies in Spain—GasNatural and Repsol—for the acquisition of Brazilian distributors CEG and RioGas, as well as GasNatural ESP, a distributor in Colombia. For Repsol and GasNatural, these operations consolidated an expansion strategy in Latin America that lies at the core of its principal business. This partnership is important for Iberdrola, buttressing its expansion strategy into new markets and businesses, where gas distribution is one of its principal objectives.

In partnership with Southern Electric (US) and the Opportunity Investment Funds, the AES Group acquired 32.96% of common shares in Cemig (14.41% of its total capital). The power utility for Minas Gerais State—one of the most highly developed parts of south-east Brazil—this is one of the most efficient companies on the Brazilian market.

Another significant partnership was established with Tractebel and Edelnor (the Southern subsidiary in Chile) to build a gas pipeline linking Chile and Argentina, paving the way for this Chilean generation company to build a 240 MW gas-fired power plant, burning fuel from Argentina.

The strategy of the Reliant group involves associations with local partners in order to ensure that corporate management takes local customs into consideration and meets the expectations of both consumers and staff.[18]

In 1997, the Enron Group took a major strategic step forward in the Southern Cone through its partnership with international companies, Bolivian distributors and Petrobras, established to lay the Bolivia–Brazil gas pipeline.

---

[15] Spain's leading energy group, Endesa paid US$ 1.5 billion for stock control of Enersis (Chile). This agreement set up a joint venture owned by Endesa (55%) and Enersis (45%), making this group the largest foreign power operator in Latin America (24% of power generated in Peru; 6% in Colombia; 16% in Argentina; and 46% in Chile). (Gazeta Mercantil; 27 November 1997). For more details on this operation, see www.tercera.com/.

[16] Codemsa (distributor) and Emgesa (generator) were spun off through the unbundling of the Bogota Power Company (EEB), responsible for 25% of power generation in Colombia.

[17] (Gazeta Mercantil; 22 September 1997).

[18] Taken from www.houind.com.

In partnership with the FondElec group, the CMS Energy Corporation (USA) established an investment fund to underwrite its investments in the region, called the FondElec Essential Services Growth Fund LP.[19] The CMS group has been implementing various investment projects focused on gas pipelines, power, natural gas distribution and independent power production, particularly in Argentina, Chile and Uruguay, through its subsidiaries CMS Electric and Gas Co. and CMS Generation.

In Brazil, CMS Electric and Gas signed an agreement with Cataguases Leopoldina covering the acquisition of 42.6% of Energipe[20] for US$ 180 million, purchased in December 1997 in an auction by Cataguases Leopoldina. This acquisition gives CMS appreciable clout in the operations management of this distributor, which holds 2.5% of the market in north/north-east Brazil and 0.6% of the Brazilian market as a whole. However, the CMS had sold their shares to Alliant Energy Resources, another north-American utility that has arrived recently in Brazil. CMS remains active in Brazil with last October's acquisition of a 77% ownership interest of CPEE, a small group of electric distributors in Southern Brazil.

Prior to the acquisition of its holdings in Energipe, CMS bid unsuccessfully in three privatisation auctions for companies in south-east Brazil: CEEE-CO, CEEE-N/NE and Enersul, this latter in partnership with Light. The high bids submitted by the CMS Group reflect the strategic importance that these acquisitions would have had for its entry into Brazil, due to their proximity to the other Southern Cone countries where CMS has a marked presence in the natural gas segment.

III. Strategies of Companies Acquired By Foreign Operators in Brazil

The Brazilian power sector requires a special analysis due to the relative size of its market compared to the rest of Latin America, its abundant energy resources, geographical size and common borders with a large number of countries all supplement its potential for expanding power demands. These factors make the Brazilian market into a key factor in the expansion strategy of all the companies mentioned above.

III.A. The institutional context

Brazil's power market has traditionally been characterised by its centralised decision processes and the hegemonic presence of state-owned

---

[19] This fund will be managed by FondElec, with technical consulting services from CMS Electric and Gas, in order to assess investment opportunities and prospects.
[20] Energipe is a small power distribution company in north-east Brazil with 0.59% of the national market.

companies, despite the diversity of its players.[21] This institutional context imposed relatively stable strategies for the companies in this sector, as their areas of operation were limited by concession contracts, with decisions frequently assigned to government agencies rather than management.[22]

Over the last years of the 20th century, sweeping changes began to appear in the institutional framework. This transition period was characterised by the concomitant implementation of new rules and institutional roles, in parallel with a privatisation program which, as shown, has already generated some US$ 32 billion by October 2000, through the sale of twenty-two federal and state power utilities.[23] Additionally, a new Electricity Regulatory Agency (ANEEL—*Agência Nacional de Energia Elétrica*) has been set up, and the complexities, uncertainties and diversities of the decision process have increased through the arrival of new players in this sector, within a context of redefinition of rules and shifting market structures.

The nature of this process is reflected in the duality of federal government objectives: a sector-wide shake-up resulting in enhanced economic efficiency through competition in certain market segments, private corporate management and regulation through incentives in segments offering a natural monopoly, while at the same time bringing in the largest possible amount of revenue through privatization.

The implementation of these objectives clearly reflects the high priority assigned to generating revenues through the sale of assets, to the detriment of regulatory modelling and sectoral rules. Examples include the federal government financing mechanisms offered to potential bidders in

---

[21] It is important to stress that the nationalisation of Brazil's power sector dates back to 1964 when Eletrobras was incorporated. Prior to this, the sector was relatively fragmented, with several private companies, many foreign-owned, operating in various states as 'electricity islands'. In the early 1960s, the government strategy was to federalise the entire sector. However, its attempts met with only partial success, nationalising half the power generation and transmission sectors, while distribution remained in the hands of the states, in an 'unconcluded federalisation' process.

[22] Until the recent restructuring, Brazil's institutional model consisted of a central holding company—Eletrobras—which was responsible for sectoral financing and coordination of power agents, with control of the four generation companies, each allocated a specific region (50% of the total national installed capacity). Additionally, each state set up its own distribution company whose concession areas were aligned with State borders. The distribution companies in São Paulo (CESP), Minas Gerais (CEMIG), Paraná (COPEL) and Rio Grande do Sul (CEEE) also accounted for appreciable portions of Brazil's power generation capacity, giving them ample political clout in sectoral decisions.

[23] The total amount brought in also includes federal government minority holdings.

privatisation auctions, as well as drafting concession contracts that are reasonably attractive to new investors.[24]

Despite these incentives, the lack of definitive regulations has resulted in some uncertainty affecting the strategies of companies eager to operate on the Brazilian market. This includes fuzzy criteria for future tariff revisions, as well as the pace and extent of sectoral reforms currently under way.

The functioning of the newly-established Electricity Regulatory Agency (ANEEL) is currently hobbled by start-up difficulties. Although Brazil's National Congress has approved the appointment of its directors, giving them temporary stability in their positions with autonomy and independence of decision, other factors undermine its regulatory activities: absence of a regulatory tradition for public utilities in Brazil, and lack of qualified personnel to handle regulatory activities.

III.A.a. New sectoral rules

In general, the new sectoral rules establish very distinct regulatory principles for market segments, depending on the intended level of competition for each of them. For instance, tariffs will be free of constraints in the generation segment, and will be defined by the regulatory agency in the transmission and distribution segments for captive consumers with demands of under 10 MWh and which will be serviced at voltages of 69 kV or more.

In the generation segment, tariffs should reflect long-term marginal costs. To do so, the Wholesale Power Market (MAE—*Mercado Atacadista de Energia*) will start up operations in the near future, as well as a spot market where surplus power in each inter-linked system will be freely traded. Operational planning, scheduling and dispatch on this market will be the responsibility of the National Power System Operator (ONS— *Operador Nacional do System Elétrico*), which will also manage all transmission assets owned by the generation and distribution companies.

The Wholesale Power Market will include all generation companies with a capacity of 50 MW or more, all retailers (power distributors and sellers with annual loads of 100 GWh or more) and major consumers with demands of over 10 MW, with this limit dropping to 3 MW from 2000 onwards. The blocks of energy marketed among them will be covered by

---

[24] The National Bank for Social and Economic Development (BNDES) has been financing 50% of the minimum price of privatised companies. Although concession contracts make provision for a price-cap tariff mechanism, they also guarantee automatic reimbursement of operating costs for all concessionaires over the next four to five years (the tariff reduction factor was defined as zero for these early years in order to foster productivity); they have also been relatively timid in defining the investment plans needed to modernise these companies. For further details, see Peres (1999b).

financial contracts called Electric Energy Wholesale Market Contracts (CMAE—Contratos do Mercado de Atacado de Energia Elétrica).

In addition to these contracts, the new model makes provision for bilateral contracts between power buyers and sellers which, in contrast to the CMAE contracts have pre-set energy prices and are long-term. Their purpose is to hedge against uncertainties caused by volatile prices on the Wholesale Power Market, reflecting the risk of shortfalls and system capacity in proportion to demand. For instance, prices on the Wholesale Power Market will vary widely between rainy years (low prices) and dry years (high prices).

Due to these swings, it is felt that the total amount of energy traded on the stock market should not exceed 10–15% of the market total. In practice, this will probably involve surplus energy and possible contracted requirements of agents in the power sector.

In order to avoid a power price hike through immediate implementation of constraint-free contracts, the government established a transition period of five years. During this time the current supply contracts between generators and distributors will be maintained, after which volumes will gradually shrink by 25% so that Brazil will have a free power supply market after nine years.

The initial contracts offer the additional advantage of boosting the profitability of the generation assets to be privatised, as the new private agents will enjoy guaranteed revenues and can forecast their expenses during the contract duration horizons.

For the transmission segment, the government set reference prices for transmission and distribution charges (use and connection) scaled by geographical location.[25] Their purpose is to ensure the feasibility of non-discriminatory charges for transmission networks in order to ensure that these tariffs allow the transmission grid to function independently of ownership, indicating location costs for demand or generation in different zones (or nodes) of the system.

In order to ensure the neutrality of the transmission segment, consultants suggest that the integrated companies should be unbundled or at least have separate accounting systems for distribution and marketing, in order to streamline the expansion of non-captive markets. All the distributors (the current concessionaires) will be obliged to allow the transit of blocks of energy traded by these retailers, charging appropriately for

---

[25] The general access contract conditions covering the use of and connection to the power transmission and distribution systems were established by Resolution No. 281/99, which attempts to stipulate the definitive outlines of this issue, including fresh investments in transmission facilities, as Resolution No. 142/99—based on Edict No. 459/97—had already defined the initial values constituting the permitted revenues for each transmission utility. For further details, see Pires (1999).

Table VIII.3. Operating control of privatised companies in Brazil.

Company/ Shareholder (Market)	Duke	AES	EDF	Reliant	CSN	Endesa	Iber -drola	VBC	Rede -Inepar	Trac- tebel	Enron	EDP	Cata- guases	Outros
Escelsa (2%)												71,15		28,85
Light (8.7%)	27,3	22,5	22,5	14,37										13.33
Cerj (2%)						10						30		60
Coelba (3%)							39							61
Ceeeco (2.21%)		100												–
Ceeene (1.77%)								33,3						66.7
CPFL (6.47%)								45,32						54.68
Enersul (0.9%)												71,15		28,85
Cemat (0.82%)									100					
Energipe (0.59%)													100	–
Cosern (0.75%)						12.2								87.80
Coelce (1.70%)						10						30		60
Elektro (5.5%)											100			–
Celpa (1%)									100					–
Bandeir (8%)								19,94				56		24.06
Metropol (18,3%)	27,3	22,5	22,5	14,37										13,33
Gerasul (6.8%)										100				–
Paranap (4.9%)	100													–
Tietê (5.6%)		100												–

The percentage of the Brazilian market serviced by each concessionaire is given in brackets.

the use of their power lines. Should it not be possible to unbundle the power distributors to the desired level, they should set up separate companies for various fields of business.

The captive consumer distribution segment will be regulated by ANEEL. It is expected that the tariff revisions scheduled for 2003 will be somewhat controversial, as the regulatory agency should stipulate the revenue reduction factors for each of the companies, no longer ensuring full allocation of gains on cost reduction and higher productivity.

Finally, ANEEL issued a regulatory standard that will have a decisive effect on the strategies of companies operating in the Brazilian market. This resolution limits the control of power distribution and generation companies by a single group to 20% of the national market, curbing the expansion strategies of various groups already bidding in privatisation auctions under way. In regional terms, a generation or distribution agent operating through the interconnected system in the south, south-east and mid-west regions may not hold more than 25% of the respective installed capacity or sales of the system. For agents operating in the interconnected north/north-east system, this ceiling is 35%. Additionally, no company may hold more than 30% of the total distribution and generation facilities nation-wide. Should this occur, the law sets a deadline of one year for one of the assets to be sold to another group.[26] The current stock control structure of recently-privatised companies is given in Table VIII.3.

III.B. New management strategies for power utilities in Brazil

In view of the alterations in the institutional framework and the strategies of utility companies in Latin America defined above, a series of strategies can be identified in the new management of recently-acquired power companies in Brazil. These strategies are slotted into a complex network of interactions among the various agents in the Brazilian power sector (Fig. VIII.1). Often intermingled, in general terms they consist of:

1. partnerships and shared management;
2. recovery of commercial losses and more consumers;
3. management of demand and energy conservation;
4. cogeneration and ensuring customer loyalty;
5. enhancing the potential of hydropower plants;
6. administrative adjustments, outsourcing and renegotiation of contracts;
7. diversification of activities;
8. verticalisation;
9. generous dividends policy;
10. going private;
11. seeking new financing strategies.

III.B.a. Shared management: benefits and conflicts

An analysis of the results of the privatisation process of power distributors shows an appreciable associative participation among the players: foreign power operators, state-owned company pension funds, power-intensive consumers, financial groups and private Brazilian power operators.

---

[26] These decisions were covered by Resolution No. 094 issued by ANEEL on 30 March 1998, as the government was concerned with the future strategies already outlined by various players in the privatisation processes already under way. A good example is the declaration by the Business Director of Camargo Correa, a major power consumer and recent purchaser of the CPFL power distributor in São Paulo State, jointly with the Bradesco financial group and Votorantim, another major power consumer. On the day after its successful bid in the auction of CPFL, he stated that 'energy is a business that demands production scales in order to ensure maximisation of gains and, once the privatisation phase is over, there will be a trend towards mergers and acquisitions that will finally result in half a dozen distribution utilities'. (Gazeta Mercantil, 8 November 1997).

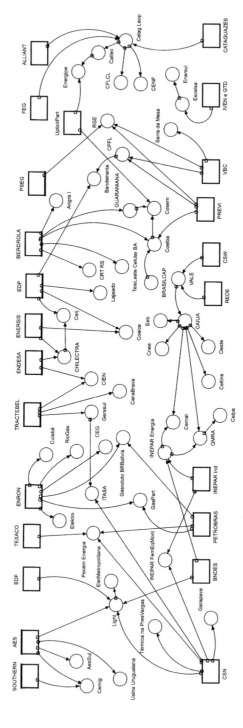

Fig. VIII.1. Brazilian power sector: interaction among major players.
Source: Adapted from de Oliveira (1999).

The first phase after privatisation typically consists of trimming costs and ensuring operational continuity on more efficient bases. During this stage, the views of the various members of the winning consortium tend to be very similar. After the initial adjustments, the second stage opens with the preparation and implementation of long-term strategic planning. During this phase, varying risk propensity levels aming the stakeholders may result in differing business visions and investment decisions. These discrepancies may trigger corporate reshuffles with interests sold off either to other stakeholders or to third parties.[27]

These associations have prompted the various groups to share the management of recently acquired companies, which has proven to be a factor in corporate modernisation as well as a source of conflict. The former situation covers Cataguases-Leopoldina and the Rede/Inepar Group, while the latter—situations of conflict—includes most of the privatised utilities, particularly Escelsa, Light and Cemig.

Outstanding among the cases where shared management has enhanced business modernisation gains is Cataguases-Leopoldina. A long-established company run along traditional lines, it is nevertheless an example of an aggressive strategy in both the power market as well as its diversification into other infrastructure sectors. It recently introduced a series of innovations in its organisational framework and business management practices, adapting to partnerships with foreign operators. This is a flagship company as, prior to the privatisation of Brazil's power sector during the 1990s, it was the private company with the largest slice of the market (0.3% of total power distributed in Brazil).[28]

Additionally, as mentioned earlier, Cataguases-Leopoldina entered into an agreement with the CMS group in the USA, selling off 42.6% of its stock control, paid by the Fondelec Group Inc. investment fund, for which CMS is a technical advisor; it has also taken strategic operating positions in Energipe. Prior to this transaction, Fondelec purchased 23% of Cataguases,

---

[27] In the case of Eletropaulo and Light, divestment of the CSN stake is expected at the time of writing, with the other shareholders having right of preference. Additionally, further reshuffles are expected, with EDF taking over Light and AES retaining Eletropaulo (Gazeta Mercantil, 18 November 1999). The reasons for these clashes will be discussed later. Recently, Reliant sold all their shares in Light and Electropaulo to EDF and AES.

[28] In the power sector, Cataguases-Leopoldina originally worked with power generation and distribution at Zona da Mata, Minas Gerais State. With annual revenues of US$ 58 million (December 1999), its first step towards expansion was the acquisition of stock control in the Nova Friburgo power concessionaire—CENF in Rio de Janeiro State, which brought it up to a total of 300,000 consumers. More recently, it acquired the profitable Sergipe State distributor (Energipe), with 0.6% of the Brazilian market, at an auction with powerful strategic interests in play with heavyweight bidders: CVRD and Coelba.

with prospects of taking over a further 13% after closing the CMS/ Cataguases deal. As is discussed above, CMS had sold their shares to Alliant.

The need for funding to underwrite its expansion through a process of mergers and takeovers, while seeking new partners, has ushered in sweeping cultural changes for this family-run private company whose track-record dates back to 1907. By inviting its new foreign partners— the CSW Group (head office) and Alliant (Energipe)—to sit on its Board, Cataguases is moving into a new era, sharing decisions that seek gains in both scale and productivity.

As the new owner of the Tocantins State power distribution concessionaire (Celtins), the Rede/Inepar Group is implementing a strategy very similar to that of Cataguases. In the power sector, this group acquired shares in CEMAT (Mato Grosso) in partnership with pension funds, at an auction where its bid topped the Cataguases Leopoldina offer. The company already operates a hydropower plant in this State, while the Rede Group also retains holdings in three other hydropower plants in Cubatão and Machadinho (Santa Catarina) and Dona Francisca (Rio Grande do Sul).

Similar to Cataguases, the Rede Group is also negotiating a seat on its Board with a foreign operator: Enron, a partner in several ventures of one of its subsidiaries (Inepar). Through another subsidiary (Vale Paranapanema, which holds 22% of CVRD) the Rede Group is already involved in a partnership with Central South Western (USA).

Particularly noteworthy among the cases of shared management generating conflicts is the situation of Escelsa, where bumpy business administration is due to disagreements between Pactual and Icatu. These two banks set up the Iven Group for the pioneering acquisition of Escelsa during Brazil's privatisation process in 1995, sharing management with the GTD Group of pension funds.[29] These disagreements explain why Escelsa did not take part in the Light auction. The Pactual bank is studying a proposal to sell its holdings to the Previ pension fund and CSN, which are already associated through Light. Nevertheless, the current partners sold 73% of the shares in this group to EDP.

Another similar case involves the administration of Light. The management agreement was drawn up by three foreign groups (EDF, AES and

---

[29] The Iven Group comprises of the following banks: Pactual, Bozano Simonsen, Icatu, Itaú and Citibank, Opportunity Capital Partners Financial Group, Central Bank Pension Fund (Centrus) and Argentina's Perez Companc, each with a one-eighth share of the capital. The Iven Group holds 45.05% of the company's capital and drew up a management agreement with Geração, Transmissão e Distribuição Participações S/A—GTD Group, comprising of 11 pension funds set up by various private and state companies owning 25% of the company's shares, as well as others recently privatised in Brazil.

Houston) and a major power-intensive consumer (CSN steel-mill). Shared management has been running into serious difficulties. Some can be explained by marked differences in the management styles of EDF, its US partners and CSN, with particular regard to the pace and direction of the company's expansion. While EDF is eager to focus on São Paulo and new generation projects, the other groups prefer to acquire additional assets, regardless of their geographic location.[30] Finally, EDF is coming under heavy fire in marketing terms as it appointed the Managing Director of Light, which is currently facing serious supply problems in its concession area. Possible reasons for the somewhat turbulent management of the company include discrepancies among the controlling groups, as positions were shared out with little concern for synergy among directors with different strategic objectives and administrative cultures.[31] (*Jornal do Brasil*, 4 February 1997). The 1999 acquisition by Light of the largest power distributor in both São Paulo State and Brazil (Metropolitana) prompted a reshuffle of directorships at Light, with Houston taking over the commercial side, while the financial division was assigned to the administration sector under CSN; EDF retained the CEO position and AES took over as Chairman of the Board, in an attempt to settle simmering management conflicts.

Another example of shared management resulting in conflict is Cemig. These difficulties are basically focused on the new commercial guidelines of the private groups and its public utility admission heritage handed down by the state government. The management agreement involves the AES, Southern and Opportunity groups on one side, and the Minas Gerais state government on the other. The new partners hold four of eleven seats on the Board and appoint three of the nine directors. However, Board decisions are taken by a qualified vote, meaning approval by eight Board members and six directors. AES plays a decisive role in the business activities of Cemig, particularly through the Operations Director. This shareholders' agreement was suspended through a lawsuit filed by the new government, elected in 1998, which did not agree with the power of veto held by the private groups over the management of this state-owned enterprise.

Outstanding among the conflicts that assailed this administration is a clash that took place in early 1998. Eager to beef up its coffers at the start

---

[30] Despite its interest in the Rio–São Paulo axis, the premium in the Light bid in the CPFL auction was based largely on funding made available by CSN, as the French executives of EDF were jittery about this deal.

[31] The former Administration Director was Brazilian, appointed by CSN; the Distribution Director was French, selected by EDF; the Generation Director was American, appointed by AES; the Financial Director was American, appointed by Reliant. The Chairman of the Board (Brazilian) represented Vicunha/CSN/CVRD while the CEO was French.

of the year, the state Government found a solution through receiving some US$ 29 million advance payments of ICMS tax from Cemig. This measure was adopted for all state-run companies in Minas Gerais State, in exchange for the benefit of postponed subsequent payments. The private shareholders were deeply displeased by this measure, which knocked Cemig preferred shares down 8.22% while the São Paulo Stock Exchange Power Index (IEE) fell 6.27% in January–February 1998.

Reconciling the dynamics of asset appreciation by private enterprise with the management commitments of a public utility does not seem to be an easy job. A good example of this is the fact that the 1996 Cemig balance sheets show a 3.6% reduction in investment in year-round power supply improvements in the Jequitinhonha Valley (one of the poorest parts of the State) from 1995 to 1996, although total corporate investments rose some 19% over the same period. According to articles in the press, it seems that the new partners in Cemig wish to transfer to the state government the company assets linked to the year-round water supply dams, representing 12% of the fixed assets of Cemig.[32]

III.B.b. Recovery of commercial losses and increase in number of customers

The power distributors of Latin America suffer serious energy loss problems, mainly commercial, inherited from state-run management that turned a blind eye to covert connections among the less-favoured sectors of the populace. In the specific case of Brazil, the state governments which owned most of the distributors were unwilling to face the political fallout caused by disconnecting clandestine consumers in *'favela'* slums and other poverty-stricken areas.

A strategy for recovering commercial losses is firming up among these recently- privatised companies (Table VIII.4). According to declarations by foreign executives—Endesa and Iberdrola, for instance—the acquisition of power distributors with high commercial losses forms part of a strategy of acquiring only companies with ample potential for management upgrades (bloated staff structure, heavy system losses and high potential market growth.

The most impressive examples are the companies acquired by Endesa. Since purchasing EDENOR (Argentina) in 1994, its management tagged the recovery of losses as top priority. In the case of this Argentineans distributor, this item absorbed some 33% of investments in 1996, followed by access for new consumers (21%); upgrading network structure (19%)

---

[32] Articles 63 and 64 of State Decree No. 41,109/57 state that 'the assets and facilities used in the production, transmission and distribution of power are linked to these services and may not be withdrawn, divested, disposed of, assigned, granted or mortgaged without the prior, express authorisation of the Grantor Authority Agency.'

Table VIII.4. Energy losses privatized power utilities (%).

Company/Year	1998[a]	1997	1996	1995
Cemig	8.5%	8.3%*	9.0%	9.5%
CPFL	6.7%	6.2%*	6.3%	6.5%
Escelsa	8.5%	9.3%	9.3%	10.2%*
AES Sul	8.9%	10.0%*	not given	not given
R.G. Energia	11.7%	12.6%*	not given	not given
Enersul	14.0%	14.7%*	14.1%	14.7%
Light	14.5%	16.1%	18.7%*	15.9%
Coelba	15.5%	16.5%	16.1%*	14.3%
Cerj	19.1%	25.3%	29.4%*	22.9%
Cemat	22.5%	25.0%*	26.8%	25.0%

Source: BNDES (1998,1999) and Gazeta Mercantil 28 September 1998.
Note: (a) Losses for January – July
* Year of privatisation.

and network communications support (13%). Despite a 12.5% cut in investments for 1996 over the previous year, losses nevertheless shrank by 34%, while revenues rose 9.1% from 1995 through 1997.

This strategy grew even stronger after entering into a partnership with the Enersis Group (Chile). The controllers of this Chilean Group have ample expertise in this area.[33] More recently, it trimmed losses at Edersur (Argentina) from 26% to 10% in just five years. In Brazil, Endesa management of Cerj followed a strategy similar to that used for Edenor (Argentina). It assigned top priority to buttressing its commercial area, combatting energy losses and re-registering customers. Under new management, losses at Cerj shrank from 29% to 26% in one year.[34]

Despite its brief experience managing Coelba under private administration, the Iberdrola Group has also focused on an energy loss reduction strategy, although its efforts have not yet produced the expected benefits (losses fell only from 16.1% to 15.8% in two years) and extending its customer listing (up 4% over the period).

As a way of buttressing this strategy, the Group is modernising 180 Coelba substations by implementing a modern network management system which will also be adopted by the Rio Grande do Norte (Cosern) distribution utility. These distribution utilities will be the first power companies in north-east Brazil to be controlled by an automated system which will interconnect the substations to the computerised control centers.

Belonging to the same consortium, EDF and the AES group which manages the Light and Metropolitana power distribution utilities in Brazil,

---

[33] For instance, the new Enersis Group controllers managed to trim the energy loss rate of Chilectra from 23% in the early 1980s to only 9% over an eight-year period.
[34] Cerj management forecasts a loss rate of 12% for 2001 (America Economia, December 1997).

are also striving to reduce commercial losses in order to ensure rapid payback of the investments required to acquire these utilities. In fact, commercial losses at Light fell 4%, down from 18.7% to 14.7% between 1996 and 1998, with its sales area controlled by EDF.

The AES Sul (AES Corporation) and Rio Grande Energia (RGE) distribution utilities decided to channel their investments into repairing the grid and reducing losses during the first year after privatisation, as well as replacing meters and wooden light poles, replacing transformers and conductor gauges. These investments reduced power outages from 23 hours/year to 15 hours/year (Gazeta Mercantil, 11 October 1998).

III.B.c. Management of energy demand and conservation

Traditionally, Brazilian power distribution concessionaires have earmarked much of their revenues to surveys designed to keep pace with the expansion requirements of this sector. Current technology-based projects now stress the optimisation of the installed park, minimising the need for further investments in the power distribution area.

Additionally, demand management measures have always been adopted individually by the utilities. The difference is that they are now deployed at the institutional level, forming part of a specific project for 1999/2000 launched under the government-run Program to Combat Wasted Energy (Procel).[35] For instance, several power distribution utilities are discussing the transfer of some peak-hour industrial power consumption to other times.

The new shared management of Cemig is introducing a power conservation system that is new to Brazil. This no-top system allows power to be stored in batteries through converting the alternating current carried by grids to continuous current. From 1999 onward, this is intended to ensure sufficient power for peak-hour consumption.

Similarly, Light plans to introduce a demand management system that will benefit commercial and residential users consuming off-peak energy through discounts and scaled rates, designed to fine-tune grid performance, avoid summertime power outages and encourage rational energy use (Gazeta Mercantil, 11 October 1998).

The Bandeirante de Energia utility will introduce a 'yellow rates' system under which customers pay lower prices for lower peak-hour consumption within the system.

---

[35] ANEEL published a resolution establishing a minimum of 1% of the operating revenues for investment by the distribution utilities in power conservation programs, such as new types of rates and tariffs that help reduce peak-hour demands on the system in the late afternoon and early evening.

Finally, Eletropaulo will have invested US$ 25.5 million by year-end 2000 in shifting industrial consumption to cut peak-period demand by 25.8 MW. It is working with its customers to determine how much electricity they could save. In counterpart, the customer can choose between having the amount of electricity saved supplied at some other time, and lower monthly bills.

III.B.d. Cogeneration and customer loyalty

As shown, the new rules for Brazil's power sector established the Wholesale Power Market (MAE—*Mercado Atacadista de Energia Elétrica*), together with the possibility of consumers with demands of over 10 MWh retailing their energy (from 2000 onwards, this limit drops to 3 MWh).[36]

Thanks to this new institutional model, trends are appearing in this sector seeking new customers while still maintaining old contracts. Partnerships are being established for this purpose between the distributors and their industrial customers through cogeneration projects. In order to reduce the uncertainties inherent in large-scale power generation projects, many of these contracts are Power Purchase Agreements (PPAs), guaranteeing the purchase of specific amounts of energy on a long-term basis at pre-set prices.

To this end, Eletropaulo signed an agreement with an major power producer—Rolls-Royce Power Ventures—through which the distributor guarantees the price of all power it will have to purchase on the free market from 2003 onward, when the volumes of the current contracts will start to be available for free negotiation. The energy traded will be generated by the natural gas-fired thermopower plant installed at the Capuava plant of Petroquímica União, under the agreement signed with Rolls-Royce.

Similarly, Light is negotiating the construction of sixteen cogeneration projects, which will use natural gas to produce electricity and other by-products such as hot water, steam and carbon dioxide, as mini-plants to be installed in industrial complexes and malls. The company is adopting an aggressive customer loyalty policy and actively seeking out new conquests, offering technical and operational support for these cogeneration operations.[37]

---

[36] Law No. 9648/98.

[37] For its negotiations with the Peugeot plant, Light made its technical staff available to this auto-assembler in order to ensure that the final design was based on the most power-thrifty formula. A working group was also set up to develop specific services and solutions for its 500 major consumers, stressing service and quality as the twin factors for keeping these consumers. It has nevertheless been lowering the rates charged to large corporations. In addition to keen competition in this sector, the company is also concerned by the fact that its partner CSN—which is also its largest customer—in bringing a thermopower plant into operation at the end of the year, will prune its expenditures on energy by 40%.

III.B.e. Repowering hydropower plants

Another strategy emerging among the power utilities is repowering—boosting capacity—hydropower plants. With the new techniques being used, Brazil's power generation capacity could increase by up to 30%. These corporate strategies are based on an awareness that Brazil's energy park is over twenty years old and investments in repowering postpone fresh investments in building dams, in addition to boosting power generation capacity and avoiding unnecessary environmental costs.

As an example of this trend, Voith S/A—which has just started to operate on the Brazilian market as a supplier of turbines for hydropower plants and paper-making machinery—set up its integrated refit and modernisation services division for hydropower plants, signing a contract with CESP at the start of the year covering the repair of two locks on the Tietê–Paraná waterway.

Similarly, in mid-1997 Light signed a US$ 70 million contract with a consortium (ABB, CBPO, Mecânica Pesada, Engevix Harva) to refit the Ilha dos Pombos hydropower plant. This upgrade is expected to boost the capacity of this plant by 30%. (Gazeta Mercantil, 21 October 1998).

III.B.f. Administrative adjustments and renegotiation of contracts

Companies in Brazil's power sector have been implementing a broad-ranging administrative adjustment process with some emphasis on lay-offs and outsourcing. This process began prior to privatisation of these companies, achieving a 17% cut in the nation-wide sectoral headcount through layoffs between 1994 and 1996.

Regardless of pre-sale downsizing, new controllers have implemented adjustment plans in all privatised companies.[38] The new management of Cerj and Light trimmed the staff structure and outsourced appreciable portions of the technical tasks of these companies. In the specific case of Light, some 4,100 workers were laid off between May 1996 (privatisation period) and March 1998, a cut in staff of 37%. (Rosa *et al.*, 1998.)

Similarly, the new management of Coelba intends to lay off an additional 300 employees during 1998, despite staff cuts of 40% during the pre-privatisation preparation process.

These layoffs have worsened power supply problems—already critical—in the Cerj and Light concession areas, resulting in widespread consumer dissatisfaction. In 1998, Cerj was fined 0.1% of its revenues and was audited by ANEEL to check non-compliance with the concession contract; it had to comply with over 40 recommendations to upgrade its services, under threat of scaled punishments.

---

[38] For eight power distributors privatised in 1997, the total headcount shrank by 22.1%.

It is even possible that many of the problems faced by both these companies are linked to the implosion of their *esprit de corps* and the disintegration of their technical heritage, caused by the resignation incentive scheme launched immediately after privatisation in June 1996.

Light established a joint-venture with Alstom—a French company specialising in technology and transportation infrastructure—and Altm S/A for providing electrical installation and equipment maintenance services, in order to outsource its activities and assign high priority to power distribution. The type of outsourcing adopted by Light is designed to assure savings when signing up maintenance services, as the distribution utility itself owns 49% of the new company. (Gazeta Mercantil, 14 July 1999).

The new management of Cemig has also introduced outsourcing and across-the-board layoffs, with almost 2,000 people leaving between 1996 and 1997, bringing its headcount down from 14,500 in 1996 to 12,550 in 1997, and with a further 500 layoffs scheduled for 1998.

III.B.g. Diversification of activities

Power companies in Brazil are drawing up strategies to offset the loss of markets through the arrival of new agents (independent power producers and major consumers) as well as the virtual elimination of the monopoly over distribution, based on free access to the transmission grid.

The general trend is towards diversification of services, following trends in the more developed countries. Power companies are equipped with the infrastructure needed to operate information highways, leasing poles and conduits for data transmission and cable TV channels. In fact, with their current infrastructure, these companies could boost their revenues, distribute cheaper energy more profitably and become partners in these new businesses.[39]

In São Paulo, CPFL plans to exploit its distribution networks with data transmission and cable TV facilities, through the strategic interests of its controlling shareholder, the Bradesco financial group. This will supplement its recently-launched activities in the information technology and telecommunication sectors.

Cataguases Leopoldina is moving into the cable TV and sanitation areas, incorporating a new subsidiary in partnership with WCCI (USA), which specialises in cable TV. This subsidiary will bid in tenders for cable TV licences covering towns in Rio de Janeiro, Minas Gerais, Sergipe and other

---

[39] For instance, the Paraná State power distributor (COPEL) intends to invest US$ 300 million in building a fibreoptic ring in Southern Brazil, in partnership with the State telecommunications utility (TeleParaná) and private enterprise. The purpose is to make good use of the existing power transmission structure consisting of pylons and networks for electronic data transmission, data communications, etc. (Gazeta Mercantil, 15 July 1997).

north-eastern States, as well as privatisation auctions selling off water and sanitation companies servicing towns in upstate Minas Gerais.[40]

One of Brazil's leading manufacturers of components for the energy and telecommunications areas, the Inepar Group stresses partnerships with major market players and technology providers at the global level. Its strategic planning looks ahead to the convergence of the energy and telecommunications sectors, with a single company simultaneously servicing the power and telephony areas. Following this strategy, the group will bid for both power and telephone service concessions.

Diversifying its activities to an increasing extent, Iberdrola is involved in fields ranging from telecommunications to tourism. The controlling shareholder of Infovias Serviços de Telecomunicações S/A, this group is moving into the tourism sector through Setur Brasil—a company being established in partnership with Spain's Serhs. It also holds a stake in the basic sanitation segment in Brazil, and is already operating in this area in Chile. Finally, through its subsidiary Tracol (Coelba) it is specialising in transformer refits and repairs, as well as power sector engineering projects. (*Gazeta Mercantil*, 20 July 1999).

III.B.h. Verticalization

An analysis of the strategies of recently privatised distributors sold to either Brazilian or foreign private groups stresses a verticalisation process, or reductions in the needs to acquire power supplies. This is the case with Cerj, Light, Cataguases Leopoldina and Escelsa.

Cerj set up a subsidiary to expand its self-sufficiency, currently limited to 30% of its demand. Following EDF guidelines, Light is seeking to implement generation projects that will boost its power self-sufficiency, today hovering at only 18% of its total demand. Another example of this is the agreement between this company and Comlurb covering the construction of a gas-fired power plant (a scheme already under way in France), fuelled by gas drawn from urban garbage dumped at the Gramacho/RJ landfill. With investments scheduled at some US$ 6 million, this should have a rated capacity of 12 MW.

Although only partially privatised, Cemig has contacted major consumers in its quest for the strategic alliances needed to meet the expanded generation requirements of its system. Six partnership projects are currently under way, involving 840 MW at a cost of US$ 1,043 billion.

---

[40] According to Chairman Ivan Botelho, the Cataguases diversification strategy is similar to that adopted by US companies. 'This is the trend followed by companies in the USA. The same employee calling to read the light meter can also check water consumption and sell TV services and even insurance. We have to use our workforce better'. (Gazeta Mercantil, 4 December 1997).

A striking aspect of the Cemig strategy is that the company intends to remain verticalised, although it also plans to set up specific business units for power generation, transmission and distribution under a parent company incorporated in Minas Gerais State.

The Escelsa controller—the Iven Group—is concerned with boosting its generation capacity and plans to build a 300 MW thermopower plant at Campo Grande (Mato Grosso do Sul). This group is also participating in the construction of a 750 MW thermopower plant, jointly with Eletrobras, Light, Cerj and Cataguases Leopoldina.

The Iberdrola Group intends to build a gas-fired thermopower plant with a capacity of 240 MW. This project forms part of its strategy to generate 30% of the power required by its distribution utilities—Coelba and Cosern—as 98% of the energy they consume is currently provided by Chesf.[41]

Currently purchasing 100% of the power it consumes, Eletropaulo Metropolitana will invest some US$ 223 million in building a thermopower plant with a capacity of 700–900 MW.

At Uruguaiana, on the Brazilian border with Argentina, AES Sul is building a thermopower plant fired by natural gas, at a cost of US$ 250 million, while Rede/Inepar Energia is implementing nine power generation projects and one transmission project[42] (*Gazeta Mercantil*, 21 October 1998).

Eager to increase its generation capacity, Cataguases Leopoldina will assign top priority to building small hydropower plants. This decision is based on the fact that the construction process is less entangled in red tape, as it is easier to obtain environmental licences and other authorisations in addition to lower geological risks, although thermopower plants have not been completely discarded. This company will hold 5% of the Norte Fluminense thermopower plant in northern Rio de Janeiro State and plans to build another power plant at Aracaju (Sergipe).

III.B.i. Generous dividends policy

The new controllers of some privatised companies have clearly decided to adopt a policy of distributing generous dividends to shareholders, shortening payback periods for investments in privatisation.

---

[41] The location for the thermopower plant will be assigned to the State offering the best tax breaks (Bahia or Rio Grande do Norte). This gas-fired plant is the fourth in-house power generation project implemented by Coelba. The two largest are the Itapebi hydropower plant and Termobahia, absorbing investments of US$ 300 million through a partnership with Petrobras. (Gazeta Mercantil, 7 October 1998).

[42] Outstanding among the various Inepar projects is the Campos Novos plant, with a capacity of approximately 880 MW, to be built with Brazilian partners in Santa Catarina State.

This is the case with Cerj, for instance, where the economic and financial indicators for its first year under private management show that shareholders benefited from its strategy of focusing primarily on recovering commercial losses and renegotiating supplier contracts. In 1998, its net revenues rose 28% over the previous year, with a 10% increase in new customers over the same period. In parallel, it posted net profits of R$ US$ 23 million, compared to a loss of US$ 256 million in 1996.

The downside of this strategy is the fact that higher dividend distribution reduces the amount of capital available for new investments (profits withheld). This is particularly serious in the case of Cerj because its investments in the distribution network proved insufficient to keep pace with rising demand during the past summer, as its facilities were virtually reduced to scrap through minimal investments during its final years under state management.

At Light, the top priority for 1997 was a rapid reward for its shareholders through dividends that were close to munificent. The company posted a net profit of US$ 290 million (87% more than the previous year). However, the downside of this approach was an audit process with fines imposed by ANEEL, forcing the Board to draw up and implement an Emergency Plan in order to resolve power supply shortages that had triggered waves of criticism and complaints from angry consumers.[43]

III.B.j. Going private

Privatised enterprises—particularly those sold to European bidders—have been adopting a policy of repurchasing stock on the market. In October 1999, Iberdrola repurchased 32% of the shares issued by Coelba and indicated it had similar intentions for Cosern. Controlled by Duke and CPFL, Paranapanema also announced the repurchase of its shares.

The adoption of this strategy—known as going private—is designed to endow the restructuring of the company with greater flexibility and agility, while defusing any opposition from minority shareholders. According to market experts, the immediate objectives of these trends are to make good use of the premiums paid at the privatisation auctions (as these amounts can be entered in the accounts as expenditure through the incorporation of the investor company), reducing its income tax and improving the average price of the shares which—due to these premiums—are overvalued. For instance, Duke paid US$ 19.01 per 1,000 shares

---

[43] During the early weeks of 1998, Light assigned almost its entire advertising budget to the first six months of the year (US$ 993 million) to refurbishing its battered image (Jornal Folha de São Paulo, 12 February 1998). Curiously enough, one of its controllers—the CSN steel-mill which is a power-intensive consumer—lost 30,000 tons of steel through state-wide power-cuts (Jornal O Globo, 23 May 1998).

when the Paranapanema generation utility was privatised, well above the prices stipulated in the repurchase announcement of US$ 7.97 and US$ 6.32 per 1,000 common and preferred shares respectively (*Gazeta Mercantil*, 27 November 1999).

III.B.k. New financing strategies

Due to their long maturation periods and the need for heavy investment, power projects can rarely be funded by the companies themselves, necessarily depending on long-term financing.

The financial globalisation process underpinning national economies and corporate strategies during the 1990s triggered a demand for financial innovations and partnerships that diversify and minimise the various risks of these enterprises (foreign exchange, interest rates, etc.). At the same time, the multilateral credit institutions have moved away from their role of encouraging investments, generating a new financing profile, as the credit market (bank loans) and government funding has shifted to the stock market (private papers). (Pinto, 1997).

Within the general context of the infrastructure companies, a trend is appearing towards the use of new funding uptake tools on the international market, through the issue of corporate financial papers (bonds, euronotes, euroyen, commercial papers and debentures) absorbed by private institutions such as mutual funds and pension funds.

These papers have become attractive to companies due to their high yield, light regulatory constraints and low market placement and trading costs. Additionally, the development of secondary markets (derivatives) helps spread the risks of these papers through countless agents (Biasotto *et al.*, 1997).

In parallel to the launch of these papers, the companies have developed other financing techniques that are intrinsically linked to the strategy—analysed above—of seeking partnerships and cooperation agreements, in order to define long-term contract relationships for specific periods covering payback of the capital invested, allowing even distribution of the amounts invested, costs, risks and benefits.

Outstanding among these types of partnerships[44] is project financing,

---

[44] Various types of partnerships have already been firmed up in the power sector, including: *Build Operate Transfer* (BOT), where a private agent P1 runs the enterprise until the payback on investment is guaranteed, and transfers ownership directly to company P2, which manages the venture; *Build Transfer Operate* (BTO), whereby the company handling the construction (P1) returns the equipment to P2, which in turn transfers its operation to another company; *Build Own Operate* (BOO), whereby the entrepreneur builds and operates the equipment (e.g. power generation concession scheme); and *Buy Build Operate* (BBO) whereby the entrepreneur acquires government-owned equipment—generally under a concession—for operation and expansion.

which is a type of financial engineering contractually supported by the cash flow of a project. Under this financing system, a financial institution grants a loan to cover the implementation of a project, which is paid back by future operating revenues brought in by the enterprise. Its major advantage over more traditional forms of financing is the fact that companies are not tying up their assets, as the collateral is based on the expectations of future profits brought in by a Special Purpose Company established specifically for the project (Borges, 1998).

With regard to power utilities operating in Brazil, a variety of strategies may be noted for bringing in investment funding and/or paying off debts incurred through the acquisition of the assets of the privatised companies.

Reflecting lower risks in terms of uncertainty about the regulations imposed by Brazil's institutional model, halts in work schedules and the stability of real rate values, construction companies are seeking project financing to implement various power projects. For instance, the Group Rede/Inepar will invest 30% of its own funds with the remaining 70% brought in through project financing being negotiated with the BNDES and the International Finance Corporation (IFC)—the World Bank—covering the implementation of ten projects that should add 4,561 MW to Brazil's power system and a further 240 MW in Argentina, absorbing US$ 303.5 million.[45]

However, the international credit market has become restricted—particularly after the crises in Asia and Russia—hampering the conclusion of further project financing.[46] Regardless of project financing, many companies are seeking foreign funding to finance their investments to a greater or lesser extent.

Most power utilities have been selling off preferred stock and/or issuing eurobonds or ADRs (American Depositary Receipts, traded in the USA). An outstanding example is the AES group, which entered into a major commitment with third parties in order to underwrite a series of acquisitions of assets throughout Latin America. This requires certain precautions, particularly after turbulent times of peaking interest rates and crashes on international stock exchanges. It should be stressed that AES

---

[45] A notable example of project financing was the establishment of a Special Purpose Company to build the Dona Francisca plant and operate it for a 35-year period. Called Dona Francisca Energética S/A, this consortium consists of Inepar Energia (30%), COPEL (23%), Celesc (23%), Santa Felicidade Comércio, Indústria and Exploração de Produtos Siderúrgicos (Gerdau) and Desenvix. Scheduled for conclusion in 2001, this venture will absorb fresh investment of some R$ 150 million. (Gazeta Mercantil, 31 August 1998).

[46] One aspect that blithers project financing risks in Brazil is the fact that most funding is taken up in US dollars, while power utility rates are not indexed to the US currency in any way as foreign investors would prefer, wary of sudden hikes in the foreign exchange rate.

Table VIII.5. Power utility debt and risk assessment (June 1998).

Utility	Net Debt/ Equity Ratio	Foreign/ Total Debt Ratio (%)	Total Foreign Debt (US$ million)	Short-Term Foreign Debt (US$ million)	Risk
Cerj	247	66	436	360	High
Metropolitana	112	52	912	296	High
Light	59	93	1.200	16	High
Cesp	38	78	3.927	478	High
Bandeirante	52	82	304	0.87	Fair
CPFL	22	21	112	53	Low
Coelba	15	69	120	18	Low
Cemig	11	59	550	not given	not given

Source: BBA/Paribas Bank (1998) in gazeta mercantil (2, August, 1998).

brought in foreign funding to finance its bid in the CEEE and Cemig auctions, with these loans not yet paid.[47]

Additionally, Metropolitana will issue debentures in order to bring in US$ 672 million on non-domestic market in order to underwrite its privatisation expenditures (Gazeta Mercantil, 16 October 1998).

Enron was also obliged to jettison its financial strategy based solely on self-financing through the share market. A good example of this is the fact that Enron is bringing in US$ 350 million through KFK (the German Eximbank), guaranteed by Overseas Private Investments (a multilateral credit agency) for investment in the Cuiabá thermopower plant.[48] It should also be stressed that, thanks to its vigorous diversification policy, its shares dropped during the last financial year due to fears that fragmented investments would increase the company's exposure to market risks, dispersing its efforts in activities outside its core competency. (Gazeta Mercantil, 2 August 1998)

In the case of Iberdrola, most of its investments—including those allocated to the purchase of assets during the privatisation process—were funded in-house. However, for the investments in grid modernisation and power generation discussed earlier, Coelba intends to assign financing provided by funding from equipment suppliers, mainly Spanish, in addition to US$ 47 million and US$ 96 million respectively of its own funds (Gazeta Mercantil, 4 August 1998). Additionally, Coelba is gearing

---

[47] Another example of indebtedness: in July 1997, the group brought in US$ 325 million in Senior Subordinated Notes and some US$ 350 million through a common stock offering. In March 1997, the group had already brought in a further US$ 390 million in papers (TECONS).

[48] Investments in this enterprise total US$ 560 million, of which US$ 210 million are funded in-house. The advantage of the Overseas loan is that, being a multilateral agency, the costs are lower than those for bond issues and other market operations.

up to bring in US$ 300 million on the foreign market. This transaction will take place in Europe and the USA through the launch of bonds. This money will be used to pay off the loan taken out last year by Coelba to purchase Cosern.

In the case of Tractebel, this company introduced a novel type of insurance for the construction of hydropower plants. Known as the Owner Controlled and Contracted Insurance Package, this policy also protects the financier, because its controls the cash flow of the contracts. A single broad-scope package covers all project risks, ranging from environmental damages to guarantees for future operations, with US$ 363 million coverage for damages and loss of revenues.[49]

According to a 1998 study carried out by the BBA/Paribas bank, as a result of their foreign financing commitments most of Brazil's power utilities are wide open to risk exposure compared with their foreign debt levels and a turbulent global financial situation.

As shown in Table VIII.5, Metropolitana, Cerj and Light are the privatised power utilities most exposed to the global financial market crisis, while the least vulnerable are Coelba and CPFL. Other debts include that of Cerj, mainly in US dollars in order to purchase COELCE, Metropolitana, in order to deal with the liabilities inherited from the state-run administration, and Light, in order to acquire Metropolitana.

IV. Conclusion

The power sector in Latin America today slots neatly into the strategies of the main utility companies on the global power market, thanks to trade liberalisation, prospects for energy integration, and opportunities for profit through privatisation of assets. Foreign investment is booming, encouraged by the prospects of expanding power demands in these countries, as well as the fact that power companies in the more developed nations are struggling against heavy competition on deregulated markets with obvious hints of stagnation.

Thanks to its strategic importance, size and easy access to natural resources, among many other advantages, the Brazilian market has been enjoying special attention from major international players, despite the institutional framework of its power sector in transition.

The winds of liberalisation are blowing through Latin America, introducing new players and increasing the complexity, uncertainties and decisory diversity of its agents. In contrast to the traditional model, with

---

[49] The policy issued by Bradesco Seguros in May, reinsured with the Brazilian Reinsurance Institute (IRB—*Instituto de Resseguros do Brasil*) and major international reinsurers, covers any risks to this project, in addition to possible future loss of profits up to two years after the start-up of commercial operations in January 2003.

a strongly centralised decision process, the hegemonic presence of state-run companies and relatively stable strategies, the current scene features an expanding plurality of organisations, with a wide variety of corporate strategies and capacity-building that is reshaping administrative and managerial cultures. Groups moving into Latin America wield similar strategies, based on diversification, vertical integration, acquisition of assets and strategic partnerships.

In the specific case in Brazil, traditional local operators have already been implementing reactive strategies both in-house and for outside operations, facing up to the challenges of this new situation: administrative adjustments, outsourcing, consortia, partnerships and diversification of activities, all seeking synergy with other industrial segments, particularly the telecommunications sector.

With the arrival of foreign players—many associated with state-owned company pension funds or major power-intensive consumers—a wide range of strategies is appearing, much of which represents a breakaway from state administration of public utilities. However, many cases of shared management where operating gains are important are undermined by the conflicting profiles and objectives of their partners, exemplified by Escelsa, Light and Cemig.

Striving to further their strategic interests under new ownership, Brazil's power utilities have been assigning top priority to cutting costs, boosting revenues and diversifying activities, among many other measures. All the privatised companies have renegotiated with suppliers to reduce costs under service and materials contracts, while also laying off staff.

Similarly, companies are seeking fresh reactive strategies to deal with the new credit risks triggered by Brazil's foreign exchange crisis and the weakening of the emerging markets, while also guaranteeing their markets in view of the modifications in the institutional framework of Brazil's power sector, particularly the measures designed to introduce constraint-free retailing of power supplies to major consumers.

To date, these privatised companies have posted impressive economic and financial returns, particularly in view of the need for heavy investments over the medium term due to the physical condition of much of the networks acquired. So far—as is the case with Light and Cerj—shareholders have been able to assign themselves generous dividends over the short term, due largely to the fragility of the concession contracts signed with the Grantor Authority.

Literature

Bajay, S. (1994), *Desempenho e Reestruturação Institucional do Setor Elétrico em Diversos Países – Elementos de Reflexão para o Caso Brasileiro*. II Congresso Brasileiro de Planejamento Energético, UNICAMP; 1995.

Biasotto Junior, G. & Magalhães Junior, M. (1997), Concessões: Financiamento e Novos Elementos. Relatório Final, IPEA, in *Perspectivas da Reestruturação Financeira e Institucional dos Setores de Infra-Estrutura*, IPEA Brasília.

BNDES (1998), *Cadernos de Infra-Estrutura*. *Fatos Le Estratégias*. Setor Elétrico Ranking 1998, Edição Especial.

____. Privatizações in Brazil 1991/1999. Secretaria Geral de Apoio à Desestatização, 1999.

Borges, L. F. (1998), *Project Finance e Infra-Estrutura: Descrição e Críticas*, Revista do BNDES, June.

Chevalier, J. & Salaün, F. (1995), Recomposition des Industries Électriques: internationalisation, nouveaux entrants, diversification. *Revue de l'Energie*, No. 465, January/February.

de Oliveira, G. R. (1999), *As Novas Estratégias das Empresas Privatizadas do Setor Elétrico Brasileiro*. Tese de Mestrado, Coppe/UFRJ.

Gazeta Mercantil, various issues from 1997, 1998 and 1999.

Jornal do Brasil, 4 February 1997.

Jornal o Globo, 23 May 1998.

Jornal Folha de São Paulo, 12 February 1998.

Pinto Junior, H. (1997), Novas Modalidades e Fontes de Financiamento para a Indústria Elétrica Brasileira: Inovações Financeiras e Estratégias Empresariais, Relatório Final in *Perspectivas da Reestruturação Financeira e Institucional dos Setores de Infra-Estrutura*, IPEA Brasília.

Pires, J.C.L. (1999a) *Reestruturação Competitiva e Regulação nos Setores de Energia Elétrica e de Telecomunicações*. Tese de Doutorado. IE/UFRJ.

____ *(1999b)*. Capacity, Efficiency and Contemporary Regulatory Approaches in the Brazilian Energy Section. The Experiments of Aneel and ANP Ensaies BNDES No. 11, December 1999.

Revista América Economia, December, 1997.

Rosa, L., Tolmasquim, M. & Pires, J. C. L. (1998) *A Reforma do Setor Elétrico no Brasil e no Mundo: uma visão crítica*, Ed. Relume Dumará.

Internet
www.edp.pt (Electricidos de Portugal)
www.tercera.com (La Tercera Journal. Chile)
www.houind.com (Houston Industries)

Chapter IX
Strategic Development and Regulatory Challenges in West-European Electricity Markets

ATLE MIDTTUN, JAN TERJE HENRIKSEN and
AUGUSTO R. MICOLA

I. Introduction

The previous case studies have presented evolution of business strategies under regulatory developments from more or less closed national systems towards more extensive competition in European regions. This development has implied both a redefinition of the role of the state and the market, and a shift from public-service orientation towards competitive behaviour, which also includes mergers and acquisitions and international strategic positioning.

This chapter pulls together some comparative observations and reflections on similarities and diversity of national business strategies and industrial configurations under new market exposure. However, as already mentioned in Chapter 1, the complex semi-competitive environment that emerges from the subsidiarity-oriented European deregulation creates a very special context for strategic configuration. Furthermore, as the emerging business strategies also have implications for governance and public welfare, we will conclude by passing a few remarks on regulatory challenges facing the West European commercial regimes, including environmental issues.

II. Competition under Institutional Diversity

As already mentioned in Chapter 1, two major factors serve to make competition in the European deregulated electricity markets very much competition under institutional diversity. Firstly, there is the partiality of the EU deregulation and the subsidiarity in applying this partial market opening to various national contexts. This implies that market rules and market institutions are extensively shaped to national taste. Secondly, national and even sub-national municipal idiosyncrasy also characterises the players in the electricity markets. The market players are companies with varying mixes of public and private ownership, with varying financial constraints, and with different combinations of political and commercial mandates.

This diversity has come about not so much by conscious design as by continuous negotiation. After attempts at systematic and radical deregulation, EU deregulation ended up with a mixed and gradualist approach, moderately aiming at a market opening of 33% in the course of ten years (EU Commission Directive, 1996). According to the subsidiarity principle,[1] member countries were allowed to choose between three basic models of market opening; the regulated TPA model, the negotiated TPA model and the single buyer model.

The very cautious pace of market opening, and the plurality of models open to national choice, indicated a soft tone *vis-à-vis* national vested interest. The member states were here clearly given the possibility to limit competition both in generation and supply, allowing them considerable control over the construction of new capacity and the fuel mix. Referring back to the analytical distinctions presented in Chapter 1, Fig. I.1, the result has been a variety of regulatory trajectories and energy policies running side by side in Europe, some implying stronger competitive exposure in domestic markets and others implying semi-competitive internationalisation.

The Nordic deregulation took a radical direct and structural perspective with an emphasis on full free-trade competition between several decentralised players.[2] Major parts of the Continental European development, however, seems to take a more gradual 'contestable market' path, where market deregulation rather takes the form of gradual market opening under few structural constraints. The English and Welsh reform could be characterised as somewhere in between, with radical change in ownership structure, but without sufficient market deconcentration and consumer participation to fulfil strong free-trade criteria in the first round. However, the English and Welsh reform has

---

[1] The principle of subsidiarity is, as far as we know, borrowed from the Catholic Church and prescribes that tasks should be solved at the lowest possible level of decision-making within the system.
[2] It should be noted, however, that the radical deregulation in Norway did not include the ownership of hydropower facilities. Public ownership to such resources continued to be protected by special concession laws.

opened the market to new consumer segments at a much higher speed than Continental Europe and has recently implemented a Nordic-type full opening as compared to the Continental opening to 33% of the customers as an end state.

As opposed to the Continental development, where the attempt has been to deregulate and internationalise in the same movement, the British and Norwegian deregulation projects were one-country projects. Norway then subsequently moved into a Nordic market, when Sweden, Finland, and gradually also Denmark followed it in deregulation six to nine years later.

As well as differences in market scope and regulatory regimes, the European scene is also characterised by extensive differences in company ownership. Crossing ownership with centralisation gives us a matrix of four ideal types that delimit the options open to company organisation (Fig. IX.1): oligopolistic capitalism, free-trade capitalism (defined as free trade and private ownership), etatism and municipalism.

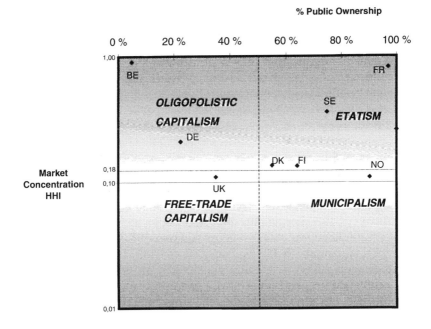

Fig. IX.1. The political economy of national generation industries in Europe.
Source: National Chapters (II to VIII) and Electrabel's Annual Report 1997.
The ranking of market concentration along the vertical axis is based on the Herfindahl–Hirchmann index which is calculated with the following formula:

$HHI = \Sigma \, (m_i \, / \, M)^2$; where $(m_i \, / \, M)$ is the market share of the i-company in the market.
The vertical scale is calculated on the amount of electricity generated on a logarithmic scale.

Based on aggregate figures for national industry in the West European countries here treated as closed economies Belgium ranks as a locus for monopolistic capitalism, France as a typical case of etatism. The German industry is characterised by oligopolistic capitalism,[3] the Dutch by regionalism, the Norwegian industry by municipalism and the UK industry by free-trade capitalism, in the intersection towards oligopoly. The Swedish, Danish and Finnish industries hold more intermediary positions. Sweden ranking as modified etatism and Denmark and Finland in the intersection between semi-public/semi-private free-trade/moderately concentrated systems. It should be noted, however, that the Danish private ownership is decentralised consumer ownership. The European electricity markets are gradually opening up, and the domestic market share therefore no longer necessarily represents the relevant market context. Nevertheless the domestic market shares illustrate the large discrepancies in starting points at the outset of the market reform. Furthermore grid transit-restrictions across national borders as well as large price differences in wholesale spot markets indicate that the pan-European energy market is still far away.

The positioning of national companies in this matrix obviously affects mandates, financial positions, and conditions for capital accumulation. Municipalistic organisation may typically imply a local focus, where companies are oriented to serving local needs and are influenced by municipal political processes, including local needs to extract dividend to finance other non-commercial sectors. Etatist organisation exposes the company to state policies, where industrial strategy has traditionally been more developed than at the municipal level. However, general welfare concerns and political preferences may result in mandates, constraints and possibilities that are very different from those of privately-owned companies. The principle of *specialité*, which restrains EdF from pursuing multi-sector strategies in France, is a good example of such a limitation. However, state ownership may also imply patient and long-term oriented capital investments that allow companies to pursue demanding positioning without critical exposure to short-term profit orientated investors. Both EdF's and Vattenfall's nuclear programmes and broad positioning in European markets are examples of this.

Companies in oligopolistic or semi-oligopolistic positions do, of course, have many of the privileges of state companies, without the

---

[3] Before deregulation, German firms enjoyed regional monopolies. The German deregulation in its first stage included distance-based tariffs that undermined competition and supported oligopolistic market control. Later, after the distance tariffs had been removed and Germany was divided into two trading zones, there were large mergers that sought to restore oligopolistic market power.

latter's political constraints. The largest German wholesale and generation companies have, accordingly, been in a position to accumulate large capital assets which can now be employed for long-term strategic positioning, with few political limitations on their strategic planning.

Free-trade exposed companies, such as smaller and medium-sized private companies in the Nordic market, are obviously pressured to develop high static efficiency, but they are also highly exposed to signals from short-term oriented capital markets, and are vulnerable to takeovers. These companies are therefore likely to be included in and subsumed under strategic configuration designed by larger and less competitively exposed companies.

As a consequence of the high diversity, both at the regulatory regime and firm level, the European scene is therefore one of multiplicity of strategic configuration and strategic developments. This diversity at the national regulatory and company level points at a co-evolution of regimes and company configuration along several different paths. Possible convergence between these paths depends both on political and commercial forces. On the one hand, political decisions to open up to more radical competition across national boundaries will confront companies with more similar contexts, and hence push for structural isomorphism (DiMaggio & Powell, 1991). On the other hand, companies may themselves, even within diverse national competitive contexts, devise cross-national strategies that undermine national regulatory boundaries and thereby work to homogenise the European electricity industry. The EU Electricity Market Directive, together with more radical British and Nordic market deregulation, has opened up an interplay between these mechanisms.

III. Market Structure in Regional Trading Zones

The institutional differentiation of European markets and the limitation of transmission capacity between parts of the European electricity system imply that the strategic context for European electricity industry is complex and segmented. Fig. IX.2 indicates the transmission capacities across national borders as a percentage of domestic consumption. Switzerland and Austria are described in a separate Fig. IX.3 because their trade relations are especially complex.

A first segmentation of the West European electricity market in the case of Great Britain, the Nordic Countries and the Iberian Peninsula is fairly obvious for geographical reasons. The British insular and the Nordic peninsular positions are only moderately compensated by inter-linkage through offshore cable capacity (Fig. IX.2). The Iberian links to Southern France are weak and hindered by mountain chains. Subsequent

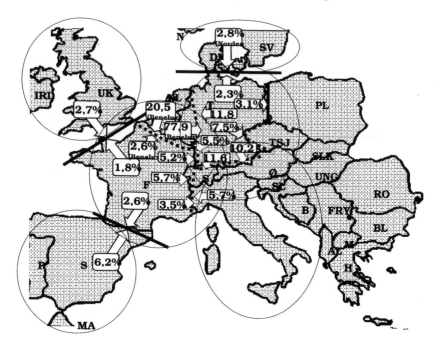

Fig. IX.2. European transmission capacities and trading zones.
Source: IEA (1999) Monthly Electricity Survey, *January; UCPTE (1998)* Statistical Yearbook 1997.

segmentation of Continental Western Europe is more open to discussion. We shall here depart from France-centred and Germany-centred regions, which are ultimately merged into one, and then focus on the two southern regions: the Iberian peninsula, and what we have termed the Alpine South, including Italy, Switzerland and Austria (Fig. IX.3).

As can be seen from Fig. IX.3, Austria and Switzerland are so extensively linked up to the neighbour countries that in terms of grid capacity we may speak of them as subsets of other markets and/or transit countries with the potential for integration with other markets.

III.A. The English and Welsh and Nordic trading zones

As indicated in Fig. IX.4 below, both the Nordic and the English and Welsh trading zones appear fairly open to free-trade competition. Even taken as closed national system, England and Wales barely crosses the border into moderately concentrated markets by the standards of the Herfindahl–Hirschmann index (HH index), traditionally used in US competition law. As noted in Chapter III, the extensive lowering of concentration in generation from a highly concentrated market in 1995 is a

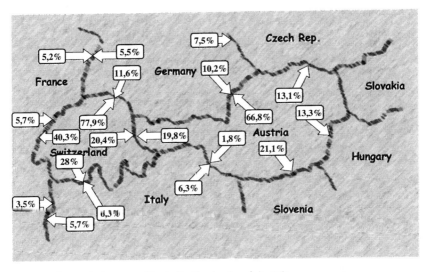

Fig. IX.3. Transmission capacities in Switzerland and Austria.
Source: *IEA (1999)* Monthly Electricity Survey, *January; UCPTE (1998)* Statistical Yearbook 1997.

consequence of the regulator accepting extensive build-up of gas-based electricity generation capacity with the RECs, and the limitation imposed on the incumbent generators' expansion.

With an installed interconnection capacity of approximately 2,000 MW, or 2.7% of its total generation capacity, the UK market is fairly weakly linked to France and continental Europe. Assuming that the French connection across the channel is counted in its full capacity as a player in the UK market, the index would come down slightly (grey-shaded column in Fig. IX.4) but still within the moderately concentrated market range. However, if the cable were opened to free trade between numerous small actors, the HH index would come down considerably.

The operation of this connection as a one-way export from France into the UK market with a bid-in price of zero to the UK Pool limits the strategic options on the use of this cable. However, such use of the cable implies that much of the free-trade effect of the cable on the British market is achieved, though with apparently little success as far as price competition is concerned, as we shall see in the following section.

Three of the Nordic countries have a market structure that remains largely unproblematic from a free-trade point of view, although Finland and Denmark, like England and Wales, figure in the lower end of the moderately concentrated market. Sweden, however, largely because of a dominant role of the state company Vattenfall, figures as highly concentrated. The Swedish concentration level falls extensively under open trade over existing connections, but only if these connections were

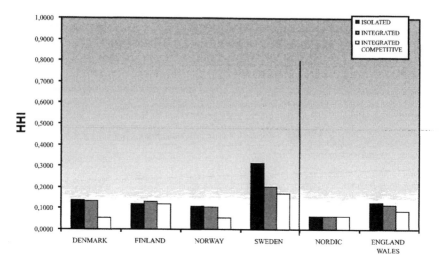

Fig. IX.4. Market concentration in the English and Welsh and Nordic trading zones.
Sources: IEA electricity information 1997. UCPTE. Annual Reports National Companies.

operated under full free-trade conditions (white column in Fig. IX.4) would the Swedish market rank as moderately concentrated, and then only be a small amount.

However, with the integration into Nordic market, organised around a common Nordic Pool, the Nordic market ranges well below the limit for decentralised organisation, and is thereby prototypically suited for free trade. The fact that there exists a common Nordic spot market, freely accessible for all Nordic players (with some limitations for Denmark) makes the Nordic context, and not individual Nordic countries, a realistic context for business strategies for Nordic companies (Hjalmarsson *et al.*, 1999).

It should be noted that internal transmission capacities within this market are not always sufficient to secure price equalisation across the whole area. The assumption of internal competition within the Nordic zone therefore does not completely hold.

Like the UK market, the Nordic market, with a transmission capacity of approximately 2,400 MW to Germany or about 2.8% of its total capacity, is also fairly weakly linked to the larger Continental markets. Furthermore, the lack of full third-party access on continental connections serves to further limit integration of the Nordic and Continental market.

III.B. Germany and extended region

As indicated in Fig. IX.3, free trade in Continental Europe is less limited by grid connections than in the two above cases. Germany, for example, has links to its neighbour countries with a total capacity of close to 55,000 MW, or more than 50% of total installed capacity.

As a closed system, assuming full domestic grid access, Germany figures as a moderately concentrated system of electricity generation (Fig. IX.5). This system is, however, under rapid concentration following the recent mergers between RWE and VEW and between VEBA (PreussenElektra) and VIAG (Bayernwerk). The structural consequences of this integration are indicated by the dashed line shown within the German column of Fig. IX.5.

However, the strong international links could have extensive implications for strategic positioning in the German market. With decentralised free-trade operation of all international connections, the German market, in principle, stands out as fairly decentralised (Fig. IX.5). At the same time institutional factors limit competition in Germany. Accordingly, the German zone-based electricity tariffs tend to limit trade and undermine the emergence of a national market. The real market concentration in the German market(s) is therefore *de facto* much higher than the aggregate HH index would seem to indicate.

The two neighbouring German-speaking countries, Austria and Switzerland, are also relatively concentrated, as far as internal electricity generation is concerned. However, both Austria and Switzerland are strongly linked to other markets (Fig. IX.3). The concentration of their domestic markets therefore falls dramatically if full free trade on all international connections is assumed (Fig. IX.5). However, these countries are far from free-trade regulated, and institutional factors therefore limit competition extensively.

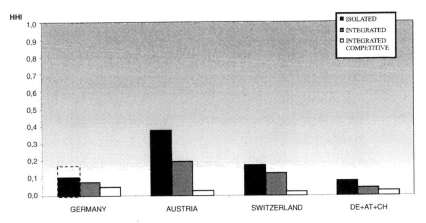

Fig. IX.5. Market concentration of German and attached regional markets (1998).
Sources: Muntner, J. (1997) IEA electricity information 1997. UCPTE. Annual Reports National Companies.

Integrating all three markets into a larger German-centred trading zone would make for a clearly decentralised market, if internally free-trade regulated. The extensive external connections of this region (white column in Fig. IX.5) would serve to reduce its concentration level even further. As with the previous discussion of the market structure of the Nordic zone, we have based our calculations on an implicit assumption of full internal availability of transmission capacity within the zone.

III.C. France and extended region

Because of the size of its market, France, like Germany, constitutes a natural centre of gravity in north-western Europe. Given the dominant role of Electricité de France, the French market features as extremely concentrated. In terms of market structure, EdF therefore has a uniquely protected strategic position in Europe.

Nevertheless, extensive interconnection between France and surrounding countries could potentially bring down the French concentration index considerably if operated on a free-trade basis. As with the German market, the French is also conceivable within a larger context. A first expansion might be to include the Benelux countries into an enlarged, French-oriented west European region (Fig. IX.6). This would modify EdF's monopoly somewhat but the market would still feature as strongly concentrated, even under the assumption of sufficient transmission capacity to secure free flow within the region.

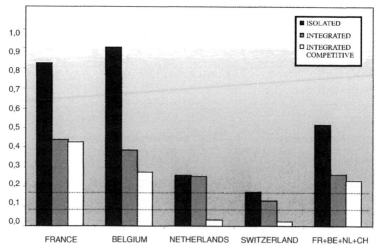

Fig. IX.6. Market concentration in the French and attached regional markets (1998).
Sources: IEA electricity information 1997. UCPTE. Annual Reports National Companies.

Even including Switzerland, such a region would remain highly concentrated. Only with free-trade operation of its international interconnections would such a region come anywhere near moderate concentration.
As opposed to Germany and the extended German region, France and
the extended region retains with limited competition, not only for institutional, but also for structural reasons.

III.D. Iberia and the Alpine South

South European energy markets stand out as highly concentrated (Fig.
IX.7). In line with French policy, they follow a Latin tradition of etatist
governance of this sector, which makes for highly centralised systems
under market economy. With two companies sharing the bulk of the
generation market, the Spanish market ranks in the lower end of a highly
concentrated market. Taking external grid connections into consideration
can considerably lower the HH index. However, even with fully decentralised free-trade organisation of foreign trade, Spain does not reach the
border for a moderately concentrated market.

With only one company controlling the bulk of the generation, the
Portuguese market stands out as even more concentrated. Even though
relatively more exposed to international trade, the Portuguese market still
remains highly concentrated even under open decentralised free trade
with Spain.

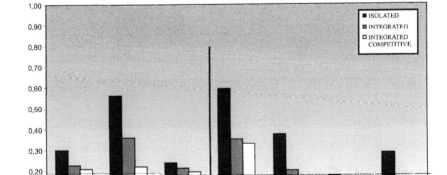

Fig. IX.7. Iberian and Alpine South.
Sources: IEA electricity information 1997. UCPTE. Annual Reports National Companies.

Taken together, under the assumption of full availability of internal transmission capacity within the region, even a larger Iberian integration of the Portuguese and Spanish markets does not suffice to secure a semblance of free-trade competition. It hardly even reduces the HH index to the upper level of moderate concentration (Fig. IX.7).

Because of its high inter-linkage to Austria and Switzerland, the Alpine South is in a different position. Italy, taken in isolation, remains in the Latin tradition with a highly centralised market. ENEL's dominant position in electricity generation clearly precludes free-trade competition. However, given stronger integration with the bordering Alpine states, Austria and Switzerland, and full internal transmission capacity, the Alpine region could reach a moderately concentrated level and even be characterised as non-concentrated, depending on the degree of free trade on external connections.

III.E. The West European electricity market

The argumentation for subdivision into regional trading zones, following a first partial opening of national boundaries, probably holds for the present and medium-term perspective. However, it is the expressed wish of the European Commission and some major players in the European market to gradually see a more systematic opening up of trade across the whole of the European market space. The so called Florence-process, where European system operators, main grid operators and the EU commission have met to explore possible standardisation of European grid access has made some progress towards the pan-European market goal. After all, commercial or contractual relations can be fairly easily decoupled

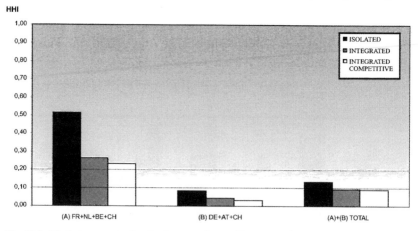

Fig. IX.8. Market concentration in the central west European electricity market.
Sources: IEA electricity information 1997. UCPTE. Annual Reports National Companies.

from physical flows of electrons, as long as there is sufficient transport capacity to balance the systems.

If such wider integration of Continental Europe would take place, with sufficient transmission capacity to secure internal flows, the HH index indicates that there is room for including even the present French structure without structurally undermining free trade (Fig. IX.8). However, this assumes extensive trade over present grid connections across to other European markets.

IV. Markets and Prices

The argument that the strategic context for Western European competition in electricity remains regionally segmented is fairly clearly supported by regional differences in electricity wholesale and retail prices. As far as wholesale prices are concerned, the differences may be registered between zones both in terms of weekly averages over the year and in terms of hourly prices over the day.

Fig. IX.9 indicates weekly average prices registered in six European trading points. The ESIS or UK spot price, Nord Pool spot price (Nordic area), the German CEPI index (parts of the German market), Swiss SWEP index, (trade at the Laufenburg central), APX index (Amsterdam) and the OMEL spot (Spanish Pool) are included. The extensive differences between the high UK spot price and the lowest Nord Pool index show that there is limited access between these markets. This again means that players positioned with fairly good access to both markets are in a position to harvest great arbitrage.

The Spanish OMEL spot price is also extensively higher than both the Nord Pool price and the Central European indexes such as the Swiss SWEP and the German CEPI indexes, indicating the relative isolation of the Iberian market from Central Europe. The Amsterdam APX index also ranks considerably higher than the central European indexes, indicating considerable barriers to trade even between the neighbouring German and Dutch markets. The high-price high volatility development particularly in 2000 may be explained by preferential treatment of incumbents in international transmission access. Dutch distributors, relying on early subscription contracts with German generators found themselves denied grid access and therefore had to buy at high prices in the domestic market.

It might be argued that the some of the differences between European electricity prices could be explained by different fuel mixes. The difference between the dominantly thermally-based UK, German and Dutch electricity generation *vis-à-vis* the lower Nordic and Swiss prices might be justified by the differences in marginal production costs. However, the

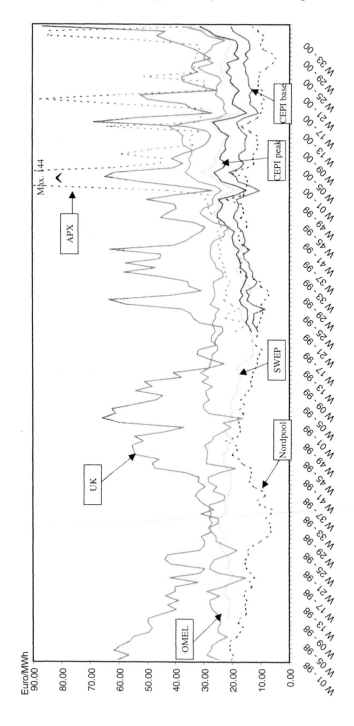

Fig. IX.9. Weekly prices in European trading zones (1998 and 1999).
Sources: UK: ESIS (www.ngc.co.uk), CEPI: *Dow Jones (ww.dowpower.com)*, APX: APX (system@apx.nl), *Nord Pool:*
Nord Pool (www.el-ex.fi), Spain: OMEL (www.omel.com/es).

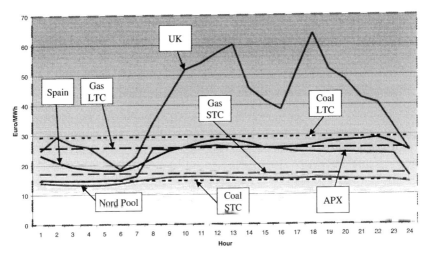

Fig. IX.10. Hourly prices in European trading zones.
STC: Short term (marginal) cost, Source: NOU 1998:11, Energi- og kraftbalansen i Norge mot 2020, p. 311
LTC: Long term (marginal) cost, Source: NOU 1998:11, Energi- og kraftbalansen i Norge mot 2020, p. 311
Sources: UK: ESIS (www.ngc.co.uk), CEPI: Dow Jones (ww.dowpower.com), SWEP: SWEP (www.egl.ch),
APX: APX (system@apx.nl), Nord pool: Nord-pool (www.el-ex.fi), Spain: OMEL (www.omel.com/es)
Average 98 and 99 prices for each hour of the day

difference between the UK, APX and CEPI prices cannot be justified in such terms.

It might also be argued that the European pools are at different levels of development with the UK and Nordic pools therefore reflecting price levels of wholesale trade more accurately than the more recent CEPI and APX markets. Nevertheless, as EU-electricity markets now are effectively open to free trade at the wholesale level although be it within a limited geographical domain, the spot prices will be an alternative price to the parties negotiating bilaterally and thereby have an important price-setting function. After all, the Nord Pool system originated in exactly this way.

In addition to the extensive price differences between weekly averages, the European markets feature very different prices over the day (Fig. IX.10). Lack of available data only allows us comparison of hourly prices for four price zones: the Nord Pool, the UK Pool, the Dutch APX index and the Spanish OMEL spot market. Firstly, a striking difference between Nord Pool and the other indexes is that hourly price-variations are on average almost non-existant for the Nordic market, while the Dutch, Spanish and UK markets have a very distinct difference between night and day. The British variation is the most spectacular, with a variation of up to 1:3, but the Spanish and Dutch prices also vary extensively. The difference between base and peak load in the German CEPI index also indicates some variation, although lower than for APX and OMEL. These differences are further indications of limitations in European trading resulting from capacity and institutional restrictions across trading zones.

V. Functional Configuration in the European Electricity Industry

As pointed out in the introductory chapter, deregulation of European electricity markets has created a basis for new strategic configuration, as traditional limitations on sector, geographical, organisational and economic scale and scope diminishes.

The regulatory regimes in most European countries, are now opening up for sector reconfiguration by allowing electricity companies to take new positions in other sectors or value chains. We are therefore seeing integration between oil and gas companies, merging into broader energy companies. We are also seeing joint ventures between telecommunication companies and electricity companies to utilise the electricity grid for transmission also of telecommunication.

By removing national barriers to trade, the deregulation process also encourages expansion of geographical scope. We therefore see European energy companies making new engagements in markets outside their

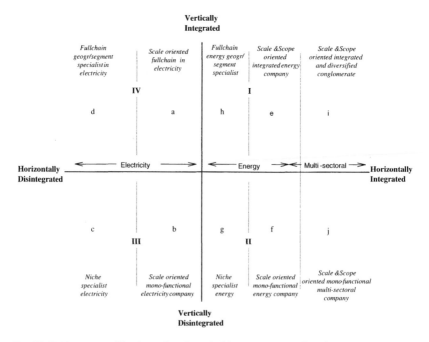

Fig. IX.11. Variations of horizontal and vertical integration in value chains.

traditional supply areas. Regional and municipal companies have engaged themselves in other regions and areas within their country, but also within other European countries.

Organisationally, European companies have increasingly adopted the shareholder model, although remaining dominantly publicly owned. However, some companies have also been privatised and/or sold out to foreign interests. In addition, companies have developed subsidiaries and a more complex profit-centre structure in order to manage multiple alliances and commercial engagements.

The first chapter of this book spelled out some of the theoretical possibilities space for strategic reconfiguration along dimensions such as scale and scope *versus* flexible specialisation, and horizontal *versus* vertical integration, and also presented a graphic scheme for multidimensional ranking of strategic reconfiguration of the European energy industry. The scheme standardises the overview of strategic configuration along two dimensions (vertical and horizontal integration), and then differentiates between various multi-sector combinations: electricity, energy and miscellaneous (Fig. IX.11). Other dimensions discussed in Chapter 1 require more qualitative analysis, and will be commented with reference to specific cases.

To briefly recapitulate from Chapter 1:

Quadrants IV and III on the left-hand side present a simple typology of horizontal and vertical integration in electricity supply and generation industry. Quadrant III-c here represents niche specialisation within a single function, such as small-scale generation, local sales companies, etc. Quadrant III-b also represents functional specialisation, but at large scale.

Quadrants IV-a and IV-d and both represent vertically integrated approaches within the electricity value chain. IV-d represents a small-scale approach, e.g. within a restricted geographic area, whereas IV-a represents a large-scale orientation.

The right side of Fig. IX.11 represents wider integration into energy and other related sectors. Analogous to quadrants III and IV, the quadrants II and I represents various mixes of scale/specialisation with different degrees of vertical/functional integration. Quadrants I-h and I-e represent respectively full-chain specialist or scale- and scope-oriented integrated energy companies. Quadrants II-g and II-f represent, respectively, a niche specialist in energy or scale-oriented mono-functional energy companies.

Finally, the far right section represents further diversification beyond energy, both integrated and diversified conglomeration in I-i and monofunctional multi-sector companies in I-j.

Given the scope of the European market and the thousands of market-players, we can only discuss a few selected companies in this

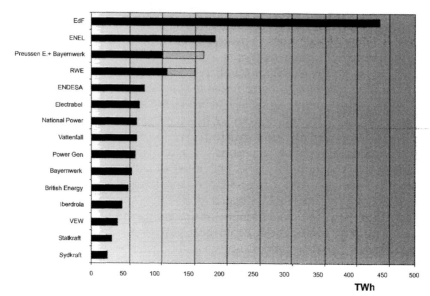

Fig. IX.12. The largest European electricity companies.
Sources: IEA electricity information 1997. UCPTE. Annual Reports National Companies.

comparative analysis. The previous chapters containing national case studies have already presented selected national electricity industry in greater detail.

As shown in Fig. IX.12, the largest 15 European electricity companies range from EdF, with a production of almost 450 TWh and supply and distribution in the same range, to Sydkraft, with less than 30 TWh. We shall concentrate our discussion of strategic configuration for the top ten largest and then address remaining parts of the industry on a more structural basis.

V.A. *Configuration of large companies*

A comparison of the largest national companies indicates widely different market positioning and strategic development (Fig. IX.13):

Some of the larger European companies are striving for *scale advantages through horizontal and vertical integration*. EdF, for example, takes a position in the upper right quadrant IV as the largest European company, with more or less full hierarchic internalisation of the electricity value chain. On this basis, the company has been able to support Europe's most ambitious serial nuclear programme with obvious scale advantages.

The Italian company ENEL and the Spanish company Endesa have also taken more or less vertically-integrated and dominant positions in their national markets, but without similar nuclear ambitions. In less dominant positions, PreussenElektra (Germany) and PowerGen (UK) also belong to this group.

The volume of the square III-b (scale oriented mono-functional), and more so the integrated square IV-a (scale oriented fullchain integrated) group clearly gives them considerable financial muscle. In addition, this integrated large-scale position also provides a large resource base and a wide scope of competencies, which again give them important strategic positions in their national and regional markets. However, very large organisations run the risk of inefficiency and loss of innovative flexibility in each of their multiple functions. Without extensive organisational redesign, and a push for internal efficiency under competitive market exposure, they become vulnerable to specialist competitors. These competitors may be more strongly functionally optimised under competitive market exposure, and thereby gain leverage in certain market segments.

Another group of large national companies is characterised by *less vertical integration, but still European-format in scale.* This includes firms such as the largest German company RWE, the Swedish state company Vattenfall, two large British generators, National Power and British Energy, the Belgian Electrabel. In the British cases, weaker vertical integration relates in part to regulatory policy, where de-verticalisation was a major part of the liberalisation policy (see Chapter III). In this case, the fall of the golden share limitation on the large generators and a change in policy on vertical integration might create a rapid structural transformation. The German and Swedish cases reflect a certain division of labour with the municipal city works and their strong engagement in electricity supply and distribution and large central generators. However, following deregulation, Vattenfall worked to complement its one-sided portfolio by supply acquisitions (domestically and in the Nordic countries). Extensive competition in the German market is moving the large German generating companies in the same direction, although more by direct end-user marketing than by acquisition of suppliers.

As far as *integration into broader energy engagements* (in quadrants I and II) is concerned, we find that the principle of *spécialité* in France limits EdF's ability to integrate into related business in other sectors. However, the existence of the twin companies EdF and GdF establishes the conditions for quick and powerful electricity–gas integration in France if/when the *spécialité* principle falls.

In part through large mother companies, the large German generators, notably PreussenElektra/VEBA and RWE Energie/RWE and even the smaller VIAG/Bayernwerk, have traditionally held broad energy engagements with extensive petroleum engagements complementing the electricity portfolios. This reflects the German tradition of industrial clustering, where industrial groups integrate multi-fuel engagements as part of broader, highly complex industrial engagements.

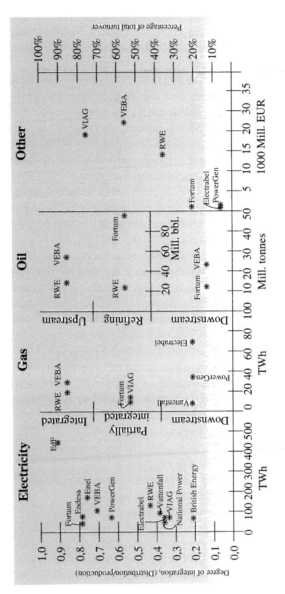

Fig. IX.13. Strategic configuration of selected large European companies.[4]
Sources: IEA electricity information 1997. UCPTE. Annual Reports National Companies.

[4] The figure illustrates the vertical and horizontal integration of the respective companies. Axes for electricity have degree of vertical integration along the vertical axis and size of production/distribution (whatever the largest of the two) along the hroizontal axis. Gas has three levels of integration along the vertical axis and size of production/transmission/distribution (whichever the largest) along the horizontal axis. Oil has three categories describing the vertical integration of the respective companies; upstream, refining and downstream. The horizontal axis shows size, in million barrels for upstream and refining, and million tonnes for downstream, all measured in oil equivalents. Other describes the respective companies involvement in areas outside electricity, gas and oil; such as telecom, water, chemicals to mention but a few. The size of the engagements is given along the horizontal axis in million EURO and the vertical scale measures the involvement in percentage of total turnover.

However, as the German case study describes, there is now a tendency towards more focus in the German electricity industry, which was the traditional cash cow of the industrial clusters. The new focus may nevertheless be wide enough to include a broader engagement in several energy activities. This specialisation process takes place at the same time as German industry scales up and consolidates into even larger units.

The gas engagement of PowerGen, which also broadens the company's vertical base, is more directly the result of the liberalised British gas market and gas supply surplus that made gas-based generation an attractive option. Other actors in the British electricity industry have also followed this strategy.

The Swedish state company Vattenfall ranks toward the lower end, both in volume and degree of integration. So far, it is only engaged in gas distribution and supplies to a limited extent. This reflects the reluctance of Swedish energy policy to move into deeper gas engagement.

Although more limited with respect to vertical integration, Electrabel is the company with the largest position in gas. They are also in the businesses of water supply, cable TV and district heating.

However, the broadest engagements in other industries beyond the energy sector are still to be found in the German groups. This is a further consequence of the German industrial group tradition, with broad energy and industrial engagements. Thus, petroleum and chemicals represent a major activity for RWE, running close to 50% of turnover. Other major activities are mechanical, civil and plant engineering, construction, mining and other raw materials. In addition, RWE is also engaged in waste management and telecommunications. Moreover, VEBA presents engagements in chemistry, logistics, real estate and water. The announced VEBA–VIAG merger will boost VEBA's position in all markets, making it one of the largest energy industry conglomerates of Europe.

V.B. Strategic configuration in medium and smaller-sized European companies

The strategic positioning of medium-sized European companies is no less diverse than what we find for the larger players.

As previously described in Chapter IV, in the case of the Dutch utility SEP, the company is being dismantled and the four smaller producers that were co-ordinated under the SEP umbrella are being integrated in larger European industrial networks or merged under the Dutch suppliers. SEP will now, under the new name Tennet, run the transport grid and become the system operator for the Netherlands. The Dutch SEP case is, in other words, a case of scaling down and following re-integration of the parts into new domestic and international configurations, where the domestic configuration implies a move towards vertical integration.

Larger Nordic companies like the Swedish operator Sydkraft and Norwegian company Statkraft also become fairly small players in the European market. Of the two companies, Sydkraft is the most vertically integrated, with almost complementary engagements in supply and generation, as well as integrated grid management. Like many other Nordic companies, Sydkraft is, as already noted in Chapter II, under increasing acquisition by PreussenElektra and Statkraft, as part of an emerging North-European alliance bridging the Scandinavian and Continental markets.

Statkraft has until recently been fairly one-sidedly engaged in generation. Only after recovering from heavy losses in the early phase of the Norwegian market reform is the company engaging more actively to acquire supply (through acquisition of the Bergen-based BKK) and to scale up in generation. Acquisition of 24% of Sydkraft is also part of this.

The Danish companies, Elsam and Elkraft, are to some extent in SEP's position, in so far as they represent co-ordination boards, rather than owners of generation. However, the two Danish companies are working to become major players in the Danish North European markets and have recently integrated East- and West-Danish large scale generation capacity into two large companies Energi E2 and Elsam. Parallel to this, they have developed independent divisions that take on responsibility for main grid operations.

Bayernwerk is expanding its interests in regional gas utilities in Germany and as an energy service provider at various stages of the value chain in the gas business. For instance, Bayernwerk owns interests in Rohöl-Aufsuchungs-Aktiengesellschaft (Austria) and Erdöl Erdgas Gommern GmbH (Germany), both engaged in the exploration and production, storage and marketing of oil and natural gas reserves. Other business where Bayernwerk is present include chemicals, packaging, transportation and telecom.

Iberdrola is the second largest Spanish utility. It also carries out activities outside the electricity industry, either through alliances or direct investment: in the energy sector, Iberdrola has established an equity exchange with Electricidade de Portugal (EdP) and a partnership including generation, co-ordination of facility management, marketing activities, diversification business and internationalisation, especially in Latin America. Iberdrola also has a joint venture with Repsol, one of the ten largest world oil companies, and Telefónica, Spain's biggest telecommunications provider.

The business areas outside energy where Iberdrola is active include construction and operation of co-generation plants, hydroelectric mini-stations and wind parks; real estate; telecom operations (fixed and mobile telephony and cable TV); aerospace, automotive, wind, electronics, and IT industries, plus public and corporate consulting.

Electricidade de Portugal (EdP) is a smaller company that also follows a broad international and multi-functional strategy. It focuses extensively in Brazil, acquiring, among others, the fourth largest distribution company, Bandeirante de Energia. Moreover, EdP owns a controlling stake in EEGSA of Guatemala, in co-operation with Iberdrola and TECO (US) and the concession of the water and electricity supply in Rabat, Morocco. EdP carries out some other investments in Macao, China.

EdP's diversification strategy includes telecommunications, where EdP owns a stake in E3G, the second telecom operator in Portugal, and a joint venture with GdP, Transgas and Natural Gas, where EdP holds a 29.74% participation in Transgas, the high-gas pressure gas monopolist in Portugal.

The German city works (stadtwerke) to some extent mirror the larger generators in their multi-sector engagements, but obviously in the small-scale end of the continuum. The vertical imbalance of the city works is also inverse to that of the large wholesale generators, namely on the supply side. These two groups of companies have hitherto been complementary, with the large generators, such as RWE and PreussenElektra, as wholesale suppliers to the city works. However, with the latest opening of the German market to end-use competition, the wholesale generators have taken initiatives to compete directly with the city works in their local markets.

Like in the German case, the smaller-scale players in the British market, too, mirror PowerGen's gas-electricity engagement. Drawing on the easy access to the liberalised gas-market as well as a guaranteed market of locked-in end users, the REC have built up gas engagements through gas-based electricity generation and thereby considerably increased competition for generation in the British market.

Given the failure of reaching a consensus among Dutch suppliers for building up a larger SEP group, Dutch generation is small scale at a European level, and the same goes for Dutch electricity supply. Dutch suppliers, however, have a strong inter-fuel engagement as they supply gas directly and also produce gas-based electricity generation.

The Nordic countries also have a fairly decentralised electricity industry originating from a tradition of municipal engagements in electricity production and supply. While Norway stands out with a strong monolithic hydro-based electricity production, the other Nordic countries have greater variation in fuel and energy technologies.

VI. Structural Diversity in National Configuration

The scale of the European electricity industry does to a large extent reflect the scale of national markets, although modified by different traditions

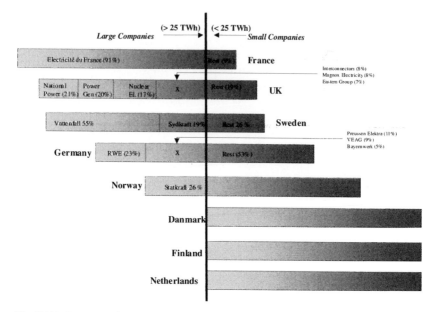

Fig. IX.14. Structure of European electricity industry (generation) for selected countries. *Sources: IEA electricity information 1997. UCPTE. Annual Reports National Companies.*

for national and regional organisation. Small states thereby tend to have industrial players at a scale that is highly incongruent with the industrial scale of companies in larger states. This incongruence may further increase if national styles in small countries dictate, for example, municipalistic decentralisation.

Fig. IX.14 and IX.15 group European generators and suppliers into two groups: for selected West European countries large (>25/>20 TWh), and small (<25/<20 TWh). We may here observe that small countries such as the Netherlands, Finland, Denmark and Norway, host electricity industry that falls more or less systematically in the small-scale end, both in generation and supply. On the other hand, countries such as France, the UK, Germany, and for generation purposes also Sweden, host companies that systematically fall in the large-scale end.

In closed national economies these differences could co-exist, given reasonable efficiency in performance, and/or national values attached to one or other of the models. However, a gradually integrating economy with semi-oligopolistic competition creates a different environment, where the co-existence of such structural diversity becomes more debatable.

The structural asymmetry of national industrial configuration therefore implies challenges to small states in large markets in the form of vulnerability to takeover and in terms of national governance of

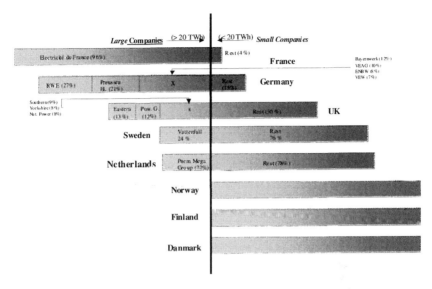

Fig. IX.15. Structure of European electricity industry (supply) for selected countries. *Sources: IEA electricity information 1997. UCPTE. Annual Reports National Companies.*

industrial development. The threat to medium-sized European companies is probably more strategic than economic. There is hardly any reason to believe that many medium-sized companies, given alliances and elements of network economy, may achieve efficiency performances at least on a par with, if not higher than, many large companies with a basis in large states. However, there is reason to believe that medium-sized companies will have problems in defending their integrity against larger players with strategically motivated integration policies.

VII. International Takeovers and Alliances

Facing the gradual internationalisation of electricity markets, European companies are now moving into trans-national positions, through alliances, acquisitions and mergers.

Most extensive takeover activities have taken place in Britain, which experienced early market deregulation and where there has been fairly free access to international capital transactions after Government left the golden share protection of the RECs (see Chapter III). The Nordic market, which was also among the early deregulation experiences in Europe, has been less open to international capital transfers, although municipal owners are increasingly seeing the value of selling out or merging into larger units. Some of the larger and medium-sized Swedish companies with extensive institutional ownership have longer experience in internationalisation.

The other European markets are still only at the start of the deregulation process. However, this has not prevented extensive mergers and acquisitions. We shall here briefly review major trends in each of our case studies.

VII.A. International engagement in the UK market

Following the expiry of the Golden Share in the regional electricity companies there was a rapid change in ownership in the electricity supply sector in Great Britain. The vacuum created by the limitations on vertical integration strategies from UK generators obviously enhanced foreign takeover in the British supply market. As indicated in Chapter III and Fig. IX.16, a majority of the RECs were taken over by US firms. This included:

1. Southern's and Scottish Power's joint takeover of SWEB and SWALEC;
2. Central and SW Corp's takeover of SEEBoard
3. Pacificorp and Scottish Power's joint takeover of Manweb;
4. Texas Utilities' takeover of Eastern;
5. Avon Energy's takeover of Midlands generation;
6. Dominion Resource's takeover of East Midlands;
7. CalEnergy's takeover of Northern;
8. US Utility Consortium taking over Northern; and
9. Texas Utilities' takeover of The Energy Group and Norweb Supply.

More recently, Electricité de France has become a major stakeholder in UK energy through its acquisition of London Electricity and SWEB supply.

The UK generation market has been more extensively protected from international takeovers by extended golden share regulation, but hampered by government policy which only very recently allowed them to diversify into distribution and supply in Britain. However, all three major generators have taken up engagements overseas. As pointed out in Chapter III and Fig. IX.16, National Power was divided into two companies. With Innogy focussing on the UK market and International Power Group focussing on overseas markets, including Poland, Spain and the Czech Republic; PowerGen has engagements in Australia; British Power has engagements in the US. In addition, the National Grid Company has a joint venture with France Telecom and the US Sprint company in developing electricity grid-based telecommunication. The recent division of National Power into an international and a UK company and further plant sales

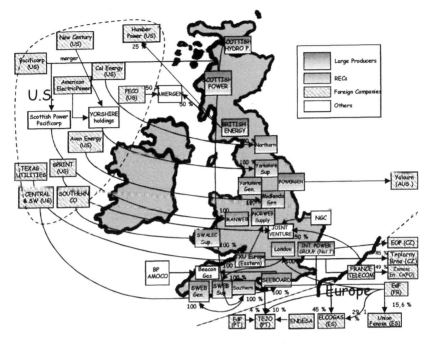

Fig. IX.16. International ownership in the UK electricity industry.
Source: Annual reports and internet pages of the respective companies.

may indicate a weakening of one of the cornerstones of the UK electricity industry.

VII.B. *International takeovers and alliances in the Nordic context*

Because of extensive public ownership as well as political protection of public ownership in Norway and Denmark, there have been less international takeovers in the Nordic than in the UK market in spite of the fact that the Nordic countries were also among the early pioneers in electricity deregulation. Nevertheless, there has been extensive international engagement, both across Nordic boundaries and by acquisitions from larger European multinationals into the Nordic market. Given the large institutional ownership in the Swedish electricity industry, Swedish firms have been particularly open to international engagements. Fig. IX.17 summarises some of the major international engagements in the Nordic market. As already noted in Chapter II, the second largest company, Sydkraft, has been the object of rival bidding between the German PreussenElektra and the French EdF. The latter finally pulled out and took a dominant position in the smaller Graningeverken, leaving Sydkraft

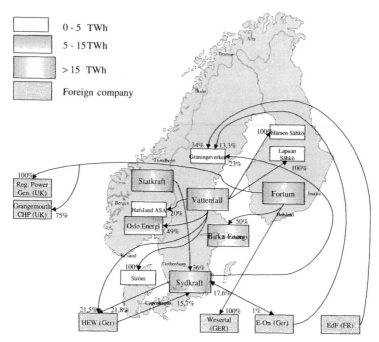

Fig. IX.17. International takeovers and alliances in the Nordic electricity industry.
Source: Annual reports and internet pages of the respective companies and TDN news.

to PreussenElektra and the Norwegian Statkraft, which entered Sydkraft after EdF had pulled out.

Another major international move into the Swedish market has come from the Finnish state company, Fortum, which has acquired the medium-sized company Gullspång and also 50% of Stockholm Energy, thereby gaining controlling influence in a Swedish company, Birka Energi, which comes close to Sydkraft in volume. Fortum also has controlling influence over Birka Kraft, a Nordic-oriented trade and wholesale company.

Vattenfall, the Swedish state company, has engaged actively to take up positions in neighbouring Nordic countries. In Finland, it has control or major influence in three medium-sized suppliers. In Norway, Vattenfall has matched Fortum's Stockholm strategy, by acquiring 49% of Oslo Energy supply, as well as taking up major positions in a medium-sized generator, Hafslund, and a medium-sized supplier, Fredrikstad Energiverk. Vattenfall has also taken a position in the Danish energy market through its 12% acquisition of the large East Danish company NESA, which again controls major production capacities in Sjællandske Kraftværker as well as a trading company Ström.

The lack of even more extensive international mergers and acquisitions in the Nordic market is probably due to extensive public ownership, and to strong political restrictions on capital assets of power companies in Norway and Denmark. In Norway, the so-called concession laws provide the State with a right to take over total capital assets of hydropower production without compensation after the expiry of the concession period if the company is privatised. In Denmark, the threat of expropriating (by way of taxation) the revenue from the municipal sale of the NESA company actively prevented a takeover by Vattenfall.

VII.C. Internationally-oriented German alliances and takeovers

Given their size and scope, it does not come as a surprise that the large German electricity companies and their mother holdings are developing active ownership ties within several European energy markets (Fig. IX.18). We have already commented on Preussen/VEBA's dominant position in the Swedish Sydkraft. In addition they have important positions in BKW FMB Energie AG in Switzerland as well as extensive positions in Hungary and the Czech Republic, through the partly-owned Hamburgishe Elektristätsverke.

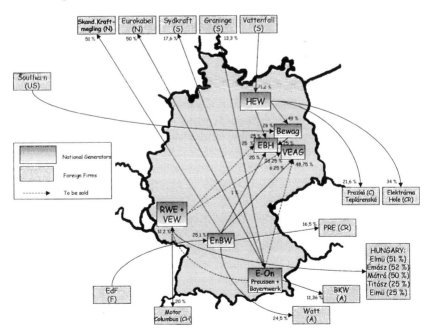

Fig. IX.18. International clustering in the German electricity industry.
Source: Annual reports and internet pages of the respective companies and TDN news.

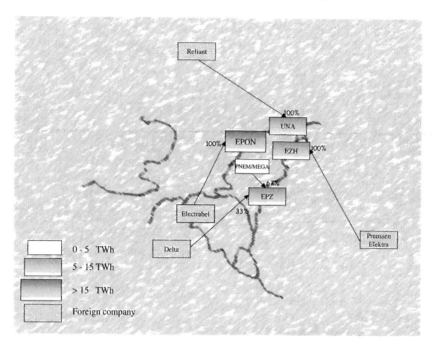

Fig. IX.19. International takeovers and alliances in the Dutch electricity market.
Source: Annual reports and internet pages of the respective companies and TDN news.

The other large company, RWE, also holds major positions in Switzerland through a 20% share in Motor Colombus AG as well as extensive positions in a number of Hungarian companies.

The merger between VEBA/PreussenElektra and Bayernwerk, E-ON, marks a major attempt at consolidating the German electricity industry into larger groups. In this consolidation process E-ON constitutes one pole and RWE the other. RWE's merger with VEW therefore comes as a natural follow-up, although at a much smaller scale. The two polar groups meet in VEAG, the old East German electricity supply, which was collectively colonised by West German industry after reunification. Given the strong rivalry following the market reform, this collective ownership is challenged both by the government, as part of antitrust policy, and by rivalry between the companies. Government therefore has demanded that E-ON divests BEWAG, and VE-A6; and that RWE/VEW gets rid of EBH and VEAG. The new owner will, however, have to take over considerable accumulated debt, which poses a considerable threat to the profitability of the company, especially after the protection against competition from West Germany expires in 2003.

VII.D. International alliances and takeovers in the Netherlands

Following the Dutch failure to consolidate generation into a large national company, the Netherlands has been characterised by a major sell-off of generation capacity to foreign firms. As noted in Chapter IV, the only remaining Dutch-owned generator (EPZ) became integrated with supply companies PNEM/MEG and Delta, while UNA, one of the two smallest generators, was taken over by the US company Reliant. PreussenElektra has bought EZH and Electrabel has taken over EPON.

VII.E. French engagements in Europe

Like the large German electricity companies, Electricité de France is also taking central ownership positions in the European electricity market. EdF now holds major positions in ESTAG (Austria), Motor Colombus (Switzerland), Graninge (Sweden), London Electricity and SWEB (UK), ISE (Italy), Tejo Energia (Portugal), Elcogas (Spain), and EnBW (Germany). In Eastern Europe, France is also engaged in Edasz, and Demasz in Hungary as well as ECK-SA in Poland.

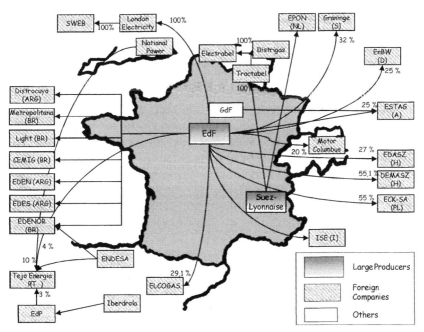

Fig. IX.20. International takeovers and alliances involving the French electricity industry.
Source: Annual reports and internet pages of the respective companies and TDN news.

The two multifunctional water companies Suez-Lyonnaise and Vivendi have been cautious challengers to EdF's quasi-monopoly position in the French market. These companies are also truly international in scope and also have broad engagements in other European markets (Fig. IX.20).

As described in Chapter VI, Lyonnaise has, until now, operated local power generation in a few French towns (Strasbourg, Monaco, Grenoble and Bordeaux). The merger of the financial holding company Suez and the technical firm Lyonnaise in June 1996 integrated French operations in the electricity market with control over the Compagnie de Belgique. Since 1988, this gave Lyonnaise the control of 50.3% of Tractebel, a position that was increased to 100% in September 1999. A later merger of Electrabel and Distrigas has provided a basis for a complete multi-energy company. Lyonnaise has also recently strengthened its position by acquiring Dutch EPON. In addition, Suez-Lyonnaise is the world leader of water management via its subsidiaries Calgon, Narco and US Filter.

The other French water company, Vivendi, moved into electricity through its subsidiaries Compagnie General de Chauffe, which manages 55 GW of thermal installations, and Esys Montenay, which has been restructured through a new entity, Energi Services. However, more recently, because of pressure from financial markets, Vivendi has been getting rid of its energy activities and is planning a compelte withdrawal from the energy market.

VII.F. Intercontinental engagements and alliances

Business strategies in electricity industry have increasingly become global in orientation.

Although this book is primarily focused on European developments, it therefore makes sense to illustrate some of the major links between the European and overseas markets. We have here included two non-European case studies, the US and Brazil/Latin America. The first study highlights the background and preconditions behind some of the major non-European investors in the European electricity industry. The second study highlights a major arena for European investments abroad.

VII.F.a. US engagements in the European electricity industry

The US engagements in the European electricity industry must be seen against the background of an active restructuring of the US electricity industry, facing increasing commercialisation of the US electricity market. The strategic trends reviewed in the US chapter include, among other things, the consolidation of investor-owned utilities (IOUs) through mergers and acquisitions, huge divestitures and repurchasing of generation by IOUs and the diversification of IOUs into telecommunications (see Chapter VII).

With a few notable exceptions, apart from British companies, international firms have not been major investors in the US market. One exception is Tractebel, which has over 1,200 MW of generation in operation and over 1,100 MW planned or under development.

In recent years, US companies have, however begun making extensive investments in electricity production and distribution facilities in Europe and elsewhere. As noted in Chapter VII, although some of these investments have come from traditional overseas investors like US oil companies, most have come from traditional IOUs and affiliated US generation developers.

US regulation has in some ways stimulated foreign investment by exempting them from strong regulatory controls and restrictions imposed on the national utility industry. The general slowdown in the expansion of the US electricity industry sector has also motivated expansion in growing markets abroad.

As noted in Chapter VII, the major US companies that appear most committed to international expansion include CMS, Central and South West, Duke, Edison International, Entergy, GPU, PSE&G, Reliant, NRG, Southern, Texas Utilities, AES, and Enron. As we have seen previously in this chapter, and as also noted in the US chapter, over half of the UK regional electricity companies, by value, are now owned by US firms. In addition, US firms also hold strategic positions in the Dutch market. Edison Mission Energy is currently one of the two largest owners of independent power projects world-wide with major holdings in the UK, Spain and Italy as well as outside Europe.

VII.F.b. European engagements in Brazil

As noted in Chapter VIII, Latin America's power market is drawing increasing interest from major utility corporations, due to the investment opportunities opened up by privatisation processes. The authors of Chapter VIII argue that the Latin American market plays a strategic role in the expansion plans of major global power operators thanks to its growth potential. They also point out that the developmental dynamics of the Latin American market indicate the formation of a single energy market over the long term.

It is only natural that companies from the former colonial powers play a major role in Latin America because of cultural and linguistic affinity. Endesa, Iberdrola and EDP therefore hold major positions. In addition, companies like Tractebel and EdF invest in Latin America as part of an extensive global scheme, while US companies like AES, Houston, Enron and Duke Energy also play a major role on the South American continent.

The foreign engagements in Latin America are characterised by diversification of activities, acquisition of assets through privatisation and by strategic partnerships. It is, for instance, clear that Endesa's engagements in Latin America are part of a global strategy. The company strives for market presence in related sectors such as gas, telecommunications, basic sanitation and co-generation in their home market. Its international market engagement, acting through Endesa International, is centred on investments in the electricity business.

Like Endesa, the Iberdrola Group has been diversifying its activities and expanding its international activities. Iberdrola also targets primarily the energy sector in Latin America. According to Tolmasquim *et al*, the international activities of Iberdrola in Latin America contributed over 25% of the total revenues of the group.

Hampered by regulatory constraints and a surplus market at home, part of EdF's strategy is centred on acquiring the assets of power generation, transmission and distribution companies in emerging markets. As shown in Chapter VIII, EdF now holds major generation, distribution and supply assets in Argentina, as well as distribution assets in Brazil.

All the utility groups studied in Chapter VIII frequently work through strategic partnerships set up to channel investments or acquire assets in Latin America. Examples are the strategic alliance between Iberdrola and two other natural gas companies in Spain—Gas Natural and Repsol—for the acquisition of Brazilian distributors CEG and RioGas as well as Gas Natural ESP, a distributor in Colombia. Another significant partnership was established with Tractebel and Edelnor (the Southern subsidiary in Chile) to build a gas pipeline linking Chile and Argentina.

To date the privatised companies in Brazil have posted impressive economic and financial returns, particularly in view of the need for heavy investment over the medium term due to the physical condition of much of the networks acquired. So far—as is the case with Light and Cerj—shareholders have been able to assign themselves generous dividends over the short term, due largely to the fragility of the concession contracts signed with the Grantor Authority. However, in the case of Light, the national regulator, ANEEL, has imposed fines, forcing the Board to draw up and implement an Emergency Plan in order to resolve power supply shortages.

VIII. Strategic and Regulatory Challenges

The extensive strategic re-alignment of the European and global energy industry following deregulation has left governments and international policy makers such as the EU with fundamental regulatory challenges. They range all the way from the problems of competition, via natural monopoly regulation of grid businesses to international environmental regulation. Finally, these challenges also feed back on the governance systems themselves and their governance efficiency faced with the dynamics of international markets. We shall, therefore, end the chapter with a brief comment on these issues.

VIII.A. The scaling up problem and possible transition to contestability regulation

The increasing integration of electricity companies facing the strategic challenges of European deregulation may, in the long run, have serious consequences for the reform itself. The basic argument for market orientation is that decentralised competition would force companies to provide customer service with maximum efficiency. The argument for maintaining national companies intact even after deregulation has been that they will be competitively exposed in a larger European market. And indeed, as we have argued previously, this assumption holds, if we presuppose open access across national borders for a sufficient amount of countries.

However, with rapid integration and strategic alliances even by the larger European players, we may in the medium and long term be facing problems of market concentration even at the European level, which may undermine the competitive pressure on the firms. In this perspective one may see the European market integration and deregulation of infrastructure industries as opening up a temporary window of opportunity for European competition which is subsequently undermined as companies integrate to develop larger units. The idea that decentralised markets will govern Europe through free-trade competition may, in other words, hold for a transitory period, before we are back again with complexity of oligopoly regulation, but now at a higher level. A possible scenario is therefore one of European scale oligopolisation of electricity industry and reversal to market regulation by contestability rather than by direct decentralised competition.

In central western Europe, we are already seeing the first moves in the large German companies: PreussenElektra's acquisition of Bayernwerk and RWE's acquisition of VEW. We have also noted EdF's engagement in the UK market, as well as RWE and EdF's attempts to seek control over Swiss production capacities through the Motor Columbus acquisition. Latin Europe is highly concentrated, and unlikely to be split up.

Private organisation of the electricity industry was in many countries substituted with public governance in the first half of this century, partly out of fear for monopolistic behaviour, but also motivated by the need for central co-ordination. However, it would be difficult to revert to the public governance model at the European level. Public ownership and public service management is hard to conceptualise in a European context, since the nation states are probably not willing to put up sufficient capital and concede that much power and influence to European players. There is, in other words, an asymmetric relationship between liberalisation and socialisation in terms of the political obstacles and transition costs.

However, if the European market is effectively integrated in terms of transmission capacities and deregulation of institutional obstacles to free trade, we could stand extensive mergers and acquisitions before concentration troubles in terms of the standard HH index. Even large mergers between the four biggest companies would not lead to unacceptable concentration, given that the market opening was sufficient to achieve a broad *de facto* competition in central continental Europe. However, the peak load problem seems to create extensive challenges in a competitive context. The recurring price-peaks in the UK market, sky high over European and Nordic prices in spite of acceptable concentration ranking on the HH index, seem to indicate that power markets may need more restrictive structural conditions than traditionally assumed for other markets. Recent geographic price differentials in the Nordic electricity market also indicate the need to look into strategic aspects of grid-generation coordination

VIII.B. Configurational complexity and multi-sector regulation

With deregulation and competitive exposure, companies are basically induced to experiment with combinations of industrial activities in order to gain competitive advantage. The previous case studies show that such experimentation quickly leads them to expand beyond given sector boundaries, inherited from their public service past, and into active pursuit of multi-sector strategies. Indeed, leading European electricity companies are now orienting themselves more broadly and redefining themselves into energy—and even infrastructure—firms.

A long-term consequence of adaptation to market conditions may be the complete erosion of sector boundaries and the emergence of different types of multi-sector engagement. Multi-use grids are particularly critical, in this connection, as grids have traditionally been considered a natural monopoly and therefore regulated according to cost-related principles. When several activities are integrated in one grid, it becomes very difficult to attribute specific costs to specific activities. The case studies have pointed to emerging development of multi-grid systems, in the use of electricity grids for telecommunication, and with the coming deregulation of gas we may see flexible interplay between gas and electricity grids as a basis for energy supply.

Another development towards cross-sector integration reported in the case material is to integrate several services at the customer interface. Billing systems and market communication may thus come to encompass electricity and petroleum products, as well as other services such as water supply, telecommunication and banking. If these sectors are unequally exposed to competition, there may be incentives for cross-subsidies with a following need for regulation.

In sum, the broadening of companies' activities across sectors creates an asymmetry between commercial and regulatory organisation, which is traditionally mono-sector oriented. One regulatory response to cope with increasingly broader strategic configuration may be to broaden the organisation of the regulator. The British case, for example, reports the emergence of new broader multi-sector regulators such as the British regulator for electricity and gas. Another possible development may be to lean back on general competition regulation. However, even abandoning sector regulation to competition regulation is no easy way out. The multi-sector complexity of advanced strategic business configuration challenges even competition–regulation to assess the strategic interaction effects of cross-sector engagements. Furthermore, regulation must remain light as it might otherwise become a cost-burden as well as an unnecessary limitation on commercial experimentation. How well the EU and state regulatory apparatus will be able to devise advanced regulatory strategies to cope with the complexity of industrial structure is still an open question.

VIII.C. Industrial diversity and greening issues

Apart from the challenge from oligopolistic and multi-sector competition, one of the most fundamental challenges to the European regulatory capacity comes in the environmental policy field. The failure to adopt systematic, market compatible environmental regulation to go along with the energy deregulation policy is striking both in the pioneering Nordic electricity market and in the larger European context.

Given the diversity of production capacities in Nordic electricity production, effective environmental action, through environmental taxation, would put burdens on each country's electricity industry and hence provoke reactions from industrial losers. This is probably why the ambitious Nordic environmental energy taxation, with its broad democratic appeal, has been so strongly modified by industrial interests who have efficiently succeed to loophole general regulations with special exceptions (Midttun and Hagen, 1997).

The failure to develop efficient common environmental policies to go with the expanding energy market programmes has also characterised the European Union. The Commission's proposal for a combined carbon/energy tax ranks as one of the most general and ambitious attempts to introduce an environmental dimension in European energy policy. However, it also ranks as one of the most controversial environmental regulation attempts made by the EU, and after strong industrial opposition, backed up by national political representatives, it was taken off the agenda and buried.

The dissimilarities of ecological vulnerability and abatement costs imply that collective strategies through unanimous multilateral agreements are hard to achieve, as the countries' commercial interests are too diverse to find a common ground. It may, in fact, be argued that with weak central governance at the relevant market level, the ability to take effective measures in environmental regulation is weakened by the liberal, deregulated regime. As companies with different resource bases that would be highly unequally hit by common measures compete in the same market, the more polluting system becomes exposed to very high 'green costs' which undermine its competitiveness. Even if strong environmental policies were to be supported through idealistic electoral politics, such policies are likely to be loopholed through the negotiations between the state/union and industrial vested interests.

There seem to be two developments, however, that counteract the obvious European state failure in environmental regulation of the energy industry. The first relates directly to the emerging trans-national business strategies that we have observed in our case studies. The gradual transformation of industry from national championship to multi-national enterprise may tune down the nationalistic positions and lead to gradually greater acceptance of neutral, collectively-oriented European positions on environmental regulation.

The second development relates to the emergence of alternative modes of regulation. The failure to reach common authoritative environmental regulation of the expanding energy markets in the Nordic countries and in Western Europe has led to a search for alternatives. A characteristic of some of these alternatives, which include tradable permits, green certificates etc, is that they can be designed to considerably soften the distributive problems of common regulation. A characteristic of other alternatives is that they originate outside of the state apparatus and rely on voluntary, market-based interaction. NGOs may also have a catalytic role in furthering such regulation, by designing licensing procedures for products, spreading information about them, and exerting normative pressure on the population to make use of them.

Facing internationalisation of the economy and increasing complexity of modern economic systems, the move away from exclusive reliance on strong authoritative methods towards supplementary use of softer negotiated and endogenous methods may be necessary to achieve results.

VIII.D. Multilevel regulation in a multilevel governance system

Given the present phase of building up European governance, the dual process of liberalisation of the electricity market runs parallel to a process of Europeisation. While the European electricity market is being formed, although with many imperfections, there is, at the same time, a complex integration process taking place, in order to forge a united European regulatory competence on top of the national governance systems.

As argued by Majone (1996) the governance at the international level is likely to be indirect and market-oriented, rather than direct and plan-oriented. The reason for this, he argues, lies in the limited legitimacy carried at the EU level compared to the nation state. The EU has neither the cultural capital nor the taxation possibilities of the national state. Given this governance deficit, strong interventionist governance from the European level would quickly lose legitimacy and inevitably run into conflict with the diverse interests of the European nation states. The European regime must, in other words, be liberal, because this is the minimum common denominator which European states may, at most, agree upon.

The European Commission has learnt, through painful retreats in the case of the energy directives (Midttun 1997) that it can only reach control through indirect market forces. However, by gradually exposing European industry to European market competition, the European Union is *de facto* expropriating the interventory power of the nation state and eroding its control over the electricity sector.

Companies spreading out across European boundaries stimulate the transfer of *de facto* regulatory power to the European level. By doing this they acquire some sheltering from national regulation, and come under more general European regime. As illustrated in the US case study, this is quite parallel to US practice, where energy companies are divesting within states and investing across states to come under Federal regulation.

The strong interventionist and even operative nation state is in other words not likely to reproduce itself at the EU level. Europeanisation therefore implies a move from stronger and more directly governed nation states to weaker, like indirect federal-governance. Governance at the European level is therefore critically dependent on the success of regulatory and not etatist intervention. If market-oriented regulatory intervention fails, then Europeanisation may, in other words, imply 'state failure', since there is no European etatist alternative in sight.

Literature

Di Maggio, P. and Powell, W.W. (1991), 'The iron cage revisited: institutional isomorphism and collective rationality in organisational fields', in DiMaggio, P. and Powell, W.W. (eds), *The New Institutionalism in Organisational Analysis*, University of Chicago Press, Chicago.
EU Commission (1996), Directive 96/92 on common rules for the market for electricity. *EU Bulletin L27/20* of 30 January 1997.
EU Commission (1998), Directive 98/30/EC on Gas. *EU Bulletin L204* of 21 July 1998.
Hjalmarsson, L., Midttun, A. and Svindland, E. (1999), *Nord Pool: Issues and Dilemmas*. Report No. 6/99. Norwegian School of Management. Sandvika, Norway.
International Energy Agency (1997), *IEA Statistics: Electricity Information*.
International Energy Agency (1998), *IEA Statistics: Energy Statistics of OECD Countries*.
Majone, G.D. (1996), *Regulating Europe*. Routledge, London.
Midttun, A. and Hagen, O. (1997), 'Environmental Policy as Democratic Proclamation and Functional Practice. A Comparative Study of Environmental Taxation in the Electricity Sector in the Nordic Countries'. In *Scandinavian Political Studies*, vol. III.
Midttun, A. (1997), *European Electricity Systems in Transition*. Elsevier Science, London.
Muntzner, J. (1997), *The Swiss Electricity Supply Industry Development and Structure*. Swiss Electricity Supply, Zurich.
Office Fédéral de l'Énergie Suisse (1999), *Statistique Globale Suisse de l'Énergie*.
TDN, Licensed database on European Energy Industry, supplied by TDN Kraft & Power, Oslo. TDN Kraft is owned by AS Norges Handels og Sjøfartstidende.
UCPTE (1998), *Statistical Yearbook 1997*, downloaded from http://www.ucpte.org/.

Appendix

Annual reports

British Energy (1998).
Electrabel (1996, 1997, 1998).
Electricidade de Portugal (1996, 1997, 1998).
Electricité de France (1998) French version.
ENDESA (1996, 1997).
Enel (1998).
Energie Ouest Suisee (1998).
Iberdrola (1996, 1997, 1998).
London Electricity (1998).
National Power (1998–99).
Omel (1998).
PowerGen (1998).
RWE (1995–96, 1996–97, 1997–98).
Scottish Power (1998–99).
Statkraft (1996, 1997, 1998).
Sydkraft (1996, 1997, 1998).
The Energy Group (1997).
Unión Fenosa (1996, 1997, 1998).

Vattenfall (1996, 1997, 1998).
VEBA (1998) German version.

Internet sites

Association of Swiss Electricity Producers: http://www.strom.ch/italiano/
Atel: http://www.atel.ch/
Bayernwerk: http://www.bayernwerk.de/
Beacon Gas: http://www.beaconnected.co.uk/
BKW: http://www.bkw.ch/
BP Amoco: http://www.bpamoco.com/
British Electricity Association: http://www.electricity.org.uk/
British Electricity Map: http://www.powercheck.demon.co.uk/
British Energy: http://www.british-energy.com/
CKW: http://www.ckw.ch/
Department of Trade and Industry, UK: http://www.dti.gov.uk/
East Midlands Electricity: http://www.eme.co.uk/
Eastern: http://www.eastern.co.uk/
EGL: http://www.egl.ch/
Electrabel: http://www.electrabel.be/
Electricidade de Portugal: http://www.edp.pt/
Electricite de France: http://www.edf.fr/
EnBW: http://www.enbw.com/
Endesa: http://www.endesa.es/
Energie Ouest Suisse: http://www.eos-gd.ch/
Energis: http://www.energis.co.uk/
EPON:http://www.epon.nl/ ESIS: http.//www.ngc.co.uk/
European Environmental Agency: http://www.eea.dk/
European Union: http://europa.eu.int/
EZH: http://www.ezh.nl/
Federal Energy Regulatory Commission, US: http://www.ferc.fed.us/
Federal Trade Commission, US: http://www.ftc.gov/
Fortum: http://www.fortum.fi/
France Telecom: http://www.francetelecom.fr
Gas de France: http://www.gdf.fr/
Gas West: http://www.gaswest.co.uk/
Iberdrola: http://www.iberdrola.es/
International Energy Agency: http://www.iea.org/
London Electricity: http://www.london-electricity.co.uk/
Lyse Energi: http://www.lyse-energi.no/
Manweb Electricity: http://www.manweb.co.uk/
Midlands Electricity: http://www.meb.co.uk/

National Grid Company: http://www.ngc.co.uk/
National Power: http://www.national-power.com/
NOK: http://www.nok.ch/
Nord Pool: http://www.nordpool.no/
Northern Electric: http://www.northern-electric.co.uk/
Norweb Electricity: http://www.norweb.co.uk/
ODIN, Official Information Norway: http://www.odin.dep.no/ OMEL:
http://www.omel.com/es
Peco Energy: http://www.peco.com/
Powergen: http://www.powergen.co.uk/
Red Electrica Espana: http://www.ree.es/
Repsol: http://www.repsol.es/webrepsol/esp/home/
RWE: http://www.rwe.de/
Scottish Power: http://www.scottishpower.plc.uk/
Scottish & Southern Energy: http://www.scottish-southern.co.uk/
Soprolif: http://www.soprolif.fr/
SPE: http://www.spe.be/
Sprint: http://www.sprint.com/
Stadt Zürich: http://www.stadt-zuerich.ch/kap08/elektrizitaetswerk/
Suez Lyonnaise des Eaux: http://www.suez-lyonnaise-eaux.fr/english/
Swalec Electricity: http://www.swalec.com/
SWEB: http://www.sweb.co.uk/ SWEP: http://www.egl.ch
Swiss Federal Office of Energy: http://www.admin.ch/bfe/
Telefonica: http://www.telefonica.es/
TIWAG: http://www.tiwag.at/
Transco: http://www.transco-bgplc.com/
Union Fenosa: http://www.uef.es/
Union for the Co-ordination of Transmission of Electricity:
http://www.ucpte.org/
United Utilities: http://www.unitedutilities.co.uk/
Vattenfall: http://www.vattenfall.se/
VEAG: http://veag.de
Veba: http://www.veba.de/
VEOE: http://www.veoe.at/
VIW: http://www.viw.or.at/
Wiennet: http://www.wiennet.at/
Yorkshire Electricity: http://www.yeg.co.uk/

Subject Index

417

Printed and bound by CPI Group (UK) Ltd, Croydon, CR0 4YY

12/05/2025

01866864-0001